Grace Stone Coates

Coates

Her Life in Letters

෧

LEE ROSTAD

ACKNOWLEDGMENTS

Thanks are due to many—
the late Kay and Ardella Berg of Martinsdale; Leonard Llewellyn;
Rick Newby; Dave Walter; Joyce Massing; Mary Clearman Blew;
The Montana Historical Society library; the University of Montana;
Montana State University; Harry Ransome Humanities Research Center at Austin,
Texas; A.A. Knopf Collection; The University of North Carolina at Chapel Hill;
the Stephen H. Hart Library of the Colorado Historical Society;
and especially Sara Timby of the Stanford University Libraries.
I am also grateful for the medical information provided
by Dr. Lee Harrison and Dr. Marc Steinberg.

TO ORDER COPIES, PLEASE CONTACT:

RIVERBEND PUBLISHING
P.O. Box 5833
Helena, MT 59604
Toll-free 1-866-787-2363
www.riverbendpublishing.com

*D*EDICATED TO

Julie, Caroline, Whitney, and Sam

∾

GRACE STONE, CIRCA 1895

INTRODUCTION

When I came to the Musselshell Valley to live many years ago, I met Grace Stone Coates, who lived quietly in Martinsdale, a recent widow in her early seventies. Grace had long gray hair that she wore in a roll around her head. The once svelte figure now showed her age and she wore nondescript housedresses. She wrote the local news for the two weekly newspapers, attended the Community Aid meetings and sometimes took the bus to White Sulphur Springs to work on the paper there. Someone told me that she was a nationally published writer, but no one seemed to have any of her work. She, herself, had loaned her books once too often and they had not been returned.

I was in my twenties and she in her seventies, but age was no barrier. We became good friends and visited about such things as literature, the best way to cook young cattails, where to find the best mushrooms, the need for funerals—never about the gossip of the valley or the social affairs. If I failed to drop in for a time, she would send me a note and enclose a stamp for a return answer. I often kept the stamped envelope and made the twenty-mile trip into Martinsdale. When she first married, Grace told her father she had come into an alien land. After a year of graduate work in London and then living in Japan with my Air Force husband, I sometimes felt that I, too, had come into an alien land in this very structured life of the Musselshell Valley. But we didn't discuss this—it was just there.

Then, in the early 1960s neighbors found her wandering in the night in her nightgown. Some of her problem was due to malnutrition—she would forget to eat. She told me she would get in bed at night and try to remember if she had eaten that day. One time when she was ill, neighbors had offered to bring soup. She said, "What I really wanted was a great, big baked potato. I just hungered for that, but they brought soup instead. They didn't understand."

When her husband Henderson died, Grace had made arrangements for both Henderson's and her own funerals. She also arranged to go to Bozeman to live in a retirement home at some point in time, and after the night wandering affair, her well-meaning neighbors decided it was time. She lived in Bozeman from 1962 until her death in 1976 at the age of 95.

Very few of her papers went with her to Hillcrest Retirement Home. Marion Coates, Henderson's niece, took most of the papers and books and put them in her garage. She sold the books to a used book dealer and some correspondence and clippings went away in the book boxes. Fortunately, the book dealer recognized their worth and sent them to the Montana Historical Society in Helena. Some of Grace's collections of poetry in black notebooks were left in her house, to be rescued by the new owners, who in turn gave them to me. More photographs and some clippings came from that family's daughter many years later. One of the scrapbooks of poetry she had given to a niece in Oklahoma, who loaned it to me later to make a copy. The few letters and clippings Grace had taken to the retirement home went to Montana State University. Leonard Llewellyn later bought Marion Coates' home in Martinsdale and found some boxes of papers and a large number of the poetry volumes and issues of *The Frontier* in which Grace's work had appeared. He generously shared those with me.

Kay and Ardella Berg, who owned the building that housed the Coates store, were cleaning the attic and found some photographs, unidentified for the most part; with them were Grace's diplomas from the eighth grade and high school and her life teaching certificate issued in 1901 by the state of Montana.

I put together a slim volume of some of her work and bits of her life after she died in 1976, but in the ensuing years I have gathered more of her letters and work, and now I feel I know her better than when we visited together. After reading her letters and other papers, I know the Grace of youth, marriage, and as a writing success.

Enough letters held clues to her correspondence that I was able to go to other sources. In the papers of H.G. Merriam, James Rankin, William Saroyan, Frank Bird Linderman and others were copies of letters they exchanged with Grace. From Caxton Press came a few more pages—most of their files had been destroyed by fire years earlier. All of these portrayed a different person.

Grace Stone Coates was well known for her poetry and her novel, *Black Cherries,* but it is in the spontaneity of her letters where the real story of Grace is found. She remarked it was "…her soul's delight—spreading myself on letters." She often sent stamps with her letters and advised a friend who was seeking information about Charles M. Russell, "…and remember that, to strangers, a stamped, self-addressed envelope is a pulling power that sometimes makes them answer a letter; the envelope lies looking up at them reproachfully every time they turn around, and finally in sheer self-accusation they say something and send it back. Not everyone indulges to such an extent as I in what J.T. Shipley of the *New Leader* characterizes as 'the whoring of the artistic spirit,'—i.e. letter-writing."[1]

For quick messages, people of that day sent telegrams. Even when Martinsdale finally was connected with the world by telephone, Grace had none in her home. She had to go to the corner booth or across the street to the hardware store.

Piles of the papers were hard to collate into order. Grace saved paper by using both sides, putting a large X on the side discarded. Loose papers with "snippets" of color and random thoughts I have included with little or no notation—her writing is better than my interpretation.

To H.G. Merriam she was both a student and then a co-worker as she assumed the role of Assistant Editor of *The Frontier*, to William Saroyan she was a mentor and guide through the first very formative years of his writing, to James Rankin a guide to the sources for C.M. Russell's work and history, and to Frank Linderman a fellow writer who shared an interest in Montana literature and teaching. Then there were the many others with whom she shared the love of poetry and the art of living. Unlike her published writing, the letters are full of dashes, underlining—expressions of joy and dismay—her feelings bubbling through the words. Her poetry comes from her soul, her letters from her spirit. And in all her work there is humor—often ironic, often mordant, but she did laugh at herself and the world.

Through her writing and letters and occasional trips to New York, she was in touch with the literary world of Scott Fitzgerald, William Faulkner, Theodore Dreiser, H.L. Mencken and many others. The art of letter writing has vanished with the electronic age, but this was Coates' tie to the literary world far away from Martinsdale life, although she commented that writing as literary production and letter writing do not go hand in hand. She felt that letters are the most alluring temptation to time-wasting a writer is subjected to, but Grace was able to be a part of the national writing scene with her vast correspondence and still continue her work. She wrote to Saroyan about his own feeling of despair and shared hers,

It has been my experience that I work for long periods blindly, in the dark, and suddenly all that I have done becomes the determining factor of a new phase of life, for me. I am working blindly right now, and you do not realize the difficulty and despair and futility (apparent) and hardship of my life. But I work. I am what I do. I have to be myself. I do not say I will not, but I can not become a housekeeper and a model wife and a bridge enthusiast and a church member and—I work. I remain myself. I submit to many things, but underneath I will never submit. And all at once, just before I die once more, some one sees in me something to utilize, as Knopf is using my book. Ask nothing; expect nothing, except this one courage, never to deny thrice what is your inmost self. Protect it by lies, if necessary; by subterfuge and outward yielding, if you are a woman. Oh, you will suffer beautifully before you die; and "success" will be ashes when it comes to you, unless this is your success; to be wretched and alone, and unrecognized, and still work and not care.[2]

The bulk of her literary output was done in the 1920s and early '30s, and after 1934, the only writing was "newspapering" and historical pieces—and of course the letters. One would wonder about this extraordinary outpouring of intense, passionate writing that came to an abrupt halt. In one of her letters to William Saroyan, she referred to a period of "maniac depression."[3] Many studies have been done on the relation between manic-depressive illness and the artistic temperament. Dr. Kay Redfield Jamison wrote, "The grandiosity of spirit and vision so characteristic of mania, coupled with manic drive and intensity, can add an expansiveness and boldness…Under unusual circumstances—and circumstances under which genius is bred are by definition unusual—this can result in a formidable combination of imagination, adventurousness, and a restless, quick, and vastly associative mind."[4]

To Robert Burns,

> The fates and character of the rhyming tribe often employ my thoughts when I am disposed to be melancholy. There is not, among all the martyrologies [sic] that ever were penned, so rueful a narrative as the lives of the poets.[5]

The list of those afflicted is long—John Keats, William Butler Yeats, Samuel Taylor Coleridge, Poe, Lord Byron, Virginia Woolf, Herman Melville and many more.

"The fiery aspects of thought and feeling," Jamison stated, "that initially compel the artistic voyage—fierce energy, high moods, and quick intelligence; a sense of the visionary and the grand; a restless and feverish temperament— commonly carry with them the capacity of vastly darker moods, grimmer energies, and, occasionally, bouts of 'madness.'"[6]

After this tremendous crescendo of work in the early 1930s, Grace again suffered from depression and paranoia. The second novel she wrote was never published. She wrote a friend that "…Knopf turned it down, questioning its salability. They did say it had some beautiful writing. But that washes me up with Knopf and I'm sorry."[7] In 1935 another crisis in her health, and she made another trip to the Mayo Clinic, and again in 1938.

Did Grace stop writing because an illness abated or only because she had said all she needed to say? Her writing reflected her inner self, and perhaps by writing she expunged the emotions of her childhood and dealt with the "alien" life she lived in Martinsdale. Pictures of her throughout her writing life show a serious, almost haunted look—there are none with smiles.

Or was she unable to write for some other reason? In 1938, she wrote to Saroyan, "Not writing is for me a way of being dead. Being dead is all right, but not while one is alive."[8]

Perhaps there was no longer the need for the therapy of exposing her soul or perhaps she had used her experiences. F. Scott Fitzgerald was said to have drawn from his own experiences and when he had used them up his writing became lifeless.

In 1957, she wrote to Merriam, "As for my inner life, for some reason I have found a degree of tranquility, an inner happiness that persists even when I'm tired or irritated or momentarily crying outside. Sometimes I feel luminous inside...."[9]

In my conversations with her, Grace always revealed how frightened she was of losing her mental capacity. She didn't fear death, just that other loss. In a final visit one wintry afternoon, we talked about such things and she discussed matter-of-factly how she would soon need more care and progress to the next level of care at Hillcrest. Then suddenly, she was walking in a garden and chatting with old friends. I left in tears.

Her letters reveal her life—they are her conversations with her far-flung friends.

The train came through Martinsdale in the middle of the night and went the other direction early in the morning. Grace's day began with the morning mail.

∞

Village Satiety

Satire sits on a satin cushion,
  Cups her chin, and looks at the street;
Questions: lethargy—or devotion?—
  Prisons me here on this window seat

To watch the villagers empty ashes,
  A wagon rattle to two white horses,
Purse-gut grocers strut like Pashas,
  And willows stagger the water courses.

Satire broods at the empty window:
  I will be *thus*, and I shall do *so*,
Hug my knees as wise as a Hindu,
  And watch stupidity come and go,

While I live a hidden life more sparkling
  Than lights that scream on a city street,
With secret ways of thought, more darkling
  Than crypt where cavern and river meet.

Ergot is on me. I shall be festive
  While life conceived in me is dying.
When I sit passive I shall soar restive
  Till I look down on great birds, flying.

I am deception to those who see
  Only coifed hair and tints that perish,
A flat bosom and crooked knee.
  In me is what the gods cherish.

CHAPTER ONE

Grace Stone had vivid memories of her childhood—those of the Kansas plains and the family that lived in disharmony there, her father dominant in all those memories. She wrote her feelings in poetry as easily as in prose.

Mutation

Winds that childhood knew
    Pageant grasses bending
Once were all that blew;
    There my thought had ending.
Now the winds I know
    Circle all the earth;
Never do they blow
    Back departed mirth.

When the friendly posts
    Past train windows speeding
Were my only ghosts,
    Ended there my heeding.
Tho my thoughts outrace
    Their far-shining wires
Side beside them pace
    Ghosts of old desires.

Once the sudden tear,
    Checked by bubbling laughter,
Knew no graver fear
    Of Before and After.
One soft kiss could steal
    Sorrow day had wrought;
Colder kiss must heal
    Memory and Thought

Untitled

Well do I remember saying to my father—
    He my grizzled mentor, I just flushed with youth—
That I wouldn't barter all my pleasing fallacies
    For his bitter wisdom, granted it were Truth.

I was wrong and knew it, said it to be wilfull
    But behind it lay conviction, unexpressed but clear
That no knowledge wholly wise could make a man so desolate
    And no fancies wholly vain could make my world so dear.

Arrogant he called me, half a fool, or wholly,
    Children flout instruction from their elders, was his theme,
And I sometimes smile at it, now that I am Mentor,
    He grown heir to other wisdom, dust, or star, or dream.

Wisdom isn't bitterness, nor illusion comfort!
    Shut your gaze to grim things, just to dream they glow?
    Truer eyes and finer meet their challenge steadily,
"Thus you are? Our joy stern friends, then to know you so!"
(This is full of rough places still—Henderson is here and
I have to write him a rhyme.)

Grace brought these obsessive memories with her when she married
Henderson Coates of Butte, Montana, and moved with him to the little town of
Martinsdale in 1910. She lived with those while coping with a new way of life.
Shortly after marriage, she wrote her father that she had been brought into an
alien land. "Henderson does not understand, of course; if he did it would cease
to be alien. And indeed, we look at each other as strangers when I say it. This is
not a complaint, for I amuse myself with the butterflies and pebbles of this
quiet shore, and with the curious, long legged nameless things that are not mine;
or at most, only mine when I am universal."[1]

The close-knit valley of the Upper Musselshell could be a supportive
community, but it could also be a demanding one in conformity. Still, Grace

lived in Martinsdale until 1962 when she entered Hillcrest home in Bozeman. It didn't matter where she lived; she transported her own spirit and brought her friends back through her letters and writing.

Coates was born Grace Genevieve Stone on a wheat farm near Ruby, Kansas, on May 20, 1881, to Heinrich [Henry Charles] and Olive Augusta Sweet Stone. She said of herself,

> On her father's side she descended from classicism and nudity in art, on her mother's from Samplers and furniture that came over in the Mayflower...and became the favorite battleground for Agnosticism against Puritanism. Her father disliked her mother's sturdy morality even more than the mother deplored the father's moral idiocy.
>
> ...Through her father...German, Polish, Bohemian and Russian blood. Through her mother, English and early Americana. By the alchemy of love and childhood, she found each parent perfect.[2]

Her early years were portrayed in her novel, *Black Cherries*, a collection of stories that were written from the viewpoint of a child. Veve [Grace] is five when the story begins and twelve in the second to last chapter. She is the last of four children.

Olive was the second wife of Heinrich. He always spoke of his first wife as his "wife" and remained so loyal to her memory that it created an irritating barrier in his second relationship. He even resented the acceptance of his two children of their new mother. Into this charged atmosphere were born Olive's children, Helen and Grace. Helen soon became a player in the game of winning parental love and approval but Grace was the indulged baby—as much as anyone was indulged in the Stone household.

Heinrich, or Henry, was the son of a professor of Greek in Berlin. Henry told his sister in 1919,

> I was born in Koenigsberg, East Prussia—north of Danzig—close in by Poland, while William, Natalie and you [Jennifer] were born in Berlin. Our parents sailed from Hamburg in the ship Leibnitz in the spring of 1847, in April of that year and we were 49 days in coming over. The Mexican war was still on, for I remember the newsboys crying out "Great battle in Mexico!" in N. Y. We remained for a few days in New York, with a certain "Madam Tasch" or Tache—just as the name may have been French or German,—both pronounced Tash though I believe she was German and conducted a sort of a German house. Cordelia I believe was born in Buffalo, for we lived there about a year. There is where I remember father pulling up the (to him then) nauseous tomato vines with ripe fruit on them and flinging them over before he died. We

are to all intents and purposes a Polish and not a German family. Our paternal grandfather's name was Kamnienski, and had fled from Poland when the Russians Burnt [sic] Warsaw, and settled in the little city of Angersburg, at or near the lake of that name—Angersee—he changed his name to its German equivalent, Stein, leaving of the "sk" which in the Polish is the equivalent of the french "de" or the German "von"; his wife too was Polish of course.[3]

The senior Stein tried farming and his sons followed in that profession. At some point the original name Stein was changed to Stone.

When Heinrich's first wife died, he turned to a school marm for a mother for his children. There was no strong love as he had had for the first. The way he found her reflected his devotion to the first.

Stone's first wife had been a good businesswoman and, while her husband tried one after another scheme, to make money, it was she who amassed the property. When she died her children were very small and she left her property to them.

Henry saw a picture of the one who would be his second wife in the home of friends. Amazed at the similarity in looks, he immediately began writing and in short order went to Wisconsin to claim the school marm who so resembled his first wife. Both wanted sons—Olive felt her life incomplete and her grief for her brother Warren, who had died young, an "unresting thing until she had born a man-child." Henry wanted sons to carry on his name and although he professed his children dear to him, none of them suited him, except for Grace.

Henry was a tough taskmaster with his children by his first wife, setting them tasks too advanced for them. He wanted to further their education, but could not lower his expectations to their level of comprehension.

Olive did not at first interfere with his abusive handling of the two older children. Although she would not allow him to touch the daughters Olive and Henry had, Helen and Grace, Helen was emotionally abused and physically overworked. Because she was a reminder of his dead wife, the oldest daughter was sent to live with her maternal grandmother when she was twelve.

In the story *Black Cherries*, Grace tells the story—from the mind of five-year-old Veve—of an encounter her mother had with Henry over the treatment of his older children.

Father was sitting at the table by my brother, teaching him square root. I knew it was square root, because Carl [Charles] was crying onto his slate. Mother went through the kitchen with a washbasin in her hand, and a towel. She went to Augusta's [Olive's] room. When she came out I asked her if Augusta had a headache, and she said, "Yes. Keep out of her room."

Father and Carl had a worse time. Father said, "I can make you see it with a strap. He said that whenever he taught Carl. Mother did something that seemed strange, as all the rest of the evening had been. I had never known her to help Carl, before, when father was teaching him. She said in a clear voice that sounded loud. "Carl, put up your books. Wash your face and go to bed." Carl looked at her with his mouth a little open. She said again, "Put away your books." His eyes were round, and he tiptoed when he crossed the room.

After he had gone, mother walked toward the porch door. A strap hung beside it, high on a nail. The strap was long, and had holes in one end. Mother took it down and rolled it in her hands as she walked toward the stove. She was saying, "You shall never touch a child again, yours or mine, as long as I live in this house." She lifted the stove lid and put the strap on the coals. I wondered why she said yours or mine.

It was to Grace that Henry turned his attention and love.

Grace and Henry took long walks, and he taught her the names of plants and trees and recited poetry. He read mythology to her until she could recite the work by memory. Her poetry over the years was greatly influenced by this mythology background, as well as her feelings for her father. In some ways he was lighthearted, building castles in the sky and working day and night—and then he would be morose and dark, shades of Grace's own moods in later years. Still, they both loved the plains.

Although she was only nine when the family moved from the farm, memories of the sweep of the Kansas prairies, the flowers, the Indians that passed through all remained vivid to her all her life. Grace remembered always the buffalo wallows, deep and soft with wild buffalo grass, delightful places to wade in after summer storms. She used to creep up to them, hoping to find a wild buffalo. Instead she saw Indians, often stopping on their way to Wichita during a session of court.

Grace was afraid of the Indians and the young men knew it, teasing and terrifying her until the old chiefs called a halt to the play. In later years she said the prairie years were the only years she really lived, so lonely and disrupted were her days after they moved to Kansas City.

As she grew, Grace gradually came to realize how sour was the relationship between her parents.

In an unpublished manuscript Grace told of her parents,

"My mother was a leprechaun, my father was a friar," chants Miss Millay. In the case of my parents the roles were reversed. My mother was of the blessed company of martyrs; my father, in her eyes, the devil's advocate. She bore her children in the fear of the Lord, and the more immediate fear that they might be like their father. He reared them in love of Truth, hatred of sham, creeds, and maternal relatives, and the anxiety least they resemble their father. Because she had given us such a father, our mother shepherded us the more diligently toward God. She established in me a conscience and a soul. These lay, like the liver and the gall bladder, but higher in the chest—no such noisome organs of gore. The soul was a crystal, singing blue that made me happy; to conscience was duller and muddier. God was a gigantic seated figure, above the clouds halfway between the zenith and the horizon in the southwest quarter. His feet, His legs, His shoulders I could always image. His face eluded me. I approached his inspection always from the feet. He was an intensely personal God, equal to summary punishment if it were worthwhile.

There WAS a God, yet something whispered, "maybe not." Spring mornings came when I put the matter to the test. Swinging under the peach trees, made with motion and with sunshine, I would "let the old cat die" and sit listening, listening. Then I would whisper "Darn God" and listen again! Would it thunder? Then I would throw myself on the grass, sobbing because I had "bothered" God when he was having the peach trees blossom.

God the avenger ceased forthwith. We were unintrusive friends until my adolescence. By a trivial incident at my baptism, my mother discovered that the God I had was not the one she had given me. Commotion followed. The rites of the church were ridiculous to me. I couldn't help thinking they were funny. She couldn't help feeling I was damned. In the storms that followed I threw God overboard. Fortunately, He treated me less cavalierly, and sent my sense of humor to the rescue. It bade me to my way in security, and seek Him later from the vantage point of an ordered life.

At the wheat farm in Kansas, Henry was a gambler and in one year gambled his first wife's property and his own on a single year of wheat. When storms destroyed the crop, he could not pay the mortgage and was ruined. His wife Olive who was a strong, somber woman found little joy or beauty in her life and made no secret of her fear of debt and failure. In *Black Cherries,* Grace said of her mother,

> She was less visionary than you [father]. She launched no yachts on the Mediterranean in face of blistering winds, and hail, and mortgages. Solvency and honor were one word to her, and impending failure held no humor.[4]

With his family, Henry became more niggardly. Many years later, Grace remembered the boys' shoes Henry bought for the children because they wore better than the girls'.

I couldn't help clumping when I walked across the floor on account of the heavy boys' shoes which I wore. I didn't leave my seat when I could avoid it. Occasionally I ventured to the dictionary when I wanted desperately to know something. One girl who sat near would point to my shoes and laugh. Perhaps she didn't intend that I should see her but she is the only person in the world whom I hate, and I don't even know her name.

However, during the farming years, Stone had invented a flywheel for the binder, which kept the binding operation going even when the horse-drawn machine was slowed or stopped, saving annoying handwork. He had sold his invention to a machinery company, so when the farm was lost, he moved his family to Kansas City, and went to work for the Plano Manufacturing company as a salesman for his invention. His job took him many places and the family was much alone. Helen became the dominant one in the home, caring for her mother who was often ill and unable to cope, and for Grace whom she protected and cared for like a mother hen. Once, after the girls were called to their mother's bedside, Helen ran sobbing to her room.

> Veve [Grace] asked, "Is Mother dying?"
> "I don't know. Probably not. It doesn't make much difference, either way. If father doesn't kill her this time, he will next. I wasn't crying about that. If you had been called to mother's bed as many times as I have, you would understand how I feel. I have been told to 'guard your little feet' until I hate your little feet. To night, when mother said that to me again, I asked who had ever guarded mine. You have been the baby, always, until I've hated you. I've hated everything. Yet, if things could have been a *little* different for me, I might have liked them. I don't care, any more, and that was why I was crying, *because I don't care*."[5]

As soon as the family was settled in Kansas City, Henry left to exhibit machinery for the company who had hired him, and was home only a night or two in two or three weeks. He moved the family next to Chicago, closer to his office at Pullman, but was still home only occasionally. Charles ran away, leaving only the two girls at home. Henry went to Russia for his company, coming home in time for the birth of a new baby that was stillborn. He was to have said, "It is what a man might expect from an old maid school-teacher!"[6]

Henry finally took his family back to Olive's hometown, Darlington, Wisconsin, where Grace graduated from Darlington High School in 1897. She then went to Oshkosh Normal (Wisconsin) and the University of Chicago. (She also attended a summer session at the University of Southern California in 1913 when she went to visit her father.)

Helen went to Montana to teach school and Grace stayed home with her
mother and went to the University of Chicago. She made plans to join Helen.
Together, they planned to make a new home for their mother who had become
both uncomfortable and unhappy living with Henry. Grace and Helen were
teaching in Stevensville, Montana when they received a telegram telling of their
mother's death in 1902. She was fifty-four.

> It was impossible for the girls to make the long trip home, and there was
> no service they could render to their mother. Except for their father's letters
> no messages came to them. Their Aunt, though estranged from her sister,
> had been bitterly hostile to what she called their desertion of their dying
> mother, and her driving tongue had set their few acquaintances coldly
> critical...When school closed in the spring, Helen returned to Darlington to
> arrange with her father the settlement of her mother's estate...They settled
> their financial affairs without friction. Their father preferred to keep the house,
> preferred to give his daughters the money that stood in their mother's name
> in the bank.[7]

Henry then proposed to Helen that she accompany him to see his eldest
daughter in Pennsylvania.

> I went with him, even when I didn't really want to go. And when we got
> back, and I kissed him, and thanked him for being so good to me. He had all
> the expenses down, every five-cent street car fare. And places we had gone
> just because I thought he wanted me with him he said he had charged entirely
> to me, as he had merely accompanied me without desire on his part, wishing
> only to further my education. I had to pay him. I'd have died of humiliation
> if I hadn't—and now I've spent money that was yours as much as it was mine.

The parting was acrimonious. Helen, especially, blamed her father for the
penury of the family over the years and the unhappiness of both her mother
and herself. She was unforgiving.

When Grace saw her father again after many years, she evaded his questions
about Helen, who did not want to reconcile with her father. When Henry spoke
of her mother, Grace answered levelly, forcing herself to words,

> I dream of her, always the same dream, That Helen and I are hunting for
> her. You have hidden her from us, and will not tell her that we cannot come,
> because we do not know where she is. She turned, and saw his face distorted
> with anguish. She was sorry she had spoken. "He understands," she thought.
> "Probably he had dreams about his wife, his first wife, when she died."[8]

Helen and Grace both stayed in Montana to teach. Grace had been teaching for about two years in the Stevensville-Hamilton area when she applied for a Montana Teaching life certificate in 1901.

Grace started teaching in Butte in 1904. She taught at the Grant School and at the Monroe School, doing extra work in the summer. Some isolated schools met in the summer since winter weather precluded a full year during the winter. One summer she taught at Ada, near Forsyth in eastern Montana. Years later she recounted that experience to a friend.

> This is authentic: Many years ago I taught a summer school at Ada, Mont., (now probably no longer existent as a post office) and lived at the Jacobs ranch—big sheep outfit (his wife was a writer before she ran away). By the kitchen door, on the panel at the left, on the long dining room side, hung a sheet of paper, perhaps 30 inches x 24. It was covered with minute lines, and I often thought, without stopping to examine it, that whatever it was was diffuse and ineffective. But one day I stopped to look, and began to exclaim… "But this is *good!*"…"What is this?"…
>
> It was a sheet of thumb nail sketches by Russell; bits of studies; a horses head—a hoof—a cowboy picking up a rope; a coil of rope—a hand—the angle of a horse's hock—hundreds of small sketches.
>
> By degrees they told me: Russell, a cowboy, had worked there. He was eternally drawing. If he was waiting for dinner, squatted on his heels he would pick up a smooth rock (boulder is the western word even for a glacier-scoured rock, two inches long) and cover it with sketches—then aim it at a rooster or a cactus plant and twirl it off. Folks got to watching where he tossed these and retrieved them. He would sketch on his boot heels, on his saddle, on whatever lay convenient to his pencil. And they had saved this sheet of sketches. I wanted it but they laughed at my presumption. So much for Russell—there were plenty of stories. He had modeled an elephant, and put it in a saloon window. It didn't sell, but a cowboy wanted something—not an elephant, a cayouse. Russell wanted $20 for the elephant, and the boy had only $10 to spend. Russell had no more wax, and couldn't buy any till he sold the elephant. So he agreed to break the elephant down and use the wax to model a horse. He would sell a horse for $10 but he'd be damned if he'd sell an elephant for $10. That's a typical Russell story.[9]

The lady in question did indeed run away from her husband with the wool buyer. Grace would have sympathized with the story of a woman caught in her own alien land.

After marrying Henderson, Grace returned to teaching in 1913, and taught until 1917, after which time she served as county superintendent in 1919.

Helen Stone married Louie Hyde in 1914, a rancher at Salesville near Gallatin Gateway. Louie remembered his family coming to Gallatin City in 1882—the first thing was a crowd of Flathead Indians bartering pelts of various kinds for groceries and dry goods at General Wilson's store. Wilson had been an officer in the U.S. army during the Civil war, and was always known and addressed as General Wilson. Gallatin City had two stores, a saloon, a hotel, stage station, feed lots and barns, a post office and a flour mill. It had once been the county seat of Gallatin County.

Grace's half-sister Olive was living in Pennsylvania and her half-brother Charles in California. Henry had also moved to California where for a time he was in an electricity business with his son and later moved to the Soldier's Home. Olive later moved back to Kansas to keep house for her Uncle William Stone. All of the children carried the scars of their childhood many years. Henry finally made peace with Charles to some extent and with Helen and Grace. Grace may have had the added burden of her father's melancholia.

By the time she was married twenty years, Grace wrote of herself,

Her occupation is housewifery; her delight, writing; her passion, music. All she has learned in 20 years of housekeeping drops from her in one half-hour's intense writing, so that she has to learn her business of housewifery each morning anew; and all she knows of anything is drowned in one half-hour of music.

Fortunately, her husband is sane. He keeps her outdoors, fishing, duck hunting, and deer hunting; and when she is away from her Martinsdale home, she remembers, never the dingy meanness of a western village but the tremendous sweep of valley from the Belt mountains to the Crazies; or the Musselshell, swimming in moonlight, below Gordon Butte.[10]

⸰⸰

Grace Stone

At Breakfast

"Where were you, last night?"

"I was in bed…sleeping
Beside you…of course!

"And I was leaping
Broomsticks, and burying Jesus,
And patting Godiva's horse."[1]

CHAPTER TWO

Grace was teaching school in Butte when she met Henderson Coates. He had come to join his brother John in the Syman Dry Goods store.

Both John Coates and his wife Josephine worked in Butte at the Syman store—John starting as a clerk in 1900 and working his way to a management job. Josephine worked in the mail order department. Henderson moved to Butte in 1909. Coates was a good-looking man who not only worked in the dry goods business, but augmented his income as a gambler. Grace and Henderson were married September 14, 1910 in Great Falls and moved to Martinsdale where Henderson and Jack [John] built a general store, selling everything from nails to derbies.

Grace was twenty-nine and Henderson forty-six when they married—Grace a slender woman with a sensitive, intelligent face and a quantity of blond hair and Henderson a short, broad, dark-eyed man.

Grace had not seen her father for ten years when she married, but his presence and memories were still with her. She wrote in a short story,

> The night of her marriage, serio-comic, came near to tragedy. At the touch of her husband's arm across her body she had known the black well of a stairway below her, she had felt stair steps cold under her bare feet, and heard her father's voice, "Do not come down," and her mothers, faint, after a pause outside of time "But you will come quick, if I call you."
>
> What happened next she did not know. What next she remembered was standing backed into the remotest corner of the room, transfixed with horror; her husband in the light, intent on her with sharp suspicious eyes. In the engulfing darkness that follows lightning flash she remembers that her mother had not called.
>
> He thought, not unnaturally, that his bride was passionately regretting an earlier lover. His suspicion was the only factor of the situation that seemed normal and tolerable to Veve, a rope that led her to reality. Suspicion she could understand and reassure. Her nervous crisis ended in violent nausea. This was an unromantic denouement within her husband's comprehension. He was a reasonable, matter-of-fact man. He took her word for it.[2]

The relationship between Grace and Henderson was one of good friendship as well as deep love. They were both deeply disappointed that there were no children.

Henderson Coates

Many years later Grace told a friend that she might not have married if she had known there would be no children. She became consumed with her writing.

When asked if he understood Grace, Henderson would say, "Hell, no, I don't understand her. I just love her." He indulged her, but did not understand her compulsion to write. Nor did he understand her need to feed the soul and mind as well as the body. The first thing she would do in the morning, even before dressing, would be to grab a book and read a paragraph or verse.

In turn, Grace once related to H.G. Merriam,

> …if Henderson and I weren't irrevocably good friends it would be out of place to say this. I no more criticize him for not being somebody else, than I criticize the Doxology for not being a motorcycle. But the compulsion I am under to write, regardless of money, is a value that has no validity for him; and if I try to sell a story, instead of giving it immediately to The Frontier it is because I want to get out of that atmosphere of being indulgently humored in something half way between a vice and an imbecility, when I write.[3]

> Always, before I sleep,
>
> My thoughts must find a place to stay.
>
> They go to you,
>
> But when you are unkind
>
> They circle restlessly
>
> Or huddle, chilled,
>
> Making me dream.

Another written for Henderson,

> I am never lonely when you are gone.
>
> Then you are all mine, perfect, like laughter or dawn.
>
> Only, sometimes, when you are far away, being near,
>
> Loneliness clutches my heart and chills it with fear.

When the general store was built, the brothers built identical houses back of the store for their wives, while up the street stood the livery stable built by their brother William, his house beside the livery building. A lumber yard-hardware store was subsequently built across the street from the Coates houses.

William and Talton "Talt" were the first of the Coates brothers to come to Montana, coming west from Missouri, where their father and grandfathers had ventured from Kentucky and Tennessee. Talt had been taking his father's mules to New Orleans for sale every spring, but when he was twenty he determined his next trip should be west and not south. Talt, William, and F.M. Blackwell fitted out a prairie schooner and joined a wagon train then preparing to cross the plains in 1875.

William Coates began to work for a stage company and Talt became a freighter for the Diamond R Freight Company, Col. Charles Broadwater's line between Helena and Fort Benton. After eight years of freighting, much of it during Indian uprisings, Talt returned to Missouri in 1884.

After Talt returned to Missouri, William settled in Old Martinsdale and had several mail contracts to deliver mail. And when the town moved to the railroad, William moved his livery business to the new location, the first building in the new town. He had married in 1890 to Margaret De Cou and they had a daughter Marion, born in 1900.

John Q. "Jack" Coates, the third brother to reach Montana came by way of Salt Lake City in 1891, and Henderson in 1892.

Old Martinsdale was a treeless village a half mile or so from the Musselshell River, becoming a service center for the ranches along the south fork and north fork of the river, notably the Smith Brothers to the west and the Charlie Bair sheep holdings to the east and north. A two-story hotel had been brought in from the deserted mining town of Castle; about twenty-five miles to the northwest, but most houses were one-story homes without electricity or plumbing. There were no trees or grass, and the limited water was saved for vegetable gardens and flowers.

To the south and west were the Crazy Mountains and to the northwest the Castle Mountains offering fishing and hunting opportunities—both enjoyed by Grace and Henderson.

In 1876, Frank Gaugler had built a general outfitting store near where the South Fork of the Musselshell joins the North Fork and added a hotel a year later. The settlement served the few ranchers who had settled in the Musselshell Valley and the travelers who used the Carroll Trail between Fort Benton and Helena. The road came from Helena over White's Gulch, down the North Fork of the Musselshell, and turned north at the Forks to Judith Gap and on to Fort Benton. Richard Clendennin moved his family to the Forks and established a store and hotel directly across from Gauglersville on the South Fork. Clendennin bid for a postal route and in 1879 a route was inaugurated between White Sulphur Springs and Martinsdale and soon extended to Lewistown. Another route went to Coulson [Billings]. It was Gaugler's store, however, that was the first polling place for the first election held in the Musselshell Valley in 1878 with twenty-one votes cast.

By 1885, there was a lively town at the Forks and the settlement was named Martinsdale after Martin Maginnis, one of the first representatives from the Montana Territory. Maginnis put the lively young settlement on the map by giving it a post office, and "the post office Martin gave us" gave the town its name.

The Montana Railroad was built through the valley in 1899. The line originally was planned to run from Helena to Castle to ship silver ore out. The line was dubbed the "Jawbone" because it was said the builder, John Harlow, had built most of the line on "jawbone" rather than ready cash. The line was built to Castle in 1896, only to become obsolete when the silver panic destroyed the silver mining industry. To salvage the project, Harlow proceeded to build down the Musselshell Valley to Merino [Harlowton] and in 1899 reached the Forks of the Musselshell. The tracks ran two miles south of Martinsdale, so the town was packed up and moved to the tracks to "new" Martinsdale. Grace used this wealth of history later in her life to write articles for the newspapers.

About 1910, the Montana Railroad was sold to the Milwaukee, connecting Martinsdale further to the world. The Milwaukee Road changed the track to run directly north of the buildings—a change from one end of the main street to the other.

The Upper Musselshell valley was a tightly knit community of people with mainly Norwegian backgrounds. Both the community and the Coates family did not readily accept outsiders and Grace remained so for many years. It was a factor in her writing—seeking companionship and mental stimulation through her writing and letters.

> When I'm idling at nothing important, like baking
>   Or doing a wash or painting the floor,
>   My visiting neighbors draw back at the door;
> "I don't interrupt you; your time I'd be taking;—
> I just came to show you this rug I was making,—
>   I'll come over later and visit some more.
>
> But when I'm alertly intent keeping quiet
>   To hear little night things discussing the dew,
>   They drop down beside me: "I'm glad you are thru
> With your work, Here's some music—I want you to try it.

The words are no good but the jazz is a riot.
Don't *sit doing nothing, it makes one so blue!*
                    (Or...)

People

Still I reach, still I grope,

Still they elude me.

My hands drop, empty, defeated,

To reach, grope, explore again.

I intrude me,

And hesitantly withdraw, uncompleted.

I could rend their flesh

To come to the hidden kernel

The inner self

That makes each one no other,

Between us comes the eternal

Chatter—

Courtesy bringing magazine and match

And serving superfluous food,

To smother all that is rude

In each;

All that would rip the soul

Bare, and shatter

(To make things whole)

The conventional business of living,

The bland, impersonal mask

Affably giving

All…but the thing I ask.

It was difficult to become a part of the community when she was barely accepted. William Coates' wife Margaret was established as the "matriarch" of the community and withheld her approval of her new sister-in-law. Grace became involved in her teaching and also served as Superintendent of Schools for Meagher County from 1919 to 1921. During this period, she built an extra room on the house and tutored high school classes. Her students loved her.

Grace penned "A Word to God":

Dear God, some day when You are done
With greater things, set right this one:

If there are women who like to sew,
And pile fresh linens, row on row;

And make hooked rugs and needle-point,
And crinkle pies, or trim a joint;

Grant finally that each one win
A home to love and keep things in.

But if a woman likes to walk
Even wet streets, and stop to talk

To the florist's boy or the organ-grinder;
Then saunter on again, to find her

A glimpse of the sea—a place to ponder
Why some take root, and some must wander;

Or an empty church she doesn't belong to
With a saint or two to make a song to;

Or a jeweled breast to question whether
Gems are a chain, and love a tether;

Give her the whole sky for her wishes,
But never a roof—with brooms and dishes;

Then wrap all women in Your compassion
Who weave Your garment in various fashion.

Martinsdale continued to grow. The bank had been organized in 1910 and the Hickes Hotel was built in 1913. W.B. Galvin put in a lumber business in 1916. A picture taken of the main street in 1916 also showed a small building at the south end of the street that was ostensibly the "red light district." A bar or two

MARTINSDALE, MONTANA, CIRCA 1916

and William Coates' livery building soon finished the establishment of the new Martinsdale.

Nineteen sixteen was a dry year. The Smith Brothers Ranch bought C.M. Bair's sheep and were wintering their combined flocks of 300,000 near Forsyth. They shipped the hay raised at Martinsdale by train.

Helen continued to live at Salesville, but her school was far enough from the ranch that she lived in the teacherage during the winter months. Their roles reversed, as Grace became the sister that advised and cautioned.

GRACE TO HELEN: UNDATED

Dear Helen:

Take good care of that cold. I am sorry for it. DO BE CAREFUL and stay in bed if you need to. I am returning pictures. We had them.

You have written the loveliest letters this season. I saved parts of them. What is your little great big moose? Your sense of humor? Love you. Am sending magazines. 4 or 5 bits of me in the Lariat. See if you find them all. And my HARP. There is lots more snap to getting a poem in print quick.

Henderson says look out for that cold, the world needs you and a cold is a dangerous thing. Shame we don't see you but once a year. I'm going to visit you some time. SAVE THE MAGAZINES.

Grace

… I got up early to beat Henderson and got the stove cleaned out—took all the top off and got the ashes out and the thick soot, and cleaned the under part. I like to do it and want to be alone with my job while I'm doing it, too. Didn't make much mess. Well, here I go—Life is full of good things to do.

We have only today—only today to be happy in, to be good looking in, to be clean in. It takes daily practice to be these things—AND MY HAIR IS FULL OF SOOT, and here I go fishing!

Love to you both—my good wishes and love to Louie—and my dearest love to you Helena.[4]

GRACE TO HELEN: JUNE 1, 1950

Dear Helen:

Not unnaturally, I think of you all the time, in spite of promising not to h'an't you. I hope you do not feel around for me. And I hope we didn't annoy you and tire you out.

H. went out and got a fish today after a hard struggle. They are not fat like those in your stream; we ate roast venison and put the fish in the freezer. The venison was wonderfully tender and good. It is 5 p.m. and soon time for the news, then the weather reading (it is raining.)

Anna[5] brought the HOLIDAY back promptly and Alberta[6] wants it—there I'll have to keep prodding; and then you shall have it. I think you'll enjoy "Brooklyn" too. Jimmie and I walked across the bridge one night, and landed at what was the old dangerous "Five Points" one of the roughest, most gangster-ridden part of the city. Oh, yes, and do read Satchmo in the front—you want to know more slang, there, you have it. It's entitled "Europe—With Kicks." They did well to keep his own words, not efface the flavor by re-writing.

This is June 2—same time of day—H. at breakfast—it is time that I drift away from the table to look around for the word or so that will feed my soul for the day. I picked up Harry Hartman's Lantern to look for his address (I'm ordering "Conquest of Fear" and if I can, and "I will lift up mine eyes" by Glen Clark—in fact I came in to start doing what Clark says) and read a quotation from Pelligrini's "Of Bread and Wine" "There is yet no evidence that the experience of the war years has had the salutary effect for which some of us hope. The American still wastes and continues to trample under foot whatever does not measure up to his gigantic illusions....nor does he yet see with any clarity that, in his uncritical devotion to big things, he has neglected the trifles which in their totality constitute a principal ingredient of human happiness."

His book was reviewed under the title I gave, but is really called "The Unprejudiced Palate."...

Henderson came in with the mail—your two cards—how well your writing looks—it always peps me up a lot to come and visit you. We both stay too close to home, and get so short of clothes we can't go out to buy any! It is not good for you to stay in the house weeks at a time, and *you are the only judge of what you can do.* And it is not good for me, or any one else, to stay too long in one place with no relief. I asked Dr. Sabo [of Bozeman] if it would be hard for you to come to visit me and he said "Absolutely not. Best thing in the world." He also said your heart was in excellent condition, nothing about it to worry about or be concerned about.

I weighed myself today and found I weighed 134—the last time I weighed I was crowding 140, and that is too much. I haven't been really following any diet, tho I have cut down on salt a lot. That diet emphasizes meat, with 25% fat, and eliminates sugar, salt, and flour. I wouldn't mind getting down to 125 or even 120. Henderson once climbed up to 165, but then reduced to 155, then 150, and is now 148.

You will feel a lot better if you can once get on a more normal plateau of appearance and contacts—in other words, you will be better if you are better—simple isn't it? If you feel better you'll feel better. Some advice! The *un*vicious circle…I just sent for Conquest of Fear—sent to The Lantern because I so like their little pamphlet that we get free. I found some mushrooms when we were out.

Maybe you can come home with us when we come over in July—we would love to have you, and perhaps it wouldn't be hard for Luie [sic] to stay alone a while—or come along with us—only I know that summer is garden time, and one can't be away from it too long. Anyway, both welcome; and I do expect to be proud of you when I see you again. (You needn't be of me.)

Love to you for this time, and more letter with more love later.

Grace

L.T.C. [Loving Tender Care] is on frail, sick baby charts in the hospital— for babies that need cuddling. G[7]

Several years after marriage, Grace started writing to her father who was in the Soldiers' home in California where she visited him in 1906. Olive, the eldest of the Stones, had married at eighteen and was now thirty-nine. Charles, thirty-eight, married at thirty-two—his only child was a son not christened Henry or Charles; Helen didn't marry until 1915. Grace had married at twenty-nine and had been married now for three years. She had married a man who rested her, she said, and suddenly she tired of being rested, tired of placidity, and wanted the old clash of wills, the vibrant interchange she had known with her father. She wrote him that she was

…hungry for the old atmosphere of my childhood, but that atmosphere was you. I am a child, alone on the seashore. The ocean is forever present for my wonder. But it is vast. It is incomprehensible. There is no companionship for a child in its incessant roar. I content myself looking curiously at stones and shells and pebbles—overturning a stone to see grotesque things scuttle. But no companion comes. I am alone.

Her father's letter came immediately, explicit in its response to hers.

She answered by telegram: "See where your life broke off from mine, how sharp the splinters keep, and fine. I am leaving, tomorrow to visit you."[8]

Grace found her father living in a little cottage in the heart of a eucalyptus grove, where he went when life at the Home grew irksome to him. He had not wanted her to visit him at the Home. "He complained of encroachment of the years—he had lost a lower tooth, a molar, and the corresponding tooth above, making it impossible for him to chew properly on that side—but he would buck through without submitting himself to the exploitation of that trade union, the dentists."

Grace wanted Helen to be reunited with her father and the two began corresponding and eventually healed the fracture between them. He eventually visited both daughters in Montana, and made a will leaving his small estate to Helen. This, perhaps, to make up for the childhood of hard work and care for her mother.

In 1921, after finding a housekeeper for Henderson, Grace joined her father in San Francisco to sail to Hawaii on the S.S. *Sonoma* after spending a few days visiting Charley and his family.

Helen had written her father, concerned about Grace.

> I'm very much worried about Grace—and I'm writing to ask you if you can manage to see that she has as much absolute rest—I mean rest from people as possible. She needs quiet and perfect rest—I've been through one of those beastly nervous exhaustions and I know so well what they mean that—I came near writing her to stay in Butte and sleep instead of visiting me and interrupting her sleepiness—which is the only road to recovery…let her have long spells undisturbed by casual visitors, exciting sight-seeing and especially conversations or reading that make her use her brain much…she said to me "It [trip] seems to me like an absolutely impossible task." …I'm writing this to you rather than to her for no sick person is fit to care for himself and this is doubly true of a person ill as she is of "nerves." Her letters to me sound so tired and not a bit like her.[9]

Grace felt well enough to take classes at the University of Hawaii and to share some observations with her brother-in-law.

> But they do have cattle, and when you saw them, you would not imagine what they lived on until a native explained. On the Island of Oahu—that's the one Honolulu is on—there is a railroad running along the south beach to Haleiva. Here I saw cattle, scrubby little wooly beasts, that must have been stocked from Scotland; in fact, I think they said that they were a Scotch strain….I think Helen would like to read you Robert Louis Stevenson's Life of Father Damian; it is not a "life" really, but an impassioned defense of a wonderful and ill appreciated man…there is also a good Honolulu story running in the Saturday Evening Posts, full of local color and accurate nomenclature, that it wouldn't hurt a school to have read to them. It is a blood and thundery thing, but if she will read it I will send the Posts, if she can not get the back numbers elsewhere…Write me any time, if there is any thing I can tell you about.

Although Grace may have tried to rest, she would be at the Mayo Clinic in February of the next year.

Her first poem had been accepted for publication in 1921. She told about it to William Saroyan many years later.

> I wrote verse from the time I was a baby, for—I can't say pleasure, any more than I would say a child breathes for pleasure. I was sitting at the machine writing a "poem" when Mr. Coates (…my reference to him as friend husband—f.h.…) Mr. Coates passed and in the jocular condescension usually extended to persons different from ourselves, said: 'Writing another bum pome?' I said, 'Maybe not so bum' and sent it, more out of curiosity and loneliness than anything else, to POETRY (Chicago). Miss Monroe accepted it. I sent nothing more any place, but 2 years later a Gwendolen[10] Haste, then living in Montana and now in N.Y. (Howard McCann publishes her first vol this fall) wrote me about the poem, characterizing it as beautiful or what not. At the time I was in a Minneapolis hospital, and her letter was forwarded to me there. The outcome of the letter was that she visited me here [Martinsdale], and poked me up to write…She prodded at me, and I began submitting work to the minor magazines. I have always done that, and made no effort to reach the pay magazines. Most of the time I am writing only because someone is asking for this or that. But there would have been no trouble getting into print if I had had anything ready to submit. I mean I have always had more publicity than I was justified in getting. Brentano and Simon and Schuster have both asked me for a novel, The American Mercury for articles—I had nothing and was too—something—to supply one.[11]

The first published poem that was noticed by Haste, appeared in *Poetry: A Magazine of Verse* in 1921. Like Coates, Haste wrote of the loneliness of the west. "The Ranch in the Coulee" shared *The Nation* poetry prize in 1922 and her one volume of poetry, *Young Land,* includes works that tell of the wind swept lands of Montana and the often bleak and barren lives lived by the women of the West.

Gwendolen Haste was born in 1889 in Illinois and graduated from the University of Chicago. She helped her father edit *The Scientific Farmer* both in Wisconsin and when the family moved to Billings in 1915. She moved to New York in 1925, and served as the Secretary of the American Poetry Society from 1928-1929.

In February of 1922, while Grace was in Rochester at the Mayo Clinic[12] she wrote to Gwendolen:

> You delightful girl:
> Don't you ever put off a charming letter so long again. Here I am at the clinic waiting to hear the verdict "Live" or "Die."

("All stealthily death

I heard her heart sob

Was watching her breath")

And how you would feel to have a good letter come back to you all crossed *Deceased!* So my little glimpse into Death's face has taught me this. Do the lovely thing quickly.

Your entire letter interests me. But I am so unaccustomed to writing with a pen (since I use my typewriter altogether at home) and really so over-taxed by my imperative letters that I am going to ask you to let me merely acknowledge it now, and answer adequately later.

There is a prolific field for poetry in the aspect of our Montana Wives. It happens that I have touched on that field also and will send you a bit of verse. It is indeed a pleasure to clasp your hand across our Montana chains. I was in your vivacious city last fall. Billings is like San Francisco on a small scale. Butte like Seattle.

If you feel like writing again to me here, your letters will be doubly welcome on my loneliness and illness—and when I am home again I'll be more legible...[13]

Back in Montana, Henderson took Grace on a summer trip through Glacier Park to help her recovery, stopping to visit Henderson's friend Charlie Russell at Many Glacier. The Coates brothers had known Russell in his cowboy days. William (Billy) Coates had figured in one of Russell's tall tales. She told a friend of the visit in a later recollection.

The last time I saw him [Russell] was in Glacier Park—where one of his $15,000 pictures hangs in the Lewis hotel.[14] With a stranger from Iowa who had courteously attached himself to Henderson and me, we were crossing the lake. He had seen this painting and stood overwhelmed before it for an hour. Russell was on the boat; and when we left it Russell and Henderson were squatting on the pier—Russell cowboy fashion on his heels—high-heeled boots, bright scarf at his waist—.

...While I and the Iowa man sauntered around, finally coming up to them. We introduced the Iowa tourist, and told him, off hand, that this was Charles Russell, who had painted the picture he had been admiring. I thought he acted funny, and later he told me he thought we were kidding him and playing him for a greenhorn. He evidently wanted to go back and meet Russell all over again.[15]

Then it was back to the typewriter again at home, although Grace admitted in a letter to Haste, "...I must stop. The mechanical side of writing is still hard for me...typing is still so hard for me that I have to do it on the sly when my husband can't catch me at it." Her recovery was slow, and in the fall, her father wrote that he was sorry her health, both physical and mental, was in such poor state.

Haste and Coates were supportive of each other, and Grace wrote when there was some mention of Gwendolen marrying. The two also made plans for Haste to visit in Martinsdale.

COATES TO HASTE: APRIL 30, 1923

Dear Gwendolen Haste:

You have a generous heart and an understanding soul. Combine this with good taste in notepaper and you'll see you're going strong—Yes, this is the paper I like. I hope, selfishly, that you are not considering a permanent address in connection with a change of name. It would leave you less free to play with me this summer. But then—Montana Wives!—of course you aren't.

While I am on the subject of visiting—if you went from Harlowton to Judith Gap the next thing to do would be to go from Judith Gap to Harlowton, and keep on coming till you reached Martinsdale. Martinsdale is on the main line of the Milwaukee, 28 miles west of Harlowton. In pleasant weather the easy way to reach us is to take the stage[16] to Roundup, which is also on the Milwaukee, and take the train and that leaves only a short train trip over here. There must be numerous "prune peddlers" who drive between Billings and Harlowton. Any grocer or hardware man could tell you. They have their regular schedule and traveling men are notably accommodating. (If you should ride with one, I'll wager he'll begin within the first half mile an account of how he first met his wife, and deposit you at my door on a detailed description of the last baby's latest tooth. One even trailed me out of the car with a really overwhelming collection of family pictures and insisted that Mr. Coates also—ah, enjoy them!

But to get back to the real business of life. Your suggestions were exactly what I wanted. As I told you I have submitted nothing to any magazines—practically nothing; so tho I appreciate very fully your mother's interest and encouragement, there is nothing available for her use. I am sorry. The little newspaper stuff I have done is of purely local and momentary interest, without any general significance.

As you must already have surmised, there is no library here, and I have access to no magazines except the limited number that come in my mail, or my friends'. I have wanted the address of several of the magazines you mention, especially the Lyric West. I am familiar in a general way with the Dial and have a few things I would like to submit to it. I had never even heard of the Midland. It would be such a help to me if you would take time to send me all these addresses. If you will do this it will surely galvanize me a bit. I realize that all my excuses are excuses merely. I have been trotting around the country and could have informed myself on markets. But something has restrained me; sickness to a slight extent, and the inertia that it brings to a much greater degree. If you will send me the addresses I will get hold of some of the publications so that I can see their general trend. Just now I see something in your letter that had escaped me—that you would send me some of these magazines. Indeed, if I ever have a laurel wreath I shall keep only one leaf and give the rest to you. I hope that you do not know how trying it is to feel that in your neighbors' eyes, you fall somewhere between lunatic and imbecile. But if you don't, neither can you know how a letter like yours restoreth my soul.

I looked for you at Missoula during the Editors meeting but failed to find you. We were on our way to Glacier at that time. Cars are running from Billings to Harlowton all the time—autos—Get into one and come and visit me. I want to know you. You were so very good to write to me in the first place, and so very understanding, that I sincerely wish to expand our acquaintance. It is my loss that your letter to Minneapolis missed me.

Are you writing? I feel ashamed that I am doing so little. Perhaps your encouragement will prod me up a bit.

Sincerely your friend, Grace Stone Coates[17]

COATES TO HASTE: JUNE 21, 1923

Dear Miss Haste:

I am in a hurry for you. Do have an elastic schedule when you come. It has been raining for almost a week, and if it happens to be raining when you come you must be prepared to outlast the rain.

I had over-prepared the event—

that much was ominous

With middle aging care I had laid out just the

Right books,

I had almost turned down the right pages..

(Beauty is so rare a thing…

So few drink of my fountain)

You remember? Poor Ezra! I did more. I blacked a stove.

What is the quality in some personal courtesy that brings tears to one's eyes? I had a (long delayed) letter from Mr. Frederick that did just that. By the way-speaking of these here now editors, did you see that verse ending

He loved and sang and loved, that throstle blest,

> Till from an ivy tod
> His wife cried, "Oh, my God,

Do stop your noise and help me with this here dratted nest."

Hazel Hall is doing good things in the New Republic. Oh, dear, the art so long, the craft so hard to learn—tho I misquote—"the life so short, the crafte" etc.

Things are growing a bit too vigorous around here for my taste. They were elusive and lovely a week or so ago. But the radishes are fat and pop when you bite them, so come along.

Sincerely yours, Grace Coates[18]

The note referred to was from John Frederick, the editor of *The Midland* magazine, published at the University of Iowa...

...I have just returned to Iowa City and have been reading the accumulated mss. I have been reading yours. And I want to tell you how deeply "After Quarrel" has stirred me. It is a deeply lovely, perfect thing. Oh—I know what you mean! The prose is genuine and satisfying. Will write you more formally about these things, of course. But I want to send you this note tonight.[19]

Haste made the trip to visit Grace and Henderson and later related the account of the trip. Her narrative of the visit tells of the difficulties of travel in Montana at that time, and gives a good description of the village of Martinsdale.

Today, the motorist drives from Billings to Martinsdale, a distance of about 120 miles ,in a couple of hours. Haste took the "stage" to Roundup, a town about 50 miles from Billings, and from there a train to Martinsdale.

On we jolted, over the dusty, primitive road, around and over hills, some sage-brushy, some dressed in drought-bedraggled wheat, some left to the jack rabbit and the sere remains of old crops, until Roundup appeared with its pleasant tidy homes and casual business blocks around the Milwaukee station. And, of course, the train from the east was late—hours late. The July sun burned on and I dallied with a good lunch, a few words with a young woman who was also lunching, then boredom and heat in the station until the Pullmans and day coaches rolled in, with more hours to go while we followed the cottonwood-lined Musselshell through Lavina, Ryegate and Harlowton to the whistle stop at Martinsdale.

...We spent the days in pleasant literary and non-literary talk. Grace had been finding markets for her poems and was interested in learning of new outlets. I had brought two recent novels as a guest offering, but I doubt if she ever read them. Her bulging bookcases were filled with sociology and economics and showed none of the titles of my history-fiction-poetry interests. As we chatted, her background emerged from the early days on a Kansas farm with her German-educated father and New England school teacher mother…As a young woman she had taught school in Butte, and since her marriage had taught in Martinsdale and had been county superintendent of schools for Meagher County with her office in White Sulphur Springs…

When we weren't talking we were riding around the dramatic country in the Coates' busy little Ford. What the roads are up there now I don't know, but in the twenties they were almost as God made them. You got where you wanted to go with no difficulty when the sky beamed, but come a thunder and hailstorm out of the Crazies and the car slithered in greasy mud.

…Henderson's interests were hunting, fishing, poker, making a living from the store and reading the Saturday Evening Post. He played a good game of bridge and was friendly with his wife's guest, running us around the precarious roads calling on this and that acquaintance tucked among the hills. One evening Josephine Coates, the sister-in-law next door, asked us over so that I could read some of my poems. Her husband was tending store, but Henderson accompanied us, the polite host, not one bit interested in poetry.

We sat around the dining room table, under the kerosene lamp, and, as the reading progressed I saw I was capturing the male part of my audience as well as the two women. Whenever I glanced up Henderson was listening eagerly, his dark eyes shining. After I had read "Dried Out" he leaned across the table to his wife: "Grace, isn't that just like that son-of-a-bitch from Shelby I was telling you about?" Said Grace, afterwards: "I knew he would like those poems."

Dried Out 1922

This place was the first home we ever had,
And I was sick of farming for other folks,
First in Wisconsin and then in Dakota.
It looked so pretty when he broke sod that day.
There wa'n't only three sides to the house,
But what did I care!
There was sunlight and wet rain and a coulee full of springtime
Where the children could play.

Seven full years, says the Book, and seven lean—

And we come in at the end of the full ones, I guess.

There ain't no crops where they's no rain.

And the stock died in the big blizzard.

So now we're goin'

Back to Dakota to farm for other folks.

Oh God, the nice white ranch house with a floor

We was to have! The roses by the door!

One of the excitements of my visit—Henderson's excitement—was the arrival of minute trout from an eastern fishery to stock Meagher County streams. They were to arrive on the night train from the east, which might—or might not—reach Martinsdale in the small hours. Henderson was to retrieve the huge fish-and-water filled drums and we would escort them into the hills to the elected streams. As I remember, we were to start out in the dead waste and middle of the night since the sooner those young fish were in their natural habitat the better chance for them to grow up and sacrifice themselves to Henderson and other dedicated fishermen.

We did go to bed for a few hours sleep but roused around train time. No train. The Milwaukee, as always, was being leisurely. All through the night Henderson plodded over to the station of the latest reports. No train. In the dawn Grace and I drove east along the highroad for a few miles and returned in the sunrise. Finally the limited dawdled in and the drums were transferred to the car along with Josephine, Grace, Myself and Henderson. We started out, but some signal had reached Henderson of an all day poker game starting in one of his haunts. "I guess I'll stay," remarked Henderson. "You don't mind, do you?" Did we mind! Free of male ideas of just how a proper excursion should be properly conducted we bounced off with the fish, west into the hills away from the main road to White Sulphur Springs, to the Findon Road, over a hilltop and down the other side at a truly terrifying angle.

One of Grace's women friends driving this road for the first time with her husband beside her, fortunately, saw what was ahead, or below, as she topped the rise, gave a shriek, took her hands off the wheel, and covered her eyes. But the Ford's brakes were good. We pitched down and soon decanted our first drum of fishlings into a stream. The tiny things followed their instinct and headed into the current. And after stocking another stream we headed for home.

…among our many topics Grace told me tales of sorrow, death, and sickness of heart in the surrounding community. Many of these stories sparked later poems, but one which has pleased critics and editors and pleases me is

"Outcast" because it is really Henderson and his friends—men who came out to that unsettled country in earlier times before the day of the small ranch, worked at various jobs, some of them dangerous, hunted and fished, played poker and faro, and loved the country.

Outcast 1925

Old man Carver
Came from the East
He never sat
At their thundering feast.

He never knew
Their whiskeyed nights.
He was farming stones
While they hunted fights.

When they told of bloody
Bar-room rows,
Carver could only
Speak of cows.

His words of seed corn
Were nothing beside
The story of Jed
And the grey wolf's hide.

So he sat dumb
In the crossroad store
While they spun shattering
Tales of gore.

They granted Carver
Could farm like hell,
But he had no beautiful
Lies to tell.[20]

In these early years, Grace joined poetry groups and visited around the state. She appeared at women's clubs to read Haste's poetry and promote her work as well as her own, and appeared in more poetry publications. Haste was helpful in giving her names of magazines to submit her work. Poetry was a fashionable form of literary expression in those days, and there were many small publications that "came and went." Most paid a small stipend for the poetry and charged for the finished publication.

During the 1920s Grace was in print often. From the first acceptance in 1921, her verse appeared in publications ranging from *Breezy Stories* to the *Christian Science Monitor,* and was copied in the *New York Times, Detroit Free Press, Virginia Pilot, Michigan Courier* and Montana newspapers. Braithwaite's Anthology for 1925, 1926 and 1927 contained certain of her poems.

Among poetry acceptances were "Diathesis" printed in *The Lyric West* and "Toys of Hoersel" printed in *The Harp* in 1926. "Incompletion" was in the *Will–o'-the-Wisp* in 1930 and in 1929 *Muse and Mirror* printed "To a Musician," "Mould," "Articulate" and "Wound." She also appeared in *The American Mercury, New Republic,* and *The Greenwich Village Quill.* Coates was published more than a hundred times from 1926 to 1931.

The June, 1925 issue of *The Midland* was dedicated to Grace Coates. The six page booklet contained "Eagles and Cat-Birds," "The Cliff," "The Freighter," "Strangers," "Loneliness" and "A Child Tastes the Loveliness of Life and Fashions a New Dream." In the biographical note, Grace said she writes, "because a Montana hamlet offers exceptional opportunities for reflecting upon the universe!"[21]

During this period, Coates began to form friendships with others in the profession. Two especially close friends were Dr. Israel Newman, who wrote poetry and published a small magazine of poetry, and Pierre Kuchneroff, who wrote under the name Eddie Custer.

In a letter to Saroyan, Grace told of her friends,

> Pierre Kouchneroff is Eddie Custer, of no fame, a musician. Russian Jew. TB. Denver. Now in N.Y. [1930] A friend of Israel Newman, whose brief letter I enclose for the good word of your story. If you are in N.Y. when Dr. Newman is there, he will be glad to meet you. I care a lot for him. Like you, he is a part of the rest of me that happens to be living in a different place that the other rest that is I."[22]

Grace shared her thoughts about Newman in a letter to Helen, and sent the poem she had sent to him. "Helen: a man with a ringing in his ears, striking a man in the face because he hears no noise."

Prodome [23]

The sleeper stirred, sat upright; suffered all
Confusion. Gongs were clanging, cymbals crashed,
Harsh voices shouted numbers. Ever clashed
That ominous bell's recurrent rise and fall.
He stumbled to the window, within call
Discerned a lonely passer-by, and lashed
His questions on him; but the lad, abashed,
Denied all word of uproar, great or small.

His questioner wrenched a panel from the sill
And hurled it at the luckless boy below,
Who half-affrighted, half-indignant, fled.
The haggard face leaned from the window, still,
Demanding that the quiet midnight show
Commotion—that was only in his head.

Good wan ? What? I am swamped with work. You get the less letters. Oh, Israel and I had a battle royal. I think he is crazy. This sonnet is the way he acts. I sent it to him.

Love and love again. I am glad YOU appreciate my nice letter. I got even. He was contrite and sent me some lovely pictures saying they might inspire my verse. I sent them back and said that by the time I had spun rhymes about the reproduction of a reproduction of the embodiment of another man's thought my inspiration would be attenuated. It happened oddly enough that he had a line of a poem printed, very like a line of subscriber's poem. I sent him a post card and said, "What is a line of poetry between friends? You and George Sterling better play a game of seven-up for that line of poetry." It got his little goat, but his goat is a dog. (Just as yours is a Moose) We cannot both get pleasant at the same time. He is father right over again, too.

Coates took correspondence work with the University of Chicago, doing the bulk of the work for that class that would ultimately be *Black Cherries*.

With the advent of *The Frontier* she appeared in there regularly. In 1929, Grace placed two stories in Edward O'Brien's *Anthology of American Short Story* and four in 1930, more than any other writer.

COATES TO O'BRIEN: MAY 10, 1930

> Dear Mr. O'Brien:
>
> To my formal permission, herewith given, to include The Way of the Transgressor in "The Best Stories of 1930", I add my delight and gratification that you want it. Mr. Merriam will be as pleased as I that this story will be included in your yearbook, and his confirmation will reach you promptly.
>
> I believe your unexpected encouragement will start me seriously to work this year.
>
> *Sincerely yours, Grace Stone Coates*[24]

∞

Circles

The wind-evading grasses sway
   Curvate intaglios on the snow.
My thrifty spirit feels dismay
   That loveliness be wasted, so,
   On paths where broom in hand I go
To sweep the night-borne drifts away.

Each small blade makes a fairy ring,
   Tiny, but large enough to hold
Much purity. The tall stems fling
   Their interlacing patterns bold.
   Not Sirius through the midnight rolled
Nor Ursa of the North can swing

A fairer circle, arc more true,
   Than wind-blown grasses delicate.
Must I efface their beauty new?
   I pause, brush lightly, hesitate—
   Then smiling smite, content that fate
Bids housewives round their circles, too.

CHAPTER THREE

When Grace Stone Coates met H.G. Merriam, the relationship helped take her out of her humdrum world in Martinsdale and introduced her to a another new world of writers that became good friends and correspondents.

H.G. Merriam came to the University of Montana in 1919 as chairman of the English Department, and the young scholar recognized the needs of the region and its cultural potential, and prodded Montana to know itself, according to Professor Edmund L. Freeman.[1]

Merriam was born September 6, 1883, in Westminster, Massachusetts. The family moved to Denver, Colorado, for his mother's health and the family bought a grocery store, where the young Merriam helped out behind the counter and in deliveries.

He entered East Denver High School in 1898, intending to become a medical doctor. To prepare for college, he took the high school classics curriculum course which required four years of Latin, three of Greek, four of English, two of French, and history, science and mathematics. To further prepare for a medical career, he went to the University of Wyoming in Laramie in 1902. There a geology professor encouraged him to take the examination for a Rhodes scholarship. He was accepted, and left for Oxford, England, with the first group of American Rhodes scholars.[2]

Merriam received a Bachelor of Arts degree in 1907 and his Master of Arts degree in 1912 from Oxford University, teaching at Whitman College in Washington from 1908 to 1910. He also taught at Beloit College, Wisconsin and Reed College in Oregon where he met and married Doris W. Foote in 1915.

During World War I, Merriam went with the YMCA to France where he taught English to French officers, and later in London assisted American officers and enlisted men in entering British universities.

Merriam was hired by the University of Montana in Missoula in 1919 to teach English and to head the English department. He introduced creative writing into the curriculum and started *The Frontier* to publish the students' work. After seven years of being a student's publication, Merriam made *The Frontier* a regional magazine that soon achieved national acclaim. In 1933, *The Frontier* took over *The Midland,* a magazine that had been edited by John T. Frederick at the University of Iowa and continued as *Frontier and Midland* until its suspension in 1939.

In 1927, as the change was made to a regional magazine, Merriam asked Grace Stone Coates to work as assistant editor. He also had her take part in the summer writers' workshops at the University of Montana.

The correspondence between Coates and Merriam was basically about poems and stories for *The Frontier,* but there are many personal communications about Coates' own work and Merriam's help in editing. When he asked her to work as assistant editor, she was thrilled.

(today)

It is impossible for me to put on paper/the enthusiasm I feel about your new venture. When I offered to help, what I meant was help the magazine, not help myself, as you have permitted me to do. Of course I'll undertake the work; and of course I'll send manuscripts as soon as possible; and try to disagree with you so suavely that you'll never have to give me one of those looks that subdue students.

I am sick today, and nothing less than your letter would have got me to the typewriter. I'll write at length soon.[3]

Coates and Merriam didn't always agree on the work that was submitted to *The Frontier.* In his letter to ask her to join *The Frontier,* he said,

You and I see and report differently: I consider that an advantage. But of course we shall have to be in more or less agreement about aims and means. My chief aim is to become a publishing center for young or old writers whose work is excellent, writers from Wyoming, Montana, Idaho, Washington, Oregon, chiefly, but also from anywhere: secondly, to get this section of the country interested in itself and its writers interested in reflecting its life...[4]

When Grace did comment on one submission, Merriam answered:

Grand! The joke's on me, for if there's one thing the English instructors here at the U stand for in the eyes of students and townspeople, is their FEAR OF SENTIMENTALITY! So it is a real joke that I should be found sentimental in my choice of verse. I see what you mean, tho, and I'm sympathetic with your criticism. A poem (?) like DEPENDANCE in the last issue makes you writhe. It does me. Every once in a while an editor gets trapped, or caught so that he can't refuse without too big a price to pay. That's part of the tale. But there's more of it. You like brittle emotion, hard crystal thot, subtle and experimental wording. You also delight in phrases, in the flavor of words. You prefer tempered emotions—tempered not necessarily by living but by thinking. Now I don't generally like these qualities. At times I do. I have read verses of yours possessing these characteristics, and liked them. I don't like poems like Shipley's FALL CRESCENT, in the November issue. You do. To me his poem is as soft sentimentally as and far less true of life than even

H.G. MERRIAM, CIRCA 1930

387(XII):2, H.G. Merriam Papers, K. Ross Toole Archives, The University of Montana—Missoula.

DEPENDANCE. As for the degree of emotion demanded by the situation or idea, you couldn't have more nearly struck the phrase I use daily, almost, with creative writing students. But you see, in the end who shall determine what is the EXACT degree of emotion demanded in a situation or by an idea?

But isn't it fine that two of the editors of the same magazine should find themselves thus opposed, if opposed we are, temperamentally? We can check one another.[5]

Merriam counted on Grace to provide work for *The Frontier* as well as Frank Bird Linderman, who gathered and retold Indian folklore, and Lew Sarrett, Wisconsin poet who became a contributing editor, among others.

Both Merriam and Coates not only encouraged the writers to publish in *The Frontier* but also helped direct and place contributors' work in paying publications. Grace helped many poets and writers refine their work and see it in print. They had to go through a lot of material to find the stuff they thought should go into *The Frontier,* and always, as with Will Saroyan, Grace tried to help the writer even as they were rejected. They both became adept at soothing the rejected authors, although Grace did admit to Merriam:

> Personally I'm STRONG for rejection slips and nothing else. As soon as an editor tries to be kind to fools he is lost; and only fools expect an editor to be kind—I mean "only fools call the wind kind or unkind"—who wants sympathy any way! As soon as I tried to tell B. what I thought was wrong, she hurled at my head that she had sold this for $16 to Whosis and that for $17.93 to whatsis; and that was supposed to be [sic] the unanswerable answer to my suggestion that what she had written was windy trash. So I told her to go ahead and sell this, it was all right with me. This was long ago. We are entirely good friends, and I sympathize with her deeply; but her logic——she reminds me of Ralph Cheyney pressing the sale of Lucian's poetry because she had just had her tonsils out. I am sorry for everybody's spines and sick legs; but as a writer I don't care a whope—or a whoop—to have an editor know I just had a tooth out. I don't know how I got started on this—inertia—got started and kept on going. Mary pity editors.[6]

Generally over the years, as the correspondence evolved it showed a comfortable friendship between Merriam and Coates.

One of the writers Grace tried to get for *The Frontier* was Taylor Gordon, a native of White Sulphur Springs who had made a name for himself as a black spiritual singer and had written of his experiences.

Taylor Gordon's father John had said that his forefathers were Zulus. John went to England as a young man of 18 and worked for a wealthy Scots family as a domestic servant and came with that family (and his father) to the United States. The Scots family lost their money and sold everything they had, including John Gordon and his father. After the Civil War, the younger Gordon went to domestic science school, becoming a chef. John Gordon married Annie Goodlow of Kentucky and they moved to Fort Benton, Montana, and later to Rocker, Montana, where John worked as a chef for a large gold-mining company until the company moved its headquarters back to Chicago.[7]

The Gordons liked the wide-open spaces and decided to stay in Montana, finally ending up in White Sulphur Springs. John worked at the Higgins Hotel until 1893 when he left his family in Montana and went to Canada to cook for a Canadian railroad, only to be killed in an accident.

Mrs. Gordon was left with a family of five boys and a girl, cooking and cleaning for other people and taking in washing to support them. One of the boys, Taylor, or Manny as he was called, found early employment as an errand boy for the red light district, running errands for the girls and delivering water. He had other jobs growing up and when he was a young man worked on a ranch, learned mechanics, and had a job driving passengers from White Sulphur Springs to the railroad at Dorsey. When the Ringlings (of the circus Ringlings)[8] came to town he drove for them. A year or so later he worked as a porter on the railroad and then on the private car of John Ringling. After taking voice lessons, he went on to a career of concerts and singing, making his home in New York. It was here he wrote his autobiography that came out in 1929.

Coates saw Gordon in New York when she visited there, and the two corresponded. However, Coates had sent a letter, which included a "ditty," to Taylor Gordon and when it reached New York, he had gone on tour. The letter was returned much the worse for wear and open to anyone including the censorious postmistress. Grace was out of town, and when Henderson received the letter, he burned it. She later told a friend,

> The letter was open to the world; Mr. Coates' father had slaves—lots of them; and Mr. Coaters read the letter. His horror at my casual chatter with a Negro, and my horror at his attitude, each revealed to the other in that lightning flash have never been modified in the slightest degree. He would feel degraded that his wife could feel unconscious of a negro's color; and I feel demeaned that he is capable of race prejudice—and here we have lived with each other years, and discovered these characteristics in each other by accident.[9]

Grace recalled on one trip to New York. "I was terribly down, one day, when Taylor took me down to 'Brass town' and we stood on the street corner and ate dill pickles till my world was restored—at the expense of my stomach."[10]

Coates did a newspaper item on Gordon's career and Gordon kept Coates apprised of his career and wanderings.

GORDON TO COATES: APRIL 16, 1927

> NEW HOTEL VINCENNES
> And annex
> VINCENNES AVE., 36th St. AND ELLIS PARK
> CHICAGO, April 16, 1927

To the Talented, G.S. Coates Of course you will pardon me for writing befor I send you the books.

But here tonight I am thinking of your interview, how much more interesting to me than the one I had today, yours didn't seem to be a interview of music, and art, so much as it did one of the characteristics of a certain kind of people.

I don't know why but that what came to me about 3.40 this a.m.

I meet lots of charming people all over the country, and I am very interested in them and what they are trying to do.

It grieves me much if I think I did not do all that was in my power to help them.

But I like to be sure I know what they realy wont before I move, that's why I am cautious then, there is places where I use much more tack than outhers. As you are aware, "with you self in your writing."

You have the spark that is required to be a great writer.

I do hope you will let it burn, and burn bright.

"the gods are with you," I can't hardly wait until I can get to N.Y.C. so I can get the business addresse of the best publisher so you can send your proofs.

You must put out one of 1927's big hits

Life is always chasing me away from good things, why didn't fate leave me longer in the west where I was enjoying myself. I am glad there is another day coming.

Oh I must close this out here for me to attend one of these pre-concert parties; I love them but I like other things too.

> ByBy, You will have a great success
>
> *Yours Sincerely, T.G.*[11]

2-36 PM: LONDON JULY-2-27

Dear Mrs. Coates.

Just a few lines to let you know I am still alive and hope to see you sometime this year again. We had a fine artistic success here and we will be here until latter part of August. I would like to get one of your letters telling me all the news of Montana.

I am sure you would like Europe you must come some time after you finish your book. I have meet many a writer here our first party was by Somerset Maugham. It was too great Lady Aschuof was there she is the Berries. I will have lots to tell you I must say Rebecca West is in Italy at present.

Did you write Carl and Mary in nyc? Let me know.

And drop me a line. Put Air Mail Stamp on it and I will get it in 10 days.

The women here are Vamps and they don't use any powder or paint. They are very tall Oh so tall. Most of them. The Blood look like it was going to come out their cheeks.

In Paris. Oh the one different the more no clothes. No place for a pious boy like me. I am to cautious.

Mr. J is well and like it very much. He lived here before.

I must close I am going to a party but I did half to drop you a line so it would get on the next tot July 4

GS ByBy lot of kind thoughts

y.s., Taylor Gordon[12]

GORDON TO COATES: AUGUST 24, 1927
6 HAYMARKET, LONDON

To that one woman, Grace Stone

Dear lady, yours of today thrilled me through and through, at last the long silence is broken, and you are living, that's so nice.

How sorry I am that I am not there to help you pick those nice, red berries, that any chance I might get my lip stained by some magic way. But never to forget the impression of the process of staining. HaHaHa,

No, no, kidding I really know love, to pick currants. I use to pick lots of them in W.S.S. when I was a kid.

I am sure you can make a fine currant cobbler, if you want to.

Well you want me to tell you about myself. I dislike that but I must do a few things you would have do so here goes.

As you know we left nyc for Paris, the heaven on earth, you must go there some time, or else you will never know all of it, we spent just a few days there and then here to London, and England, its mason self, so mascular in form, and ways, and blue in tone.

I almost decided the first nights here they locked the town up on me at 12:30. you know new york city is not the quietest place on earth an their paree, where your Russian noble blood will leap with joy. And all the wildness, of your ancestors will rush through your brains, to tickle your soul.

But I found out anything is done here behind closed doors, and it not half bad after you get in, it grows on you. We are having a grand time now, that we know the ropes, sorry you are not here, to join in.

We have been to some fine country places they use every inch of the ground. They are fine people Oh I can't tell you all on paper. I write too fast, But you see I am to be a writer and all fast writers are good writers HaHa

You would like the country here "But in a town like Harrogat, or Leeds, if you should get full one nights and try to go home, you would try every key hole in town before you found your own house. They all look a like. Oh it terrible, London is although different

Radcliffee Hall and you are a great deal a like, see her sketch. You must wore a suit like that to when you are the big authoress, Ha

You could go as the young sister. She is OK You will like her, Oh, fine lady, I can't tell you all on paper I shall half to wait until we meet, then I will tell you all

You are so kind to write so much about us, I never will forget you, chief sends regards

Inclosed, are a few clippings—I will send you more later.

Write me again soon, please and tell me anything; we will be here until Sept. 20 I know I thought I would be in Montana in Sept. But fate is mean to me, for some reason.

Your poem is too beautiful

I think I can really understand it. Clearly, too clear,

Sincerely, Taylor Gordon[13]

Coates told Merriam,

He [Gordon] writes me for instance (when I asked him to please confine himself to letters that I could drop without blowing myself up), "The reason I write the kind of letters I do is because I am so healthy. Most writers are always sick in bed half the time. I will have to catch me a bad malaise and be a writer. It wouldn't be any tougher than this singing job."

If you do institute the range ask Taylor to contribute. He, at least, sacrificed 6 heifers, once, to his fear of ghosts, and it is a good story. You see Taylor is a Montana boy, and he knows a lot beside spirituals.[14]

Both Merriam and Grace were anxious for Taylor's appearance in *The Frontier*. Merriam had told her:

Don't let Taylor Gordon rest until you have his story of the sacrifice etc for us, please. That would be invaluable. And we'll print it exactly as he writes it, spelling and all, if that won't anger him![15]

Taylor Gordon

Castle Museum, Meagher County Historical Association

Unfortunately, Gordon never sent material to *The Frontier.* His story of the ghost and the six dead heifers was never revealed, although he remained a life-long friend of Grace.

Grace submitted to many magazines, as well as asking Merriam's advice about getting an agent. She submitted work to *Palms,* beginning a friendship with Idella Purnell.

Palms was started by Purnell. Raised in Guadalajara, Mexico, by her American dentist father, she attended the University of California at Berkeley, and then returned to work in Guadalajara at the American consulate. In 1923, she started the magazine with the help of former classmates Barbara Burks and Vernon King as associate editors and Witter Bynner and Agustin Basave as contributing editors.

Purnell met John M. Weatherwax in 1925 in Los Angeles where she spent a summer working in the public library. They married in 1927 and Purnell and her magazine moved to Aberdeen, Washington. In a letter of submission, Grace wrote to Purnell in 1927,

> It delights me that you have come into the west...I am sure I will not seem half such a nut when I write you, now that you have foregone that slightly exotic and disconcerting atmosphere that hung around you in Mexico; that impelled me to do weird things with postage...[16]

In a later exchange,

> Brief experience convinces me that writers usually have more reason to curse and tear their hair after an appearance in print, than to thank their editors. Contrasts pleases me very much, and it gratifies me to know that a magazine which I respect would use something of mine.[17]

Weatherwax divorced Purnell in 1929, but the two collaborated on 19 books between June 1929 and October 1930, when Weatherwax sent Purnell to New York to find a publisher for their manuscripts. There she met Remi Stone and it was love at first sight. They married in 1932.

Grace had mentioned having a cousin in New York, so Remi Stone may have been related. Her niece mentioned years later that she corresponded with a "relative" at the University of Texas where Purnell was located.

In the meantime, Merriam recommended Curtis Brown of New York as the best agent for short story work for writers already established and suggested Grace also send him some poems. He also recommended Bryan and Kilpatrick of New York City.[18]

COATES TO MERRIAM: MAY 26, 1927

Dear Mr. Merriam:

Even before addressing the agencies you mention I shall thank you for your two letters—yes, and for the check from the Mercury that came tonight. Thank you most for the adverse comment. I had been wondering whether I was deceiving myself about wanting it, but I wasn't. The praise is like cold hotcakes, but the criticism makes me glow. I know too well how to evaluate the praise! "In Irony"—I shall evolve a better title—the New Republic wrote me a note about that, too. They liked it, but no individual but you has seen anything in it but words. Couldn't see what I was trying to get at.

If you are familiar with Jean Christoff you know what Rolland says about all genius being ridiculous—and indifferent to being so.

What you say, in general, about the prime weakness of my work is no doubt true, and the saying helpful. It's five minutes or nothing for me, on a poem; not that I want to work that way, but who's going to get the dinner? It astonished me to find that I could do decent work just as a task, a class exercise. Some of the things that seem to be commended were done solely as a duty. They were more finished and logical, probably, than things that arise out of inner derision. I hadn't supposed I could do it. It is interesting to see how Gwendolen Haste works—completely outlined before she begins. (That is only part of it, of course; but in general it is true of her work.)

You hit more of the spots I considered weak than any one else has ever done, in the comment on the various verses. And I'd necessarily respect you for singling out "inmost ways are anybody's street" for approval. Several of the words you reject were makeshifts, as I inwardly acknowledged at the time. I'll sing the rest of it to Mrs. Merriam. She may not be as tired of us as you have reason to be. Mrs. Merriam wrote me a delightful letter which I shall answer soon.

Sincerely yours, Grace Stone Coates[19]

MERRIAM TO COATES: JUNE 13, 1927

Dear Mrs. Coates,

I have been wishing to catch a minute or two on the wing ever since receipt of your letter of May 27, for I don't believe you have quite understood my attitude toward your "prime weakness". Five minutes might be quite enough time for the production of an eight-line mater-piece, provided that masterpiece has been brewing in the subconscious and conscious mind for some months or years, or it springs out of a situation that has been thoroughly digested spiritually over a period of time. The reason why you found that you could do "decent work just as a task" probably lies in your ability under such stress to choose to write about material which had been thus germinating in your emotional and intellectual experience. What I wished to state about your work was that more frequently than necessary you wrote on the spur of the moment with the emotions and ideas of the moment, caused by some present irritation or "inner derision", unrelated to more permanent emotions and ideas, or insufficiently related.

Jove, what a sentence!

Cordially yours, HGM[20]

Grace sent material to Merriam from the Maine psychiatrist and poet Dr. Israel Newman, hoping it would be printed. Newman and Grace had started corresponding during the 1920s, after she submitted a poem to his poetry journal. She later spoke of him when she was consoling William Saroyan about loneliness.

Few persons have mitigated my loneliness. I could always turn to Dr. Newman. I must tell you about him sometime. It was he, more than any one else; or rather my experience with him, that made it hard for me to write to you at first. My impulse was to write to you with the easy frankness natural between us; but I had written to him so, and he had wound up with an (actual) attack of pseudo angina, and I had so far reflected or simulated his physical condition psychically if you can untangle that mass of words, that I had mentioned to Mr. Coates that I must consult a physician. Henderson whose one panacea for all life's disorders in Chamberlain's liniment offered to rub me and I said, "You can't rub a pain that hovers two inches from my body." So I have that remark to convince me that the experience wasn't a constructive memory. At the moment of going to sleep I was, for two weeks, stricken awake by the characteristic smothering, anguish and struggle of pseudo angina. The entire thing disappeared when I learned that Dr. Newman had experienced the attack (concurrently) and overcome it.[21]

It was probably with Grace in mind that Newman wrote:

Tight-Rope Walker

Perverse she was and bitter, seemed to lack

Those kinder traits whence lovers' lives are wrought.

Some buried something seemed to hold her back

From what she might have rushed to. He had sought

A lump of lead and found a coiled up spring.

He thought she was unbalanced. Could he guess

Her Life was but a constant balancing
As her who walks the tight-wire in distress?

"—Fell in my arms at last", he proudly said,
"Which proves her judgement is mature and sound."
They break, who fall from those high wires they tread
When there is neither saw-dust on the ground
Nor arms wherein to land. How could he tell
She had been broken long before she fell?

Grace had an amazing way of separating her life in Martinsdale with her correspondence. She spoke of Newman years later when she wrote,

Yesterday I met a man who makes, made, me ache. Cosmopolitan, New Yorker for the moment, crook probably but not positively; promoter evidently. We just took one look at each other and lost the roomful and began to flirt. The trouble was that time was brief. It is only one man in 87,942—I've counted—that sees past my crowsfeet. (One poet [Newman] in N.Y. did write three pages to those very crowsfeet, and life pinched us quite a bit for a few years because we accidentally tumbled too far over the edge of a love affair.)...Anyway, deathbed repentance, I wind up in a sonnet in Henderson's bed. That gets you by with the church."[22]

Grace burned her letters from Israel Newman, but she sent a poem to Saroyan she wrote about Newman.

Spring Scimitar

One I loved—I loved, and love, and shall love—
Named for me an unfamiliar flower;
Named for me the golden flower, Forsythia,
As he raised its tangled, showery branches.

Once he teased me that my simple palate
Craved the chartreuse-colored Chinese love-nuts.
In my hands his violets and freesias
Caught the tears we scorned to heed, at parting.

A fat Jewess lived with him, unmarried.

Since one time she studied agriculture

She knows which side pumpkin seeds are buttered

Before planting…Spring's gold sword, Forsythia!

In November, Merriam returned Dr. Newman's poetry with extensive editing notes.

I immensely desire to use something of Dr. Newman's, but I honestly do not find anything just suited to our magazine in this material. I'll give you my criticism and you can pass on to him whatever you think best. (I shall certainly desire personal contact with him, too.)

Merriam went through each of the poems and made extensive notes such as,

Pioneer Woman—excellent quality, and I should like to use it. But I should want the catchy reiteration of sound in "pots and pans" of line three changes: "pans" almost picks up "hands" of the preceding line and yet is not the rime. Secondly, I do not understand even faintly, "Entangled in fine stands." "Stands"—of what? Even if "strands" were meant, what meaning would the phrase have? Am I dumb? Thirdly, I can't be sure of the reference of "their" in the fifth line. Again, am I dumb? These two matters destroy all meaning for me in lines 4,5, and 6. Could they be "fixed"? We go to press on Nov. 10. I'd genuinely like to use this poem; it has flavor and fine phrases and significance…

…I can't tell you how much I hate to write this to you. I deeply appreciate Dr. Newman's generosity. I hope that his name will be under excellent work in our magazine soon. Can't Pioneer Woman be helped and returned at once?

Cordially, HGM[23]

Coates was gracious about criticism from Merriam, both for herself and her friends.

Thank you especially for your letter of November 3. You will find out (if it is my privilege to work with—or for—you) that I can tolerate truth in maximum doses. When you are crowded for time, don't even bother to be suave.

I'm glad you think Israel is worth while. His work is uneven, but much of it is unique and some of it beautiful. I am wiring him to work on Pioneer Woman and send it to you direct. It may not reach you in time, but if it doesn't, it doesn't. "We do our possible!"

The only special consideration I would ever ask for any friend is that you give their stuff the once-over even tho you are busy. It would be be-littling to all of us if you couldn't be honest of course, and the meaning seemed clear to me. "Your heart, entangled in fine strands of memory—or memories—that even tug your hands away from their (present uncongenial) work, leaps wildly; yet tho these memories tug at your heart and hands like strings (strands) you are not their marionettes."

Don't feel unduly concerned about the contribution. If Israel can make it please you, we will both be glad; and if he cannot, something else will, some time. (I hope you like that construction!) Israel and I have furious quarrels behind us, and they started over just such a thing as has come up now. He asked me for a contribution, thought what I sent him was third rate, and instead of refusing it, used it. He was indignant at me for sending him what he thought was poor, and I was indignant at his using what he thought wasn't good. We said quite a few things to each other about it.

(Forgive me for being diverted to personal matters) To go back to your criticisms... they have raised my opinion of Israel's verse, and made me question my own so cock-sure judgments. I am happy over them.

Dr. Newman "introduced" me to a patient of his, "Petya",[24] to whom I write. The boy is dying probably. He is a musician, so he will appreciate the little joke of the title given the verse I mailed him this morning. It is not an aspirant for the Frontier—and I send it for fear you aren't getting enough amateur verse to read!

Modulation

Israel was the one I loved
　As I love the gloom of night
When the wind is whispering,
　That retains no dream of light
To remember or desire.
　Israel was one I loved
As I love the caves of thought
　Where no other mind has moved.

Have you seen a cereus bloom
　Drowned in silence, on the floor
Of the pale enchanted sea

That the moon knows how to pour?
Beyond gesture, beyond breath
     Drenched in magic beyond reach?—
(Israel Petya) was that motionless
     Ecstasy upon my beach.

Flush beneath the breasts of dawn,
     Jewel on the spider's span,
Twinkling of the leaves at noon,
     Music when the shadows ran;
Fragile patterns in the dust
     Where a whirlwind passed away—
Petya is the gossamer
     Happiness across my day.

          Will they laugh?
     Sincerely yours, Grace Stone Coates[24]

Merriam liked the last two lines of the first stanza and the next four, which he said were "Beautiful four lines. They should be salvaged—and used in a less "occasional" poem."[25]

COATES TO MERRIAM: NOVEMBER 3, 1927

Dear Mr. Merriam:
     This was one thing (of three) that I didn't send you—One of the other mss was something I like, but wanted revised a bit. By the way, Israel has a hard time with punctuation, and will not resent any changes in that.
     Please be assured that in my opinion the only decent standard to maintain in editing a magazine is to take only what comes nearest to the thing you want. I think I could despise an editor who compromised—except when he had to!
          Cordially yours, Grace Stone Coates[26]

There was continual discussion of the magazine and its contents. Grace promised Merriam the next decent thing she wrote, recalling that *The Midland* had four of her sketches,

     …that you would have been more welcome to.

There is hope for Mulcahy if he is under twenty but not if he's over fifty. What I'm going to say doesn't need an immediate answer—but sometime tell me what you think. First, about rejection ships: there are two angles; one, that my greatest difficulty is the mechanical side of typing—I'm always on the verge of trouble with my hands and arms. The Miner, just tonight, took exception to my carbon copy I've been slipping them to save typing. The other side of the rejections question is that a rejection slip is far less offensive than an equally brief letter—and what is there to say to the hopeless ones? It is easy enough to give encouragement to the fairly promising ones. Personally I think it is a waste not to use slips.

There are a number of other things—but my mind has become a blank. I am impatient to see the new magazine, and hope to get a copy before Saturday. By the way, did you know that Harold Hersey was born in Bozeman—or does his name mean anything to you. He is now writing Frontier ballads, has no patience with poetry that every body can't understand, and is at the head of the Cowboy, Ace-High, and Ranch Romance group. Anyway he has had an interesting life, spent all over the world. What is the length limit for prose, for the Frontier?

Thelma Lucille Lull is a Bozeman product, too; writes from Iowa. She had to leave college, financial difficulties, and take boards for a living. Evidently she refused to be subdued by fate, and writes:

With imagined hoofs I spurn the earth

(For actual hoofs I've lacked from birth)

And kick up the soil for all I'm worth,

For spring is in my spine, O!

I like her spirit if not her expression of it.[27]

In November, Merriam announced that the new magazine would be out the next week. He went on to answer her question about who to contact for future contributions to the magazine.

THE FRONTIER will be off the press early next week and I will immediately send you copies, enough to use as specimens at least in your talk on Nov. 26th. You needn't be "ashamed not knowing the real Montana writers". In general, there are none "doing genuine work, as opposed to aspiration and pious hopes". Most Montana writers are busy getting established. Of the more established writers there are Sexton Bailey (Butte), Will James (?Powder River), and Frank Linderman. There may be others but I don't know of them. I think that probably you yourself are as established as any of the others.

Aside from those you know, I would mention [Henry] Jason Bolles [poet and English instructor at Montana State University], perhaps Mr. Ivins of Lewistown, Joe Allen, a butcher in Missoula who has done some good pieces of work but none of fine note, Grace Baldwin (Kalispell), the poets who were in the MERCURY. If there are prose writers other than these I have mentioned I don't know of them. There was a man Bozeman who was making about $5,000 a year on stories for magazines like ADVENTURE but I can't think of his name.

In previous years I have tried to know who earlier writers of Montana are and I confess that they all wrote so badly that I myself would not care to recognize them as "Montana writers".

I see that I'm not helping you. I'm sorry.

Sincerely yours, HGM[28]

Grace was delighted to receive the new issue of *The Frontier,* and immediately wrote to Merriam.

This is a eulogy and an impertinence. Praise to one's superiors is always an impertinence. Because it is Thanksgiving time, (I suppose), I first said to myself concerning your editorial: One would think a thing so packed with meaning would chew like hardtack instead of fruitcake. But I don't have to be culinary even if I do have to cook. Your editorial is like a perfect wave, that swells and recedes, and lifts itself beautifully again in the closing paragraphs.

At first I thought,

"The best paragraphs are at the last where they belong;" but the dirt and soil and mold kept me from saying that, and your fine challenge to the attitude that the ardent joy of writing is an escape from life, in the second paragraph, made me put the high point there. You had already won me by the quotation from Thoreau, whose words have been on my lips a thousand times.

I do not expect to be panegyric and personal very often, so let me say that it is most reassuring to know that whatever the failures of the Frontier, while you direct it they will not be failures of taste.

Reassurance conveys something I didn't mean, but I have an engagement with the breakfast dishes right now, and can't escape from life any longer.[29]

Merriam to Coates

NOVEMBER 29, 1927: DEAR MRS. COATES,

I kept Love Came Like A Landlord because of the clever quirk in the last line. Really, that line is pretty well packed with poetic significance. I did not by any means think the poem among the best in the issue.

Let me answer your questions as them come.

I should like very much to have a list of "the various writers and near writers and, more especially, obscure editors". I can't put them on the mailing list for this issue, because it is so nearly exhausted; but I should like to pick them up on next February's issue.

We have-not for this issue planned "an expensive exchange list", but again I should like to have that row; and sometime in off moments if you care to make suggestions I should be glad to receive them.

The criticisms which you have sent me on material that has been returned to me have seemed to me to strike at the strength and weakness of the pieces. Now you can use what has appeared in this first issue as somewhat of a "basis of comparison".

Financing the magazine this year is not difficult; however, if we get out six issues instead of three issues next year the financial problem would be serious. I have put out feelers with the idea of attracting some "angel", and it has been my plan to bring one down out of the blue after the second issue has appeared. But you know it would take an appalling endowment to run the magazine, not less that $30,000. Do discuss magazine fineness with whom you know who knows about them.

The verse at the end of your letter is well under way. I don't think that any of the three words "salute", "accept", and "admit", is the right one for the fourth line. I think the rhyme of the last stanza in ...all and second rhyme in—all is unfortunate to—gives a ticking effect.

If Mrs. Anderson would like to have us use some material I should be happy to see it, of course. I have had two or three pieces offered me for money that read well but, of course, I have no money.

Someone should very soon compile data on Montana writers. I think that perhaps you know more about them than any other person in the state, and I don't see why you shouldn't do it aptly and well.

I'm a little worried about the historical material for the next issue, since I have nothing at hand and prospects are not very good. I shall eagerly look over John Moro's ditty. Naturally, I should prefer material from some other state than Montana.

It would give you great encouragement to see the number of inquiries that are coming in about our venture. Every mail brings more than one letter.

Cordially yours, HGM[30]

∞

Possess the Day

Earth's dazzling winter gladness puts to shame
    Consuming though and inward brooding eye.
The tinkling gullies twinkle into flame,
    Bare trees commit their beauty to the sky.

Hark, overhead a music fine and faint
    Rises and dies—the wind-plucked wires' drone!
They mock our messages in laughter quaint,
    Their grey utility to beauty blown.

Each frost star flashes up a smile to greet
    The lacquered magpie tilting to and fro;
And what such blue on blue of sky could meet,
    Except the deeper blue themountains know!

Are you too dull to love the hurried leaf,
    The snow-spin and the vibrant elfin song?
Salute the sun—its radiance is brief;
    Possess the day—the winter night is long!

CHAPTER FOUR

*T*he *Frontier* became a consuming passion for Coates as she critiqued poems and short stories. While Merriam was the final arbiter of what went in the magazine, he relied on Grace's good editorial skill to make the first judgment. The year 1928, Grace put her all into making the magazine work.

While the work itself was rewarding, it also added to her circle of friends. There were also some interesting friends to meet through the DuRand Dude Ranch, just a few miles west of Martinsdale started in the twenties by Courtland DuRand.

DuRand was born in Minneapolis in 1877, and came to Montana with his parents at the age of fifteen. He and his father handled twenty-horse freight teams of supplies for the construction crews of the Jawbone Railroad—a line that was originally built to haul the ore from the mining town of Castle to a smelter in East Helena. When the mines closed, the line was continued to Merino (Harlowton) and Lewistown.

DuRand attended Columbia University where he earned a degree in civil engineering and a reputation as a polo player. After college, he was in partnership with his father in the DuRand Mining and Smelting Company with properties in the Little Rockies. An international mining conglomerate employed DuRand and he traveled the world supervising prospects. Stories later circulated about suspicious stock transactions. It was never proven, but the story followed him back to Montana when he started a dude ranch and a game farm with elk and bison from the federal bison range at Moiese. There was overcrowding on the range, and with the help of Senator Thomas Walsh, DuRand was able to get eighty-six elk and fourteen bison for his game farm.

DuRand trained the animals for packing and taught pairs to pull wagons—one of those teams he would take back East for parades to advertise his dude ranch. At the Big Elk Ranch, he entertained his guests with a water rodeo. The local paper reported,

> A diving platform, water corals, and fish-hook chutes have been constructed, from which buffalo, elk and horses dove into 15 feet of water …dudes were able to catch the buffalo and elk and ride on their backs across the lake. One elk was lassoed, and it pulled a row boat with two passengers.
>
> Mary Brosseit, a professional roper who entertained at President Roosevelt's garden party on the White House lawn last spring, gave an exhibition of roping on a specially constructed platform in the middle of the lake.

An airplane flew low over the heads of the crowd, covering them with confetti.[1]

Grace could see DuRand dressed in his khaki-colored knickers, high laced boots, a wool plaid shirt and a Stetson hat, often with neckerchiefs and leather cuffs decorated with silver-colored rivets, come to pick up his guests at the Martinsdale train depot. Although she had no quarter for sham or show, she was entertained by his display. In turn, Grace and later Marguerite and Alberta Bair were pointed out to guests of the ranch as important people of the community.

The same train that brought guests brought the Coates' mail, and Grace was quick to return edited mail to Merriam.

Coates to Merriam: January 5, 1928

Your registered enclosures came this morning. Why am I always feeding guests just when interesting mail comes? Anyway, I burned only the potatoes, hovering over your letters—manuscripts. I did not know you had been in the hospital. I was rather waiting for some suggestion from you. Thank you for your good wishes to us. Good things are on the way for us all. I feel them. I have any amount of verse for you to select from; and I feel sure there will be some prose. I wrote you a

"Midland" story—Windfalls—and just then Brandt & Brandt wrote for more material, and I let it go. I am under this necessity: of making my work command respect. I do not want indulgence. I want the right to my time. Rather, I want my right to my time respected.

You must be overwhelmed with work. Let me do anything I can to help you. I was greatly surprised to know you were in the hospital, and hope you will regain your strength quickly.

The rejection slips are better than most of the mss they will ride with. They are good enough until we get others.

I will send the mss to you soon. And will go to work on something to enclose with this for you to pass on.

Of these I am sending, Mr. Frederick may have BARRIERS and PAST HEALING. If you care to take out all you even *may* want, you are welcome to keep them as long as you wish, and reject later if you find better stuff. Then if you will, send me the rest. The Harp wants something, and some others, and I'll give them the skimmed milk. And as soon as Mr. F. remits, you can have the other group. You will like some of the things. Some of these you have seen. (I have not mailed an editor a poem since the Mercury business, except those, last week, to J.T.F.)[2]

There was still a teacher-student relationship between Coates and Merriam as he critiqued her work. When Grace sent a story to Merriam in January of 1928, Merriam sent it back with an apology.

MERRIAM TO COTES: JANUARY 10, 1928

I fear I'm going to be disappointing. I really don't like the story! You seem to me throughout it to be aiming at more than one target. Are you directing the reader's interest to a clean-up in morals, and suggesting one for this country? The story reads that way. Your note indicates that you intend to direct your reader's attention to the prodigal way America uses, or fails to use, its immigrant man-power.

Thruout the story Jean is depicted as a gentleman not only by nature and by cultivation but by occupation; there fore the last sentence shocks without driving home the idea. Furthermore, isn't the idea quite new to the reader as you pop it at him?

I don't think you need worry about offensiveness to Jews, altho certain magazines wouldn't touch a story even indirectly suggesting race prejudice—not that yours does but that editors would fear it might. My experience is that the Jews who are real Americans recognize the objectionable in lowdown Jews more quickly than we ourselves. I can't see, as to the other query, why any man would object to having such a story written about him.

Lastly, I'm not sure that I see a story in this material. Certainly this handling of material is an account rather than a story.

Forgive the harshness; I mean all right.

Sincerely, HGM[3]

And the next day he wrote,

MERRIAM TO COATES: JANUARY 11, 1928

I don't see why *Stubborn Thistles* shouldn't place, unless it should be an editor's fear of offending G.A.R-ites by display of a bluecoat who isn't ideal and never was! I suppose too that the less courageous editors would fear to print such a heartless—so it would appear to a reader, an average reader—conversation between a daughter obviously well off and an old man who is all but spiritually down-and-out. I'm not criticizing; I'm explaining an assumed attitude of a mythical editor. I think *Thistles* a better title. Perhaps *Castle of Indolence* would be shrewder still. I don't like the ending at all; the implied symbolism won't carry over. To me the old man should be bent but not broken. I think he should be given some ironic remark that would show that the old stubbornness and blindness could never be rooted out—some remark like, "I'm getting, getting old indeed." Or some shrewd, ironic record in the journal. I know that you expect the record you have given him to do just that, but I believe it doesn't.

Why not send it to B & B, if it returns from Scribners? By the way, has that firm placed anything for you? You know that it's considered professionally bad to place your material in the hands of an agent and continue to try to place other writings yourself. This is merely a caution; I don't assume that you sent the story to *Scribners*.

One Without etc is good man's humor. Oughtn't the story to end less stiffly, and less arrangedly? Couldn't it end in a great bubble of mirth? And isn't the beginning of the story carrying too much irrelevant material, irrelevant to the real issue of the story. The bridge and the dining, which you mention but do not use, should be turned to use—to show perhaps, how the town would be shocked at the incidents of the story, and thru the town how the "ladies" involved would take it? I don't know; it just seems to me that the beginning could carry fuller relevancy and much, much more humor. So modified the story should find a ready market in such a magazine as the Elks; I'm not sure but what it might be funny enough for the Sat Eve. Post.

Thanks for the poems. I haven't got over them yet. I wrote at length to Dr. Newman today. Thanks for your help.[4]

And after receiving more material, he picked what he wanted to appear in *The Frontier.*

MERRIAM TO COATES: JANUARY 15, 1928

Oh, delightful. I shall surely want THE VISIT. It is human and witty and finely written. Do you mind if I make a suggestion or two? You enjoy writing subtly—and I enjoy reading subtle writing; but you sometimes don't give your reader a sense of surety. Now I maintain stoutly that surety and subtlety are friendly; in fact one gains by the presence of the other. (Read Thornton Wilder's THE BRIDGE OF SAN LUIS REY. It is the surest piece of art written in America. Hergesheimer tried similar writing and failed—he succeeded in all but one chapter in LINDA CONDON, his most artistic work; and Thomas Beer tried it—SANDOVAL—but go Saturday Evening Posted, at least for the time being. But the BRIDGE is superb.) Now then, you write, "Something had happened while mother was away, that father and she were not happy about; and eating the peaches seemed part of it." The reader doesn't know and hasn't been given a sure enough hint what happened, and the symbolic value of eating peaches if therefore only confusion for him. Can't you give the reader a sense of surety here? I know that you may defend the tale by stating that it is told from the child's point of view and that she honestly did not know the only reply is that the story will gain in both force and charm if, nevertheless, the reader does know. I have read the story to three people of fine intelligence and virtually they have said the same thing, that what happened is only a vague guess with them and therefore that the story is not thoroly satisfactory. Again, the "alone with Carl" is a thrust with vague intention: was Carl only her half-brother? The parents surely weren't afraid of sex trouble? Were they simple afraid of—what? And just what thrust does this push at the father's relation to his children? Please don't become too explanatory; it's only a touch or two that the story needs. And I'll print it exactly as it is if your judgment tells you that it shouldn't be changed. I like the story immensely.

Of the verse I am keeping *Barriers*—please let me know if Mr. Frederick does want it, *Under Trees*—the best written of the lot,—*The Road*—a straightforward bit of charged realism, *The Cloak*—about which I don't feel quite sure, and *Encircled*—also beautifully written. On the other poems I have suggested magazines which might accept them. I am grateful for the generosity of your sending and your proposal. I'm going to use you this time as all editors who write get used: I'm going to print the story surely, you willing and hold the poetry and print it this time or in May as the make-up of the magazine may determine. You don't mind?

Mr. Frederick's editorial is indeed gracious. He must be veritably what the English use as their highest praise, a scholar and a gentleman. I shall write to him. I'm delighted that you have rated O'Brien; the call for biographical material surely means the inclusion of a story.[5]

COATES TO MERRIAM: JANUARY 22, 1928

Dear Mr. Merriam:

I felt gratified, more—pleased—that the Peaches story was in it. Those stories are so closely mine that I might as well try to tell the color of my eyes without a looking glass as to know whether those stories are good. They started as letters to Israel, because he asked me about my childhood; and when he praised them I utilized them for credit work with Chicago—the earlier ones; then Mr. [John T.] Frederick got hold of some of them and that was the way they grew. Mr. Frederick comments on their "patina" and Israel [Newman] on their poignancy; but you are the first one to mention (what is the central meaning to me) their humor. If there are any tears in them, the tears trickle down and lose themselves in the corners of a wide grin.

I *did* shy around the explanation of why the man ate the peaches, in the original story.

Your entire discussion of subtlety interest me very much—let me thank you for the time you give me—and I agree entirely, of course; not to orient a reader, is to leave him in the place of a child, and no reader will tolerate that.

You mentioned the same defect in—*Plaster of Paris,* but I believe I had remedied—or attempted to remedy that—already in the version I sent B & B.

I am sending the new version, and the original. Other editors usually ask that; so there

Sincerely yours, Grace Stone Coates

Henderson this moment came in with, among other things, a letter from Archie. He and the Chagnons found themselves congenial, and more warmly at one than that. Archie is capable of unusual courtesy and deference, and he exercised both whenever he spoke of what you had done for Montana. He asks me if I care to read any of his mss before he sends it off, so I surmise his "Gallant Troupers" is almost completed. If he has luck there, it may be the making of that boy; but, oh, dear, depending on any Irishman who drinks is""leaning your elbows on the wind." So I expect nothing, not even a letter; and then whatever comes is so much to the good. Am I wrong in believing that suspicious persons can't be trustworthy?

I'll observe all your suggestions about news notes; and I'll get busy on them right away. I'll do some thinking and write again promptly to see what I can suggest…

Apparently some people had asked Merriam if Grace had a degree. She replied to him.

I had a year in the Chicago university, a year in which I tried to take care of my mother, who was ill, and make up two years of Greek. My mother died, and so has the Greek. And I did a term's work in the U of Southern Calif. I've had a pretty steady diet of correspondence work—by the way, Black Cherries was done for English VI, Chicago university. That's how it happened to be written.

This letter has grown too long to accommodate anything about the status of my own writing, which I wanted to tell you about. But I can't now; and will some day when telling you seems important.

Sincerely yours, GSC[6]

COATES TO MERRIAM: JANUARY 27, 1928

Dear Mr. Merriam:

I didn't "sic" E.E.R. on you; all I told her was that if the Frontier exchange list became extensive enough, she would be included; she has asked to be put on the exchange list, you remember. Or did I?

I sent [Rosa Zagnoni] Marinoni to you because I had no lime in my spine. (I have been reading the Great American Ass, you can imagine with what pain and delight, since I have experienced both the physical and the intellectual environment at first hand. And both Kenyon's advice, and the author's theory of creative writing are worth pondering)

Marshall is a *find*. Baranoff has beauty, but it fails to lead anywhere. It is galling not to be able to publish the Saga of Seattle unexpurgated and entire. Why isn't he selling such stuff as that? Hersey (Harold) 799 Broadway;, N.Y., would jump at it I think. He may not be editing, at present, but he knows the markets.

Yes, Nason. An empty parenthesis like this, hereafter, (   ) means I've crawled under the table with my head drooping.

From now on I'll try to save you more work than I make you. Miss Nason's stories will reach you o.k., because I registered them.

A Paris magazine, "transition" with a small t took some of Norton's work. He will be happy. His uncle, Edward Custer, asked me to convey his thanks to you for the criticisms and suggestions you sent.

Writing is a dream world. Why do I have to live in it?

> *Sincerely yours, GSC[7]*

Grace wrote to Merriam,

I want to say a (quite unnecessary) word about Dr. Newman, because your criticism means so much to him. He writes me that they have been very helpful, because he always understands what you mean, and begins to see what you are getting at. He adds with accustomed candor that you are a better critic than I. Dr. Newman's deficiencies have always reduced me to impotent, inarticulate rage, and he has never been willing to admit (strangely enough) that my dancing around him and shaking my fist was legitimate literary criticism. I have the feeling that his failure is never in the man, but in his phrase, and because I love him it makes me furious…that he should let words betray him. When I am trivial or vulgar or cheap, it is from unworthiness inherent in me; words have not done it to me. But this is not so of Israel. I believe I really care more for the help you give him that for the help you give me—there's such a lot of me that can't be helped! So I want to thank you for it.

…I want like everything to send the enclosed story to the Atlantic Monthly, since they have said a nice word or two to me. Don't you suppose I can write you another one? I have one in my head—but of course that might be good, too![8]

MERRIAM TO COATES: APRIL 27, 1928

Dear Mrs. Coates,

I've lost track of your goings and comings. Where are you now? I've missed the privilege of sending you submitted poems, which have been coming in faster and thicker than I have been able to care for them. And what are the results of your trip? Especially, have you a poem in your pocket by Gwendoline Haste?

Proof is at last all read for the May issue, which will be distributed next week-end. It carries material by Floyd Dell, [author of Paul Bunyan yarns] James Stevens, [arctic explorer Vilhjalmur] Stefansson, [Frank Bird] Linderman, and yourself, among the "known" writers. Send me your criticism of the magazine after you've thot about its stuff. I've used *Under Trees* and *The Cloak* by you. *Mea Culpa* was put into type but had to be abandoned for this issue. I'm enclosing a few poems that I shall not wish to use, and keeping those— Encircled, Fracture, Color of Kisses, Dream Fears, Wild Honey, and if you want to send out any of these, let me know; it isn't fair to you for me to hold them. I appreciate, however, having some coin in the cash-box.

I wish that the editors of *The Frontier* could consult and make joint decisions. I've made a few: we shall issue four times next year—November, January, March and May, going to press on the seventh of each proceeding month. This regularity and frequency are necessitated by entrance into the privilege of second-class mailing. That will keep me hustling—an issue every nine weeks during the college year. I want to get the November issue practically complete by the end of July, when I stop teaching, and shall probably leave town. And I shall want considerable material ahead for the other three issues. Can't I count on a story from you? Do you know Will James? I want to approach him for a story. Whom else do you suggest? I think I can get editorials from [John] Erskine and [Robert] Frost. Another decision: the price will be $1.50 for the four issues, forty cents a single copy. I'm thinking of other plans; what ones occur to you? Is there any chance of getting any advertising around your part of Montana?

I shall be much interested in a report of your New York visit.

Cordially, HGM[9]

MERRIAM TO COATES: MAY 16, 1928

Dear Mrs. Coates:

Here are a few verses; I got pretty well cleaned up a short time ago, and this week not much has come in.

Please don't get the "too-modest" habit. Understand now for once and all that you have been a great help to me in *Frontier* work and will be increasingly a help. Your judgment in verse is good; your criticism is keenly analytical; your phrasing of that criticism illuminative. I rely strongly upon your criticisms. And more and more I shall hope to get all verse to you for your judgment before its final acceptance. Let's understand that matter and call it settled.

I shall count on you for a story in the November issue. We shall go to press on the dot next year—we must in order to get the second-class postal rate— on the seventh of the months of October, December, February, and April, and our issues will carry the dates of November, January, March, and May. That means an issue on the press just a fortnight after the opening of college, a very busy time for me. I shall therefore have to have all material on hand ready for the printer really before the opening of college—by the middle of September! The sooner I see your story the better. I shall make a vigorous effort to get during the summer enough material for the two first issues.

I very much desire something from Will James for the first issue.[10] Have you means of getting to him? If you have or if you haven't will you undertake to get his interest—and a story? If so I suggest getting at work on him at once. What other known names can we try for for next year? I think that I shall be able to wangle an editorial out of both Mr. Frost and Mr. Erskine. I can get something else out of James Stevens. But who else?

I'm awfully sorry about Miss Haste's sad experience with THE MERCURY because of our Montana poetry. Would she consider appearance in McClure's? I've just sold two of Jim Marshall's poems there for $75 each! If she can't sell the long Vigilante poem I'd be delighted to have it. Will you handle this matter, and let me know results as soon as you can?

I think I'll open a new section of the magazine and call it THE RANGE, and print in it original contributions from cowpunchers and others which have freshness and authenticity but not literary skill. What do you think? The devil of it would be the ease with which I could be taken in by spurious cowboys et al! What other new feature do you suggest?[11]

COATES TO MERRIAM: MAY 20 [1928]

Dear Mr. Merriam,

I know you are overworked. Don't write me an unnecessary word. I am not personally "touchy", and I'll go ahead and do what I think might be of service to the magazine without bothering you any more than I need to. Sorry that you couldn't stop—it makes no difference to me if you step on the morning train, or if you stop in the afternoon and talk all night and take the morning train—but it may to you. But personally I do not object to irregular hours and night conferences. So if you have a chance to be here, do not let unearthly hours prevent you, except for your own sake.

Where do I address Will James?—if you happen to be writing. I'll approach Taylor and the rest, and perhaps ask you to also prod Taylor along. Really, I wanted Mr. Shipley to see your first editorial. Maybe I can locate a copy for him. Perhaps he will write us something on the meaning of the "modern" drama—something about Cummings—I apologize, cummings!

Let me have Mrs. Harwick a little longer before I comment. I believe at first reading, that running such a story may get us a lot more stuff, better than this, elicited by publishing this.

I will return the story soon, and have sent on the poem with a word or so of appreciation.

Sincerely, Grace Stone Coates[12]

It was invigorating to Grace to speak before groups, and she was a very popular speaker around the state. She wrote to Merriam after her return from one engagement.

Home. Fine Trip. Lots of laughs (when I talked) so I am engrossed in the question of what makes groups laugh. They laugh, always, when I am making an entirely serious statement. It should be easy for me to establish myself as a humorist, then by always being in earnest. I watched Brown on that, wondering at the simplicity of things that brought laughs. Always, when the crowd laughed I was unmoved or faintly disgusted; when I choked my laughter, they were silent. But with Burt, who seemed profoundly amusing to me, the laughter didn't materialize.

(You can see I've been on a vacation, to start off so at random "Soil so quick-receptive—not one feather-seed, Not one flower dust fell but strait its fall awoke Vitalizing virtue—")…

Sincerely yours, and always gratefully, Grace Stone Coates[13]

Merriam, too, enjoyed getting out and addressing various groups. He reported to Grace after a trip to the west coast.

Time for only a note. Mrs. M and I drove 1400 miles in Henry, old style; met about thirty writers who are interested in what we are trying to do. Profitable, I'm sure. This note won't touch any matters about which you have written me; letter later. I am trying to clear out my contributions basket. It would amaze you to see the amount of material that comes in, little of it completely trash. Thanks for handling the material I am enclosing. I haven't looked at the Shipley material yet but will try to get at it tomorrow.

Rupert Hughes, unsolicited, wrote congratulating us on "the high level attained," and continued, "Mr. Matthews' two sonnets seem to me to be classic nobility," Not bad.

Clarke, literary editor of *McClure's* thinks the magazine "coming on splendidly." O'Brien is going to star all four stories in the May issue. He didn't mention the other two issues, but I'm hopping he intends to star work from them too. Stevens *Romantic Sailor* gets three stars, *Mike* and *Years* got two stars, and *Hans* gets one. I don't think *Romantic Sailor* the best by a long shot.

James Stevens gave me another article—I haven't read it yet! And he promises more. Dick Wetjens [Albert Richard Wetjen, northwestern regionalist author of sea stories] said he would send us something; said he had a story that was "too good to find a market." I'm leery of such. We'll see. I found the Coast people generally very cordial and cooperative.[14]

Grace had been considering the possibility of combining her stories, and then Merriam put the idea into words in a letter in June of 1928.

> Here's a proposal—dangerous! Why not publish four of your "family" stories this year in the Frontier, and then add three or four of them and the ones already in print, and let me present them to Herschel Brickell, of Holt and Co., formerly of the N.Y. Post.? He's asked me for book manuscript. Whatsay you say? Go ahead? *The Horn* is unquestionably the best. If printed O'Brien will triple star it, anyway. *Trees of Heaven* you can make more pointed and cleverer with more childish reactions. I'm returning it, in case you agree with me; but am keeping the other two. If you give me choice of course I'll take *The Horn*...
>
> Item etc: I'll send "Gwendoline"[15] a note; and you a copy of it. I want her vigilante poem, badly, but I'm willing to try to market it for her if she'll give me something else. Sure, if Mary Roberts Sillyhart[16] will give us something, let's grasp for it. She ain't my style, but her name would be worth three months of publicity endeavor for us. Tackle her, please. Linderman, who knew James, is after him. I doubt if FBL can pull him thru; but a young fellow here, I've discovered has spent weeks with WJ and been helped in his artwork—he's an illustrator—by WJ; and thru him I may land WJ.
>
> Don't let Taylor Gordon rest until you have his story of the sacrifice etc for us, please. That would be invaluable. And we'll print it exactly as he writes it, spelling and all, if that won't anger him!...
>
> ...And my great god, what a story Guy Holt might give of his mother trouping thru Montana in a covered wagon. I just must have that story! Gorgeous stuff! The rickety performances, the greased scenery, the hellbent audience, the purveyors of ART—oh jiminyjiminy! Can't you get it?
>
> And why not a cartoon by Mr. Munson? I'm going into the picture business, modestly, in this year's issues. Oh yes, a cartoon.
>
> There, if you do all that, the structure of the 1928-29 Frontier will be yours. I can't tell you how appreciative of your interests and your efforts I am. You're a genuine "Co-worker"—a nice word, better than "co-operator".
>
> Let me try to do something for you, now.
>
> I'm sorry that a class is waiting for me, for I wanted to send you an account of our Coast trip. Pack up and come over to Missoula for a visit, so that we may talk. Maybe I can get into the middle of the state later, but I'm doubtful.[17]

The idea of putting the short stories into book form had been an idea of Grace's as well. She wrote to tell Merriam that Brandt and Brandt wanted her to do a novel, and then handle a book of the sketches after the novel. She went on to explain,

> If I can get started on the novel, I believe their advice would prove good— that the short stories will sell with a book behind them, and not without. They want to handle all one's stuff or none. I think I will get those sketches together and let you have them, however; unless I get deep into the other book and see a chance to follow B&B's advice. I'd be glad to have you handle my poems, but—surely B & B have enough since they don't want verse, anyway—don't like it. I have two or three salable things I'm working on that I'll ask you to look over.
>
> I might be able to get the Guy Holt story. His mother herself might do it for us.. She is a wonder. They are great friends of the Heywood Brouns.
>
> ...You *have* done something for me. By permitting me to work with you on the Frontier you have offended the Greater Gods—Goddesses—of Martinsdale. I am pained (?) to say that Margaret hasn't voluntarily spoken to me since she found it out. It's a funny story but too trivial to write.
>
> I think I was unintelligible about the mss offer. What I tried to say was that I was still half tied up with B&B, but that the situation there would work out sooner or later. If they can't do the business, I'll be more than glad to have you use you good offices with Holt & Co. I don't know whether I could stand it to have PLASTER OF PARIS in the Frontier. Maybe. Take THE HORN by all means—but it needs some work.
>
> Lord, I'm tired! And perceiving the length of this letter think you may be too.[18]

Grace quickly recovered and was soon back working on *The Frontier.*

> I have a lot of schemes for helping the Frontier—if I don't procrastinate. Things are coming my way a little bit.
>
> Don't think that I ever question your subtlety of handling "clients", your feeling, tact, discretion or judgment; or the composition of these that constitutes taste. I mentioned the slips on the various poems, because I ran out of clips to fasten them to their moorings, and didn't want to be party of a justifiable oversight. With Pamelia, of all persons. She did get sandpapered at the meeting. And when one idiot finally tried to heal the breach by making her and Mrs. Wintergreen or whatever her name was life-members of the Association, and Mrs. T. promptly urged the organization not to begin gumming up the future by any such precedent, putting her suggestion finally in the form of a motion; Pamelia rose to the occasion and seconded the motion, getting for the first time a spontaneous whole souled tribute that

brought every body in the room to their (all right, his) feet. I do like to observe women fights.

I am writing under pressure—people do waste such a lot of time for their friends—It is all right about the Shipley stuff," Grace wrote in the summer. "I didn't think the prose in line with The Frontier's range; nor that it was Shipley at his best by any means. When I asked for material, I said, "Don't send anything unless I can feel free to send it back with a grin in case M. Merriam doesn't want it", so you see there was no occasion for embarrassment whatever happened. He is the secretary to the president of the Orthodox Jewish College from whom emanate the messages to American Jewry.

[Benjamin] Musser didn't send anything—yet. A second letter from him funnier than the first says he will send something. It happens that he has become enthusiastic about my work, so it was easy to tell him we didn't want to have to pump up polite phrases in case his work wasn't what we could use. That was what I meant about leaving the door open for refusing it easily. (By the way, I got a check for $11 tonight from Commonweal for a poem that didn't get a look in at the Butte Scribblers' Club.)

Taylor[19] may or may not write. He keeps C.P.T. (colored peoples' time)— if you have read [Carl] Van Vechten. Did I tell you I met Van Vechten and Chanler who was painting him? Your letter was far from too fresh. If Taylor answers you'll know it wasn't! All of your letters are effective, of course—far more so than that *wet* paragraph. What an opportunity lost if I had only known! I'll write Taylor again, I hoped for an advance chapter of his book. I had to ask him to stop writing to me because it annoyed Henderson so much. And Taylor may not swallow his grievance even for impersonal writing....

Gwendolen [sic] will send something—when she gets ready. I like your letter to her. I gave her a write up when I got back to Montana and sent her the clippings. I am sorry that the item you sent went into the state press one day too early for most effective handling, but it will be better done in the local papers I think. I have not written Will James, because I didn't do it. No other reason. I'll let the other man handle it. Yes?

A man here who is a notorious liar said Mary Roberts Rinehart was to be here (in Martinsdale) this summer. That is why I mentioned her. Rorty was once of Butte? Yes, and wrote the Misson Play? I met him in Los Angeles— but he wouldn't remember me, the contact was incidental and slight. Munson might do something just for fun. Clark of Butte illustrated the SHOETT HOMESTEAD. It should have gone to you, but Musser has it on his wall, he says. Clark wrote me recently: "I'm glad you did not enclose any of your poetry. It must be awful to be cursed with the ability to write serious verse."

I haven't added my word of delight at the success your magazine is attaining; but you know that I am pleased.

6 a.m.—I recall a joke about Bonnet Rouge—if you remember the story where the child's hat drops into the soup? A young Chicago University man, now selling tea, visited in Martinsdale. He sat for hours reading my verse—I could see him from the house—and at last came across the street to look at the animals. He analyzed the various poems, and asked point blank questions like whether I was really sick of Henderson, and then he analyzed the stories. He was impressed with the astonishing fact that I didn't mind making myself ridiculous in print; and secondly remarked that my characters showed their nature in even the smallest matters—for instance the child had used her remaining nickel to buy a hatpin, not to TIP THE WAITRESS. The suggestion was so novel to me I pass it on. Every man, writes Shipley, recites his age (generation). This was the poem he left to the last, and pinned my domestic unhappiness (?) onto. Perhaps I sent it to you.

Turnstile

After Rabelaisian shaft
   And a kiss in mockery
To my crazy room, as daft
   Comes my body troubling me.
Must the turnstile of my hell
   Click its worn, accustomed way
Past the dolt who can not spell
   One bright word of Rebelaise?
(*not for print*)[20]

Merriam depended on Grace to represent *The Frontier* at the state press meeting in the summer of 1928 and urged her to get in touch with the Eastern group of writers and speak at their convention.

"It's a nutty affair," he told her,

Mozor is the president! And Camelia P—good heavens, she's a pro and a nut…but the convention may be fun, and Dick Wetjens will be there (drunk, as per) and James Stevens and W.L. Davis may be out on outskirts writing scurrilous attacks on the meeting. I think it would be unwise for me to go—and I can't manage going, anyway, but I do want THE FRONTIER before the writers.[21]

COATES TO MERRIAM: SEPTEMBER 23, 1928

> Dear Mr. Merriam
> You must be busy—turn over to me any work I can do. I am momentarily mired down, but I'll wiggle out. I know Verne Bright—met him in Portland, and he spent an hour or so with others (Maring, Richards, Fuller etc) in my room. Shows how hard it is for me to make associations with names! He is painfully bashful the others say, but he seemed all right so far as I could see...
> ...A letter still unmailed tells you that I regret giving Mrs. Guerin "access" to you—and even more, to myself! I said (more politely) that SUPERSTITION seemed to peter out at the end, and she tells me Sherwood Anderson does it that way; before getting that bit from her, I dared say her incomplete sentence structure was a weakness, not strength, and she tells me all good European stories are like that. In the mean time, for the good of my own soul, I had spent a morning analyzing the complete flop of one of her stories. When her next letter came complaining that I didn't like her stories when she had been nice and liked mine (!) I just ditched the criticism and mailed her story back with a few polite words. I don't know anything about criticism, but I'm trying hard to learn. Richards' Principles of Literary Criticism is interesting, especially in spots. But A. Sullivan Hoffman is her level in his Fundamentals. Borghild's story is charming; just one spot—"John's day" jarred. It is even confusing, as well as obscure. Perhaps if she would repeat the "today" it would center the thought better. Firty [sic] years old today—today—*John's* day. I know this—that as she has it it not only made me look forward for the explanation, but also back and around; and was to that extent a loss. But it is lovely.
> ...We tramped for six hours straight today—I did—in hip boots, and if I were not so tired I could have said this whole thing in twenty words.
>
> *Yours sincerely, Grace Stone Coates*[22]

As a writer for the state newspapers, Grace was able to develop more publicity for *The Frontier*. Merriam sent her material to develop.

> I am sorry that in the hurry of the opening of college I have not been able to send you the publicity material for
> *The Frontier.* Mr. Fitzgerald, who attends to most of the publicity, has been ill in bed for a week, also. I will give you a little publicity. It [The Frontier] was given to the Missoula papers an hour ago. I shall run Gwendolyn Haste's poem called *Gold* which you know. There will be your excellent story, *The Horn.* James Stevens contributes another sketch called *The Romantic Road.* I shall run two poems of Joseph T. Shipley; poems by Cortland Matthews and H. M. Corning, both of Portland. Corning is giving me the title poem of his forthcoming volume of verse called *The Mountain in the Sky.* I am running also

a ballad picked up in the woods by a woodsman called Joe Mafaw, with the music. There will be a series of sketches called *Oil Field People*. I am establishing "The Open Range", a new department, in which will be a cowboy tale by "Pink" Simms. There will also be a double spread historical and romantic map of Wyoming by Grace Raymond Hebard. Mrs. Hatwick will have that humorous story called Salt *and Pepper,* and I have another Western story by an Oregon woman, Edna McBrian. Jason Ballis will have a poem. And in the historical section there will be an article by Professor Archer T. Hulbert called *Western Trails.* Mr. Hulbert is head of the Stewart Commission on Western History and there will be another overland diary. That together with the recognition that *The Frontier* has received this summer, of which you know, ought to give you a pretty good story, probably more than you can get handled.

I am going to write Mrs. Guerin a rather severe note soon; I will send you a copy.[23]

Merriam and Grace continued to disagree on material for *The Frontier,* although Grace told Merriam it would be the devil if one had to like the poem because the other did—"that being a pastime reserved for the happily married." She was so moved by one poem [Ben Musser] that she cried. The first time, she told Merriam, that she had cried over anybody's verse but her own.

You see, he writes from the same sore spot that I do; and writes better. Life galls our shoulders in the same place. I don't know Musser; but I'll bet he is exactly the same type of lean, sad-eyed humorist that A.J. Clark is—and when he says he did start a poem once, that died aborning, it is his own life of course. My understanding his poetry makes it neither better nor worse; and you are the better judge of literature in general.

I know how insidious is the temptation to pat the back that pats yours— do you get that?—but searching my soul I don't find it operating here. His enthusiasm for my verse had puzzled me, because I had had only second rate stuff to send him—until I read these. Then I knew that Ben saw in my verse the inner thing that crowded me to expression. I see the same inner thing in his. He has the same ruinous thing that I have, a sense of humor *toward his verse*—and will you show me one person who wrote greatly who conveyed or even harbored derision toward what he was doing? That, I believe, is the basis of the thing he said to me too often "I can never tell when you're sincere." For me Musser's stuff is far ahead of Trent's or Cheyney's—just temperament that happens to be suited with his.

I got an eyeful of Mrs. Dail's Frontier last night, and was happy to see my "Fault" under Bud's Thistle. Shipley, Trent, Cheyney, and Musser if he ever qualifies, would make an arresting young-Jew group! (Echo has suspended, by the way, as perhaps you knew. My eye just fell on Raffelock's letter) I'll be sending you more subs soon, and will comment on the magazine later. Really you are doing a remarkable piece of work with that magazine…An interruption, but during it a woman said to me, "How much The Frontier is going to mean to Montana."[24]

Merriam was still not convinced about Musser's work—they did not ring true to him.

They sound to me as if the man were shallow natured, a rebel by determination rather than conviction, a writer who wished to be clever. But let's agree to disagree violently and self-respectingly!

I like REAL MARKET much and should like to publish it. If you think he wouldn't be offended by choice of a single poem please return it to me.

OLDER WOMAN, HERETIC, SINGERS ALL, BRAVADO, THE DEACON ring to me as bravado. THE SAGE and NARCISSUS don't say anything that isn't terribly trite. THE WATCHER I would like if I could really get hold of its meaning—in fact, if it were satisfactorily explained, either emotionally or intellectually, I would publish it. CLEAN LINEN IN PUBLIC I should like to publish, mildly like to, but only mildly, because again the idea and the expression do not seem to me fresh, and I dislike the title. APRES NOUS is the sort of cynicism that I despise. LINE TO E A I haven't the faintest idea of the meaning of; I like the rithm of it the best of the lot; but the only meaning I can get is trivial.

This is awfully ungracious of me to write so bluntly about each poem, but we'd better be teetotally frank with one another.

And—good god—I feel much the same way about Trent and Cheyney, only they seem to me younger. Well, no I don't. I think FARM WOMAN very good, and I want it. What angers me about them is the unctuous assertion, "We are rebel poets." Real rebels don't have to keep reminding themselves and other people that they are rebels. Let's return PREGNANT. Cheyney's HILLS I don't recall; I'm not supposed to have it, am I? I do recall ME DAMES JUDAS, and fairly well like it. I should like some satire for the next issue. Will you please decide whether to accept one of the other of the two or both—I'd be happy with both if you thot them up to it. You please correspond with these three poets, at least until my eyes are better opened to them. Please don't put me in bad with them. We want them for FRONTIER friends, surely.

Out of nine stories printed last year O'Brien is double starring six and reprinting one. Not Bad. You get triple stars on BLACK CHERRIES and TRUTH; and double on LATE FRUIT, CRICKETS, NYMPHS and PAN. You are there fore on the Roll of Honor. Fine.[25]

COATES TO MERRIAM: NOVEMBER 5, 1928

Dear HGM

I hate like the devil to give Wetjens' letters up. I don't wonder at the varied things his friends, near-friends, and enemies say about him. And he can write. I'd like to keep his letters at hand to prod me for a few weeks, and to flatter myself that I have said all and still more than he has about poetry magazines. That was what started my "quarreling" with Dr. Newman. (I wish if you had time you'd read his letter that I enclose, by way of sidelight on personality—and return it.)

I agree with a lot that Wetjens says. I agree about the controversial stuff being vigorous—commanding attention. The historic material? W e l l, maybe. It is often the thing we save—carefully—to read at that indefinite dusty sometime that never arrives. Yet surely is has worth. In a letter to you that I discarded, I said this issue of the Frontier was the only one I had really read. And like Dick, I haven't read GOLD. I went to sleep when Gwen was reading it to me, also.

Tell Dick Wetjens that only considerations of delicacy restrained you from fronting THE HORN with a woodcut of Miss Davidson's HAMADRYAD, familiarly known as her vaginal tree! Dick is as soothing as a mullein leaf. I like that about him.

But how Frank Ernest Hill would loathe Wetjens!

GSC

P.S. Don't retort that considerations of delicacy seem inoperative with Wetjens and me![26]

COATES TO MERRIAM: UNDATED

Dear HGM

My entire understanding of the way Wetjen's letter was sent on made your apology unnecessary—however fully appreciated. I am not sex-sniggery, myself, nor am I prudish; and referred to his allusion only that words might thud less heavily than silence on your (possible) discomfiture. I enclosed good old Israel's letter to take the bad taste out of your mouth.

Dick's forgiven. His comment was between men. Long ago I weighed the vulgar connotation of that title, and dismissed it as childishness Frontier readers might be assumed to have left behind someplace in the fourth grade.

Sincerely yours, GSC

I am reading the Second American Caravan: Carolus Elston, in Jonathan Leonard's The Meddlers: "How can intellectual beauty expand from vice? And if it does, vice was probably the wrong name to give the raw material."[27]

Grace could be as tough with criticisms as Merriam, for she was forever honest.

…if I am free to express myself as I feel, and as vigorously as I please—I am so decided in my likes and dislikes that I am unjust sometime, I know—I may go far astray at times, but at other times I may be right.

She admitted as much to Merriam.

Thank you a lot for the advance items. If you knew what I did with the rest you might not have been so good! I infuriated Gwenna—now calmed down—and got 2 pages from Pinkie Simms telling (not irately) what I did to him. Answered that, also.

B & B sold a silly lyric to Plain Talk.

I note you are using PLASTER OF PARIS. This is—for reasons you will find apparent—confidential in a way: The bit of statuary that story hangs on is a genuine (what other kinds could there be?)—an original Houdon. You may have noted that some of Houdon's pieces ran as high as $450,000 on the occasion of his centennial, last April or May. If I can establish its authenticity, what beautiful material for a press agent! Having left my house wide open all these years, during our hours away from home, on the open fact that we had neither money, silver, negotiable paper, jewels, furs or home brew to attract attention, I am not eager to advertise a possession that might be worth stealing![28]

Mr. Shipley and I had a nebulous idea of issuing a joint volume. That started the hand-in-hand business of our verse, to do a bit of preliminary attention-calling. Knopf have asked him for a volume; and the idea of a joint volume seems rather less nebulous than it did. Use the CANCELED if you want to, and not if you don't. Vinal—nothing; I have no time to toot my own horn at this moment. I'm getting into print more easily than I did, and getting requests from time to time for stuff.29

Merriam continued to give Grace more and more work for *The Frontier,* asking her to contact her friends in Portland and Seattle for work.

Well, well, I should say Helen Maring was thr-thr—i-i-i-ll-lled! Let's get next to this source of good stories. James Stevens writes that the School of Journalism at the U of W has anathematized him. Wehtall? Is McKenzie that sort? Let's find out. Could you approach, thru Helen Maring, those five writers and interest them in Frontier? I shall fool round for an approach that might be profitable, to McKenzie.—profitable to us, I mean, of course, and approach to McK.

I don't at all know the verse of Ellen Carroll. If you think I could, ask her for some. I'm still pretty well stocked with verse, especially with verse that is not definitely western in tone. I'm returning Helen Maring's verse, I should

like to use it when, and if, rewritten—I'm writing of THE MATRON. CHILD
WISE I think has purpose and emotional conviction; do you? If you think it
excellent please adopt it; if you don't let's wait for other Maring verse.
SURPRISED seems to be very good; if the last two lines should be recast, I'd
like to see the poem again. BACHELOR is all right with me; accept it if you
think itgood. I admit that it's a bit trite. The sixth line evidently has been
miscopied from the original. COAL MINE—by all means, let's have a poem on
coal mining. This one isn't it. Can't she make the images clearer cut in this one?
And can't a stiffer, stubborner rithm[sic] carry the sense of mining? And I don't
see what the idea of a lover trudging has to do with the poem. But I do want a
coal mining poem! Please urge her to work on one for Frontier. We must develop
a Seattle group of Frontier enthusiasts, and she's probably a splendid center for
it. There's real ability (not so much judgment and self-criticism) in her verse.

This is written in the very devil of a rush. Wetjen writes that the next time
you are in Portland he will invite you to a party of his; that last time he didn't
dare because "even my wife" (Dick's) thot "she looked too pure!"[30]

Taylor Gordon is preparing a book for Knopf. He was ordered to do it
without reference to a dictionary, and without letting one human being correct
a word. If it is as funny as his letters—and it will be—it will be great.

At the end of 1928, Grace noted that all four of her stories printed in *The
Frontier* were triple-starred in the latest O'Brien—the only author with four
stories listed.

At Christmas, Merriam again suggested to Grace that she combine about
twenty of her stories into novel form.

The tragedy or whatever you care to call it (you needn't stick to fact) of
second marriage. The story of the second marriage would come out thru the
eyes, ears, and sensibilities of the little girl (the I of the story) as she grew in
years and in observation and in judgment. That's a corking idea, and a novel
one. Each story would be complete in itself, and yet bound with all the others
thru the unfolding of the central story. The earliest stories would be thru the
eyes of a very little girl upon the eve, almost, of the second marriage; then the
relations of the father and mother would develop; the child would keep pace
in development; the reader would garner the true state of affairs and their
drift. The last installments might come when the "I" of the stories had become
eighteen or twenty years of age.

Think it over. The stories you've written could be used with not much
change, probably."[31]

⮿

Grace Stone Coates, assistant editor of The Frontier

Wild Honey

Within the man there is a boy
   Who tracked the wild bee for its honey,
On sturdy feet. It is my joy
To summon in the man, the boy;
   He holds for me the wistful, funny
Ways of affection men destroy.

A bit of rose-geranium leaf
   In apple jelly is, for him,
   Wild honey from the stolen limb;
And for the moment dear and brief
   I see an urchin's round eyes follow
   A bee's flight past the timbered hollow,
Unmindful of time's grief, time's grief.

CHAPTER FIVE

Coates wrote to Merriam early in the year,

> Gwendolen Haste writes me that I am a member of this thing [Scribbler's Club] I enclose. Perhaps I told you I expect to go to New York this month or next, to visit her. Have you anything in mind that I could be entrusted with, that would be of service to the Frontier? I will try to interest Gwendolen and her group.[1]

So in February of 1929, Grace again spent some time in New York. She told Merriam she was,

> …debunked in rather large and unrelated areas of the soul. I believe, at least hope, I am in a better frame of mind to work than I have been for some time, and more in line to give the Frontier a little decent service. Don't bother to remind me not to be over-modest, for tho you may not know how mediocre my services have been to date I do…The last Frontier does please me. Mr. Merriam, you have something there. It interests me to see how many, not of the Greenwich Village persuasion, look to the west for a deliverer. Really. I haven't read the issue entirely—just at this moment caught an eyeful of May Vontver's "kiskis". It hurts. The Russell letter is a triumph.

The Vontver contribution, "The Kiskis," was republished in twelve anthologies, translated into Swedish and printed in Sweden. It was reprinted again and again, the last time in the antholog *On the Rims* where it was described by the *Billings Outpost* as a "…moving and memorable account of teaching school in days when poverty meant no shoes."

While in New York, Coates enrolled in a finance course and took, too, a course in poetry writing…a natural thing, she explained, since a poet makes so little it is important to know how to manage the small income. She also served as a delegate from the Scribbler's Club to the annual dinner of the American Poetry Society in New York. She stayed with Gwendolen Haste. Although Coates told Merriam they were not necessarily friends but "suave antagonists," they got along well. Grace loved New York, a decidedly stark contrast to the little Montana prairie town. She told a friend several years later:

Yes, I've wandered in the Bronx. Once I didn't get off the subway train at Times Square. Guard: "Did I let you on here?" I: "No, but you didn't put me off." G: "I bet you're from Brooklyn." "You lose. I'm from Montana." Guard: "Ed, Ed, come here…She's from Montana, same as Jo…You don't talk a bit like him." Eventually "Jo" showed up—he said he had worked in the dark for 3 years. All three of the boys stayed with me until they got me going in the right direction to Columbia U. They say New Yorkers are hard boiled; but all I could find out about the rank and file of them—yes, By George, and some of the customers' men in Kidder, Peabody's Wall Street office, too—was that they are all lonely as the devil, hungry for human sympathy of some kind that they lack. I dunno…I know a Fifth Ave. bus conductor—an Italian humming snatches of opera when he assumed that the noise made him unheard—chucked me off the bus with a sudden whispered wish that I have a happy day. And a bunch of real city Jews—one can hold them speechless. And keeping a lively Jew silent is doing something…a snap shot of antelope dropped out of my purse, in a little stocking shop where I had stopped to ask directions. And before I got out of there, there were 5 of the Jewiest kind of urban Jews—the kind that deal one hell under some circumstances—crowded around me asking the queerest questions about Montana. It was like a fairy story to them; as their lives was a story to me.

In other words, I enjoy New York—I've been looking at the RCA building in the last issue of Fortune—good (not so good) Anaconda stuff in it. I do not like the paintings.

Her query stamped her as a clown;

He took the hint—and stamped her down.[2]

And later to the same friend,

…Yes, indeed: there is much you can do for me in New York—I take the NY Times; so: send me some of those Transcontinentals in wine with yeller spots, that Altman shows; and one of those crystal ball watches with a little birdie to hold it on my lapel; and a few popcorn yell'r [sic] shirts; and some of those three piece suits, one of them with the jacket tails cut off at the belt behind, and extending to the knees in front. Pick out a few bolero jackets, too; and send a couple cases of caviar, some good oyster stew from the—you know—Terminal something or other; Brand Union Depot, I guess; some Florida strawberries and a barrel of avocados (I just ate two, and that wasn't enough.) If time drags, I can think of lovely things for me for you to do.

(Henderson's eating ice cream, and I'm going to be, in a minute.)

Sincerely, Grace Coates
…I forgot to mention garlic.[3]

Publicizing *The Frontier* was also on Grace's agenda, and Dr. Merriam reminded her of this chore.

MERRIAM TO COATES: FEBRUARY 6, 1929

Dear G.S.C.

Along with the whole of Montana I have been snowed-in, both by snow and by work; so that I have not got off to you the two or three letters that I have intended to write or material that I have decided to submit to your judgment. Now it is too late. I have a few notes, however, I want to send to you.

Mr. Clack sent me a perfectly stupid write-up of the W.C.T.U. women in a cowboy camp, and enclosed another dull parody of Masefields's "Sea Fever", written by his son, suggesting that I print both in THE FRONTIER. As courteously and tactfully as I could I returned both to him. As I have had no reply I feel that I have tipped over the bean pot.

Item 2. I received from an old cowboy an account of roping a wild buffalo. Charlie Russell saw this feat and 37 years after the event painted a picture of it and wrote a letter to that cowboy. The article, the painting and the letter are in my possession, and will appear in the March issue of the "Open Range". This ought to be a knockout.

Item 3. I have a good story from Harry Huse for the May issue and another excellent one from Roland Hartley. I also have a fine letter from Bill Adams about Portland Port 30 or more years ago, which will be in the March issue. I am running your "Wild Plums".

I wonder if you have been doing anything for us by way of publicity in New York journals? That is really the most essential and pressing matter concerning THE FRONTIER at present.

I hope you had a good time and a profitable time. When shall you be in Montana? We have had eighteen days of blizzard and storm!

Cordially, HGM[4]

Returning from New York, Grace wrote,

I feel like going to work—only one thing intervened (this is a new paragraph): the doctors say my tonsils are annoying my soul. I weighed little over 100 pounds, while I was in N.Y.; and Henderson, who has had a 280 lb. Housekeeper while I have been away, looks at me and says, "Woman, I never saw so thin a person in my life!" So I'm going to Great Falls and have a tonsillectomy soon, and after that—we'll see if my tonsils will alibi me for past inertia.[5]

By March, Grace was recovered from her tonsillectomy and back at work with her writing,

If I did a crystal gazing I think I'd see that you were extremely busy. There is nothing in this that needs an answer, and you can skin to the signature without missing anything vital.

> *HGM*[6]

Grace passed on the criticism she had heard that *The Frontier* had a bit of monotony.

> By the way, the most frequent adverse criticism of the magazine that I hear is that there is a sameness about the contents in any issue. I know what the critics mean; but what's a fellow to do? What they mean is partly that they are used to high flavors in their froth, and find a full diet of sincerity too much for them. Anyway, it comes quite often. Mrs. Hey's praise means a good deal, for she is a competent critic; and reputed to be an authority on something or other, I've forgotten what."[7]

Merriam replied,

> …I reckon, tho, that there's nothing to do about that. I shall have to use the best material I can get. And of course it would be ruinous of any plans I have to try to "jazz it up." Aren't those criticisms mostly from very sophisticated people? Particularly to drop the demand for sincerity would be ruinous. However, in the natural course of things, more liveliness will creep in, I think.
>
> Please write me about Ben Mussar. All you reported was something like "Oh my god!" I have the greatest difficulty "seeing" the poetry he writes and such of that he publishes. And the Cheyney-Trent combination isn't much easier for my sensibilities. I suppose that I'm too serious and too much a believer in sincerity and taste.
>
> James Rorty won The Nation poetry prize in 1924. Verse by him, of virile sort, has appeared in The Nation ever since. He has also been connected with The New Masses (check spelling) I don't [know] a thing more about him. But I've written to him, and may learn something.
>
> Don't mind my turndowns of a person now and then that you "sic" on me. Keep on sicing, please. We never know when we are going to turn up a diamond.[8]

COATES TO MERRIAM: APRIL 26, 1929

Dear HGM

I didn't see much of Ben Musser; but met him at the Poetry Society dinner. He was kind enough to hunt me up. He is—oh-too well dressed; just the bit too much that one can't stand. And he has a nasal feminine voice; like a eunuch (I never had any experience with eunuchs, but maybe you know what I mean.) I still like his poetry, and think he suffers like the dickens from life—but maybe if he'd put on some rougher clothes he'd get over it. You see, my "O my godding" was on purely emotive grounds. Cheyney is a dead beat. Lucia may be all right.

MONOTONY. Of course I shall always pass on any adverse criticism that wakens the faintest ache in my own soul. It was the mill-run of readers that made the criticism; girls here, of university training for instance. And I had felt it faintly. But without your letter, I should have assured you that this issue (May) has got entirely away from that too-great similarity of response. I noted that, immediately.

Going back to Ben: he *is* clever; but his humor is too lively for my not too prudish bent. There is something to be said for taste.

Eda Lou pleased me with her Nation verse. And of course, I'm not in the least sensitive, in the sense of "having my feelings hurt" over any of my diamonds in the rough that you can't cut to advantage.

We are driving over to Bozeman for a few days. I hope that Henderson and I can go to San Francisco this summer.

> *Sincerely, GSC*

My story isn't good. Sentence structure is too choppy, for one thing.[9]

Along with editing material for the magazine, Grace continued to find new talent for the magazine, supporters and subscribers. There were a number of people in New York that she suggested to Merriam for further contact.

Send the surplus mss along any time. I have always had the (uninspiring) feeling that sending mss to me was a perfunctory courtesy on your part—I feel so inadequate as a reader—but if my work really helps you any I will attack it with more confidence. If we could have an occasional conference it would mean a good deal to me at least. Perhaps we can, later.

I have not read the new number—no time yet. I think Mr. Shipley would write an editorial for you some time. He and I are rather good friends, and I want him to really know what the Frontier is. He has a rather wide following of one type. I enclose his review of e.e. cummings'"him"—the only prose I happen to have of his, that you may judge his news style in case you know as little of him as I did until I met him. Anyway, I'm going to ask him for an opinion of the magazine, on the adverse side as far as possible; and as he is rather caustic and candid as well he may say something worth weighing. I have read the editorial of the May issue, and like it very much, but no one has approached your editorial—which is natural enough.

Would you care to make up the year's volume of three issues and send to Mr. Shipley, as a preliminary to my personal attack on his time? Joseph T. Shipley, c/o Stuyvesant High School, 345 East 15 Street.[10]

Don't you think James Rorty, formerly of Butte, ought to be interested in the Frontier? And Burton Braley? I am including their names in a mailing list

I enclose. Most of these are people I've met. Thru the Holts I met Ruth Hale, and had arranged an evening to meet her husband [journalist] Heywood Broun, but missed it thru pressure of other things. Anyway, Ruth and Mrs. Guy Holt are talking about visiting here next summer, and have a romantic interest in Montana. Guy Holt's mother was an old trouper—traveled Montana in a covered wagon and played one night stands. She is a remarkable woman and I fell completely in love with her. Thru circumstances I wont waste time over I had rather intimate contact with these people, and I think they will have real interest in what you are attempting in the way of a genuine literary medium.

Munsons, also quite definitely plan to spend the summer at Delpine[11] and Mr. Munson is a man worth interesting in the magazine—he isn't a writer, but an old cartoonist—and has plenty of money and a love of beauty. A Wall Street broker.

…I think Frank Ernest Hill whose new book is about ready for the press would be delighted with a letter from you and would have unusual interest in what the Frontier is trying to do. He is with Longmans Green, and that is the only address I have. The Hills are personal friends of Miss Haste, and I met them, and talked about the magazine, but not at any length. Mr. Hill is so far ahead of most of the writers I met that I wish the Frontier could have his goodwill. I mentioned Mr. Hill's book, because I know he is extremely busy until it is off his hands…

…Oh, yes, put Taylor Gordon on your mailing list. He has the reputation of knowing more people than any individual in N.Y. and he surely is a good press agent for things of Montana.[12]

MERRIAM TO COATES; MAY 18, 1929

Dear GSC,

Who is Will Burt? Should I know him? I'd like to. For he has first-rate critical judgment and better still first-rate appreciation of fineness. Would he be interested in meeting me some time when I am in Butte? The two bits of advice he gives you I second. I have desired to write you about both of them time and again but I have felt that your enthusiasms have run toward the sophisticated and I have not wished to get in the pathway. No, I don't mean just that—it isn't sophistication that I mind but"attitudinizing", which I find constantly in WAVES for example, and in the Cheyney-Trent stuff, Ben Mussar stuff, and occasionally, I have felt, in yours. However, I have felt that my close academic living had incapacitated me for understanding some of your poems, and therefore I've kept silent. I am profoundly a believer in sincerity (not necessarily wedded to seriousness). I am convinced that a writer succeeds when he really means something. I am not too unaware of human nature's functioning, either, to be ignorant of the pretences—that often it is being *deeply* sincere (subconsciously) then the everyday, second self thinks it is being supportive or even insincere. Well, well, let's talk sometime, rather than write. But Will Burt is a "real feller", in campus lingo.

I like the Lucia Trent verse well enough to accept it; but don't accept it unless you do. When dealing with that group of poets I want to rely on your judgments more heavily than on mine.

What does it matter whether GATES is a narrative poem or not? It has elements of the narrative; but obviously it doesn't tell or suggest a detailed story. It is ordinarily a reflective poem. I like its spirit, its versification, too. I'm not sure that it's yet a whole. That is, you suggest to the reader first that you're going to write about the name's tolerance—perhaps how he arrived at it; then there is the suggestion that there is to be some narrative of the people who wait by the gate; lastly, the suggestion that the man is really telling why he is so lonesome. The poem doesn't seem to be about gates, but about loneliness. You see, the significances of the elements of the poem haven't yet merged into a total or grand significance—not for me, anyway.

Thanks for the Matthews criticism.

    HGM[13]

Merriam was as pleased as Grace when her short story was cited by O'Brien for his best short stories of 1929. He was still "glowing" when he wrote to her in June.

He urged her to send on her story "The Transgressor" for his criticism so he could use it in the November issue. And send along the novel—he would get to that soon. He reported that he had heard from E.H. Taylor, the editor of *Country Gentleman,* who spoke highly of *The Frontier,* stating, "…it is one of the most interesting magazines" that comes to his desk.[14]

The development of *Black Cherries* proved to me more of a task than just assembling the stories. Grace worked to put them in order and rewrite them enough to link together better. She expressed her frustrations to Merriam in July.

I'm stuck but not discouraged. If I weren't working as hard as I am capable of working—I meant that truly, for when I work at all I work too hard—I'd not have the effrontery to appeal to you about them. I am running into difficulties that so far offer no suggestion of their own solution. In the first place the stories were written independently—each of the other—and the Red Hat and Stubborn Thistles are in a mood and manner different from the rest. As I try to write toward them I get into straight novel material. If I'm writing a novel I might as well chuck these stories, and do it; and if I am arranging a series of independent stories, to what extent may they interlock and overlap in time? Sequence?

What do you think of discarding Red Hat and Stubborn Thistles, and having the entire group the sub-idiot manner?

(I caught what you meant at last by repetition—it was between two stories, I had missed that both in writing and in comparing—in fact, I didn't compare)

Trying to rearrange those stories is like rebuilding an old house, changing one thing throws something else out of kilter. I have just received your criticism. It is reassuring to me in the way most vital to my work—on the score of material. I mean this literally. I can see nothing except boredom in these stories. When I finish one I am physically nauseated, and have no way of knowing whether the thing is utterly flat, or whether an intelligent person could read it without disgust. If you say the material is there, I am not afraid of not being able to work it up to smooth finish. (I know the story needs rephrasing etc)

But about the other comments: LIKE GLASS falls before THE HORN; so does BROKEN. If you had the mss at hand you would see that there is no contradiction or confusion in the sequence under that arrangement. 1) The farm was going to foreclose 2) We had a sale and were going away. Then comes the K.C. [Kansas City] school story. I know this wasn't what you expected, but in a way I have to use what is in me, and am embarrassed by too much material, rather than too little. I could do several K.C. reaction sketches, and perhaps that is what suggested a group all of the hydro-cephalic-infantilism manner.

(Be patient) My intention in broken was not to suggest that the father was broken, but that in a situation where every one else was, he emerged not only triumphant but arrogant, without sympathy for the ones who had met common disaster, and in this characteristic to hint at the element in his that cost him his children's affections and his wife's life; and I had in mind—(I have in rough draught—another story, in which the breach is made between all but his youngest child and him; his first fortune is made, and the element in himself, trickery and failure to respect his word, that lost him his fortune, foreshadowed.)—and I had in mind an unsuccessful situation in which his fortune is swept away in his age, and his attempt to save himself at his children's expense, as justification for their indifference.

But I still don't see how I can carry the idiot-manner of telling into and thru adolescence, or merge a story of a "mother's" death smoothly into the vivacity of a bonnet in the soup.

It isn't your trouble, I know; it's mine. And a real one. But the only thing I know is to keep on working as hard and faithfully as I can; and send you the material to ask your opinion as to its inherent value. I can revise and polish, and will; but I have to know at the conclusion of every story whether I have made an ass of myself. There is no pretense or mock modesty in my saying this. I can not judge them, until I have laid them aside and forgotten their content, on the score of either material-interest, or good taste. But I have no time to season them a year or so.

To write the sequence as I have in mind takes more work that to adopt your suggestion, about having the invention fall thru—but I believe I can do it better. There are two lines that I can follow in developing a character that justifies his children's disdain—he can be tricky about his patent, and lose the company's good will and his position; or he can reinvest his fortune and when he is "stuck" with repudiated bonds 'Imperial Valley, to get him down to California—and they did repudiate their bonds—) have him try to palm them off on his family—children (Continue to be patient) You must know that I realize you are a sound critic, and I am not. I always come, eventually to your opinion, and every competent person confirms it as against mine; but I had thought BROKEN the more consistent story of the two—It begins—father didn't cry—only the two extremes were not defeated, the man of near-genius and the po'r white. And it foreshadows a vital part of the subsequent stories, a psychic disturbance in the child that raised the devil with her thru each new crisis—My idea is that the stories have to show how the faults of the father injured each of the children, according to the disposition of each. Teressa's injury at his hands passed on to the child she was in contact with. The mother's injuries passed on to Teressa. The motherless children took their injury direct—etc.[15]

Taylor Gordon wrote to Grace to say that he has his "dummy" for the book.[16] Grace wrote to Merriam, "[Taylor] says it is grand—the only adjective he commands, so far as I have noticed. I have written Covici-Friede for a copy to review. Some of the Montana papers will want it."[17]

Taylor's book, *Born to Be,* the memoir of a "famous Afro-American and blues singer," tells the marvelous story of his youth in White Sulphur Springs and his singing career. He wrote that he never knew racial prejudice until he went to work in Minneapolis as a chauffeur. He returned to Montana to retire in 1940s.

Grace promoted Gordon's book in all the newspapers carrying her releases, but was still having a problem with Henderson's attitude about Negroes.

Grace tried again to stop her correspondence with Taylor Gordon to appease her husband. Taylor was not easily deterred and wrote in July.

GORDON TO COATES: JULY 28, 1929
LONDON

> Hello Young Lady
> Why no more letters. Because I said, I lived a lie at what N. ad HaHa will you might of misunderstood what lie. I will tell you some time.

One of you [sic] lives and sense would help me here a great deal. I have meet a lady her Radilffee [sic; novelist Radcliffe] Hall that reminds me of you. She give me one of her books. I will let you read sometimes. I guess you are scolding me because I didn't send you those book as yet but I will I was all up to leaving newyorcity.

Please excuse that mistake I am rushed and I must drop you a few lines,

Did you write Carl Van Veiter [photographer and author Carl Van Vechten] and Muriel Droper [Draper, decorator, writer, and arts patron]? Let me know Carl Ravel was your country doctor.

Write me a long letter and I will tell you all about England.

We will be here in Aug. 23—I hope you are well I will close Chief send his regards

Y S., *Taylor Gordon*[18]

Grace continued to have trouble with her own work, and Merriam continued to support and encourage her.

MERRIAM TO COATES: JULY 27, 1929

Dear G.S.C.,

I think that you are neither "stuck" nor "discouraged". You are going along nicely. The only thing I want to be dead sure of is that you will keep going along until we get a volume accepted by Jonathan Cape. Your last letter, sent with the two stories which I forwarded (and for criticism of which I thank you. I have not yet read them.) shows that you are doing famously.

I would not discard wither "The Red Hat" or "Stubborn Thistles". I see no reason for carrying the "idiot-manner" of telling clear through the volume. Good heavens, one could expect the girl to grow up! Wouldn't that be part of the story? Wouldn't light dawning upon the child be one of the fascinating features? You haven't the infantile manner in "Stubborn Thistles" and you don't want it…

I want to publish "The Way of the Transgressor" in the November issue of THE FRONTIER. I have an early version and then you sent me a version on thin paper. Is this thin-paper version the one you want to appear in print?

Good wishes,

Cordially, HGM[19]

COATES TO MERRIAM: UNDATED

Dear HGM

Your last criticism helps me get the idea. It came in time to stop my sending on the next story. I half think the next may be enough to let the series carry to the final Stubborn Thistles without too much jar. It will with one more, anyway.

I can weave the father into the school situation easily. He has a complex about schools anyway. The broken was meant to show him arrogant in good fortune, too little milk of human kindness. I forgot what I meant to do about the mocking birds—they—were the hailstorm to the child—her avenue of interpretation of what the storm meant.

—Oh, yes, and BROKEN lets in a new light—the woman doesn't say "He's done it" but that the corn knife is gone—and we'll keep all titles concrete "The Hail" etc. The man—the father—gets sardonic amusement because Mrs. Likely' worry is that suicide is against the law in Kansas, and her husband's recovery means a year's jail sentence. (That is a matter of fact—attempted suicide, one year in jail!) But don't tell me not to use what has been a family by-word for 30 years—"His swaller leaded"!

I think DESERT SON has good possibilities.

Sincerely, GSC[20]

Merriam continued to read and critique the stories for the novel.

BROKEN lives up to its name, it has a broken back: what you wish it to do is to indicate that your father and his family were broken, by the hail, and the first two-thirds of the story does what you wish, but then you shift and leave the reader concerned with "your" horror experienced in the picture of Mr. Likely that was etched into your mind. The Likely sketch is overdone; it must be subordinated to the general family breakup. Tone it down, put it in its proper place; and then end the story with something like this: your father's return from Kansas City with bad news about the invention—or something to suggest the coming old soldiers home. And I note a second fault; this story leaves the reader facing the foreclosure of the mortgage, and far back in THE HORN you indicated that the mortgage had been foreclosed. So that you do not gain time but positively lose it as your series of stories progresses.

LIKE GLASS is much nearer completion. It needs a good deal of touching up, but is very good as it stands. I think that it too needs a different twist of emphasis at the end. If your last sentence were something like, "Father wasn't singing," you would have the right twist. That, of course, won't do; it's too bold, and out of tone with your method of telling; but is should suggest the kind of twist needed.

I think that both of these stories are going to emerge as grand as the others. Please try to make a record and have them ready to incorporate with the other within a fortnight.[21]

Grace thanked him for applying the pressure.

Merriam then took some of the stories to his writing class for their observations and reported to Grace.

The story is very effective in parts but to be sure of my judgment I read it to a class and asked for reactions: about half of the students were taken up with the mother's story and the rest were absorbed entirely in the child's school experience; none of them got the two put together. What I think you will have to do is to have as a background behind all the incidents the father's reactions. For example the father would probably have had something to say about Mr. Higgins and his methods of teaching, and couldn't by some hook or crook, the father have got hold of the answer concerning the part of speech, "a millionth maybe", and couldn't he have enjoyed that hugely? Then for some of the teacher's cruelties couldn't he have had some seething comments? And at the end—the story ends abruptly—mightn't the father have had some vigorous comments on the child's having been to school and then having had to be taken out of school?

There is excellent material in the story; all it needs is a typing-together according to your underlying purpose.[22]

In August, Merriam asked about sending the book of short stories to Mr. O'Brien, Grace assured him that O'Brien was welcome to the book since B&B returned it. She also revealed to Merriam that she had written nothing for two years. But she said, "I've just loaded and unloaded and distributed two truckfuls of earth for my next year's garden."

Let me know all you have to say about the stories for O'B. THE HAIL will be that to-be-eliminated—paragraph in THE HORN—as a nucleus. (I know what I mean but am not saying it.) By the way, Braithwaite is using something of mine this year. All the kick is gone from that for me. He had the nerve to ask for $50 prepublication loan, after slaughtering the innocents right and left all these years! I hope my literary allusion redeems my vernacular. I'll send you a copy of the 1929 book, so do not buy one.[23]

Grace was in Great Falls later in the month to both speak about *The Frontier* at the Pioneers organization and see the doctor. To Merriam, she wrote,

Several notes from you are on my desk. I have spent nine days with the dentist, abscessed tooth etc., and a $125 dentist bill, which was about half what I expected it to be. That helps.

The Pioneers meeting was not fully satisfactory, but nothing is as a rule. I think you will draw some historical material from it. Mrs. Bruckert came to speak of a diary of her father(?) [Albert Bruckert] kept for the past sixty years—Montana stuff. She lives at Wilsall, and I am supposed to go look the thing over.[24]

"The value of the contacts at Great Falls remains to be seen," Grace wrote Merriam.

> Nobody was in town—clubs suspended, no university girls in town, etc. I have the alumni list from Mr. Freeman, for you. Mrs. Mallon wants to copy it, so I will send it via her.
>
> When I am immersed in those stories it is difficult for me to turn my attention to the subscription end of the magazine needs, but I'm not at all discouraged over eventual support, and think I can send more subscriptions later.
>
> I spoke to the sons and daughters and to the other group—the Pioneers. I hope to send you the book mss almost immediately. It isn't right yet. I agree with you about the PROMISES. I am at work, really I have a clear conscience on that score.
>
> Met Mrs. Hatfield and had a good time with her and Mrs. Plassman's daughter. Why doesn't Mrs. Plassman do something for us?
>
> I'll write at greater length when I have gotten the smoke out of the house. I just had an accident and almost started a disastrous fire.
>
> Mrs. Hey did move, but not until last July. She is a good booster for the magazine. I have a lot of troubles, but will tell them later. In the mean time I'll finish the mechanical work on what I have to date. Your criticism is invaluable to me. Don't be hesitant about giving it straight. I never see your encouragement until the tenth reading of your letters, and it always comes at the right moment, just as I'm starting toward the stove with the entire manuscript
>
> I'd give a lot to be nominated, or even eligible for that *World* entry.[25]

Merriam continued to urge Grace to write, and suggested that when the short stories were in book form, she might try putting some of her verse in book form.

> …If you care to make a collection of verse—*after* the volume of stories have been made up and shipped—I would be glad to get it a reading from W.W. Norton & Co., a rapidly rising firm, and from the Viking Press. I can get material to the head readers in those firms.
>
> Did you make Great Falls? And if so, how did matters progress?[26]

When Grace Coates had told Merriam she hadn't written anything for two years, it was a concern to him. His encouragement led to "The Choice" that she sent to him for approval and publishing in *The Frontier*. Merriam liked the story.

COATES TO MERRIAM; OCTOBER 25, 1929

> Dear HGM,
> I can't tell you how much your letter means to me about the story A CHOICE: and I'll tell you why.

CHOICE was a new story, had nothing to do with my childhood, the suggestion was just received—hadn't had to ripen long. I have in my home now a casualty of the depression, and there are unending stories in her—she had a little goat that turned her father's flour mill for the house; and she pulled his whiskers to make him trot fast on the tread belt, for instance. I didn't know whether if was any good or not. The story ends when the bag is empty; but I couldn't stand it. I couldn't.

I just got it back from Scribner's. I will work on it a bit more, and try ending it where the end comes—when she looks hard at the empty bag. Yes, indeed, I'll make every effort to sell it if you say it's any good. I just sent GOOD HOUSEKEEPING a really good poem not cynical nor yet sob-stuffy. The only thing wrong with it was that Goethe has done it better!—"lebendige Kleid"

So much for enthusiasm. You needn't read the longhand letter unless you wish. It is enthusiasm for the latest Frontier which is way ahead of the rest—more like an honest-to-God magazine, and not something the well-disposed think kindly of as a matter of justice. It makes me say it mustn't die. Trowbridge (Green Valley, Ill.,) says Pagany has gone out, and that The Midland may, almost will fold up before Spring. I doubt it, about the Midland. [Novelist] Jack Conroy's agent found the Pagany office closed when he went to collect...[27]

COATES TO MERRIAM: OCTOBER 30, 1929

Dear Mr. Merriam:

Because one of the enclosed poems referred to my sister, and another contained a phrase of mine, Dr. Newman, with characteristic delicacy, sent them to me first, with the request that I explain the situation to you. But his letter covering the poems is sufficiently free of personalities, I believe, that it wont be out of bounds for me to pass the entire letter on to you, for its delightful flavor. (I am very fond of Israel, as you know. He is a gentle spirit.) Since he likes my AT NIGHT so much, I'll send a copy of that for your eye. It hadn't occurred to me that it was good.

As I shall suggest to him. I shall be delighted beyond words (such banality of phrase!) if Israel can make Tight-Rope walker meet your needs.

About J.T. Shipley. Twice he has said, "If you have anything of mine you like, send it to Mr. Merriam" Well, if he is too busy to mail his things (he is working on a new book) he is surely too busy to have me get him in a mix-up sending something that is already in print. However I have two poems on hand, and one that I have mislaid that I like greatly. It isn't obvious, but I didn't like it until all of a sudden I just fell for it with crash. I'll find or type, the other. I enclosed one recent one of his.

Please return Israel's letter at your convenience.

When I wrote you, I had not fully examined the Nov. Frontier. I like it more and more the farther I go. The Chronicle is using a story I sent them of Taylor Gordon, and one I wrote of Ethel Romig Fuller. I should have sent you that one of her, but didn't even keep a copy—was in the mood and ran it off and mailed it. There is going to be no trouble getting material. Just say "newspaper" to a poet, and he erupts material. I am going to send a brief review of BORN TO BE which of course you may not care to run. No difference, I have chewed Taylor so fine one review more or less is nothing! Vinal has asked me to do occasional reviewing for Voices, and I was affable about it.

Praise for the Frontier is coming often—from Eddie Custer, Denver "It's the real thing" From Doris Bradley "Something to be proud of" from Dolly Martin "A magazine better than other magazines" I'm not thru with it yet.

I could send the Chronicle two or three short stories a week—not necessarily all about Frontier matter—but if 200 word items is what he wants—that is easy.

GSC[28]

The *Great Falls Tribune* reported on January 5, 1930,

Among writers who won Bozart prizes in 1929 was Grace Stone Coates of Martinsdale, winner of first place for the best quatrain, "Sophistication," published during that year in Bozart.

Mrs. Coates recently sold serial rights on her story "Wild Plums," to an eastern newspaper syndicate. This story was published first in The Frontier and from that was chosen by O'Brien for his best short stories of 1929. Four stories by Mrs. Coates received triple star rating on Mr. O'Brien's honor roll for 1929.

Although Grace was nationally recognized in her own right and busying editing the work of others, she still looked to H.G. Merriam for help with her own work. After helping put the stories together for *Black Cherries* he helped with the selection of poems for her two poetry volumes, and continued to critique the work she sent to *The Frontier*. Although she did not always take his advice, she was pleased to get it. Once, after receiving his critique of a story she was reworking, she thanked him for his "razzing," the critique she had requested.

Coates continued working on putting the stories into book form.

GRACE STONE COATES, CIRCA 1930.
COATES USED THIS PHOTOGRAPH TO ACCOMPANY HER NEWSPAPER ARTICLES.

COATES TO MERRIAM: JANUARY 18, 1930

Dear HGM

Story etc in the mail when your inquiry came. Reworking those stories makes me see that they really aren't integrated into independent stories. The book mss will be improved by the work I am doing on the "stories" to make them stand on their own legs.

I reworked STUBBORN THISTLE and improved it a lot. It is no good yet. It is not a story that I want The Frontier to use. I get tired of answering silly questions. Was your father married twice? Didn't he get along with your mother? Did you really say those things to that poor old man? Did your grandfather chew tobacco? There are several of those stories that I don't mind having the Midland use, that I shrink from having the Frontier, with its nearer sources of annoyance, give to the world.

This is merely by way of explanation as to why I don't give you first whack. Mr. Frederick wrote that if I couldn't sell STUBBORN THISTLES the Midland would be "proud" to publish it.

It was the difficulty of laughing off friends who eye me sidelong and ask questions, that made me so long sending you a story. I forgot. Thought I had all manner of material to select from. But every one except the one I sent was "out", when I thought of some damn fool reading it. Those stories were never meant to be read; just written.

Dolly Martin read my story chuckling. That was, and is, the way they are all intended. They aren't so "sordid" as one critic characterized them!

GSC[29]

Dolly Martin was as "out of place" in Martinsdale as was Grace. And, later that year,

Dolly Martin is my only companion here, and she and I merely slide the surface of things. I am afraid of her, and she does not understand my jibing ways. She is a Tennessee college graduate and incongruously enough teachers the village school. She is the cigarette smoking, hard drinking, hard loving, hard thinking disillusioned type, a wide reader, a lover of luxury, always in debt, always generous, always criticized and bitten by gossip. So you see how well she fits into village life.[29]

Still later that year, Grace wrote Saroyan,

She is a cracking good irresponsible live youngster; but how interesting she might be on paper I do not know. She should be writing, for she has wit, and a fine sense of the ridiculous.[30]

∽

Encircled

I wanted you to lie so still
    The even beating of your breast
Would seem an impulse of my will,
    A motion of my spirit, guessed
Through all the measure of my days;
    I wanted you so soft to lie
That when your presence shaped my ways
    I would not know you were not I.

CHAPTER SIX

One of the first prospective contributors to *The Frontier* was William Saroyan. He saw one of Coates' stories in *The Midland* and decided to submit a story to this assistant editor of *The Frontier*. Saroyan was a young man of about twenty-one and Grace was forty-seven when their friendship began and although it was an association of student-teacher there was almost a sensual tone to their letters back and forth. The similarity of their work created an immediate attachment.

William Saroyan was born in Fresno, California in 1908. A high-school dropout, he was self-educated and wanted to become a writer. He wrote voluminously but was not able to have much success at publishing. His tentative submission to *The Midland* began a relationship that affected his writing and his life.

Although at first the letters from Grace to Will were strictly professional, they soon lapsed into a more casual mode. They told each other their innermost thoughts.

Saroyan poured out his frustrations with his work and told of his ambitions and Grace responded with encouragement and tales of the aggravation of her own work. They discussed the writers of the time and other sundry aspects of the writing business. Their almost daily dialogue told their own stories. They even corresponded about their stock investments.

After 1934 when his first book of stories appeared, he had reached a point where he no longer needed the help of his friend in Montana, although he continued for the rest of his life to acknowledge the impact she had made on his work and his life.

In 1936 he published two more short story collections, and plays, *My Heart's in the Highland* and *The Time of Your Life*. *My Name is Aram* was released in 1940, and in 1941, he worked with Louis B. Mayer in Hollywood and wrote *The Human Comedy*. Saroyan served a time in the army during part of World War II and continued to write until his last memoir, *Births* (1983) was published posthumously.

Grace's first reply to Saroyan, in late January 1930, was a critical one.

COATES TO SAROYAN: JANUARY 25, 1930

Your sincere treatment of this story, and its freshness of theme makes me believe you have the ability to send us material The Frontier will be glad to use.

WILLIAM SAROYAN, CIRCA 1930

Saroyan Portrait, M0978, Saroyan Papers, Special Collections, Stanford University Libraries

This story needs further work. You have unconsciously relied on your own clear conception of the situations, and have failed to clarify them for the reader at the right time; that is you leave him floundering around waiting to get things straight in his mind. There is nothing to make a reader know that La Paloma Vineyard belonged to "your" uncle, until the second paragraph of the story tells him by inference. Consequently, in the final sentence of the first paragraph, "the place" has been assigned no particular location to the reader.

The first sentence of the second paragraph would be an excellent and illuminating opening for the story...

There is another defect in the story: practically four pages out of six have no relation, except that of background, to what your title gives as the real theme of the sketch. The title is not good. To me, at least, it conveys something of different atmosphere than the story—and the atmosphere of the story is precisely where the beauty of the story lies. The idea of—*growing up* embraces both the swimming episode and the apple picking—in fact the entire story.

Before you send this out again, certain misspellings and typographical errors should be corrected. I have checked a number of them—The opening sentence is tedious—it hasn't snap enough...

As I have suggested before, this material interests me because of the latent ability it suggests. We will always be glad to see any work you have to offer.[1]

Saroyan immediately replied.

SAROYAN TO COATES; FEBRUARY 1, 1930

...I appreciate your valuable suggestions very much...

Almost all of my stories are written at one sitting, probably because I can type fast, and this may be the reason the finished job is often rather unfinished. It is very difficult, almost impossible, for me to type a page twice. The sentences become almost meaningless and so many changes are made that I have come to believe it is best not to try to revise and improve a story, as much as I am sometimes aware of the need...

I had intended merely to reply to your very kind letter today, but since I had written the attached story this morning, I thought The Frontier might care to see it. It is not in the same vein as the other, but in the meantime I will see if I can send you something which I can feel is more likely to be what you want. Though I do not want to impose upon your good-will, it is needless for me to say that your suggestions are very encouraging and helpful, and that I hope you will give me a little of your time again.[2]

After receiving another story, she wrote,

Coates to Saroyan: February 6, 1930

Persons most worth criticizing (if criticism helps) are, I believe, the ones least able to profit from criticism. They write from an inner necessity, and their work delivers itself "whole-born". The current that drives in them is not easily deflected or modified from the outside…

The simple and naive title you used for the other story was all right *after the reader had read the* tale; but before he had read it, the title in some way cheapened the story; just as the title you suggest, "Love is Funny that Way", cheapens this story. It prepares the reader for something flippant—that does not develop. I read the story with the greater interest because my mind wasn't predisposed this way or that by the title…I'm enthusiastic about your work…[3]

Her enthusiasm about Saroyan's work found a mark. On February 12, he wrote:

Saroyan to Coates: February 12, 1930

I do not believe I can tell you how sincerely I appreciate your very kind letters and your interest in my work. Quite often, when disappointments have been many, and everything has seemed futile, I have definitely decided to quit writing. The other day I was on the verge of walking out on myself when your good letter came, and of course it revived me completely. I feel extremely fortunate to enjoy your interest and assistance, and I sincerely hope that through your suggestions I will be able to write short stories *The Frontier* will want to publish.[4]

Five days later, Grace told Saroyan how much his story touched her.

Coates to Saroyan: February 17, 1930

Dear Mr. Saroyan:

I hope I didn't give you a disappointment by returning that last story; I meant to say, in first commenting on it, that The Frontier wasn't going to use it. I sent it on to Mr. Merriam because it was worth reading and I wanted to have him see it, and you thru it. You mostly. I had in mind to say that it was a matter of no especial moment about the publishing of the story. The big thing is that you are writing them—such stories.

Mr. Merriam's discussion would have warmed your soul. He praises discriminatingly, and his unqualified word was "beautifully handled." He had no criticism of any letdown, that I felt (from my own fatigue, most likely) in he middle. I did not feel that on second reading. But the ending is not just right—I mean the wording of the ending. It is exactly right in concept.

Did you see my story in the 1930 O'Brien? Just by way of illustrating that publishing in such magazines as The Frontier and The Midland does pay, even tho you get no immediate check, that story was published in The Midland. After O'Brien spied it, the *McClure Magazine Syndicate* bought the serial rights; and several companies have asked me for a novel, on strength of the story. I have no novel, but you see if one does work like yours, and does not get too easily disheartened, goes ahead and accumulates material, when the gong strikes he is ready to go—even if he has waited years for the moment. But when the opportunity comes, have something to feed into the publishers maw. (Learn from my failure).

Keep right on sending things…the invitation is a standing one Mr. Merriam said, tho he probably did not expect me to repeat it, that if the files had not been so crowded he might have jumped at your last story, even tho for extraneous reasons it didn't furnish just the thing needed for balance or flavor or something of the kind—the last words mine—in the magazine.

I understand wholly what you mean by messing things up by trying to act on criticism.

Would it be impertinent for me to ask you your nationality? I am not sufficiently cosmopolitan to know. In fact, the reason I didn't send Mr. Merriam's comment, first-hand, was that it was written on a slip bearing that question addressed to him; and sending it would have disconcerted me…

Oh, lad, I've just read your story and think it's great. It is the humor in it, the humor that flickers thru the pain, that takes me. Of course I can not commit Mr. Merriam to anything, but on it goes to him with my blessing. It is more suitable for The Frontier than for The Midland, since we are more in touch with the coast than that magazine is. Do not be disappointed if Mr. Merriam can not use this story—but I have a different feeling about this manuscript's chances with him than I had about the other.

After you read some of my stories you will understand why yours speak peculiarly to my heart. We write out of the same impulse. I hope you will always have just enough hardship to keep your heart properly wrung, so that it drips good stories—and in the end, glorious success….

In a subsequent letter I am going to criticize minor points on your story— use of certain words—reprimand, for instance. The word suggests to me a sharp, single, formal reproof from a superior, or an authoritative reproof. I believe the mother and sister <u>reproached </u>the boy—that he feared their— <u>reproaches</u>. There are other slight matters of diction. I take it for granted that you know my good will, and that if any of my criticism seems trivial or picayunish or directed at detail, you can strug it off, knowing it was well meant. Personally I find specific criticism the only thing that helps much, and blanket criticism the least helpful.

Sincerely yours,, Grace Stone Coates[5]

Grace soon passed along news of acceptance by *The Frontier*.

COATES TO SAROYAN: FEBRUARY 22, 1930

> ...I have received good news for you. Mr. Merriam will use your ESCAPE BY STEERAGE in the Frontier. It is back in my hands for criticism, and I take it for granted you will wish to consider my comments on it, and put it in as perfect shape as possible for us.
>
> ...I am delighted that Mr. Merriam likes this story. I'm going to give myself the fun of telling you the spots that make me chuckle—the points that make it your story and no other man's.
>
> Can you make any sense out of the poem I have written on the back? I just made it.
>
> Write like the devil, now that you have two sound, if unsaying, editors watching your work and expecting much; and you know better than I how many others besides Mr. Frederick and Mr. Merriam.

> Smite my eyes with a thorn branch,
>
> But do not make me look at forsythia
>
> Smoking into color under February rain.
>
> Pumpkin seeds, pumpkin seeds, and which side to butter them
>
> An East Side Jew who studies agriculture
>
> Practices biology without a license!
>
> Freesias choke me—and never again violets!
>
> But I can forget the color of Chinese love-nuts,
>
> Twirling an absinth glass against the light.[6]

Saroyan enjoyed receiving the current *Frontier* and commented on "Corn Knife"—a story by Grace Stone Coates in the March issue. He told her he particularly liked the story and thought he was beginning to understand her work.

SAROYAN TO COATES: MARCH 3, 1930

> I shall look forward to reading the stories in book form, and it seems to me that if gathered together they would become more a novel than a collection of short stories. Roland English Harley's stories seem invariably excellent. I feel fortunate to have a story accepted by the Frontier, and although I previously stated I would rather not retype the story, on second thought I am sure it would be the thing to do.

The reason I am quite convinced I should go over the story again is because I have just received your very good letter written from your sister's. Your suggestions were most valuable, although I felt somewhat ashamed of myself for making so many blunders. I suppose it is because I write for sounds, paying no attention to grammar, that I make so many grammatical mistakes. And then again if I write for sounds how could I have repeated the word "never" twice in one sentence? The point is: your criticisms are very important to me, and I shall anxiously await the arrival of Escape so that I can see for myself what my mistakes were. Of course I hope you will mark the script so that I will be easily guided…

…P.S. It has just occurred to me that I am undoubtedly burdening you with these stories I am sending, that it takes time to write suggestions for me, to read and correct. Am I not unconsciously taking advantage of you? In submitting a story to the Frontier should I not send it to the editor? Or is it quite the same to send it to you?

W.S.[7]

COATES TO SAROYAN: MARCH 6, 1930

Dear Mr. Saroyan:

Forgive me for what I did to your other manuscript. If you will return it, I'll gladly have it retyped, if I have to send it to China to get it done! I really do consider manuscripts sacrosanct; but I mistook your rapid composition for digital expertness; and the situation was unusual; be generous and know that the unwarranted marking up of that story beguiled a painful journey for me.

I am back at the desk after a ten day absence. Your not wanting to see your story again gives me a fellow feeling. Manuscripts used to fill me with nausea. Of course you felt like a school boy under my school-teacherly ministrations. (I'm Mrs. Coates, by the way.) Tomorrow I'll get to work on my accumulated mail, and your manuscript. I can't change it—wouldn't let any one do that to me, nor would I take the responsibility of doing it.

Send anything, any time. We may not use it at once, but are open for the consideration of your material at any time. Mr. Merriam tells me that he is so filled with short story material that he can take only the especially good right now.

To continue, about your accepted story. I'll spare you as much as possible, and leave the mss not too much marked.

Thank you for retyping the "poem". They stay in my mind indefinitely. I suppose I could repeat every poem I have written (I wonder?) They come entire, remain entire, and go entire.

Probably I was more interested in what you would say you felt about the lines I sent, than in what you felt. You didn't disappoint me. I rather thought you would be honest. What I made of the poem, you had in the first version. What I didn't put in it is on the other side.[Spring Scimitar]

Cordially yours, Grace Stone Coates

In my haste and pressure (disorderly house—sick Setter pup—et alt.) I have not even touched on what you say in your letter that most moves me. Are you reading everything Ludwig Lewisohn writes? I want to. I shall be glad to be reassured about the scribbled manuscript. Mea culpa, mea culpa, mea maxima fortuna!

Your friend, G[8]

Saroyan apologized to Grace for not wanting to retype his story.

Saroyan to Coates: March 10, 1930

It is a fact that I loathe a manuscript after it is written and that it is tortuous for me to work on anything twice. I was afraid you might misinterpret my reference to feeling like a school boy, and I am glad I got off so easy. I wrote earlier in the day a letter of apology. The reason I made the remark was that I was somewhat reminded of how I felt in school when a teacher requested that I rewrite a composition. I am glad you are tolerant. I was actually quite worried until your letter came. (I learned some time ago by referring to a book containing the names of American Authors that you were Mrs. Coates, but I imagined for some strange reason that it would be correct to address you as Miss.)

Though I feel it will be impossible, I hope my story is used in The Frontier. Thank you for letting me read Spring Scimitar, but I must admit that it is yet only beautiful to me, though I understand it more now. The first line I especially like.[9]

Poetry was something that Saroyan did not attempt very often, but he was appreciative of good poetry and was pleased when Grace would send him poetry for comment.

Saroyan to Coates: March 11, 1930

Yesterday I was in a hurry to reach the mail box before the last collection, otherwise I might have written a much longer letter. Today I enjoyed studying your most subtle poem and it is difficult for me to decide which I like best. But I believe the second version is more to my taste, since it is more readily understood and since it loses none of its original charm. Of course I suppose the best poetry is said to be the most subtle or symbolic. "Practices biology without a license" is a thought very aptly put, and yet "A fat Jewess lives with him, unmarried" seems more trenchant. Perhaps this poem were best published in both versions: the second for the benefit of those who like foot-notes. Do you believe poetry can arouse thought as against awakening emotions? (Have you read what T.S. Eliot has written in the February Bookman in regard to the purpose (if there is any) of poetry? Of course I have not, although I have just read one or two sentences of Poe's in his The Poetic Principle. He has written: "It has been assumed, tacitly and avowedly, directly and indirectly, that the ultimate object of all Poetry is Truth. We have taken it into our heads that to write a poem simply for the poem's sake, and to acknowledge such to have been our design, would be to confess ourselves radically wanting in the true poetic dignity and force." And further: "the demands of Truth are severe. She has no sympathy with the myrtles. All that which is so indispensable in Song is precisely all that with which she has nothing whatever to do. In enforcing a truth we need severity rather than efflorescence of language. We must be simple, precise, terse. We must be cool, calm, unimpassioned." And I suppose quite unpoetic, and yet all this notwithstanding, I believe a good many poems are being written that achieve truth. I believe if a poem succeeds in stirring a reader, reminding him of something almost forgotten, causing him to find new values in old things, or merely make him feel funny, it is a good poem. Depending, of course, upon who the reader has been. Every poem written is apt to arouse feelings in some person, and yet some people (critics, no doubt) are liable to denounce a popular work as shallow or fake. Edgar Guest, I sincerely believe, is the greatest poet in America today, not for me, however, but for those he prefers to write for. There is no doubt in my mind but that if he cared he could satisfy the most caustic critic with sophisticated poetry. But I am afraid Robinson Jeffers would never be able to write Guest poetry.

I hope you will find the time to write three sheets to me, although I am afraid by this time you are quite tired of hearing my talking and getting no where. I am enclosing an envelope today so that you can send back the "poems" after you have looked them over. I am quite worried about the word reprimand in my story. Won't you please change reprimand to reproach for me?

Rueben Haig is my name when I write poetry—or try—[10]

It is difficult to realize when Saroyan had time to write stories when he wrote three and four page letters to Grace almost every day. In one, he went into a long dissertation about translating music into words. He tried to put Tchaikovsky's Theme and Variations Suite No. 3 in G into poetry—but he said,

I am quite afraid that very shortly you will have become so annoyed with my numerous letters written for no apparent reason, that in reply to them you will send me a Frontier rejection slip, which I believe is the polite way in which magazine editors tell aspiring writers to go to hell.[11]

Although Grace apologized for marking up his manuscript she still sent pages of comments suggesting changes and words. His disparagement of his own work brought this comment from her.

COATES TO SAROYAN: UNDATED

> Willy-nilly
>
> Criticism's silly.
>
> The more meticulous,
>
> The more *re*diculous.

About the only thing I'm out of sympathy with you about is your occasional implication that you fell disconcerted over imperfections in your writing. Why should you? Why should any body? I finish anything I work hard over, feeling a nauseated sense of having made an ass of myself. I used to humor my nausia [sic], and refuse to look at my work—but now I ignore it and go ahead with the revising and the weighing and pondering.

In general you do very little *bad* writing. More often you go astray on usage, more often still on diction; and I am not in accord with your punctuation, sometimes.[12]

Although Saroyan accepted every criticism from Grace of his work and worked to improve it, he did not accept the advice of others. He later mentioned that he did not plan to write for *Midland*.

SAROYAN TO COATES: APRIL 17, 1930

I do not like to be asked to do this in a story and not to do that. I believe that is for me to decide. Do not imagine, however, that I feel the least unkind towards Mr. Frederick and the magazine. That is not so. I may perhaps send them more stories, and I appreciate his interest, but if I write a story which I stretch to three thousand words or seven or twenty thousand words, I think that many words are necessary, even it they aren't. If I am naturally wasteful with words I don't see that I can be changed or that it is right for me to be influenced outwardly...I merely write. If it hits, all right. If it doesn't all right. I'll try again...I do not like to be influenced, in short. I think it is naturally wrong....I would like to please the magazine, but I do not believe that can be done unless I am left to myself. I mention this to you because I believe you will understand…I know I have much to learn and I am willing to learn, but I do not believe the valuable things (at least not in art) can be taught.[13]

Letters between the two became much less formal as "Dear Miss Coates, Dear Mrs. Coates" became "My friend Grace" and "Dear Mr. Saroukhan" became "Dear Will" and even "My dear lad." Grace wrote to Saroyan, "Just call me 'Dear Grace' I like that." Although Will used his ethnic name Saroukhan on occasion, he used Saroyan for his publications.

Will was embarrassed to think he had been "impudent" in his address. Grace reassured him.

COATES TO SAROYAN: UNDATED

Once I said to a good old Doctor whom I had embarrassed by asking what something or other was—that it would be impossible for me to say a vulgar thing to him—i.e. vulgarity between us couldn't exist. Our mental attitudes were such that nothing between our minds could assume that form. By parallel, nothing between you and me could be crude or inept or offensive. What's the matter? You aren't developing a complex are you? Dear Will: Dear Friend: dear what difference does it make! Why no, nothing you do is impudent, can't be, because you are not an impudent person. A person might call me dear Mrs. Coates, and be impudent, or call me old gal, and not be. Henderson surprised me once by saying "Are you the old bird that's had my hammer?" That moment has remained one of the delightful ones of my life[14]

In March her salutation was lengthy:

COATES TO SAROYAN: UNDATED

Dear—can't you give me some esoteric form of the name William that I can use without sandpapering my soul: Mr. Coates has a brother William; 'nuf said—Mr. Saroyan[15]

Grace became an extremely important element in helping the young Saroyan launch his writing career. For a year or more, he was completely under her guidance. In return, she found a kindred soul she could tell her frustrations with work and stories and hurts of her life. This was a different person than the one who wrote careful and organized letters to Merriam as assistant editor of *The Frontier*. At one point, she wrote,

COATES TO SAROYAN: UNDATED

Will, don't be too bitter. I learned early in life that no body cared a damn what happened to me but myself, so I played a joke on an indifferent world by going along and having a hell of a good time, most of the time. Accidents will happen to the best regulated spirits, but thanks to you, I didn't go clear crazy. Thank you my friend and spirit's brother, and be happy.[16]

Saroyan sent her another story.

SAROYAN TO COATES:UNDATED

I am sending you a short-short story I wrote quite some time ago. Brotherhood, I've called it. I don't want it printed anywhere, but you might like to read it. In view of its recent tragical [sic] ending I shall hide it just as soon as I get it back from you. The item (newspaper) I am enclosing appeared on April 7th in the San Francisco Examiner. My brother is quite broken He is never getting a decent break.[17]

Coates wrote to Merriam in early 1930,

COATES TO MERRIAM: UNDATED

About Saroyan: He sent me something so good that I regret it wasn't for print. Maybe he'll change his mind. It was called BROTHERHOOD, and was obviously an incident of his brother's life and his, that arose from his brother's approaching marriage. The story was arresting in its poignancy, yet without sentimentality. The reason for its suppression was made plain by a clipping attached, date April 7—from a San Francisco paper. As his brother was preparing wedding announcements for the mail, a telegram reached him that his fiancée had been killed as she returned from the funeral of a friend. Auto accident. The story, of course, had no reference to the later accident. I believe you would like that story if you had it.

I had sent back so many of Saroyan's things, it occurred to me you perhaps should see something of his.[18]

And another time,

COATES TO MERRIAM: UNDATED

I handled Saroyan's mss rather stupidly—hurried it to you under the impression that you might want to see it again before you confirmed or corrected my supposition that you had accepted it. Anyway, I think there are places in it inferior to the original. I have the original…My intention was to do the best I could with it first, and then turn it over to you. (I found the cuspidor pretty full, myself, and had meant to criticize it in my first suggestions to him, but overlooked including the criticism)…If I had a story ready for you I'd probably not be so gracious and unselfish with Saroyan. He has probably had more encouragement than I assume, and I am always over-solicitous for nuts[19]

"Your letters do me good," Grace told Saroyan, "usually amuse me, sometimes stab me with a sense of my own squandered youth of the spirit, and always interest me. Some day they will provoke me to adequate answer."[20]

At this time, Grace was editing for Caxton Press and over the next few years, edited nine books—the last being *Jugheads Behind the Lines* by Carl Noble in 1938.

Merriam was dealing with editing manuscripts as well and he wrote in February about a story.

MERRIAM TO COATES: UNDATED

I may be completely haywire, but I think that Scearce's manuscript would sell as a popular account of Alaskan experiences as it is, if published. It is full of crudities and ab [sic] absurdities; it also reveals an experienced man who is very naïf in many matters. He doesn't know how to write. I put Mr. E.R. Ormsbee, former superintendent of schools at Hamilton, at work on the manuscript and he worked nicely on it straightening out the sentences, organizing the paragraphs, but trying to leave the flavor of Scearce himself. I believe that Scearce paid him $100. The manuscript has been to publishers (as you say with my name used large and in vain) and they have thought that the manuscript had no chance of sale unless it were turned into regular fiction. I wrote Mr. Scearce that he was not capable of turning it into fiction; that whatever value there was to the material lay in its being an authentic account of a real personality in Alaska. He has been determined to turn it into fiction. Now Maule has suggested that he get a ghost writer, and Scearce has written to you suggesting that you "edit" the manuscript. Don't fool yourself; it will be no job of editing, it will be a job of turning into fiction a manuscript that has only fictive touches— you would be a genuine ghost writer.

Mr. Scearce has an enormous ego; yet he is humble in the presence of people who know about writing, most pleasant and friendly, and willing to pay for any service he received. You would have a good time with him. Ormsbee went to Ronan and stayed a week or so at his house and reported an excellent time. One simply has to be careful not to injure the man's childlike vanity. He is immensely in earnest; he thinks he has the book of all times about Alaska.

Thanks for the other information of your letter. I hope this response to your third paragraph tells you what you want to know. I know well that you will keep this matter confidential.

Are the Literary News notes nearly ready? We don't need to have them before March 1 but always appreciate as early receipt of copy as possible.

Cordially, HGM[21]

H.G. Merriam did not share Grace's enthusiasm for Saroyan's work, and only one short story, "Escape by Steerage," appeared in *The Frontier* in May of 1930.

COATES TO SAROYAN: UNDATED

Your story ESCAPE will appear in the next issue of the Frontier I think. I heaved one of my stories aside to make room for you. In other words the world loses a masterpiece, in order to hail a new genius. The rest of the story is that I really didn't have ready what I most wanted to submit. So don't be overwhelmed with gratitude.[22]

Another time,

COATES TO SAROYAN: UNDATED

...I think you will have no trouble in appearing in the Frontier more than once. I have no right to promise anything, but I am sure we can use more of your work than ESCAPE BY STEERAGE. Please send the original soon. I want to revise one or two places...You have such abundant intuitive sense of presentation that you ought to break big some of these days.[23]

SAROYAN TO COATES: FEBRUARY 20, 1930

Dear Miss Coates:

I do not believe I have had in all my life a better friend than you have become in less than a month. I am certainly more indebted to you for your generous interest and encouragement than I should ever be able to explain. I should be satisfied, I think to write stories that might never be published, as long as I could depend upon you to read them, and to offer your very good suggestions. I cannot understand why you are being so good to me, but I pray I shall always be able to think of you as I think of you today.

...After making the corrections you suggested, and after calling the story "Cheated", I mailed it to Mr. Frederick of The Midland, mentioning the fact that you prompted me to do so, and also that you were responsible for whatever polish the story had. Of course I changed the ending just as you said, and I removed the word "angelic", besides cutting out a few other things which I did not like on second reading. The sentence, for instance, regarding the young man's moustache, his ability to dance, and his affairs in the other city, which I thought quite beside the point.

Do not imagine that I was the least disappointed because you returned the story. How could I be so ungrateful when your letter was attached? Do not, please, ever feel that I shall be discouraged because The Frontier returns a story, no matter for what reason. I have been getting stories back without a murmur for so long that when there is a little encouragement accompanying them, I feel more than amply repaid for my effort.

...I read with great pleasure your story in O'Brien's volume, and it was because of it that I was prompted to mail you the first story I did. I am very glad the story is being recognized, and that you are getting offers, on the strength of it, from publishers. I shall look forward to reading everything you write from now on. I have been intending to write a novel since 1926, for some unknown reason, and I can imagine that if ever I should get any sort of an offer from a publisher, I should be able to produce one in a very short time. Which would be too soon, I am sure.

...I do not know why it should be impertinent for you to ask me my nationality. My father and mother were born in the same village in Armenia, they were distant cousins, my father was educated in a Protestant College in that country, spoke English (and wrote it) while still there, came to America in 1905, was a minister for some time in Paterson, N.J., moved to Fresno, California in 1908 where I was born on August 31 of that year, tried his hand at farming, laboring, chicken raising, moved about for several years and finally died in San Jose in 1911. Four years of my life from (my third year to my seventh) were spent in an orphanage in Oakland; I sold papers from my eighth to twelfth year, was a grocer's boy until I was thirteen when I became a messenger boy for a telegraph company, working after school, and I have since been a laborer on a vineyard, a clerk and typist, and a branch manager of a telegraph company.

That is perhaps more biography than you asked for, but I do not mention these things because I feel I am anyone of any importance...

...Your suggestion in regard to the word reprimand is excellent. I shall never want to feel that your advice is ever trivial or picayunish (whatever that is), and I assure you that I have not yet had occasion to disagree with you on any points. You are pointing out to somewhat I might find out for myself after a long time.

Before closing I must again try to thank you for all that you have done for me. I shall never want to forget what you have meant to me.

Very sincerely yours, William Saroyan[24]

In return to Saroyan's thank you for what Grace had done, she replied,

You have done more to release me from the inhibitions that were hampering me than any one else has ever done.

The atmosphere here is unfavorable for one of my temperament—not that I howl about that. Mr. Coates infuriates me by being indulgent. He made the mistake once of saying he gave me a great deal of freedom. I am usually either silent or mild of speech; but by the time I had torn myself to pieces telling him that my freedom lay in my own breast, and that no human being was the repository of my freedom—and had reduced him to bewilderment, so that he answered, puzzled, "It was only a way of speaking." I retorted, "Learn a different manner of speech, then" and now I laugh; for he and I never quarrel. But when I desperately want only that my precious precious all too brief moments be not frittered away by needless interruptions, I am treated indulgently, like an amusing child who wants to play with the clock; who isn't abruptly denied, nor yet permitted to have what it wants.

And I've lived in that atmosphere of belittling so long, that I have ceased to think of myself as a decent human being, as indeed I am not in so far as I do not force circumstances to my will instead of yielding to them. I know only too well what it means, that we must forsake father and mother and sister and brother if we care to get anywhere. It is the most harrowing, compelling thing in the world to know that one who loves you is lonesome because your eye is bright with a sonnet you are making.

To go on: I believe really you have touched off something in me that will make me go to work again. For some reason other persons give me the sense of crowding me, demanding something of me, when they praise my work. You don't. Your letter makes me want to work for the fun of it, not from a sense of external pressure. I do thank you for your generous praise. You like my work no better than I do yours: but you are less critical of both your work and mine, than I am of both mine and yours. It is a curious thing about these child stories: After writing them I am entirely unable to tell which are memories and which created work. All is true, that is true to the situation. But whether the minister did intimate anything about bringing my father to the "Truth", that I do not know....

Will you do something for me? Eight years of ardent epistolary effort went up in smoke because the letters were too good to be safe to keep.[25] But if you will, if you have room and it isn't too much of an imposition, will you keep my letters that have anything in them? Maybe we can use them for notes, sometime—essay material. I keep no notes, as I should. And so much is lost in letters that might suggest a train of thought worth pursuing. I am not systematic. I hate carbons—hate the small effort and delay. And the carbon cramps my flow of thought.

Some of these days I'll find an afternoon, and write you a letter. Last night friends who wanted to play poker interrupted me. Mr. Coates lost $75 on a full house against four sevens.[26]

Saroyan did keep the letters, but Grace never asked for them. They remained in Saroyan's papers and then in brother Aram's possession, and finally in a pawn shop until they finally made their way to the archives at Stanford University. Grace kept Saroyan's letters until 1938 when he requested them.

In an April letter, Saroyan noted the arrival of three copies of The Frontier.

SAROYAN TO COATES: APRIL 24, 1930

...I like the format and editorial policy of the magazine very much. I immediately read your very interesting short stories and was delighted; but I shall read them again tonight at my leisure, so that I may pause over each subtlety a little longer. Your style is most original, and I believe you have affected a number of other contributors to the magazine. Do you think the kind of stories I write could ever get into The Frontier? Those I have sent you, with the exception of the first one, are not out of door stories, though they are perhaps western.

A story with a title which I am sure is a little too pretentious is attached...

I have cut out a good many words from this story and I believe I have failed to create the mood I had originally intended: that of the utter sadness of all people, especially in large cities. I am sending you the story not because I expect it to be considered for use in The Frontier, but because I would like to have you read it, and to offer suggestions, which might make it a legitimate story, which I do not believe it is as it stands. I have thought of calling it The City Sobbed, but in the meantime I shall think about another title for it...

...If I get a check from College Humor (I mailed them a story on Jan. 4, which I believe must be lost in the mail) I shall subscribe to The Frontier without fail, as I like the magazine very much...[27]

Grace was still writing to "Mr. Saroukhan" when she felt close enough to ask about Saroyan typing for her. There was not much access to a professional typist in Martinsdale.

COATES TO SAROYAN: FEBRUARY 21, 1930

You mention being a rapid typist; and your work is beautiful. Is your time such that you could type stories for me, if it happened that I needed the work done? Forgive me if your situation is such that the suggestion is impertinence.

As you see, I am an inexpert typist, and my time is eaten up making mistakes and correcting them. A girl slaughtered a book mss for me last summer under one of those damnable "Oh, I'd just love to do it" arrangements, that demand double price because it's a friend you're paying (excuse me, I didn't intend to suddenly erupt my woes all over you)[28]

Saroyan replied, "Your confidence in my ability as a typist surprises me. I am a rapid typist only when I write from my mind. At all other times the work is most painful."[29]

Grace was delighted to inform Saroyan at the end of February that his story would be printed in the spring issue of *The Frontier.*

Saroyan in turn was delighted to have "Escape by Steerage" published, and asked if he should send another now.

The glow of having a story accepted probably was diminished by the lack of payment for the contribution.

SAROYAN TO COATES: UNDATED, 1930

My well-nourished hopes of getting a check from College Humor were quite definitely shattered yesterday when the little story came back to me with one of those too silent rejection slips. Tomorrow I shall get a haircut and try to look as much like a clerk as possible. Then I shall see if I cannot get myself hired somewhere. For five years I have been trying to convince newspaper editors that they ought to hire me, but they won't hear of it. How do young writers live?[30]

SAROYAN TO COATES: MARCH 14, 1930

Dear Mrs. Coates:

First, let me thank God I've found you. If ever I have been given new life it is now and through you. What I am learning from you I doubt if I might ever learn alone.

Second, let me apologize for the appearance of my manuscript. My Corona is in hock, and this old Underwood is not in very good working order. There is something the matter with the ribbon mechanism, and the impression of the letters is not uniform. I have done my best to make the manuscript as neat as possible and I hope it will seem satisfactory.

I cannot begin to tell you how fine your criticisms are, and I only wish that they are not in vain, for I feel greatly obligated to you for your sincerity. I am more than convinced now that it is just these apparently minute details which make a story good, and with your suggestions before me I must admit that the work of correcting the story was not half as difficult as I had at first imagined. In fact, I enjoyed the labor, because I felt that I was at last moving in some specific direction.

In reading the manuscript now I see the vast difference, the sharpness of each sentence, the clarity of each thought, and I feel the absence of those sentences which you have so aptly termed mutty. I believe the omission of that maudlin sentence, "He was telling himself he was unlike other young men; etc," almost wholly saves the effect of the story. I was afraid of that sentence, I was doubtful as to how the reader would interpret it, but I am sure I would never thought of leaving it out altogether had not its weakness been pointed out to me. These are most important points. By all means, please know that I want all the suggestions, no matter how minute or trivial they may seem.

I have tried not to be haywire in my tenses, and I believe the situation is greatly improved... I have tried to do just as you have suggested and I hope the story will now please you.

And thank you for your wishes of good luck. I do not find that any of the points you raised were at all debatable. Did you perhaps let me off easy in this criticism? I confess I was quite ashamed of myself when I noticed how many times I was wrong in The City Sobbed story, because it was the first time mistakes were pointed out, and I had never suspected that so much could be wrong. But now I can imagine that there is liable to be just as much wrong in the first copy of any writer. It was good of you to tell me that it is nothing to feel incompetent about. I understand this business more clearly now...

...I wonder how difficult it is for poets not to be ridiculous in seeking the sublime.

Sincerely yours, William Saroyan

The pats on the back almost spoiled me.[31]

COATES TO SAROYAN: MARCH 17, 1930

Dear Mr. Saroukhan:
At my first leisure I'll write you one of those long, divagant letters that are the devil's subtlest temptation to writers and a waste of the human creative spirit; but right now I am so busy my letter will seem brief to crabbidness [sic].

...My criticism of your mss shows how I work on my own. It was as complete and minute a criticism as I knew how to give.

...But, yes, in any writing where inner pressure is an element—where one writes because he had something to say—has felt and wants to express that feeling. Until he says accurately what he means, he has no deliverance. I doubt if any one, in any sustained writing says exactly what he means in every sentence at first stroke. (God didn't say all he meant at one stroke) He is most lucky to say part of what he means felicitously and immediately.

...Talent does what it can, but genius does what it must. I hope you have that touch of genius that makes its own rules...If you are in a prolific period, make the most of it. But I do not believe you can increase your ability to write the kind of thing that needs no revision, except by perceiving wherein you fail, analyzing that failure, and so moving always toward greater exactitude.

My opinion is that author's agents are not worth a damn to you at present. Also that any agent asking for money before a sale is probably a fake...

Write all you want to me, any time—put your return address on your envelopes, for this is a country post office, and blank envelopes invite mysterious losses!—and some day when "Oh, hell," said God, "let's be happy" instead of working all the time, I'll answer them. But not now

Sincerely yours, Grace[32]

SAROYAN TO COATES: MARCH 20, 1930

Dear Mrs. Coates:

Divigant is right. I thought you manufactured the word, it looks that unreal. I never came across it in print before.

The reason I would have liked to have seen Escape published soon is that it is growing rather old, almost in its second year now, but I think I am free now to forget it. I am enclosing the other copy. The egg sentence you may correct as you see fit. How about the ending? Does that seem all right?...

...I am learning about revising. Aren't writers those who revise the lives they have lived instead of going on living. You see, when it comes to writing I am one of those crazy fools who thinks he has so much so say he blurts everything in one incoherent gasp. That's why the keys on my typewriter are always piling. Sometimes I stop myself and repeat what the old newspaper man said to the cub (sounds like a traveling salesman story) who was so excited he would write feverously or feverishly as the case may be for a minute, tear the paper up and start writing again. Sometimes I stop myself and say "Just one little word after another, if you don't mind." It is a case of too much afflatus (Mr. H.L. Davis) and not enough system. But now and then I do have something to say, although I have not been feeling that way for a week. That is why I have been editing and retyping some old stuff in my desk. I retyped a story called Zangar, The Great today, and although it is perhaps different from the other things I have sent you, I am sending it to you, since I have nothing else which is corrected and edited. (I suppose you received The Night Clerk all right. The reason I mention it is because you asked me to put my return address on the outside of the envelope...

...I suppose I have written for all the reasons one writes: because I felt I had to write, because I liked to typewrite anyway, because I wanted to feel important and big, and for money. I have thus far earned exactly $30. in United States Gold coin by writing. Three stories, the first published in June 1928, were purchased by a magazine called The Boulevardier in Detroit for $10. each.

One of the stories was about 5,000 words in length. But I like the people, it doesn't take me long to type the sort of stuff they want to use, and as you see I am gradually making my fortune. I don't think I've spent $30. for stamps and envelopes yet. Not only that several people have heard I am a writer, and have timidly asked me how I do it.

You will have noticed by this time that I am not as yet consistent in attitude, point of view, or anything else. You will notice that sometimes I seem to take myself very seriously and at other times am quite amused at my foolishness...

...I have not yet seen a copy of The Midland, although I may get one soon from Mr. Frederick. I tried to fix up Cheated as he said and returned it to him. I have also been sent a copy of the Prairie Schooner, which seems very good. I have sent them an essay and a sort of a sketchy short story. I have even sent The Mercury a story, though I should have saved stamps. Which of the magazines you name contain Prose? Voices I have seen and do not like, nor do I much care for any of the other magazines containing poetry only. Kaleidescope sounds good...

...That wasn't really a picture of Martinsdale, was it? If it was you are most fortunate. I have been looking at O'Brien's volume for 1928 and the O. Henry selections for 1929. The latter does not even list the Midland. How Come? By the way, the picture of Martinsdale looks very much like the work of the late cartoonist Webster, does it not?

This story of Zangar, The Great, is one which was written merely to occupy an idle hour. It is not life revised.

Sincerely, William Saroyan[33]

Living in San Francisco, Saroyan could hardly fathom the picture of Martinsdale Grace sent showing the three block main street. In reply to his discussion of finances, Grace suggested to Saroyan that he write historic pieces to earn some money.

COATES TO SAROYAN: UNDATED

County papers, rural papers, circulating in the sticks, usually have an insert of more general material than their local news, that is printed and distributed by a more or less indigenous syndicate. If you go to the library, or the historical lib. if they have one, and ask to see a local paper, a county paper of almost any county, and look inside you may find this syndicated insert. It can be identified by the small print at the top or bottom of the page, usually, and a little inquiry and research (pronounced digging) will give you the address.

...I know what you mean about money. But those historic stories sell well. For instance, suppose you see in a San F. paper an item about a Montana man. If you have his address in the paper, go hunt him up, write a story about him and sent [sic] to the Montana Newspaper Association, Great Falls. Do you see what I mean? If a Mont. Old man gets knocked in the head, run over etc. Or if you see an old man on the street who looks interesting, go tackle him, be ignorant and humble, let him tell about HIS early days—and chuck him in the paper. The trick of news writing is three-year old English, facts, authority cited; and names, names, names. Never stop with involving the name of one town, if there is a way of naming. Not "Martinsdale," but ""Martinsdale, a cattle shipping station for Blank and Blank, that lies midway between Podunk and Sand Coulee, surrounded"...Henderson just rushed in to tell me the new manager of the Bair ranch fell dead just now. The one I wrote feature stories about—must stop and write him up for the papers.[34]

Grace, herself, made a steady income from the historic pieces she wrote for many years. Again, she advised Saroyan,

COATES TO SAROYAN: UNDATED

I would like a preacher. But there is money—not lots, but Bierney got $10,000 for his vigilante story in the Post, and got all the stuff right from the hist library at Helena, where I should have been instead of he—see? Go to your hist library and dig up something new and sell it to the Post...

All good wishes, and friendliness. By the way, do I need to say gain that I am completely "sold" on your writing. Every man needs one woman to think he is perfect, so when I found myself getting critical of Henderson, after I had him all tied up where he couldn't marry some other more appreciative woman, I decided I was wrong, and would thenceforth consider him perfect—and he is, for him; and correspondingly, every writer needs one person to have entire faith in him, so I have it in you and you have it in me. I mean, in me you have the person, and in you I have the faith. If you do not write a lot of good stuff, you will have betrayed my faith. I do not say "If you do not make money, — if you do not get into print immediately" I say only, "If you do not do a lot of excellent writing."[35]

Despite encouragement to write some articles for money, Saroyan continued to resist writing what he considered junk to make a living. Grace finally gave up and in a short letter, "You make me laugh. Why should I care if you refuse to write bunk for money? Good for you. I wish for this one night I could be young—and drunken."[36]

COATES TO SAROYAN: UNDATED

> July and August I'll write for the newspapers again. Expect to make 100 a month out of it…I know what you mean about making money—do not think that I do not understand the dubby side of historic event writing…I happened on an account of the naming of Fort Benton. Major Culbertson built an adobe fort, the first adobe in Mont, and gave a great party at Christmas time; at the height of the fun, suggested that since old Senator Benton of Missouri had been a good friend of the American Fur company, they name the Fort, Benton.
>
> Someway when I read that I could see the voyageurs dancing and swinging the pretty squaws (tho the account didn't say so) and so I put some of me and some of history together, and having no news item that day, sent it to a paper. It took perhaps 20 minutes to write.[37]

Grace kept her writing money separate from her account with her husband, giving her a certain amount of independence.

"Identity" was the next story Saroyan sent in March. He described it as …

SAROYAN TO COATES: MARCH 24, 1930

> …a story I put together this morning from fragments of several stories I once started but abandoned…It is perhaps too long for use in The Frontier, but I thought you might like to see it, and, to be honest, hoped you might give me a criticism of it. I am aware of a number of defects myself which I have not as yet changed. The story is in single space because with too much blank space on a sheet of paper I find there is too much blank space in my head, and I am afraid it will be difficult for you to read it. I feel certain, however, that with a single reading you will be able to discover its weaknesses and to offer general suggestions.[38]

SAROYAN TO COATES: MARCH 25, 1930

> Dear Mrs. Coates:
> …I'm glad you have confidence in me. I hope I'll be able to get into The Frontier as often as possible, and as regular as possible. I think I should be able to satisfy Mr. Merriam several times a year.
> Why should you get 2000 rejection slips? Why not checks? You know what you're doing, and I don't. If I ever break big, as you say, I'm afraid it will be by a lucky fluke, and I like that expression…

…You say: Don't forget us—me. How could I or why? I would rather write letters to you most of the time than stories. And I'd rather get them from you than to write them.

When will Escape appear in the Frontier? Can't possibly smuggle it in in the next issue, can you? Biographical note, if it is necessary: William Saroyan lives in San Francisco. Who cares about William Saroyan? Or why should they?

You also say AND SEND THAT ORIGINAL story. I sent it yesterday. It's temporarily called IDENTITY. BUT I may be wrong about it. I don't believe an original story has been written in years, except in style, do you?

I'm very enthusiastic about the story you have half-finished, and I'm anxious to write my part if I can.

Isn't it said the funniest things are written in the most despondent moods? You mention being blue. That is the time to be funny, I think, really funny, like Ring Lardner, the melancholy clown…

…Can you spare a copy of The Midland, preferable one containing one of your ***stories, such as Black Cherries or Truth? I want to write a seven asterisk story. What happened to The Little Review I notice so much in O'Brien's volumes? Plain Dealer also? All's Well likewise? About 75 writers ought to incorporate and put out a national monthly, and not be ashamed to solicit advertising either. I can't understand that point in small magazines. And the magazine ought to sell for about fifteen cents so that all the youngsters growing up in the land could buy it. I think there is going to be such a magazine soon. The Bookman is on a campaign to revive Paul Elmer More's Humanism, whatever that is, but it looks pretty much like a campaign to down Mr. [H.L.] Mencken. They are growing angry it seems. And they are sore because guys like me used to read Mencken's Prejudices instead of More's Shelbourne Essays. Young people don't like essays. They like firecrackers and Mr. Mencken knew it and knows it, although when young fellows grow up they don't care a hell of a lot for him because he forever continues to repeat the obvious. I wrote and had published in The Overland Monthly last year the nastiest essay ever written on Mr. Mencken, Mr. [George Jean] Nathan, and Mr. Haldeman-Julius. Not only was it nasty, it was also sadly immature in spots, but the editor said it was in order, and crossed out one or two lines of language he thought was pretty strong. Nothing happened, however. No one was arrested, and the circulation dropped off if anything. I was sore at Mencken, I think, because he didn't print an essay I sent him when I was seventeen. I believed he was trying to keep me down. I don't care what others think, but I believe Mencken writes, for intellectual morons. I should like to examine his latest book (the first since 1927) called, I think, A Treatise on the Gods. Now that is the simplest subject in the world to write on, and to write on sarcastically, but I insist it is a small thing to do. The subject has been over-done, no intelligent person gives a damn about how religious people interpret God, and no civilized person despises them because they do. The subject is to be treated at best with sympathy and understanding. I was an atheist when I was twelve. And so was Mencken perhaps. And I'm not much of one now, nor is he, his writing to the contrary.

Sincerely, William Saroyan.[39]

Henry Mencken, the target of Saroyan's tirade, was an influential newspaperman and commentator for almost forty years. He either received the slams of the public or the praise from those who considered him the most powerful personal influence on that particular generation. His works included literary criticism, theology, political theory and language. It is to Saroyan's credit that he would take on this influential commentator who had promoted such writers as Sinclair Lewis, F. Scott Fitzgerald and Theodore Dreiser.

COATES TO SAROYAN: MARCH 28, 1930

Dear Mr. Saroukhan

Thank you, and again, for ZANGAR, THE GREAT. It goes this minute to HGM, and unless I miss my guess he will use it. Its outstanding virtue aside from several other virtues is that it has irony without malice. I read it twice, just because I wanted to. I could read it over and over, and shall when it is in print. (Of course my liking it is not an acceptance. Mr. Merriam does the final work of saying yes or no. I mention this to avoid misunderstandings).

About memory. If I am deeply impressed with poetry I am uncomfortable until I have it all in my mind. Sometimes one reading is enough, even for rather long poems; sometimes two. Often more, but I must know them. And as a corollary, I suffer more or less from amnesia. If something unpleasant occurred, as between you and me, I would begin to find it impossible to remember your address; your name would go; I'd forget the title of your stories; all quite against my conscious desire. Not long ago a woman wrote me a vicious anonymous letter. I read it, standing in my living room. I read it, without moving from my place, but when I looked down I no longer had the letter in my hands. It had disappeared. I hunted for hours, and could not find it. I hunted, on the assumption that I had walked away, and hidden it, and when I could not find it I accepted the fact—that I had been sure of all the time—that I hadn't actually moved at all. So I stood where I had been, and looked to see what I could have done with it without leaving the place. I had thrust it thru a ripped place in the cover of a sofa cushion, but had no memory whatever of having done so.

I have forgotten my own name. I have been unable to spell my husband's name on checks, after writing hundreds of them. I have dated letters September in April; But By George, when you said there was no intelligence in Shakespeare, and also said that the man covered his head with a turban, I remembered:

The world is still deceived by ornament:

In law, what plea so hardened and corrupt

But being seized by a gracious voice

Obscures its show of error.

In religion, what damned error.

But some sober brow

Doth bless it with a text,

Hiding its baseness with fair ornament.

I have misquoted, probably.

…Yes. Writing is an escape. But it becomes reality. I got the NIGHT CLERK. It has gone back to you. I think Mr. M. might use it sometime, maybe…

There was a time, when, writing letters, I would say, what does life offer better than just this pleasure? And so, write as much and as long as I wanted to. But I am past that stage. It offers, now, the fun of holding myself on an irksome job. So I have stopped what one friend described in good anglo saxon as "the whoring of my spirit". But of course there are exceptions to the formal rule of "yours at hand and contents duly sworn at."

GSC[40]

COATES TO SAROYAN: UNDATED

I used to write such indiscreet letters that they were a joy to show, but no more, no more, I am wrinkled and old of spirit.

It's a shame to be in touch with such good material as you and not flirt with him.

GSC[41]

The letters from Saroyan continued to come, and although Grace was too busy to answer them at length, she tried to send a post card or short letter whenever she could. She enjoyed his letters when he used them as a sounding board for his ideas and aspirations. He told her he started to write but,

SAROYAN TO COATES; MARCH 25, 1930

… I got lazy and attached it to the other sheets which I wrote …. played about seven sets of rotten tennis. The courts are very close, and they tempt me. Besides I am waiting to hear from a half dozen editors to whom I have sent stuff. When I am expecting something I can't be at ease very much. (You told me I could write to you as often as months ago. It was too fine a day today (and yesterday) to write, so I went out and I liked, but when I get this far and find myself just commencing I begin to worry. I suppose writing letters is a feeble pastime, but I think it is a little superior to talking.)[42]

SAROYAN TO COATES: APRIL 1, 1930

Dear Mrs. Coates:

I have just read your good letter and the description or criticism of Identity, and it amuses me greatly to think how I am invariably wrong when I arrive at an emphatic opinion of something of mine. I believed sincerely for some reason that Identity hit the bull's eye. I don't know why, but I thought it was a knock out, and I told you so, but I'm glad you've given me the works. However, I'm certain if it isn't any good, it should have been. I had the good part in mind all right, but it must have evaporated while I smoked cigarettes. I did not, however, think Zangar was a very good story. How in hell does one tell? I have to laugh (I mean actually laugh) when I recall I wrote you that I believed Identity an excellent story...

...I am glad you are a poker player. In the right company I believe I would rather play the game than anything else. That is one of the supreme pleasures of life, I think. If Heywood Broun played the game less, however, he would write more novels and better ones than he has. But he started out as a newpaperman and they get poker in them early...

...I am tempted to argue with you about certain things in Identity. There is a story there, damn it, and I thought I wrote it, and I didn't think I didn't do it in the manner that was right, but I won't bother with the thing...

...The little poem startles me. How can you manufacture them so readily? The good thing about poetry is that the lines are remembered for centuries, while an entire novel (years of hard work of a sincere artist) are readily forgotten in very little time...

...Glad to hear about Escape getting into the next issue. But perhaps you did go out of your way to let me get in sooner than I deserved. Overwhelmed with gratitude, anyway.

William Saroyan[43]

SAROYAN TO COATES: APRIL 3, 1930

Dear Mrs. Coates:

You are right, all right, all right, all right about the way I revise stories. And I will be honest and say I have never known yet when I have written a good

sentence or a paragraph. I am always afraid something is going to sound ridiculous. Also I have seldom been able to tell when I have written something lousy, to use another healthy Anglo Saxon word. Just let me revise a story and I'll guarantee I'll flatten it plenty good.

I am sending you attached a self-portrait, drawn while intoxicated.[44]

Grace acknowledged the scribbling,

Forgive me if I do not use the right words telling you your OTHER PORTRAIT was good. I am too preoccupied and worn to write. Go ahead and make some money. I'd buy coppers if I were buying...45

When Saroyan wrote to Grace that he had returned the galley proof with his story in it, he was embarrassed to not know the purpose. She consoled him,

COATES TO SAROYAN: UNDATED

If you happen to feel foolish over returning the mag and the galley, and there is no reason why you should, but if you happen to, savor the feeling to its fullest, for that, too, is experience.

I am going to clean house. The reason I do not write to you is that I made a vow not to until I painted the pantry. My hands were not made to paint pantries, nor my head to have paint drip off ceilings. But I can do it. I can, I have, and some day I shall WON'T....I wonder sometimes how Henderson and I go on living together and being friends. Bickering, he trying to induce me to take ice cubes out of the frigidaire his way instead of mine: "...and you'd be surprised to see, when you just dip them in the pail of water, how they float right out" (I) "I'd certainly be deeply surprised if they sank!"—and the bickering splinters into giggles. Always. Our ill humors always shatter on a joke. Utterly unlike—. Less man and wife than friends.[46]

COATES TO MERRIAM: UNDATED, 1930

Dear Mr. Merriam:

Saroyan writes me that you sent him a copy of the magazine and what he supposes was galley proof. (Some time ago he told me he didn't know what galley proof was, when I mentioned correcting galley on certain poems of my own, and I told him) When he got *his* galley proof, he assumed that it was to be sent back and says he returned the magazine and the proof to you, and asks me if that was what he was supposed to do with them. The entire thing has been funny, and much of the futile correspondence on that story has been my fault.

I can't quite understand—or yes I do. Anyway, Saroyan has no Frontier. Will you send him back his galley and copy, and I'll explain to him this morning that next time he is to keep all he gets his hands on.

Saroyan is delivered hand and foot into devotion to you, or admiration, or whatever it is that gratitude makes a man feel. I am sorry that thru my fault your letter was delayed. He says, regarding his biog note, which he hasn't seen apparently, that anything you handle he leaves gladly in your hands…

…I appreciated your congratulations, and certainly am glad of the recognition Mr. O'Brien gives The Frontier in using two of its stories. I hope you will found an editorial dynasty. I'll try to have something soon for the Fall issue of The Frontier.

Sincerely, GSC[47]

COATES TO SAROYAN: APRIL 8, 1930

S'yan, my friend, you and I are twins who were accidentally born in different places. It grieves me that we were also born too many years apart. (It is my almost-for-the-first-time-in-my-life consciousness of this discrepancy that makes me keep trying to establish a different system of alimimentation for the two of us, when we really eat the same thing (are nourished by the same things if I am to be less prosaic) by reason of our agelessness.) After this I'll feed you what I eat.

I wrote with unusual fervor a story so good that I thought the Frontier was made for life because I said it could use it. I asked Mr. Merriam to tell me quickly in case he could not accommodate it to his space, that I might save the reputation of the Atlantic Monthly by letting them have it. I wish I had not forcibly forgotten his criticism of that story! So that I could pass it on to you. My guardian angel, Israel Newman, said it was "stale beer". Even Peyta Ivanovitch said it was a silly account of the most blatant type of German junker. HGM was even so cruel as to suggest that my interest in the subject of the story had blinded me to the lack of merit in the tale.

GSC[48]

Saroyan wrote to Grace,

Who is Dolly Martin? Though I suppose I'll soon find out. Tell her to write to me. I'm sure I'll be glad to meet her mind.

The incident about the letter you once wrote to a colored singer and which was returned is very interesting. I believe I should be able to tolerate racial prejudice in anyone. Some of my best friends espies [sic] Armenian. Where I was born an Armenian rates about as low as a Mexican, Jap, or Negro. But I have always enjoyed negros, Mexicans, and Japs. I like people who are different and these are. But on the whole I am interested in specific people, not nationalities. If a person is English and it has been decided among those who are supposed to know that the English are the most superior people on the face of the earth, I would not be the least bit interested in him unless there was something about him that warranted my interest. I mean, his being English wouldn't have anything to do with my liking or disliking him.[49]

In early May, Grace sent two postcards to Saroyan telling him she had no time to respond to his letters. "I must cut out letters and get busy. I run a house, read financial papers, and if I write letters other writing is crowded out."

SAROYAN TO COATES: UNDATED, 1930

I did no writing today, save a few desultory sheets I abandoned, hence the length of this letter. I shall capture soon, I think very much in something I write. I know something is ripening.

You mention having written something vulgar and stupid, but I assure you I should be able to understand anything you might write, or if I failed to understand to at least try to. What we write occurs in an instant. I can often be altogether untruthful even to ourselves and trivial. I do not regret anything I have written. I can rectify everything with a new paragraph.

Dolly Martin is most interesting. There must be a reason for her living as she does in a village. When I am in a small town it is impossible for me to live unlike its inhabitants. I cannot be cosmopolitan in a village. There ought to be much for her to write, however.

I believed you would like the manuscript. My brother's sadness is my own. It is most tragic. I could write an excellent short story about him, but shall not do it. He came home after the funeral and laughed bitterly. "We couldn't give her a wedding," he said, "so we gave her a funeral. Isn't that really funny, Willie?" Then he added, "They claim it was one of the grandest funerals in the town. One of the grandest." He doesn't believe yet that she's dead. In her last letter to him which he read after the funeral at his office she wrote, "I'd laugh if it rained on Easter." He was to visit here then and drive to the hills. As much as I know he feels he has lost something most precious, I also hold that what he has lost was his own, not hers. What he knew of her was little. What he dreamed much.

Your last two sentences affected me very much. That you write flippantly and cheaply is absurd, but that you (judging from what I have read of yours) are concealing the most tragic and somber things of your life and lives you have known seems apparent.

The reason the tone of this letter is melancholy is perhaps because your letter I have before me is also melancholy, but I am afraid by the time it reaches you you will be in another mood and so will I. There are several short stories I have on hand I might send you, but I'm all out of stamps and envelopes. So much the better, no doubt. I think I will, however, by the next issue of The Frontier have something worth while for the magazine.

Sincerely, your friend, William Saroyan[50]

SAROYAN TO COATES: APRIL 14, 1930

Dear Mrs. Coates:

I was Maupassanting in The Night Clerk. I did not find out I had done so until I was finished with the thing, and then I didn't give a whoop about it. I don't believe it was a good enough imitation to be termed plagiarizing. Boul de Suif is the story to imitate in Maupassant. I like the man, however. It is a shame to me that no one in America writes near as honestly as he wrote when there is so much need for honesty. (I must beg your pardon for the condition of the print of this typewriter but there is nothing I can do about it.)

I am afraid I have sent you too much drivel of late, but personally (and this is straight) I would rather read any writer's drivel than his best work, because in them I am on an adventure. I have not yet failed to find sparkling gems in the tenth-rate stuff of good writers. It is very interesting to look for a fine paragraph lost in a hundred that are no good at all. However, I'll lay off the drivel for a while if I am able to tell drivel from drivel…

…I sent you a story yesterday that is Lardner, though probably not much of a Lardner. I understand he works hard over his stories, but he is almost always plagiarizes himself in each story. Save for Champion all his stories are alike, character revealed through speech or attempted writing of letters. But his is reporting America and he has done fine reporting so far as he has gone, but his America is the stupid, though lovable, America. There are still 637 different angles to be worked, or perhaps only eleven.

What happened to the two yellow sheets of Incident? Don't you realize I can sue you? Don't bother to return them, however. I really don't want them. I merely wanted you to take a look at Incident. I'm not going to do anything to it but file it away with the other busts. I've got a couple of cartons full. You said Dolly Martin had Incident and was going to write to me. Well she hasn't, damn it. But I can write stories to order. If she'll tell me what she likes I'll write it for her. Anything from Anatole France to H.C. Witwer. This is wrong, but I'm glad the latter is dead. He would never have quit spoiling the language if he hadn't died. And unlike Lardner he did not even report accurately common American speech. Not only that he wasn't funny in the least. But I understand he made a dozen millions or so. Why not clip the coupon and be a writer yourself? Ask the form letters. Look what Witwer done or did.

I don't get you about writing "letters" long before Auslander started. Is that a form in poetry also? Your A LETTER is very good. I am saving and dating everything you send me, since you do not date them yourself, so that biography will be rewarded, or something like that.

Mr. Merriam sent me in the sealed letter a couple of cards that say something about a story appearing in the Frontier which I am supposed to mail to friends, but I ain't got no friends what wants to read my stories, so I'll send them to enemies just to be nasty. If The Frontier hasn't got the biographical note (what?) I sent you, I would appreciate it greatly if you would see that it is not said that I am a foreigner, and Ermenian,[sic] or anything else. Perhaps it would be best to say that I am not yet six feet in height but hope to be by the first of the year, God willing.

WS.[51]

Saroyan to Coates: April 16, 1930

Dear Mrs. Coates:

It is regrettable to me that by the time a letter you have mailed to me reaches here I have already mailed you one wholly unrelated to your letter, wholly out of tune with what you have written. That is the trouble in writing letters. What you say today is three or four days in reaching me, and what I reply to what you say today is at least a week in reaching you, and you must go backwards a week to understand what I am talking about. When we talk by mail we must wait a long time for replies, too long perhaps, because when they arrive we are talking about something else.

Will.[52]

Saroyan is lavish in his praise for the short story TRUTH.

Saroyan to Coates: Undated

Thank you, Mrs. Coates, for TRUTH. It is by far one of the most beautiful short stories I have ever read. It should live forever. It is a story any writer would like to have written. I am humble, very humble, in its sacred presence.

(This is not tommyrot. I have been greatly moved.) But I am very angry. Angry with a God Damn civilization which has not the talent to appreciate the real, the sincere, the good. TRUTH alone should have made you famous. It is unlike another story I have ever read, American or otherwise. Its treatment is superb. In this story you have done what others cannot do in novels. The pictures of your father is a masterpiece. In this story for the first time I see you as I have never seen you before. How could you say that you wrote flippantly and cheaply? Do you think another writer has ever written more tragically than you have in TRUTH? Your work is vastly more American than Sherwood Anderson's. It belongs ahead of his. It is not, I think, because you are not pushed ahead by those who control the national mind, the critics. It would be a simple matter for a volume of your short stories to be a national best seller. And it would be deserved, perhaps for the first time. It is sorrowful that a story like TRUTH was published in a magazine which is not in touch with enough people. The Mercury, Atlantic, Harper's, any of them, should have been very fortunate to get it. When you said, regarding your story of which HGM thought so little, that you believed it would save the reputation of the Atlantic Monthly you were jesting. But if it is at all like TRUTH, if it should not exactly save the reputation of the magazine it should at least strengthen it. When your volume of short stories is published I hope you will get a decent break. If you do not, I will be greatly disappointed. I do not see how an unfavorable review can be written of your work. I do not see how it cannot be acclaimed. I am very glad you sent me the story. I will return it to you shortly. I should like to show it to everyone I know, but no one I know is interested in literature at all. Mencken should write about your work. And a lot of others. You are the only American writer who has an originality which is not forced, shallow, and disgusting. I wish I could do something about it. TRUTH is the key to your work. For the first time I understand you...

...You say you are glad we have come in touch with each other, but I am sure I am more than glad. Why? Because you allow one to be oneself if possible. That is the ultimate kindness. One of my best friends, an uncle who loves literature more than anything else, once showed me a sentence in the works, I think, of one of the Russians. "Here," he said, "Willie, is one of the most magnificent thoughts I have ever read in literature." I looked. The sentence said—"and I want to suffer as I choose." Or at least something on that order. My uncle is a very lonely man also, and he suffers (as who does not most of the time?), but he is very sensitive about how he suffers.

> Will[53]

A poem was part of the answer.

COATES TO SAROYAN; UNDATED

For Willie When He Is Old

On the counter of time the coin of fame rings hollow.

Can it buy for me the ankles I did not follow

In summer dusk, when need was a drum in my body?

On the shelves of time, men's gabble of praise is shoddy.

Can the taut wire of my drawn will be twisted

To the line of a girl's breast my thoughts resisted?

So will age forever speak,

Counciling the naughty part;

If its tongue is in its cheek,

Old regret is in its heart.

I'm rather down. My own fault. Worked too hard and the old griefs [sic] hit me.[54]

COATES TO SAROYAN: UNDATED

I caught myself—was brought to myself by the slash of fresh wind across my face—just as I was starting out of the door at 2 a.m. with an empty suit case. I had started to undress, and the undressing, and the passing of a train had suggested to my inner mind that I leave the prosaic Where-I-was for the mysteriously enticing Where I-wasss't[sic]. I had dressed completely, in a fit of absentmindedness, to go look for myself. And the awareness of what I was doing expressed itself so:

The Mind's Trolls

Dark and terrible they swarm

Underneath all comely seeming;

Do not name them, for your breath

Gives them entity and form.

Shape them not even to a thought,

Lest by potency of dreaming

Dreadful power in them be wrought

Over you, of life and death.

I liked the thing, but no editor would give it a kind look.[55]

It is interesting to note that Saroyan and Coates both suffered from the same kind of debilitating spirit of depression that brought a halt to their writing.

SAROYAN TO COATES: APRIL 23, 1930

The delay, my dear Mrs. Coates, in replying to your most interesting letters (if you have been aware of a delay) has been due to a depressed condition of mind into which I fell some days ago, and which made it impossible for me to look a piece of blank paper in the face, to write three words consecutively, to read, to walk, or to live. Yes, I was quite wretched, though I quite understood my wretchedness and though I believe I could have over-come it if I had desired in work, but depression won and I merely waited, smoking cigarettes all the while. What's the use of interfering with fate? Of course, at another time in a similar mood I would have humored fate by going to town and playing cards all day and almost all night, but I lacked the necessary funds. I believe in cards and I don't care who doesn't. Also ponies and dice. I'm no good, in short, and don't care who knows that either. I would rather be no good and myself than excellent and someone else. Today, although the mood is still present, it is passing and I am able to write this letter and a short story and a couple of hundred words on Humanism which aren't necessary. I enjoyed Mr. Mencken's review of the volume on Humanism published by Farrar & Rinehart in the May issue of his magazine. I was even surprised that he gave them as much attention as he did. The matter will not drop, however, just now, I think. The principal trouble with Humanists it seems is that although they are as a class fairly well educated, they are not naturally over-intelligent, and lack downright honesty, and most of all a sense of humor, collectively. They desire among other things that mankind shall be in awe of God again, or of nature or the unseen, and they also desire that people shall feel life has a purpose if ever so faint and that it is worth while to be good, decent, patriotic, and humble. In fact they desire to revive the principles of Christianity, Buddhism, Confucianism, and Mary Baker Eddy, which is hardly the job for men of letters. Since they cannot create works of art which will inspire goodness in people, they compose technical essays on the need for goodness, a field already well covered by the various Bibles of the various religions.

BLACK CHERRIES ranks with TRUTH in my estimation. (This has just occurred to me for some reason: Relatively, I think, you give too much in too few words in each of your stories. The gems are too closely linked together so that their brilliance does not stand out as it should. I have been told that I write too long-windedly, and it is said to be a fault, and yet I believe I should appreciate all your work if it was a trifle less compact and a bit more rambling, prosey, a little unlike poetry. I'm sure you won't point out that I'm meddling and I don't expect you to take me seriously, but that is my honest conviction. Prose is prose and poetry is poetry. I haven't read one paragraph of yours yet which was not loaded with ideas, freshness of point of view, and life, so much so that it was almost top-heavy. It is quite difficult, I think for anyone but a most intelligent reader to understand and appreciate every sentence you write as it should be appreciated. I still hold also that most readers, especially when reading fiction, are not very intelligent. I'm not. But you'll understand me in this, I'm sure. You'll not think I'm trying to play the wise-man by daring to offer a criticism. This is between friends.)

LE BONNET ROUGE is wonderful.

With very best wishes, I am, Wm Saroyan.[56]

COATES TO SAROYAN: UNDATED

Dear Will—I am too what—I do not know. I start again: I am so organized that I hide shyly in my heart the things you say that mean most to me. When everything was swept away, you were there. You are an established and permanent part of my life. I'm selfishly glad that you have stopped that damned writing long enough to write me, again. My desire to write you has come flooding back.[57]

As the year came to a close, Knopf asked Merriam for a comment on *Black Cherries* for publicity releases. Alfred Knopf was not pleased with Merriam's comments.

Many thanks for your kind letter of November 13 and for the nice things you say about Mrs. Coates' BLACK CHERRIES. What you have written isn't of much use from our point of view, particularly because you emphasize the fact that the book consists of short stories and because much of what you say is cast in a negative form. I would prefer if possible, to have something quite brief from you, referring to Mrs. Coates as an authentic voice from your part of the country with a volume here to her credit of very real distinction. I think you ought to emphasize the human quality in the book and the soundness and beauty of the writing.[58]

GRACE STONE COATES WITH HER STUDENTS AT THE MARTINSDALE SCHOOL.

Merriam was quick to respond,

I'm sorry my blurb about Mrs. Grace Stone Coates' BLACK CHERRIES was no good for you purposes. Suppose I simply write—Grace Stone Coates' BLACK CHERRIES is a distinctive book. The tale told, the manner of telling and the language are all distinctive. The author reaches into the life of a child whose mind struggles in an unconscious way to grasp the meaning of family affairs. The reader responds emotionally to the child's reactions, recognizing himself often.

You are at liberty to use any portion, all, or none.[59]

∞

Conclusion

Do not be kind to me;
It is too late to be tender.
It is too late to rant
And accuse. Can you restore
The trampled grape to the vender,
Or water a dead plant?

I tell you quietly
Our life together is closing.
If I lied to you
Saying I was happy,
I deceived myself,
Supposing
Steadfast lies
Must make themselves come true.

CHAPTER SEVEN

W hen *Black Cherries* came out, dedicated to Henderson, the first to receive copies from Grace were H.G. Merriam, John T. Frederick (*The Midland*) and Will Saroyan.

Reviews were favorable. A story in the *Billings Gazette* in April of 1931 said *Black Cherries* was proving one of the most popular in number of calls of the new books added to the library.

Margaret Haughawout of the *Journal Post* of Kansas City wrote, "…So ruthlessly has Mrs. Coates seen through externals, pared away all unessentials, left the bare kernel, chapter after chapter, that one reads breathlessly…

> Grace Stone Coates was born on a Kansas farm near Wichita, and while her book is probably not autobiographic, its air of authenticity is due to the fact that she has seen just such life as she has pictured. Though now she lives at Martinsdale, Mont., she sometimes says that those were the only years she really lived so lonely and disrupted were her days after they moved to Kansas City. She still loves the plains… .
>
> …Her interest has always been in writing, and for years she has done newspaper work. She is at present busy on a series of Kansas stories based on the experiences of a Montana pioneer, a photographer, who accompanied a surveying party through Kansas and Indian Territory in the early '50s. She has thus far been best known by her poetry…"

GREAT FALLS TRIBUNE: JANUARY 4, 1931

> Mrs. Grace Stone Coates of Martinsdale will arrive in the city today and during the week will address several of the prominent local women's organizations of the city. On each occasion she will give readings of her own works,…poems, short stories and in some cases will read the last chapter of her novel, "Black Cherries," which is being published by Alfred A. Knopf, Inc. in New York.
>
> Mrs. Coates will appear before the American Association of University Women Monday evening, before the Rainbow Research club on Tuesday afternoon, before the Travel Club Thursday morning and before chapter I of the P.E.O. Thursday afternoon.
>
> Mrs. Coates is assistant editor of The Frontier, a magazine of the northwest, published at the State University, Missoula, by H.G. Merriam. She appears in

the press section of "Who's Who" in "Among North American Writers" by reason of the feature stories she writes for Montana papers, but her more serious interest is poetry and creative prose. A group of 10 poems under the enigmatic title, "Chicin and Gneiss," will appear in the next issue of Voices, New York, and a story "Stubborn Thistles" in the Midland, Chicago. Her poem, "Pretending" was among those read at the last session of the American Poetry Society in New York.

A department of literary intelligence appearing regularly in The Frontier is in charge of Mrs. Coates. She is eager to learn more about the work of Montana writers and all writers of the northwest; she believes that Mr. Merriam's work in establishing The Frontier will prove deeply significant in the development of life in the north west on its upper levels....

As Grace Stone Coates turned fifty, she was near the peak of her career. Her blonde hair had become dark—those days didn't offer the breadth of color as today—but her appearance was striking with a regal bearing. When she started to speak or read material, the audience heard a melodic, pure voice. Her reputation as an historian also grew with the years.

She wrote to a friend in January of 1931,

> One week in the dusty, frusty, basement Historical Library, searching the files of 1918-1922, gave me the flu. I came home, worked a day thinking I could ignore my condition, and went to bed for a week. Up for the first time yesterday. Well, it is the first offense since I left New York in my previous incarnation...[1]

She wrote a post card to Saroyan that she was in bed with flu, on verge of pneumonia.

> Poor f.h. [friend husband] is "mad" at me for being sick, and I'm desolate. Just got home. Work piled mountain high. No doctor no nurse no "family" to look after me, and I'm forlorn.

But she answered again in regard to him writing feature stories to make some money,

> Why the hell should you write feature stories? I like you a lot and have faith in your remaining yourself...You will be a success if you remain yourself. Ceasing to be is the one failure. I'm such a preacher when I talk to you and the Lord knows I'm not a saint![2]

C*oates to* S*aroyan*: J*anuary* 26, 1931

> Dear Will—See Knopf's spring catalogue for what he says about "Black Cherries"—real nice. Perhaps a bookstore may have it, or you send for it. I'm

too sick to type it off and will be awfully busy for 2 weeks when I get up again so you'll not hear from me for a while.

Sincerely and with warm friendliness, Grace[3]

Saroyan immediately wrote to say he was grieved to learn that she had been ill,

and ill where it is cold, where perhaps the sun does not shine these days, as I know that when one is laid low with disease, when fever acquaints or reminds one of the really significant things in life, one longs and longs passionately for the sun, symbol of life; and where it is cold and bleak this longing amounts to something like nostalgia, nostalgia for a condition, not a place. I too am forever looking to the desert as both a condition and a place for the real life of an individual, but how shall one dwell in a desert? And what of snake bites and cactus pricks?

The thoughts of Saroyan were so like those of Grace as he went on to say,

I know very well the desolation of illness, the almost horrible and intense reality of the thing; but there is good in even this and the good is that the suffering destroys, annihilates almost all superficial conventionalities one might have accepted or adopted in one's life, and is something similar to a brand new start. One leaves a sick bed new as a baby, quite as weak and perhaps as simplified. It is a time to build up a more satisfactory code of life. Except for tuberculosis O'Neill might have remained a mere vagabond and were I not so uneducated I might name dozens of other instances.

Gide, in his recent novel "The Immoralist" describes a very scholarly young man who discovers that he is tubercular on his honeymoon and while recuperating learns for the first time that he has never been aware that he was alive, he himself. He had actually never thought of himself as a living being, but had rather merely accepted that he *was*. He said that having been touched by the wings of death, as the expression put it, he had awakened to the need for his extracting every goodness from life that his form of being could get from it: and from this object the story proceeds, ending with the scholar's young bride perishing from the disease she contracted from him while she leant her whole physical and spiritual being to him, and he in turn, being selfish and now too much alive, allowing her to die without the least effort to do for her what she had done for him. The fact was that he wanted her to die, had rejected the female form as an adequate expression of beauty for him, and sought to live with a young healthy Arab boy. The Immoralist, you see. Knopf published the novel last year, it's short but rather brilliant, except that I do not like Gide's always telling a story in the first person, though he was probably learned that in this manner only can he express the individual feeling of chief characters as they experienced them.

About *Black Cherries,* Saroyan told her,

> ...I only hope that the reviewers will not be too blind-folded to see the originality and beauty of the book. I want a copy of the first edition. It ought to be a collector's item in several years, especially when your second novel appears. But about future work you must be quite leisurely, not let it trouble you, not let it burden or frighten you; then the work will be surely fine—and you won't be angry with me for saying this, will you? They have been saying that one's second novel is the most difficult one to complete, but this I believe is largely imaginary. I wish you success in all sincerity.

In his four page letter, Saroyan talked of writing and his inability to write feature stories for money. "How can I remain myself, how can anyone?, when identity is actually a condition of a moment as ever-changing as the water of a river?"

COATES TO SAROYAN: FEBRUARY 7, 1931

> Dear Will:
> Starting the days with a letter to you is sheer luxury and self-indulgence. But your letters to me have so often been the only thing right in a world awry, so often the thing that has made me keep going, that I want to write.
> Throw my foolish picture away. It took courage to send it. Exposing my face is like admitting a deformity. Sending it to you was almost an unkindness.
> You were wrong, though, about the physical sunshine here. We have had no snow; I mean literally not a flake of snow since one brief, quickly melted fall in November. I cured my illness by lying naked in a sun so hot it burned me. I am all for the sun.
> ...Yes, Oh, yes; being touched by the wings of death. I was, once.

> I like the black insistent night,
> Pressed against my window pane,
> Held at bay by my single light.[5]

That bit of verse and the rest of it came out of that fresh, new, childlike beginning after critical sickness.

> Dear Will—I am too-what?—I do not know. I start again: I am so organized that I hide shyly in my heart the things you say that mean most to me. When everything was swept away, you were there. You are an established and permanent part of my life. I'm selfishly glad that you have stopped that damned writing long enough to write me, again. My desire to write you has come flooding back.
> *Grace*[4]

Coates to Saroyan: Undated

Dear Will:

You keep me in a mood to work. I thank you for that. About the photograph. There was a certain beastliness about my sending it. One must feel that, not analyze it. I didn't understand, myself, until I bothered to think about it....But now I know part of the whole thing. Once I was infuriated by a man sending me his photograph under similar—or, yes, similar—circumstances. A snapshot. He was a poet, who had written me beautiful things. I wove phrases of his own into the octave of a sonnet, in my rage, and derided the sending of the picture in the sestet. Of a group eating watermelon

He was forever fluid in the blue

Welter of ocean, tossing sea-maids' hair,

Sea-green. Involved in the Aeolean air.

He was a scarf the June night's half-wind drew

Across her fingers. He was everywhere

(I can not recall the other lovely suggestions from his poems—conveying, at last, that he was an element always of her comfort or despair.)

He has solidified into a pose

A meaningless moment to perpetuate.

A vacuous smile wipes out all trace of soul.

The dripping crescent underneath his nose

Informs the cockeyed world what 'twas he ate.

He is involved in watermelon rind.

Imagine sending that as gratitude for a picture from a sensitive young Jew. I preferred the real knowledge, thru his writing-what you call myth.

But it was the beastly irrelevance of a picture—it is—was—as irrelevant as if I should send you a shirt. It was satirical. Not satire directed at you—at life—which is a large order. One must feel it, not be told...

I can't write more—thank you so greatly for the things you quite without intention do for me.

Grace[5]

Postcard from Coates to Saroyan: February 20, 1931

Dear Will: Glad the book came. 3 days is a long wait. I thought the previous letter was the acknowledgment. Thank you and thank you all over again for the appreciation. How…, the more persons and reviewers you call the book to…the better. It needs publicity. Sure Don't be too sure it is all good. Underscoring the a's was teasing but not the rest. Of course not.

> *Sincerely, GSC*

By all means "Ballyhoo" the book, even tho you do think it too good for the usual noise. It has to be done. *G*[6]

SAROYAN TO COATES: MARCH 2, 1931

Dear Grace:

I feel very stupid, angry with myself, disgusted with my environment, perplexed as to the future. And in this mood I write you, after having been silent for a week. I have been trying to make money and this requires a point of view alien to me: one which I am positive I shall never be able to permanently accept. With that point of view in my system I could not write you a letter; I tried but found it impossible. My mind functioned in terms of material progression, possession, activity. Today I have a day off. And though tomorrow (which is remote) I shall more than likely return to that state of mind which I loath, I write today as myself.

I want to thank you for writing the good letter. I read it with extreme contentment. I thought of how fine you were to me always, and I wondered how I might interest book reviewers in your book. If I hadn't been tied up with the absurd effort to make money I might have been able to think of something suitable to write to book reviewers here. Now the letter has reduced itself (angrily, since there is the need for a letter at all in this case) to a mere brief sentence: "I should be greatly pleased if you were to read and review Black Cherries by Grace Stone Coates." I think something of this sort would be best. What I wanted was to see a reviewer discover the work for himself; to be surprised with its beauty and to proclaim the work without any outside influence. Of course San Francisco is not America (and not much of anything else; certainly not exceedingly well-read or intelligent local beliefs notwithstanding) but it is a large city at least with quite a few book dealers. My best judgement [sic] insists that I refrain from intruding myself into the book, and still I see the need for at least suggesting its merits to reviewers. Not now, however. They should have a month a least in which to learn about it themselves; after that if they have overlooked it we might point the way for them. I must tell you, in any case, what I have done: I have loaned the book to Goldie Weisberg of Phoenix, Arizona. We have been writing to one another for some months and I have told her of your work, the appearance of the book and its beauty. I do not know whether I've had the right to send her the book you inscribed to me and if I've done wrong I beg you to forgive me. I am certain, however, that Miss Weisberg will like the work and perhaps be in a position to boost it much more than I could ever…

…The magazine I am supposed to be working for has a paid subscription of a thousand; a free subscription of two thousand. I am convinced that no one (not two people) read the magazine or pay any attention to its ads. The publisher is a wholly illiterate former groceryman; this business he understands, the grocery business. He organized a group of chain stores several years ago and falling out with his employers, somehow or other conceived the idea of founding a magazine.…I am supposed to get the big firms, national advertisers, and local organizations who insist upon a magazine's having readers. What I am supposed to do is to lie, to tell each firm that the school-children subscription contest we are having will undoubtedly increase our circulation this year some 25,000. We are conducting a contest (the editor's led) but not one actual subscripition has thus far come to the office. So there I am.[7]

The job lasted only about a couple of weeks. Saroyan wrote, "I somehow cannot any more (even for short periods) adjust myself to the hypocrisy of business, and if any man tries to say that it is not hypocrisy he is either a liar or a nit-wit." Saroyan was still in a dark mood when he wrote a week later,

With nothing to write (as if I have ever had something) I write, aware only that there is a lack of letters between us. I know you are busy and I know (as God's my witness) I am altogether out of tune and good for nothing…I don't even want to make money writing. I am as sincere as anything; and Well, it's thissa way. In any event, I would like to be able to figure out an intelligent scheme to make money or not need it.

It is quite strange-feeling not to get letters from you; rather lonely I might even say. Tell me how the book is making out.[8]

COATES TO SAROYAN: MARCH 17, 1931

Why, Will, dear, of course I think letters to you whether I write them or not. I am going to send you a letter that meant a good deal to me. Maybe it will to you. Dear Will, this isn't going to be a long letter but just a hello. I am at work and have to stay that way. I have a sick innard today—sore abdomen, without knowing the cause. Can't walk, and the jar of the typewriter isn't pleasant. Which makes me think: I'll go get a rubber pad and put under it. There. That is great relief.

I think I'll just send a poem, and stop—or shall I answer some of your previous letters. One of these days I'll send you a real letter, promise truly, cross my heart. Most of the time I'm writing I am sick at my stomach with a sense of the futility. STUBBORN THISTLES—all the time I wrote I was almost actively vomiting I was so sure the story was a dud.

I love your reaction to business. I used to do many things that way, saying things under my breath, and I got so I was saying them out loud, and had to make hasty and untrue explanation that I didn't mean the person listening.

Will, will you do something for me? Send me the March Bookman when it is out. I'll send stamps for it—yes, don't holler I will—and just ask you to remember to send it to me. Then I can dismiss the matter from my mind. I do not know why I want it but a man wrote—be sure to see March Bookman—somethin in it! That was all.

Send my letter back. My answer elicited a very explicit and frank one. Naturally. Since I had quoted Lady Chatterly's lover to him. Do you know his writings? Sea Stories. Post writer. I want to see his books.

Sincerely yours, Grace[9]

Saroyan answered immediately.

My dear Grace: I was God damned worried about the silence we had got ourselves into, and I swear, as God's my witness, that while you were thinking letters to me I was thinking them to you. But I was getting melancholy and I was saying, all right, we've cooled, we're through, that's all. You know how some minds function…

After a long discussion of his thoughts toward writing for money, he wrote,

The relationship of money to art, I am afraid, is one of the disgusting features of our civilization. Of course artists are human, they like cars, good clothes, clean comfortable homes, bathtubs, and so on like anyone else. But the minute their love for these things, the need for them, becomes greater than their love for their work, in the minute something, that indefinable something, in them snaps. That's how I look at it…I doubt very much if I shall ever manage to be a financial success. It doesn't torment me the least bit…[10]

MARCH 23, 1931: COATES TO SAROYAN

Dear Will:

You do write me the finest letters I get. This is an extra, to surprise you. I am alone, and should be harder at work than I am. The BOOK [*Black Cherries*] is about ready for a second printing, I judge. Thank you for sending to Goldie Weisberg. Of course after a book is yours you can feel free to let anyone have it—I mean that there was no reason why you shouldn't let her have your copy. Surely. If it were a very personal matter between lovers, it might be different. You might have a wife, from whom all matters of affection had to be concealed. I think when *I* get married, I'll not live that way. (I'm wearing bifocal glasses, and they deprive me of what little sense I ordinarily have. Terribly annoying.)

It is long since I have written you anything but chattering words. But you are one of the nearest friends I have, and I do love the way you use words. I really admire your style, and think you should be a great writer. Be patient, be patient. Art is long—but time—time—time that works for man, and chance that works against, some one says.

I understand about your "hustling". I can go into a strange boarding house (I am the most reserved and diffident of persons) and if there is an object in doing so, I can jabber and ask the most impertinent, pointed questions, and carry it off. Once I succeeded in getting away with asking strangers—three strange girls—what their salaries were. I talked noisily and asked impertinent, pointed questions, and laughed at nothing. They should have loathed me, but they all seemed to think I was a hell of a good fellow. There was a purpose and point in the affair—but I am merely citing it to say that I understand what you mean. I loathe "gold-digging", but once to accommodate another girl, under peculiar circumstances, I did a fair evening's job of just that—but I had to take 2 highballs, first, to do it. (I have ordered a BOOKMAN. Do not bother to get me one.) But all at once, in these roles, I turn wrong side out and can't go on—won't.

We can step out of character, as we can wear strange garments; but we do not wish to stay out of character, and a life based on such alien ground—no, no.

Yours always, Grace[11]

COATES TO SAROYAN: MARCH 24, 1931

Dear Will:

Get over the stupid idea that I am trying to do you good, or change your ideas or attitude in any way. It is farthest from my thoughts. Wetjen's letter "did me good" by stiffening my backbone. In no other way. By making me more myself, not less. The only "good" any one can do any other, is encouraging that other to be himself, more deeply, and still more deeply. I have learned something about trivial money making. If any one wants to know what I have learned, I am ready to pass it along. Several persons are making a little money, trivial, small money, because I told them how and made them think they could. I understand fully how you feel. I think it is the normal and right way to feel, and certainly the right way for you, even though you were the only human being who felt so.

I sent you Wetjen's letter for the letter. If I say a beautiful gem, or a curious icicle, or a sunset, I might think of you. I couldn't enclose these. I could a letter. Dick's letter is fine for him. I read past his letter to much that contradicts his words. So do you, or you would if you knew the man.

As for my getting through with you—why? I can not write fiction and letters at the same time. Don't worry. Your letters have meat in them for me. When they are only froth and air, I will not care for them. Until then—And it may be a single sentence, as well as a long letter, that carries the meaning I find in you—or silence.

I have always thought that to write anything except what comes of necessity—(dire, painful necessity, or overflow of joy) was prostitution. But bear in mind that I also think other of prostitution as a business than Salvationists pretend to. Prostitution is pitiful in proportion to what it destroys. I know persons who are not much but by prostitution, for nothing has been destroyed in them, except a purely physical ignorance.

Probably the March issue isn't the one I want, anyway, and I destroyed the letter that mentioned the matter. Never mind it. It is absurd to ask you to bother about it. People do those silly things. A N.Y. acquaintance mentioned Guy Holt, and his appreciation of BC, and added, "Be sure to see the March Bookman. I think there is going to be something nice in it"—so I took it he meant about BC. Never mind. If you see anything, let me know.

I must end this—All good will and friendship—and *interest*.

Grace[12]

SAROYAN TO COATES: MARCH 26, 1931

It is very nice (O very nice, as a tenor would sing) to feel that you are beginning again to write me letters, and I hope it won't end in beginning. (And, by God, it's not quite just getting letters either. I mean rather that it's nice we are again beginning to spend more time (you in your place, you said, I in mine) (you living in your self and I living in my self) communing (so?) with one another, talking, or is it really is discussing trivial abut interesting things with shut mouths.) Although now and then I believe I unconsciously stand over my typewriter and actually talk at you, or feel that I do.[13]

And to Merriam, Grace sent a short note. Despite the time spent in social letters, Grace was also conducting other business "as usual."

I am leaving Friday or Saturday for Sioux City. I do not know exactly what you mean by "profitably". For publicity, quite a few; but if I were to name persons that might come to the conference, I'd hardly know where to start. My reprints cost me so little that I can afford to scatter them widely. That is one element in the number to send—the cost. Send me what you wish, and I'll place them to the best of my ability.....What a magnificent tribute to you the Sat Review of Lit April 1 gave. I shall use that a lot.

…Yes, I'll read stories or anything else you want. Henderson may have to call on you to mail out a book or so while I'm one, since I am out…

Wish the Sat Ev man had ballyhooed me a little stronger.[14]

Saroyan was embarrassed and continued to apologize for sending his copy of *Black Cherries* to his friend Goldie Weisberg to review, since it had a personal inscription to Saroyan. Weisberg was a poet who lived in Phoenix, Arizona, with whom he corresponded. Grace did not even remember the inscription she had made in his book. She sent Goldie a copy of her own.

In God's name, Will, I'll get to Godding myself—what are you embarrassed about re BC [*Black Cherries*]? What did I say or do? Tell me Goldie's address, and I'll send her a book—love to do it. Just Phoenix? Why on earth shouldn't you send her the book? I considered it a favor. Because of what I wrote in it? I know that I wrote what was in my mind at the moment, but I have not the slightest remembrance of what it is. It suited me, so I had no reason to remember it. Why not send the book to Goldie? I thought it a very fine thoughtful friendly thing for you to do. I am glad you didn't want to give it to her—glad you wanted to keep it. When you send up the reviews, that will be a natural easy time for me to send her a book. Of course. What ails you? Maybe your not getting enough vitamins in your cigarettes! They say magnesium promotes mother love—pick around until you find something that starts you to knowing that nothing in the world would embarrass you in connection with you-and-me, if you once met me. Not—well nothing—I was trying o think of the most embarrassing moment, and did it all too well, so won't tell it. I thought you did more for me than I do for many persons who approach me with their books. That was one small pat of my gratitude. Now if you want to go on being uncomfortable, just go on being. I can't stop you—but you are being uncomfortable with no reason except a manufactured one. One thing I have always liked about you was that you were sensitive in the fine, excellent sense, not in the sense of getting hot and bothered over insignificant matters—because you pulled the wrong card or mistook the range for a radio…

…Just—now isn't this curious—(I am reading your letter for the first time and writing alternately)—and just as I finished what you said about BC, and turned for a better light on the page, I without volition laid my cheek first against your hand, then against your cheek—something as difficult to express as your desert heat and sun and Alma—then turned back and read your ALMA paragraph. It was as if I, without reading the words, had picked up the mood of your paragraph from the page and indulged it—translated the mood of the unread words into a physical sensation. Odd? But quite true. I have answered letters, before now, without realizing that I had merely handled, not read, them.

Yes, it is what Stein tries to do and fails in. You have just said what I mean—
"To one who has felt the words in his body himself" I felt your words in my
body before I read them. And why not? Ah, if I had not been ruined!

Now I remember that sorrow said to the little smile that trembled toward
you "life is cruel to the tender bodies of young smiles,"

I shrank from pain, that is from life, and killed something that was between
us, before it arose.

In you is a haunted forest,

In that forest a secret garden,

In that garden I am lying

Where (something, I can't remember) are thickest.

Monday—I was just leaving the typewriter to hunt that up—had I even
sent it to you? When a guest came.

To go back to the book—no, my sentences were not a rebuke, subtle or
unsubtle. I was desperately annoyed because a young girl had flopped herself
down on me for a visit after I told her it wasn't convenient—and my letter
would shape itself to anything but a bristle; and I see now that your blush was
for cheating Goldie, not for my remarks. Well, let's send Goldie a book. I'll
send it—you let me know her address

I must go to work.

Yours with regard—yes, to get back EMPTY HOUSE.

Grace[15]

The reference to the *Bookman* concerned an essay by Guy Holt, who
mentioned *Black Cherries* along with other books.

GUY HOLT, FLEDGLING FICTION, *BOOKMAN*, MARCH 1931

To remember childhood accurately, to recall early happenings with fresh
detail and to refrain from injecting into the recollections some adult
interpretation, is to perform a rare feat. This Grace Stone Coates has done in
Black Cherries (Knopf. $2.50), a series of sketches exquisite in texture and so
faithful to the childish mind that one derives a warm impression of the
imagined young narrator, in these tender, vivid incidents the child's dim
comprehension plays upon the event recounted, narrating, interpreting, the
happenings in a family whose common happiness is defeated by the father's
immersion in grief for his dead first wife. It is the child who records with
unabashed vision whatever comes before it; at no time is there hint of an
older, alien commentator. But the adult eyes viewing these childish revelations
reads into them the subtle implications which by their very indirectness gain

in intensity. This is admirable work, not alone because of the technical skill which produced it but for the moving quality of the material itself.

COATES TO SAROYAN: MARCH 30, 1931

Dear Will:

Poor Grocer! I am leaving tomorrow for Kansas. If I were running a store I'd say, come up and keep books for us and write as you "stand around"—but I'm not running Coates Brothers I still think you will have to thumb your way up here and type feature stories for me. I can't write now. You know what the last day is. And I do not want to write while I am away, since I want to rest and "visit" with persons in the flesh. But I know how hard it is to write, and Will, it is just as hard for me as for you and maybe harder because I am— well—we each think our chance at writing is the toughest. I think of you often and often, and will write when I can.

I love your letters, Grace[16]

COATES TO MERRIAM: MARCH 31, 1931

Dear HGM:

The Knopf ad in the Mercury is too disarmingly flattering for me to be aggrieved at that, per se. The same thing could have been said with no mention of its limited appeal or the few who would read it; and if course there is room for a difference of opinion of the sincerity of such ads, or the justice or injustice to a writer, to pick his book to go artistic on: but none of this entered into my 2-day annoyance about the matter.

In November I sent a list of 12 persons to whom I wanted the book sent for review—advance copies. Mr. Smith thanked me most graciously for the list, saying it would be of great benefit to him "later". I supposed of course he would mail the books, and was somewhat surprised that he didn't notify me of mailing them. When mine came, having had no word from him, I at once sent one to you. (Your name and Mr. Frederick's[17] headed the list) You had yours. Mr. Frederick, I found, had his. So I assumed that all the list had been supplied. My object in this western list was to get the right kind of publicity launched early—to head off the great majority of small reviewers, who are necessarily more or less influenced by what they see said of a book, from the ineptitude of assuming the book was autobiographical, and a few other things. I waited, then the complaints began to trickle in that the reviewers had no books. I asked Mr. Smith, and he said the books had been sent. Reassurances from me to the reviewers. Delay. More asseverations that no book had come. Letter to Mr. Smith. Reply that he had sent books "to almost all" the people I had named. As a matter of fact, he had sent out 2 books—yours and Mr. Frederick's. I asked for a check list—couldn't get it—just another—"almost all". I supplied the list—late, of course. Then on pressure, he names the persons to whom he says he sent books—(list, not theirs of course) But of the four he names, two I know of didn't get their books, and of course there was still further delay. And to two they sent galley proof for review, which brought me a merry ha-ha about Jews. It's all right, and all this in the face of my writing Mr. Smith that I was not in the least aggrieved about their not sending copies— if he would merely let me know who had not been supplied, I would be glad to supply them at my own expense. He answers: "Very few reviewers can sell books, and fewer lecturers"—and ignores my persistent question as to what had been sent, and what hadn't.

Then I told him the complaint from booksellers that their field man was trying to talk them out of placing orders—and sent one letter that was sufficiently impersonal so that I could—and you saw his answer. I think they didn't want to be bothered with a second printing that might only half sell. But I asked him to supply all who asked for a book *at my expense* –and this is the way he does it—letter enclosed.

I have stopped feeling sore about it—it has become funny. The only hard part was acknowledging that Smith wasn't straightforward.

I wrote him that he would never affront me by being frank—just to say "Go write a book and let me run my end of the business" but not to mislead me. But now it is merely funny. I know what kind of a man I am dealing with, and it is merely a matter of outmanaging a situation. I never did solve my problems with temper and tears—but one does hate to recognize a problem sometimes.

I was discomfited about that—"What can a column do for you?"—but three answers so far are reassuring—one:—"I don't know. I always turn to that column first, if that means anything."—"The only way I have of knowing what is going on around me" "Friends have mentioned that column to me oftener than any other feature in the magazine"—and from dear old 72 year old Andy Adams: "Nothing". The only thing I had known of the column so far was that it represented everything I didn't want in a lit. section, and that it wasn't so awful that you refused to run it!

  GSC

You note that a letter like this is equivalent to several pages of that unborn book??????????[18]

The *Wichita Eagle* covered Grace's visit to her home area and family:

"Returning to Kansas after an absence of 42 years and visiting the scenes of my earliest recollections has been the fulfilling of a desire I have entertained for many, many years," said Mrs. Grace Stone Coates of Martinsdale, Mont., well-known novelist and poet, who for the past week has been a guest of relatives and friends in Wichita and El Dorado.

The place of her "earliest recollections" is the farm near Goddard where she was born and lived the first five years of her life. This farm is of particular interest, too, because it happens to be the setting of the first chapters of her widely discussed book, "Black Cherries," which she herself describes as a "background of a novel" rather than a novel.

Accompanied by her sister, Mrs. Olive McCarty of El Dorado, Mrs. Coates' visited the rural home of her childhood, became acquainted with the members of the family who are the present owners of the land; and called on Mrs. Rosa Coleman, whose parents were pioneers and friends of the Stone family. Mrs. Coleman joyfully brought out keepsakes that belonged to the dearly-remembered past and faded photographs of old settlers whose names had almost become legends to the novelist.

After leaving the farm, Mrs. Coates called on her childhood friend, Mrs. M. Odem, 1717 West Douglas, whom she had not seen since she was five years old.

Although Mrs. Coates is now gathering material for a novel picturing early days in Kansas, her present book, "Black Cherries," which has been praised by leading American critics, has a special significance for Kansans and more particularly for residents of Wichita.

…While in El Dorado, Mrs. Coates visited her sister, Mrs. Olive McCarty, and her uncle, W.E. Stone. In Wichita she was the guest of her cousin, Mrs. J.W. Lucas and Mrs. John W. Clendenin.

Besides being a writer, Mrs. Coates often lectures for women's clubs and is a prominent member of the Montana Federation of Women's clubs.[19]

Likewise, the area newspaper that served Martinsdale did a story on her return:

GREAT FALLS TRIBUNE: JUNE 3, 1931

Martinsdale, June 2—Mrs. Henderson Coates has returned from a month's trip through Iowa, Kansas, Oklahoma and Colorado, where she filled a number of lecture engagements and visited friends and relatives. At Pittsburg, Kansas, Mrs. Coates was the guest of Miss Margaret Haughawout, head of the English department in the university.

She read from her recent novel, "Black Cherries" at a commencement tea given by the Y.W.C.A. Sigma Tau Delta, an English literary fraternity, which conferred upon Mrs. Coates the 10th degree, an honor—given only for distinction in writing. Lew Sarrett, a poet…and Mrs. Coates are the only two who have had this honor.

Mrs. Coates traveled by plane most of the time. She left Denver in the morning and the Great Falls plane met her plane at Casper, Wyo. She arrived at Lewistown in the evening, making the trip from Denver in eight hours through unfavorable flying conditions.

Mrs. Coates will assist H.G. Merriam at Missoula during the first conference of writers, to be held there during the summer session at the State university.

A first Conference of Writers, in 1931, was a feature of the summer session at the University of Montana in Missoula. Besides Grace, writers lecturing were Struthers Burt, novelist and short story writer; Frank Ernest Hill, poet and publisher; John Mason Brown, author and Broadway critic; Frank Bird Linderman, authority on the pioneer west; and Estelle Holbrook, head of the Holbrook Writers' Colony. Miss Holbrook was listed as a teacher of narrative who had years of successful experience in writing and marketing problems.

Mrs. Burt was also to be in attendance. Katherine Newlin Burt was an author in her own right. The conference was to last a week.

John Mason Brown was to lecture at the conference and also during the regular six weeks session of summer school. Merriam, of course, would also be there for the summer session, helping students with their writing problems and lecturing on the acceptance and rejection of manuscripts.

Grace enjoyed working with Merriam and Frank Bird Linderman in organizing the conference and lecturing, and Frank Linderman joined the long list of Coates' correspondents. They became good friends. Linderman was such a gentleman that he sometimes had twinges of conscience to be on such friendly terms (albeit through the mail) with a married woman. Their great regard for each other and their talents show in the correspondence.

When Grace was going to write a "blurb" about Linderman in 1935, he told her some of his life story.

>...Mine is an old American family, the first Linderman landing in 1690, Pioneers of New York State, Penn., and Ohio. Instead of going to town or mining camps I went to the wilderness where I learned Indian ways, and lived as they lived (quit the trapping when Ry. [railroad] came. Became assayer at old Curlew mine in what is now Ravalli county in 1892, later went to Butte and there became chief chemist Butte & Boston Smelter in 1894-5. Went to Sheridan, Madison county in 1896, bought newspaper, Chinook. Elected to legislature in 1902 and again in 1904. Became Deputy Secy State 1905, (acted as secy much of the time etc. account illness of Secy. Became State Agent Germania Life Ins. Co. In 1909. Came here to Goose bay, where I had earlier been trapper in 1917—
>
>Forgot to say I married in 1893, that we have 3 daughters. The first Indian I ever talked to was Red-Horn, a renowned Flathead. Didn't know if Indians were friendly or hostile, didn't know a Flathead from a Kootenai—and the Kootenais were not friendly at the time. No greater tenderfoot ever entered the wilderness than I—and I'm sure that none ever took to its life any more

surely, or more happily than I. Indians have always been my friends, even though I did have some trouble with the Kootenais during the eighties. My Blackfoot name is Iron-Tooth. The Crows call me Sign-Talker, the old Kootenais "Bird-singer", they call me Sign-Talker, the Crees and Chippewas, "Glasses" Earlier the Crees and Chippewa's called me "Sings-like-a-bird".[20]

POSTCARD FROM COATES TO SAROYAN: UNDATED

> Dear Will, Some time ago you said "Youth walks the Highway" was quoted at a reduced price. Will you tell me again what it is and get me a copy? I mean, save a copy for me, and I'll send a check. If you can—Oh, dear, I am so hampered and busy—and I think of you often. I want to go to Vancouver and can't. No hurry about the book. Whew, it got cold here, and I built a fire, and it got too hot. Rain, a fine 24 hour rain pulls us back from despair—but I forgot I was writing on a post card and mustn't be poetic free of charge of alien eyes. Make all your poesy pay, don't put it on a post card![21]

Grace appeared again in the list of O'Brien Best Stories for 1930, and in May her poem "Makers of Son" appeared with her biography in *Principal Poets of the World*—a compilation of living poets by Mitre Press, London. She was in—*Golden Stallion,*—an anthology of the Southwest, and Ellen Carroll's column in the *Charleston* (South Carolina) *Evening Post*. She was again writing the local news for the Harlowton and White Sulphur Springs papers—a chore she did off and on the years she lived in Martinsdale.

As soon as the manuscript—*Black Cherries* was off, Grace started putting together poems for the book that was to be *Mead and Mangel-Wurzel*—honey-wine and hunger-root. She explained the title in this way:

> Mead was the honey wine the gods of Olympus were soused on and mangel-wurzel were the coarse beets without much sugar content, that my German ancestors fed their cattle in good times, and themselves in time of famine. But it isn't verse that is honey wine and hunger root; it is love, which is mead when you are falling in, and mangel-wurzel when you are falling out.

Coates insisted that *Mead and Mangel-Wurzel* was a hilarious book. One eastern critic said, "There is a knife-twist in much of it—into the author, I mean—that makes of life's thrust an irony armour." Still, Grace insisted that the book was good fun—that such poems as "Village Satiety" made her wake up in the night laughing. She maintained the purpose of all poetry is to give one a chance to say, in verse, what would otherwise be said with flowers—or kisses—or a rolling pin.

Again, Dr. Merriam helped with the selection of the poems. Merriam's *Northwest Verse: An Anthology* also came out in 1931 and was advertised on the back cover of *Mead and Mangel-Wurzel.*

"I believe that the Northwest is preparing for a literary movement which for the first time will give to the life of the region honest and rich expression," Merriam declares in the preface,

> In preparation one of the necessary steps is a survey of its forces—how far its writers have progressed, which ones among them have seen the past with finest understanding and candor, which does know the present life as a rooted growth of Northwest soil, who among them are looking forward with intelligence and vision, and, finally, who have bound over their souls to understanding and beauty. The anthology of about…one hundred writers offers an evaluating moment.[22]

Both the anthology and *Mead and Mangel-Wurzel* were well received. However, when Caxton brought out Grace's book with "certain poems of appalling frankness," it was a shock to the local paper in Idaho. As Montana historian Richard B. Roeder later wrote,

> Even Grace herself was shocked by what the collection revealed about herself. While she felt the book "was a fairly coherent thing," it was also "a shocking (I mean that) revelation to me of what I'm like—the concentrated picture wasn't very pleasing." Later she wrote that the "general tone of the book is an edgy woman getting it out of her system." She regarded this as her best piece of work, but she also admitted that it was "the most annoying to nice persons."[23]

Harriet Monroe of *Poetry: A Magazine of Verse,* thought many of the poems were less than memorable, and those that were tended to be the expressions of the wrath of an embittered woman. Understandably, the review hurt Coates. She wrote to Merriam:

COATES TO MERRIAM: UNDATED

> …There is a natural antipathy…between Harriet Monroe and me. I asked her to mention me only as an assistant editor of The Frontier, and to omit any name other than GSC if you see Poetry you will see how charmingly she conformed to the suggestion, the sour old antediluvian…[24]

In a Trenton, New Jersey, paper the reviewer said,

> One scarcely looks for great literature from Idaho, but Mrs. Coates is a poet of creative power and this volume includes several dozen titles followed by appropriate verse that is never dull and sparkles with humor and fresh sentiment.

Harold Vinal in *Voices: A Journal of Verse:* Her poems are irresistible, poignant and authentic."

Robert Lesseur Jones in *Bozart and Contemporary Verse:* "The author is a unique and interesting poet. Her crisp, bitter diction, her originality and perspicacity, and a philosophy that arrives at something definite, give Mrs. Coates an ample place under the sun."

The *Oregon Sunday Journal,* Portland, Oregon: "Mead and Mangel-Wurzel is a sophisticated volume of poetry which sparkles with zest and sustains with understanding. It is far superior to the ordinary collection of verse as the fountain of youth is proverbially superior to the coarse bread of mortal existence."[25]

The reviewer for *The Frontier* said the poems were "written with energy and craft. They are a genuine contribution to modern psychological poetry."[26]

Mary Brennan Clapp, a poet and the wife of the University of Montana president, was taken by the volume itself.

> It comes in a gay, green holiday jacket carrying a design made by a co-ed of Idaho State University. And under the flapper jacket the little volume wears a strictly tailored gown of elegant simplicity. One loves the binding, black of fine texture, with clear gold printing of title, author, and publisher…you will be surprised, maybe a bit shocked, that one small volume can hold such variations of ecstasy and pain, sardonic facing of impossible situations, and absolute and perfect surrender to love that is worthy of trust. You will wish that there might have been more songs of happiness in it and yet you will know after reading them all that this road to happiness had to be a way of pain.[27]

Grace recognized herself that the book was a single poem with many parts, "approximating a novel in verse." To Roeder,

> This coherence comes from the fact that the poems are examinations of her inner life, her passions which range from ecstasy to anger. Most of the emotions, in turn, arise from her relationship with her husband Henderson to whom the book is dedicated. While the poems express a wide gamut of emotions, they are also united by a common theme of futile attempts to bridge the separation between Grace and Henderson, between woman and man.[28]

As Grace put it in "Uncalendared,"

Between them lies

A strange uncalendared day

No leap year can set right.

By the standards of the day Grace was totally unconventional. It is hardly surprising, therefore, that her explorations of emotions included sexual ones. In "Revenants" she used the imaging of a swarm of bees caressing her body until,

> Their vibrant wings explored my thighs
> And secret flower of my flesh.

Or in 'Recession' she says,

> The sun, like an ardent boy, caressed
> The virgin snow of the mountain's breast,
> Until it dissolved (like a woman's fears)
> In a flood of eagerness and tears.

Grace's electrifying poetry and captivating correspondence often caused readers to become enamored of the writing and on occasion imagine a personage other than the demure middle-aged wife of the local storekeeper. An admirer once went through Martinsdale on the train and seeing a svelte, young woman playing tennis, was quite sure this was the Grace of verse. Grace was amused by the mistaken identification and responded:

Dear Mr. Ludlow, July 13, 1936

> Cherish your dreams,
> I waddle when I walk,
> To stoop must straddle,
> Druel when I talk.

> With years came care;
> My hair first lost its glint
> And then I lost my hair—
> And acquired a squint.

> Fallen arches fret my feet,
> My chins are terraced;
> We'll likely when we meet
> Both be embarrassed.

But keep your dreams
For dreams alone are real;
In yours, it seems,
I bounce with sex appeal.

We are not all undone
Tho time's agen' us
While stock trains run
And lither girls play tennis.

But for Grace, while compiling *Mead and Mangel-Wurzel*, 1931 was also a time to "sell" her own work, and so she sent a copy of *Black Cherries* to the *Contempo* magazine, published at Chapel Hill, North Carolina.

In an article in *Contempo*, Grace explained her book.

Black Cherries falls between two stools. It is more than a collection of stories, it is less than a novel. The book grew around a single situation, whose crux is of two, married, "held in a globe of darkness, yet separated by a deeper darkness at their feet, wherein hid all that later rose between them." When the parts of the story fell into a more or less inevitable alignment, the resultant book became more than the sum of its parts, and was exposed to (just) criticism as a novel. Not having been conceived as a novel, it had not been fully integrated as one.

If *Black Cherries* had been written for publication, it would have been a more coherent book, save for one difficulty: for publication it would never have been written.

Yet to anyone who jumps to the conclusion that I have given the public my cowslips, I would say: Any sincere writer writes out of his own experience—how else?—but when he has so written, the reader is naïve who assumes he knows surely what that writer's experience has been. Photographic exactitude varies inversely with creative art.

I have characterized *Black Cherries* as the background of a novel; the surface glints from a stream that is full novel material. It is a series of attempts to convey fully (presumably to adult minds) minor situations, and through them a major situation, of which the narrator is unaware; or at best, obscurely and imperfectly aware.

Whatever worth the book has lies precisely in the thing I didn't know I had put into it. One reviewer only, Guy Holt, clarified my own mind, when he characterized the book as the story of a family "whose common happiness is defeated by the father's immersion in grief for his dead first wife." Some creative reviewers even have the mother die an unauthorized death; and one suggests that *Black Cherries* is a study of the race problem. Critical comment, unexpectedly generous in the east, has varied in the west from that of a publisher's, God bless him, who maintains that Mr. Knopf will be overlooking a lot of money on establishing *Black Cherries*, not as a best seller but as a classic, to that of a department store book clerk in Great Falls, Mont., who lifted an eyebrow at me when I inquired for the book, *Black Cherries*. "That hooey! A bunch of spinach, lady, if you ask me!"[29]

Milton Abernethy and Tony Buttitta ran the Intimate Bookshop ("over Cavalier Cafeteria") in Chapel Hill, North Carolina, and were editors of the *Contempo*, a publication for writers. In their rather avant garde magazine, they published the work of Sinclair Lewis, Theodore Dreiser, John Dos Passos and Sherwood Anderson along with many others.

Buttitta, an inspiring writer, had moved to Asheville, North Carolina, because of Thomas Wolfe's presence at Chapel Hill. Five of the students had started the *Contempo* to "stir up a little excitement on the country-club like campus."[30] One of the young editors went back to his father's barbershop in Newark, one left to bum around the south and write his adventures for *The New Republic*. Another went to Moscow with a Russian dictionary and a training manual to become a mechanic. Buttitta and Milton Abernethy remained with the publication which was printed for only two years—1931-1933. "Those are a high wind, those Contempo boys, and write me letters without head nor tail to which I reply in kind," wrote Grace.

COATES TO ABERNETHY: JUNE 18, 1931

> I read all of CONTEMPO, which is a rather remarkable thing to do to a paper. It suits me—and this enclosed verse will probably not suit you. But it's fresh and alive in me, and I can not at the moment desert other work to find something less personalistic. I wish some real people would get enthusiastic about my book.[31]

Grace began corresponding with J.A. Powers of Columbus, Ohio, who had admired *Black Cherries* and helped her with marketing in his area. She wrote to him in August of 1931:

> Frank Ernest Hill, with Longmans Green, says word of mouth advertising is the soundest and surest in the long run. I am glad you are inclined to give publicity to BC. I am glad you like the book—that, most of all.[32]

She was more humorous in a later letter.

> You are fun. I'm beginning to think I don't need to purse my lips when I write to you! This letter answers yours in part about the poetry.[Mead and Mangel—Wurzel]. Gipson wanted the book, and at this time it is useless to peddle mss around to the eastern publishers. As a matter of fact, I have never peddled my mss anywhere. BC got by on a fluke, when Knopf asked for it...
>
> Shall I tell you more about the book? I haven't even whispered to Henderson that the book is pregnant, or Gipson pregnant, or I pregnant, or whoever it is gets pregnant before a book is born. No use making him groan unnecessarily. My book, by the way, leaves a puckered taste in the mental mouth. I hardly realized how true a picture a book like that can give of a personality...

In response to Powers' Thanksgiving greeting, Grace wrote,

> I'll try the turkey—if I can catch the bird. We dined most informally on venison Thanksgiving Day; so you see we aren't conventional. Usually our Thanksgiving dinner is an apple, a piece of bread, and a strip of bacon in the woods some place—time honored custom; but this year the duck season had been shortened, Mr. Coates had a lame hip, and I was hard pressed at this desk—so it was venison instead...And have I told you that I kept thanking you and thanking you, in my heart and on paper, for a box of delightful French toilet soap—that I found later had come from San Francisco?...
>
> ...and come to Martinsdale, so that we may have the pleasure of baking you a turkey! [33]

In her letters to Saroyan, Powers, and other men, Grace sometimes engaged in mild flirtation. In person, she abided by the social mores of the day. Once, however, she confided to Saroyan:

> Years ago when I was young and not beautiful Mr. Coates looked up from the paper several times and repeated, at intervals, "I had something on my mind I wanted to say, but I can't think what it was." Then, suddenly, "Oh, yes. I know. Don't start a flirtation with Umpty umpty (discretion a tribute, here, to the local postoffice). He has a hundred relatives and they'll all be in your hair." I looked in something short of astonishment, admiration rather at his prophetic powers, and said: "What on earth made you think of that?" "I'd noticed you for the last few days, and thought I'd caution you about it."
>
> Then in a few weeks I was crying in the corner, and Mr. Coates high-hatted me for a few days; then consoled me with irritated affection, cussing the man, the relatives, and what not; everything but me. "I tried my best to keep you from being bothered this way. If you'd just listen to me..." etc. etc.

COATES TO SAROYAN: JULY 24, 1931

Dear Will,

I haven't meant to fail you; but things aren't always right with me, either. A young man, free. What more need one want? Yes, I know; the other man's chicken is turkey to his neighbor. I know how hard things have been for you, or surmise, at least.

These two semi-lesbian things are all I have—CONTEMPO took the WELLCURB, and asked for 500 words of author review on BC. (I wish I could see the Boston Digest stuff. J.H. Gipson of Caxton Printers says Knopf ought to bet a lot of money on making BC a classic—not a best seller but a classic. The department store clerks says, "A lot of hooey")

Wellcurb

The ass takes the mare's hoof to spare the stallion;
And in the ass's well is only water.

Music dissolved the wall,
Or made it transparent
To a fairer world.
The wall was no longer final.

Need found a crevice;
Longing looked thru, and love extended its fingers.

Metaled ivory, manfashioned, became vexation
To the natural shoulder,
And was tossed from the earlobe.

For an instant Need stirred, and shaken by music
The wall dissolved, or became transparent
To a fairer world, where there was no snake in the garden,
No puritan against joy,
No flaunted perversion

Silence; and again the wall, a tear's falling continued
Into the inner pool, the profound well,
But never the ass's well, that yields only water.

(That is imperfectly quoted) The other is on the reverse side of the paper.

Where No Hand has Parted the Boughs

Tranquil and rich and dark the water
Where no hand has parted the boughs;
Leave to the empty their dull carouse,
Largo, Largo, Lesbian daughter.

The oblique, imperious Sun has shaken
The hill to a garden in the sky;
A paradise where who shall lie
Rosy and rapt and strong to waken?

His oblique and importunate hand has shifted
The whited grave of the desert sink
To a shimmering lake; where who shall drink?
Compulsive and oblique, has lifted

My body's fountain to his barrage,
Disunited. Oh, Lesbian daughter,
Laved and lost in its phantom water
Who shall wander my soul's mirage?

I wouldn't have turned aside to type these for any one but you. Thank you
for being you, so that I could.

Your friend, always. Grace[34]

Saroyan immediately wrote,

The poem Wellcurb is extremely pleasing to me: I like its manner and form,
and the rhythm that does not force itself into word rhymes. The other is perhaps
the more beautiful of the two: the more regularly musical. (I seem to think
somehow you are now arranging for a volume of poetry to be published: think
it will be as unique a book of poetry as Black Cherries is of prose.)[35]

Although Grace continued to suffer bouts of illness, certainly some caused
by overwork, she still found time to write her friends. Concern was evident for
her friend Saroyan.

Will, my friend, are you terribly hard pressed? Can I help you? You are in my thoughts, and I wonder, and am troubled for you. I do not like to hear you say, "just an Armenian"—Life is damnable. I wish you had money. Fine persons should have money, and I wish you and poor Pierre Kouchneroff, beautiful musician that he is, had money for all the fine things of life.

Grace[36]

Grace was particularly concerned about Saroyan having money, because she herself was desperately writing to obtain money.

COATES TO J.A.POWERS: AUGUST 17, 1930

...people who had been good to me in the past began to need money; and a cousin to whom I am peculiarly bound in NY actually almost starved before he in his queer, still, remote way obliquely let me glimpse the fact that he was desperate. Usually I can keep enough checks coming in so that I have all the things that no one knows I need but me. The things that are essential become unnecessary. But now I have to slip this manna to him,—but hurrah for God, I have never seen the righteous forsaken nor his seed begging bread. I'll not worry about paying for books for which the contract is yet signed. And when Henderson sees my book with my name full of poems that sound like chop feed to him his eyes will be so proud of me that his hand won't notice it's signing a check. I'll rub his arm with linament! He and I are enormously good friends. This is his sonnet that closes the book:

> Only to the simple, or the very wise,
> Or those who having hungered long, are fed,
> Does Heaven open this side paradise
> And give its glory to their daily bread.
> Of these am I: never wise; my candor gone;
> But one long hungered, now in you content;
> And we have seen God moving in the dawn
> When our communion was His sacrament.
> My silence would more fitly meet your own
> But the words press, that you will leave unread
> But not unsmiled at. Never am I alone
> When you are him I seek; Uncomforted
> You do not thrust me off. If nights are deep
> I care no longer. On your arm I sleep.[37]

Letters were more sporadic between Coates and Saroyan as they both became involved with their own writing and work.

POSTCARD, COATES TO SAROYAN: OCTOBER 10, 1931

I wonder if I addressed you incorrectly in my last note? Did I tell you about CLAY, a new quarterly now looking for (unpaid) material for the 2d edition? It is a place where one needs not be ashamed to appear. Address Mr. Jose Garcia Villa Editor CLAY, University of New Mexico, Albuquerque. I hope you will feel like writing to me soon. If you do not, it will make me feel like writing a better letter to you probably. Your friend, always.

Grace Coates[38]

COATES TO SAROYAN: OCTOBER 15, 1931

Dear Will,
By no means—your fault. I am passing thru one of my periodic states of maniac-depression,[39] and that is all. I think sometimes if I could find a cave where I'd be inaccessible, I'd crawl in and commit suicide. But that would keep Henderson looking for his revolver and wishing he had it; and maybe looking for me. And so, and so, I just don't. I hope you know what that last word is intended for.
I am at a standstill, a blank, a trough, and slump, and all I have left is a friend or two, such as you and Pierre.
A woman's only friend at fifty is a bank account, and mine is overdrawn.

God bless us. Grace[40]

This is the first reference by Grace to her recurrent illness. If indeed she were a manic-depressive, she joins an elite group—John Keats, Edgar Allan Poe, Robert Burns, and many more.

SAROYAN TO COATES: OCTOBER 27, 1931

Dear Grace:
Scribner's announces for the dec. number a story by Jose Maria Villa: must be Grac—garcia, I suppose. I saw the first number of Clay at the home of Yvor Winters Sunday before last. Erskine Caldwell had a good story: Winters asked me to read it: thought it was the best he had seen of Caldwell: said he found the man unbearable as a rule. I began writing letters to Villa when I got one from him asking for a lot of things: scripts: and not mailing the, and then I dropped him a brief note saying I had nothing on hand I'd care to see in print. He wrote again, mentioning what attention, mentioning the notice he was getting from Bl. Col. Williams and O'Brien and all that, and naming all

the writers who were to contribute: a good group, the same old names, though. How was his story (if it was) in the first number? 1. I went window-shopping in San Francisco. 2. I saw a girl's face and fell in love. 3. I couldn't sleep at night. 4. And so on. The form is too easy. Caldwell did pretty well in it: Lew. Mumford did better, though, in one of the Caravan's. Too easy.

So I sent Villa a story, untitled, in single space, and all that, about nine pages, I think, and not a bad job, though I knew it could be fixed: but I don't like the fixing: if he'll print a first copy of something I do and use his own judgement about a sentence here or there, he's a good editor, and I'll shoot him a lot of stuff: otherwise I'll be exactly where I was, which isn't too bad or anything like that.

Besides I have discovered a technical form for a novel which is proving the thing for me to work in and with: I can produce now. This afternoon I am going to Half Moon Bay, about thirty-five or forty miles from here, to work in a packing house until I've saved a little money or until I get fired or the work ends.

I hope your second novel is coming through all right. I am discovering that prose is most powerful when put to paper after physical exhaustion (not quite that, though), after six miles walked, or three sets of tennis. And it comes forth with less strain and effort. All that one really needs is the technical scheme or framework, and that other thing: that private quiet immensity of identity which must be present in all great work.

I hope you will write me some letters so that if I'm lost among the steam-shovel minds who labor I shall at least have something from somewhere finer once in a while.

Contempo is puerile and doesn't know it: our writers of books are sick hysterical children and don't know it: and quite a lot of them sound like a man with cancer being flippant. The spirit behind most of these individualists is ugly: you cannot get away from their pettiness, their selfishness, their stinking dogmatism. I can't for the life of me find a really great person towards whom I can decently lift my eyes. They chirp about drinking beer, about being rakes with women, and all that sort of adolescent rot, and the truth of it is that they are lousy lovers. Mencken[41] at (and I hate to return to his name) thinks he's a gallant old adventurer. You can get it in anything he writes. Only the younger men seem to be decent. Well, I hope you get what I mean. I mean that writing isn't supposed to be, was never intended to be, a trick, a juggling of words, and that a good writer ought to be a decent fellow anyway, and the best sort of a mind he is capable of being. I see no particular reason why—I see no particular reason

Will[42]

COATES TO SAROYAN: OCTOBER 28, 1931

I am sending CLAY Return at your convenience. Your escape by Steerage was double starred by O'Brien in Best Stories of 1931. I am glad. I think I published only 2 stories that year—awful! No, I had another in Prairie Schooner but later, perhaps. You would like Struthers Burt personally. Wish you could come to Montana next summer for the writers conference. I probably will find it good walking there myself! Write when the sprit moves you, and say what you please, always. I liked your last letter for I knew just how you felt and much that you didn't say.

$$G^{43}$$

SAROYAN TO COATES: NOVEMBER 18, 1931

Dear Grace:

Your friend Mrs. J.T. Jackson sent me a note some days ago, and I replied immediately, I thought properly: though I have not had a reply. I said I would like to visit her and so on: hoped she enjoyed our city, my city. And I should feel very wretched if I made some sort of a mistake in the reply. I think I said I should not want my visit to upset her holiday in any way, and that, since she suggested it, as her note shows I might bring along a lady friend; and might not.

But I am very grateful to her for taking the time to drop me a line: and to you. If I hear from her I will let you know.

DeCasseres in the latest Contempo which you so kindly sent me again demonstrates that he is largely a dull ass. I replied to that letter, and probably made a mistake, though I think the reply is quite nice and ordinary. Nice, I mean, in language. Still, after a week or more I have come to the conclusion that it would be best if the note were not published. Do you think I might best exclude myself from such trivial affairs" Do not imagine that I took it upon myself to speak to Mr. Decasseres for his stupid slur or your note published in Contempo. No such thing. I mention no one in particular, and discuss only the question of his asserted immortality. You remember, when Sinclair died he would be dead, When Decasseres keeled he would be immortal. And also the question of the commercial value of his letter. In ten years it should be worth more than a hundred dollars, he bets. I suggested that it was already worth more than that to me, though I wouldn't buy it for a dime. And so on. Probably very improper; but DeCasseres is like the rest of his contemporaries: ridiculously deluded about himself, insensibly inconsiderate, impolite, and hysterical. And he is not a child, I mean: not a boy who might be allowed a certain amount of cock-surety. He is in his prime if he will ever be, which I doubt, not having a prime.

Please overlook the scarcity of my letters: I shall write more often I hope in the future. With good wishes.[44]

Coates to Saroyan: December 16, 1931

Dear Will—thank you for going to see ... She says pleasant things of you that please me, of course, since I care for my friends. Very soon I'll send you down M&M, so you can see what it isn't like. And soon I hope to give myself the pleasure of a letter to you. GSC[45]

Meanwhile, Grace was working on a story based on a Martinsdale ranch family, assisted by H.G.Merriam's astute guidance.

Coates to Merriam: Undated

...What ails the COWCOUNTRY is that it falls into journalese in spots. What an effective way of criticism—to turn back my letter intended to seduce your mind into reading what I intended into the story, and make it inform mine. Thank you. I'll come out of my coma one of these days.

The letter you sent, the circular, was fine. I always thought we were stung a little on those first prices. To the extent of postage, at least. I gave Mrs. Breen this note for the papers: that a Great Falls book store reports a sale of Northwest Verse to Billie Burke,[46] because she wanted to know more about the northwestern literary movement because it was attracting so much attention in the east. With other material, to extend the story. Your circular shone with a satisfying inner radiance—(I've been consorting with Rosicrucian's) and is one of the best circulars you have emitted. They are waiting ardently for you in Anaconda—I met Jason Bolles and he is fun. He hates that ROADHOUSE GIRL, and doesn't want to be known by it; he has been accepted by the Sat. Review of Lit. a series of sonnets.

I feel something good around the corner—for all of us, I hope...[47]

Coates to Merriam: Undated

Dear HGM,

Never let go of a dollar the Frontier once gets hold of. I return it for balance on postage. Meant it for that. I didn't object to the price on NWVerse except that I wished you had had it instead of Mr. Gipson, the earlier ones, I mean.

Clipping is too funny to be annoying. I did talk about NMVerse a lot, and said the first symptom of genuine interest, as opposed to a wanting to hear a stranger talk about something that had no teeth to bite the listener, was POSSESSION of the book; and I did tell a group of women who professed great interest in BC, that I was sure they were interested, since there was not a copy to be found in town. Women get great satisfaction out of hearing such comments, because each applies it to her neighbor and admires the speaker's penetration.

I was careful not to improve CATTLE COUNTRY too much, for fear you'd be encouraged over my ability and send it back. But seriously, I've done what you said—best advice I ever got from a critic. I often clarify my intentions by making a letter out of them, but seldom mail the letter.

Thank you, and I do hope the Frontier will take this at long last.

GSC[48]

HGM reported to Grace about a conference he attended in Vancouver, B.C.

MERRIAM TO COATES: OCTOBER 5, 1931

Dear GSC,

First, the Lit News section is a vast improvement over anything we have yet had. It's fine. If we can go on with it in this tone and with similar material we will be giving a column of value to the general reader as well as to writers, whereas we have been catering to the vanity of writers in the past. Thanks. I appreciate the improvement.

Helen Maring seems to have got out of the Vancouver convention about what we did. We too *had* to cut sessions, and we did so right and left where she did occasionally. And we too had to bring a lively sense of humor to our rescue while in attendance at meetings. We thot of asking Helen M. to cut with us one afternoon and also to leave for Victoria with us a day early, but she seemed to be keeping busy and we thot she might be getting more out of the Convention than we. The palpability of the organization of the League around the *Overland Monthly* and consideration of everything in the light of good or ill to the magazine was ludicrous in the face of attempted concealment of the fact.

I have a grand idea. I've not thot it out. I've not written of it to anyone. In brief, it involves the organization of an Association for Northwest Literature, with some quite definite aims, and with a book service attached—a sort of Book of the Month club. The plan would be for members to pay perhaps $5 or $10 and receive for it membership in the Association, a year's subscription to THE FRONTIER (or possibly another Northwest to publishers books by our writers—provided we could enlist 1000 members or more. That's as roughly and as fully as the idea has shaped in my mind. What do you think of it? And who could handle it? The organization would frankly acknowledge as one of its objects support of THE FRONTIER (or another magazine, if we so decided.)

About CATTLE COUNTRY. Yes, omit the last sentence, by all means; there is some fine writing in the story. Some grand phrases. But the story seems to me too unclear, to have too many threads (the gawkiness of Harvey and his love affairs; The furnishing of the cabin and improvement of the ranch; the social attitude of neighbors; the moon shining; Harvey's suicide.) I for one am not clear about matters, and rereading doesn't make me clear. It seems obvious that Harvey wasn't in on the moon shining, and yet he commits suicide just as his mother returns from her discovery. What was the immediate motive for his suicide? Harvey you may intend to have been degenerated by unfulfilled sex hunger; but mostly throughout the story he seems simply a moron—at least, a "cattle". Again, the time elements seem confused: the period covered by the story is uncertain. You get the sixth year and seventh, then you cut back to the first year for the visit of the Reeveses. (What function has this cutback here?) The paragraph after they leave runs over the seven years. One place you speak of the tenth year. The story is a grand idea, with some fine execution, but as yet it hasn't got integrated. I hope to have the story for FRONTIER. Now you've got what you asked for—razzing.[49]

Grace had a problem getting her story CATTLE COUNTRY ready for publication and was still concerned about her literary column.

COATES TO MERRIAM: UNDATED

Dear HGM,

I'm glad, about the lit. column. I wish I had the gumption to say what I think, even to archangels; or rather, I wish I respected my own opinions more, and didn't lay them aside so easily—not lay them aside, but lay them out, mute.

My idea is that every issue of the news col. might well hinge on a single theme—this one was built around regionalism (that's why it pleased you!); the next one might be on vanity publication (I do not agree with you about vanity publication—I think the crux of the thing is not to kid oneself. Buying a highpriced shot gun neither makes one a good shot nor keeps one from being one. The main thing is not to mix values.) Then, for another theme, there is the exciting experience of telling the truth—no end to that theme.

We got exactly what we asked for from those who cooperated on the column. We asked for what we should have exerted all necessary tact to dodge.[50]

MERRIAM TO COATES: OCTOBER 17, 1931

Dear GSC,

CATTLE COUNTRY you have immensely improved. I'm sure of that. I also feel that still there is work to be done on it if it is to be up to your level of attainment. I think you have toned down the irony a bit too much. The general clarity is improved. If, however, the reader understood from reading the story all that you explained in your letter to me the story would be a wallpaper. I am returning your letter with the request that each of the bits of explanation you turn into a query whether the reader will'"get" it and why and how. The ending seems to me ineffective—that is, not so effective as the ending should be. After all, it doesn't touch the dominant ideas and feeling of the story unmistakably, does it?

Again, there are fine passages and through out good writing. I'm still hoping for the story for THE FRONTIER. But I do want you when you next appear in prose in the magazine to appear at as high a level of attainment, as in the "Black Cherries" series.

HGM[51]

Despite overwork and depression, Grace could become excited about a new writer. She sent a contribution on to Merriam, who apparently didn't agree with her.

If this is good, the whole thing is exciting, like discovering a new continent. Mrs. Embrey is a Montana woman, of the kind The Frontier is intended for if she can write. She is writing directly because the Frontier opened a path for her; a year ago she wrote me timidly, asking to send me some verse. It was so-so-over timid and restrained, and more or less hackneyed. But I gave her names of pay as you enter magazines to give her a spurious thrill, and—Oh, there is a poignant story back of it all that I can't take time to tell—ultimately she had to go to Warm Springs [the Montana state mental hospital] after all, but poetry was the rope she clung to that led back to sanity. And this morning she sends me a flock of poems that astonish me with their excellence, asking if they are good enough for a little pay as you enter anthology. I held out this one for your eye.

I want her to change *wore* to *used*.

GSC

She was one of the Bowers, affluent Judith Basin family, big house Great Falls, once. I'm not meaning this is a reason to use her verse—just giving the setting that informs all she writes.[52]

HGM's penned note on Grace's letter: "Interesting. But for me it doesn't capture enough emotion. The words and phrases need to carry more feeling "

COATES TO SAROYAN: NOVEMBER 17, 1931

Dear Will,

I got your letter saying you had seen CLAY just after I had mailed you my copy. I have written another "child" story, and sent it on to HGM. He will refuse it, and I'll send it to Villa. Let's give him something good. I am eager to see your poems that he accepted.

Things go badly for me, but I keep on working. I am sleeping well, and that is something new and fine. Mead and Mangel-Wurzel will be out in December. I like the jacket design—in proof at least...

I believe you are right, a new decency will come—not that you said that except by indirection. We are born right, born fine, and degenerate until death. I hope things are well with you. I'm glad to get this book of unrest off my mind. This book of episode.

You, more than any one, have been good to me in letters. Write when you feel like it.

Grace[53]

Editing, marketing and trying to write kept Grace busy. She reported to Merriam.

COATES TO MERRIAM: UNDATED

I'm swamped—so I'll do something unnecessary.

CAXTON PRINTERS asked permission to advertise NWV[54] and Irene Grissom's opus, and I suppose a few textbooks etc. on the back of Mead and Mangel-Wurzel. I countered with the very amiably phrased suggestion—assuring them of course that it *was* a suggestion only, and that the jacket space was theirs wholly—that Northwest Verse was the only book on their list that Mead and Mangel-Wurzel would have the least hint of a chance to help sell. Maybe not that, but surely nothing else. That NWV was the one thing they had that was getting anyplace, and that if someone disliked my book they wouldn't buy Grissom on the strength of it; if they liked it, and therefore bought Grissom, the types of the two were so distinct the reader might be disconcerted; and that maybe they would consider putting only some such legend on the back as this—revised to their own

Mrs. Coates says:

A hundred better poets in NWV etc etc.

Today I have a letter saying they thought my points well taken, and they were advertising only NWV. So you see how I keep out of the rain under your umbrella.

They couldn't use the suggestion of better poets in NWV EXCEPT THROUGH ME, FOR IT WOULD BE TOO MUCH OF A SLAM AT MY WORK. I HOPE IT LOOKS RIGHT WHEN IT IS DONE.

As soon as I can you will get a long letter. Book ready for distribution around Dec. 10. Isn't that speed for you?

I'll send you my advertising announcement. I knew that verse would come in handy some day.

Love GSC[55]

When the book came out, it had the following ad on the back:

Did You Like this Book? Mrs. Coates says: Remember, there are a hundred better poets represented by their best work in Northwest Verse, an Anthology. H.G. Merriam is the editor, and it includes the states of Montana, Idaho, Washington, and Oregon. The volume may be obtained for three dollars at your own favorite bookstore or direct from the publishers. A limited number of the first editions are also available in de luxe binding at eight dollars.[56]

COATES TO MERRIAM: DECEMBER 8, 1931

Dear HGM,

I haven't had a breathing space; and now I suppose I've let slip up the one thing I thought was certainly arranged for: that was some publicity about M&M [*Mead and Mangel Wurzel*] and in this issue of THE FRONTIER. Well, it can't be helped, and nothing is going to bother me about the book, neither razzing, ill luck, or mistaken praise.

I kept Caxton Printers posted about the press date of The Frontier, assuming that they would run an ad. That left next issue for a review, hopefully from you, but from somebody. In the meantime I took it for granted that they had sent you proof sheets. I have just got a polite letter that they have no appropriation for ads in the Frontier, and that is that.

You know the book in general, since you read for it and suggested eliminations. The only reason I didn't ask you to pass finally on it—the only reasons—were

1. I wanted to put in the book certain things that I knew no well balanced person would countenance.

2. The pressure of time was very great, after we once got started.

3. I realized that books are to you what legs are to a cabby, and wanted to spare you as much as I could. I think this was the most restraining reason. This, and the feeling that the book is in for a razzing maybe, and no one else need be responsible but me.

I have lots of orders—hope they won't be stuck on the thing. The book is ready, and my 10 copies probably here tomorrow—they didn't come today.

After this is done, I am free once more to think.

I'll go over your recent notes, and see if there is something to answer. Miss— Mrs. Duncan asked me to read—you know, NW lit. You told her. I said yes.

Sincerely, GSC[57]

COATES TO MILT AND TONY (ABERNETHY AND BUTTITTA): DECEMBER 15, 1931

Everytime I tried to send a book to just one of you the other set up such a howl in my head I couldn't do it. I'll write when I am through having a book.

I am going to send you 5 to put in stock. No time to ask permission so I'll just have them sent

DECEMBER 16, 1931

Your respective letters came and lifted my fainting heart; having lifted it, you can expect me henceforth to be heartless. Well, you are nice boys and good friends, and I appreciate you; in fact, I do not hesitate to impose on you. Today I had the publisher of M&M [*Mead and Mangel-Wurzel*] send you 5 books billed to me, for the shop. If you can sell them, well and good (33-1/3 off from the list, plus carriage) and if you can't no loss to you. I'll tell you' where to put them.

A man just characterized THE MAS*TER as humor! W h e w.

I hope you like my book. I hope it does not disappoint you. It was a quick job, and errs in one or two minor matters because of the speed with which we decided to do it; but it is selling. If you can give it attention that will make it sell in your territory, I'll take off my hat to you. Mr. Knopf reminds me that not all reviewers can sell books—don't bother to publish that Tony, Knopf knows he said it.

A man in Columbus has already ordered 8 books. I wish all men were as deeply impressed. Sounds as if I were asking you to consume eight books apiece, but my conscience is clear, since I just fed you all you can digest.

I open this letter as if you two were already dead and gone, and I close it as if I had gone dead—I have but only momentarily. Tired. I hope you will have a fine Christmas. I'd like to spend one Christmas day in North Carolina. I wish I could visit you and take you up on that guest editor business. I wish I could. No. I cook beans. I feed dog. I run tractor—I mean vacuum cleaner. I review eecummings. I write letters, and never by any accident do what I most like.

Yours with long maintained regard, Grace Stone Coates[58]

Grace found another correspondent in the "man from Columbus, Ohio, who ordered eight books." J.A. Power, a great admirer of her work, was also a friend of her uncle, William Stone. Power promoted her work in his area.

MERRIAM TO COATES: DECEMBER 18, 1931

Dear G.S.C.,

It is always with more emotion than I care to reveal that I receive a book from a writer inscribed with gratitude to me. Often I feel the gratitude runs the other direction, as in your case. Your writing has been good for the Frontier, your publicity work has been invaluable, and your help as assistant editor I value greatly, and I hope that you realize I do.

I have not read M and M yet, and it will be a week or ten days before I can clean up work on my desk sufficiently to give me the leisure I want to read it.

Thank you for your suggestion that we combine M and M with the Frontier at $2.65. It will be the March issue now before we can get out such publicity. Thank you, too, for your effort with N.W.V. and for the most glorious back page of the jacket for M and M. Just after the Christmas season I will send you a check for the copies of B.C. [Black Cherries] which I have sold; will you send me a check for the copies of N.W.V. that you have sold—so that I may settle with the Caxton people.

Best wishes for the Christmas season and the coming year.

Cordially, HGM[59]

COATES TO MERRIAM: DECEMBER 22, 1931

Dear HGM,

And then you say that it is a tradition that the English Department is not sentimental! Now that I have your number, I'll write a book that you'll want to suppress and dedicate it to you.

No, every time I get a letter from you I expect to be kicked off the editorial board of the Frontier for my inadequacy. But NWV—I have sold only 1 copy. Don't settle up now. I have a new scheme and maybe will get rid of all 3 I have left of these books.

You and I do not understand each other intuitively, but only by our intellects—That's the least understanding way; and it speaks well for our respective heads that we get along at all. By the way, you said you could stand criticism, and I want to mention this for your edification: I have learned that when strangers begin: "You know Mr. Merriam personally? What is he like?" That the denouement is going to be this: that they have written you something intended to be facetious, and you have distressed the, mildly, by taking it in earnest, or they are not sure but that you have. I usually assure them that there are 2 possible explanations, that 1) you replied humorously, but your humor is too subtle for them. But with smarter persons I use 2) that your humor is limitless, but you are too busy to be diverted into what would be an interminable bypath. Of course I could be cruel and tell them that you have gone English. That's just by-the-by, but my impression is that you command a fund of goodwill that you by no means realize, and you can take all letters as animated by that high regard and goodwill.

Well, you see that M & M and the Frontier 25 off each does make $2.65.

That back page is rotten for NWV—wrong end to the REMEMBER should go with the publishers end of the ad, not mine. Remember: Mrs. Coates says thus and so. Well, it is better than a hymn to Grissom

I've sold and donated about 155 books, and have to wire for 20 today. I will keep you supplied. That makes my efforts show up more, so I can say, "I sold thus and so, what did you do?" to Caxton extremely limited.

Very busy—I just note you say, "After Christmas" settle up anent books. Good.

   GSC

P.S. Your letter did me a lot of good. Thank you deeply GSC[60]

COATES TO ABERNETHY: DECEMBER 28, 1931

  Tony, the lazy Loneseaman asked me to do a self review of M&M. I WON'T I know it too intimately. Its like asking me to discuss my, ahem, well yes, ahem. Get someone else. Please review it. Pan it if you wish. But don't ask me to, not until the 3rd book is out. I'll sell it then to ballyhoo the next one....Peace be far from you—unless you like peace.[61]

Tony Buttitta never became the great writer to which he aspired. He continued to run the bookstore with his wife Remy and did free lance writing and book reviews. In the summer of 1935, F. Scott Fitzgerald spent the summer in Asheville and Buttitta and Fitzgerald became friends. Buttitta took notes on his conversations that eventually became a book—*After the Gay Good Times: A Memoir of Asheville, Summer 1935.*

From Asheville, Buttitta went to New York where he worked as a theatrical press agent. While Tony was learning to become a press agent he asked Fitzgerald if he could do that and also write. Fitzgerald replied that publicity and writing "made a lousy gin rickey," that he considered press agents "glorified pimps—a tax deduction." For years, Tony could not get his salary without remembering Fitzgerald's words.

In 1937, he wrote Grace from New York, where he also was a feature correspondent for the *Herald-Sun* papers of Durham, N. C.

BUTTITTA TO COATES: JULY 24, 1937

  Dear Grace Stone Coates:

  Just a note to let you know that I'm still here and about…How are you and what are you doing in a literary way…I've been set back a lot in my work by rushing and the necessity of making a living, but from April 1938 on I'm not going to let that enter into the picture at all. Leaving for a small Penn. Town where the cost of living is at a minimum…Remy will garden and bring up two goats for our milk and I will devote all my time to writing and bookreviewing [sic] for the above papers and The Raleigh News and Observer.

  At the present time I'm writing a book for the Federal Theatre Project…the History of the whole damned thing from the beginning to the present day, a comprehensive official thing to be published. Next month sees the publication of a one act play of mine SINGING PIEDMONT in the One Act Play Magazine.

It is being pub. Because Percival Wilde, the O'Brien of the 1 act field, liked it. Consequently I'm dedicating it to him! Today, I just finished a final, complete revision of my first novel NO RESURRECTIOIN. It now has become SWIFT UPON THE EARTH and if it doesn't get a top-notch publisher, I'll recall it again! But I can't this time. At last I'm satisfied with it. Write us and love, Ajax[62]

In his sixties, Buttitta retired and spent half the year living in Italy and half the year in New York. Finally in 1974, his memoir on Fitzgerald was published.

In December 1931, it was announced that *Mead and Mangel-Wurzel* was going into a second printing, and Grace was gathering together poetry for another volume. She always sent printed cards for Christmas greetings, usually with a verse of her own. This year it was,

My Wishes for You

Nights too starry for fear,
Noons like a golden chime,
The confident gift of a year,
To open one day at a time,

A tree from the garden of dreams
Whose tapers are hopes come true,
Whose glitter is all that it seems—
These are my wishes for you.

Then in small print, she added the note, "Mead and Mangel-Wurzel, a volume of poetry by Grace Stone Coates, is to be published December 10 by Caxton Printers, Ltd., Caldwell, Idaho. Price $2.00."

∾

Moment-Flare

Suddenly, all that is not so,
imagined, seems more real to me
than sordid life I know and know,
endlessly, day by day by day.

I will say over and over, say
to myself the word that stabbed my spirit;
finger its edged injustice; hear it
till its insult thrusts no pain through me.

I shall move it in and out like a knife
accustomed, until no blood follows.
Let it numb itself a way through my life,
sliding, unfelt, the easy callus!

Only…only…only…only,
My heart contracts to something chill,
Desperately small and lonely,
Lost, where everything is still.

Chapter Eight

Dear HGM,

This is a leisurely letter for once. Here is my heralded nice thing—it may not meet your approval, but will amuse you anyway.

The last time I was in Missoula you conveyed a faint dissatisfaction with the way Mr. Barrows' material was coming along, or being handled. You said nothing, but from the way the back of your neck looked I had an inkling of what you didn't say (This runs in incidents)

Some time ago Margaret[1] came over very formally and announced—I mean announced—that she had the Barrows mss and would bring it to me if I wanted to read it (which I much less formally did) and would I please make criticisms on it. I said do you mean proof it? And she said "yes".

She brought the mss, in carbon, with a good many inversions in spelling—but I proofed it and returned it to her. I spent about 8 hours on it.

Two weeks: I got a letter from John in his whimsical manner, saying that he wished I'd write him what I thought of the mss, since I was the only person who had ventured an adverse criticism—something of the kind—the only woman whose comments made him sure the commentator had actually read the story. (Of course I can think of persons I'd rather have interpret my comments than Margaret.)

So I commented; suggested hesitantly the possibility of selling the story to The Tribune as a serial; and with a formality that would have meant something to any one who knows me said, "May I suggest that before submitting it to the Tribune you retype it?" or something of the kind.

Then I approached the Tribune—you know the process of being a go-between—favorable response—more letters—John intimated an acceptance of the book mss, I asked who was his publisher—he said Caxtons—I dropped that information along side what you hadn't said; John sent me a short item. Margaret used that to introduce a question I had seen glinting in her eye ever time I had wiggled out from under: "Grace, may I arsk [sic] what one pays for getting a book published?"

(I said wide-eyed, "I didn't know they paid anything? Do they?" but Margaret was on her guard and terribly afraid she had tipped something instead of hearing something.)

But of course I put that remark down the well, and the three things made a perfect triangle—which excludes me because if was framed before my time and none of my business—(I decided after reflection.) Well, I got John's minimum price, and this morning the Tribune's maximum, and by George they were identical. SO The Tribune will take John's story, first serial rights only, for $75. Please consider this confidential.

Confidential, I was saying—for I don't like to peddle prices and especially not to your young hopefuls who make it hard for us—and I do not want to peddle John's business, either. Of course all this is just as much your business as mine, and I have been waiting patiently to hear from Mr. Warden.

Next chapter: John sent me some longer stories which I submitted under his name. In the mean time Hill gave that astonishing radio review of Riding the High Country and Mr. Barrows and Leslie heard it. We didn't, Henderson or I; Jack and Will did and were talking about it in the store when Henderson came in. They were rather noncommittal—said Hill was talking about Tucker. "Was he reviewing Tucker's book?" "No, he didn't mention the book." This seemed to ruffle Henderson, though I can't see why. Anyway, I heard no loud huzzahs from any of the Coateses over the review. Then came letters about it—many of them—among them John's. Among other things he said, "...and of course Hill had to drag your name in. If you paid for this, you got a good run for your money. If you didn't, how do you do it?" If was after this that John's longish story showed up under his name—the other had been merely a news item under a Martinsdale day line—and Margaret, still haughty:— "Grace, may I arsk how that story of John Barrows' got into the paper, now does he send those things right to the paper?" And it is the radio business that explains the brevity of my answer: "I sent it in." And Margaret looked as if she were suffering an attack of mental impetigo.

One of my chapters is left hanging in the air—about the carbon—Leslie sent the *other* carbon—not even the proofed one—back to me for the Tribune, and I returned it with a letter I rewrote four times to step down its voltage. I thought that was the end of the world so far as I was concerned, but she is a fine woman and a good sport—she thanked me and came back pronto with a beautiful ribbon copy, God bless her. I liked that in her.

There is one more chapter: I am a good publicity man, and with an eye to Barrows, and to remind The Tribune that they had not yet given me a decision on his story, I made a news item about Barrows of Buffalo, now of San Diego, hearing the review of Tuckers' so-so on the air etc etc. Two days: Margaret bustled in al amiability, "Grace, I've been trying to remember to arsk you all the week if you heard Mr. Hill talking about Mr. Tucker's book..." (She had seen me only every day.) I said craftily, "Did you hear the entire talk?" "Yes." There was a pause: "Grace, may I arsk you how much newspapers pay, do they now pay so much every month or pay by how much there is in the paper?" And I, always helpful, answered earnestly, "Different ways. Each editor has his own system. And I suppose Metropolitan editors of the big dailies…." But Margaret's eye was wandering and I saw she was listening only from native politeness and sensitivity. So I changed the subject.

Page Victoria—"We are not amused."

This is the first time I've wasted in an age. All good wishes—Let me know if you think it has been unwise to sell that mss—first serial rights only—to the Tribune.

GSC[2]

COATES TO MERRIAM: UNDATED

…It is very easy, a temptation, to thrust oneself into other persons' business. Please consider this a confidence: Something John wrote made me wonder if he was contemplating paying for the publishing of his book. That is his privilege *of course,* if he does it with his eyes open. He also wrote that he wasn't going to wait too long for the Caxton Printers to get around to it. I had to correspond with them about the serial publication—and they know from my many savage letters how I feel about authors having to promote their own books except in very exceptional cases. I did quite a bit of pondering, and as last wrote Mr. Gipson [of Caxton Printers]–1) repeating what I had said many times, that Tucker was one of the few persons whom I considered justified in selling his own book—one of the few who could (his contract is straight royalty, however, the sales promotion being on his honor or dishonor!) 2) that my sole comment to Mr. Barrows had been that Mr. Gipson was delightful, personally; 3) that I had put no pebble in the Caxton Printer's shoe; 4) that I supposed he already knew that Mr. Barrows was deprived of his sight, an invalid, and quite unable to do what Mr. Tucker might easily do, —and 5) that I was in the position of thinking it probably unwise for Mr. Barrows to have Caxton bring his book out but also that it was assuredly none of my business.

GSC

Some time when you can I wish you would make a comment or so on this whole matter. I'm like Tucker "Grace, say something when; you write."[3]

COATES TO MERRIAM: OCTOBER 1, 1933

I think Caxton Printers will never get anywhere because they will take any book at a price. They have too many kinds of contracts. Tuckers is a straight royalty contract, but no royalty on the first 500 books. That is all right; but Wagner's was a prepublication sale of 500; so was Miss Blakefeather's—Fitzgerald—and so on. And I think they aren't any better than any other vanity publisher, and that is that, and I hate to find it out. Oh, not so bad as Henry Harrison, but on the wrong track—fewer books, and good ones, would be my idea.

Vardis[4] says I have a flair for doing things for other writers—a born publicity man I suppose. I wish I could do something real for Linderman— that sounds presumptuous, when he is a writer and I am merely something falling between two stools—but maybe, maybe. I feel toward him as he feels toward you. But anyway, I wangled fifty dollars out of thin air for Mrs. Wagner, and perhaps can help her to a wider syndicated sale. [Max] Lieber is going to try to sell HIGH COUNTRY to a syndicate. Lieber is a good agent, even if Shipley does say he isn't a gentleman. He is faithful and vigilant; and honest I believe. If any of your young radicals want an agent, let them try him out. (Recommend him to Dr. Lennes!)…

…It seems to me there is a lot of material in connection with the Linderman business—but lightning hasn't struck yet. Can you help me? Have you any slant on anything? There may be 1000 reasons why Mr. Linderman can't get into magazines. He knows the 999 that aren't so, but is incapable of perceiving the one that is. I think you know what I mean. You know I have told you that I hold you the one person we can all say indiscreet things to. You are the repository for pressing indiscretions, that insist on being aired.

Doing things for other people is merely smoking hop to forget what you are being too lazy to do for yourself. ? .[5]

Grace enjoyed writing humorous letters, but there were times when she wondered if she should temper her writing. The publishers at Caxtons disagreed.

CAXTON TO COATES: MARCH 6, 1933

Thanks for your letter! My Gad no, don't get the idea Jim thinks you insufferable or impertinent, we like you as is and if you change over the other ordinary stilted epistles that make up our average letters we will lose all interest in you personally and probably write you stilted letters in return prodding you only to keep on writing so we can print your books. We know they are good.

Did you ever hear the merry tale of the chap who fell in love with the extremely homely girl who sang so well? He woke up the next morning after their marriage and looked at her and in desperation shook her and said

"For God's sake Mary wake up and sing?" Well—we might feel that way about your writing if you weren't such an interesting person to write to. The average person simply bores a man to death with proper letters and we are all fed up to the back teeth with them. Your letters are different and we chuckle and refer them between us because they are so different and individual.

As a matter of fact we look forward eagerly to the time when you can come to see us and wonder how in the devil we can be entertaining enough to make it worth your while.[6]

Frank B. Lindeman and Grace Stone Coates had great regard for each other and their talents show in their correspondence.

COATES TO LINDERMAN: EASTER MONDAY

Dear Mr. Linderman,

How good you are to me to have John Day send me Stumpy![7] I read a while, then Henderson read a while, and I am getting no end of pleasure from the book. It's packed with real stuff, too.

I've not finished the book, of course, for it reached me only yesterday. Do you suppose I'll ever have books and books to my credit, as you have? And take a new book quietly, like a gentleman, without a loud noise?

Since I came from Missoula, a week ago, I've written nine feature stories and washed nine blankets. Yes, and I might add, cleaned one wild desk. I wouldn't miss the letters I get for anything, neurotic as some of them are; but unless I watch myself the tail gets to wagging the dog, and my major operation becomes letters. I understand why real writers' letters are brief and few.

"The Wagon-boss" and I send you all friendly wishes, with full hope that we will be talking together one of these days. And I hope Stumpy wags (flicks?) his endless tail all over the United States—and the rest of the world.

Sincerely yours, Grace Stone Coates[8]

The Charlie Bair family had been living in Portland—coming to Billings and Martinsdale for the summers—and now decided to make their home on the ranch at Martinsdale. They started with a house built by John Grant and remodeled and enlarged it. Grace found them a good addition to the community. Henderson and Grace and the Bair sisters had many games of poker. She told Jim Rankin in a letter:

Marguerite is the Spanish type, with an angelic disposition and a voice like an angel. Alberta plays cards and golf like a man, and that is a fine compliment—if one picks the man. She has impecable [sic] card manners, with no feminine dirt. Put all the letters you want in any of my words where I leave them out....[9]

COATES TO THE BAIRS: MAY 1, 1933

Dear Mrs. Bair and girls,

It didn't take me two weeks to sober up after your party, but it did take me two days. That was the nicest bridge party I was ever part of, because I had enough rhubarb exhilarator beforehand to make me forget that I knew nothing about bridge. I just played my hands and kept telling the world.

One of the pleasure of the afternoon was having such a good time with my best enemies. I think the charm of new residents in any small community is that they are not afraid to disregard the stereotyped village tabus, and let edgy persons play in the same stall and rub the edges off—if they'll come. Ever since your party Josephine and I have exchanged ideas about spinach, wool comforters, gangrene and sich; and I think it nearly knocked Gerry [Breen] over to see J. standing on my walk this afternoon, talking. We gave each other the dirtiest look the morning before your party!

This isn't a very formal expression of my appreciation of your friendliness, in fact it sounds rather as if I had just had another round of rhubarb. But the fact is I am merely still under the influence of aches and pains from doing and washing and digging a garden—planted a row of carrots and one of spinach, and got a cramp in my arm. I am faced by a necessary trip to the dentist—bridge out of my mouth, so I can't call on any one or do any talking. Henderson goes to Butte tomorrow, and when he comes home, I am going.[10]

In July, R.W. Pence of DePauw University asked to print "Le Bonnet rouge" in a book he was compiling for classroom use, and Pat Tucker approached Coates about a manuscript he had written. Tucker's book was a cowboy yarn, complete with tall tales. He wrote about riding, tangling with Indians and his friendship with young Charlie Russell. Grace was enthusiastic about the project, but later had misgivings as she realized that Tucker had perhaps taken some liberties in telling his relationship with Russell.

Tucker had written the manuscript and had someone edit it for him that had made a story in stilted language, unlike the Tucker story. Russell had offered to illustrate it for him, but when he read the edited copy, proclaimed, "They've ruined it, Pat." Apparently, Tucker had burned the original, so he had to start over to tell the story. By the time he finished, Russell was dead.

Grace not only edited the book for Tucker, but also arranged for the serialization in the Great Falls Tribune. *Riding the High Country* was reprinted in 1987 by the Fjord Press.

Merriam seemed to have been left out of the conversations about Tucker's book.

M*ERRIAM TO* C*OATES*: A*UGUST* 31, 1933

You have not told me about "Riding the High Country," unless, as I surmise, this is Pat Tucker's book. Will you see that the Caxton Printers send a review copy? I am surprised that they have accepted books by Eleanor Allen.[11] We should have review copies of them also.[12]

COATES TO MERRIAM: SEPTEMBER 2, 1933

This is just a letter, purposeless and pointless.

It is a good thing that you, busy, can understand what queer things another person preoccupied with business can do. If I haven't told you about RIDING THE HIGH COUNTRY, which is all I've eaten and breathed for some time, you are the only one! I have been sending the serial to Dr. Phillips, and generally pruning myself on Seltzer's illustrations. Of course the book isn't much to me, but I did get great pleasure out of Tucker's chance to hold a book of his own in his hand before he dies, if the waiting for it doesn't kill him. It ran in The Tribune as OLD COW TRAILS.[13]

Patrick Tucker's book, *Riding the High Country,* came out the middle of October. After working with Frank Linderman at the campus in Missoula, Grace sent him a copy of her novel.

LINDERMAN TO COATES: SEPTEMBER 12, 1933

Dear Mrs. Coates

"Black Cherries"—the book came day before yesterday. I sat right down with it and, eyes or no eyes, *read* it, read it all at one sitting. And I *like* it. That dear little girl (yourself of course) is *such* a fine character! She seems so out of place in her surroundings that I often wanted to go and get her—and carry her away—to give her some pretty things, the poor little kid. Oh, but our daughter Verne will revel in "Black Cherries." It's just the thing to bring Verne pleasure, and she shall read it.

It's "In Tragic Life" and yet sweet. It's the same story without the unnecessary—and it's even more beautifully written. It does what "In Tragic Life" does and does it more delicately. That same delicacy is in your poetry—and the battle too. There is a fine difference between a hay-knife and a dagger, you know (yes, you *do* know) Oh, I do like your book—and we must have it autographed. When are you coming to do this?

The Frau is reading—"Black Cherries" now, and says "it's lovely"—that she will write later.

Thanks for the treat
Sincerely, Frank B. Linderman[14]

COATES TO LINDERMAN: NOVEMBER 22, 1933

Dear Mr. Linderman,

You will excuse me for sending you post cards. Our friend Mr. Bradley isn't such a bad sort. It is hard to take notes all day, however, from a person whose yarns too often are left hanging pointless. He has had some interesting experiences but most of the exciting ones have been outside Montana. Tomorrow he will tell me about his experiences in Europe with Buffalo Bill. He is a good sort of a man, but not a tool forged to my hand so far as easy feature stories to.

And now after all that prolix nothing, I must say that I have your Beyond Law from the publisher, and take it reluctantly. Like yourself, I know all about this book business. However, I shall prize it, and shall give it all the publicity I can.

I have your clippings, and will take good care of them until I return them. Mrs. Breen said she was saving me a clipping (her work) from the Montana Standard, but she didn't bring it. She hasn't produced it yet.

If this letter is desultory, take it that I am resting from the sound of General Jack's voice—the metallic click of the keys rests me. He just showed us a knife belonging to Nelson's father—the Nelson who wrote—*Fifty Years on the Frontier.*—Henderson could see a dozen things in the knife that I would have missed—the buck horn handle, worn to a polish, the guard for the blade, also worn off a half inch.

Mrs. Keeney wrote me, also, that Bob was on a ranch (?) in Pennsylvania, selling enough to make expenses, and so maintaining his self-assurance. At least that is what I remember the letter to have said. Mr. Merriam takes a deep, almost poignant interest in Bob.

You deserve all the nice letters you will get, and many things beside. I look forward to reading your book—you might be surprised at how clearly I have Lige Mounts lined up in my mind. You were very good indeed to go to the battle, or to battle, with your publishers for the thing. What you say about literary ladies reminds me that I had a letter from your vicinity, a Mr. Lowenstein for his wife, via HGM, asking for biog notes. HGM passed it on asking that I either answer or let him know I wouldn't—so I answered; the man's letter was evidently from some one of more than average intelligence. By the time I got to, "No doubt you can borrow a copy of Black Cherries from some one, (I am not being ironical—at least not more so than usual) and you may feel free to consider it largely biographical, (although it is not.)" The man wrote at once that they would get a copy from the library; and having enjoyed saying that, he said he'd give his third cutting of alfalfa to talk to me. He was writing with pencil, because he had a fractured wrist; and said that before he came to Montana he had a fractured wrist; and said that before he came to Montana to acquire wealth on a ranch, his business had included dictating to two stenographers eight hours daily, and that it was impossible for him to think slowly enough to write in longhand. I knew so well what he meant, that his letter reached in and twisted my heart. Poor people! His ancestor's were '48ers, like mine, coming with Carl Schurz; and there is another of us—he also eating his heart out over his venture in Montana land—another of the '48ers I mean, over by Billings.

This letter has accomplished its selfish purpose. I am rested. A letter to you is always accompanied—is always written to an accompaniment of thoughts of Mrs. Linderman—she fills in the background like a nice song. I know she is glad it is you I put letter burden on, instead of her. Do not bother with my letters—except to take my thanks for your friendliness in insisting that John Day Company send me a book.

> Now I'll go unleash Jack.
> *Sincerely yours, Grace Coates*[15]

COATES TO LINDERMAN: NOVEMBER 24, 1933

Dear Sign-talker,

I had to read your book at two sittings, when I wanted to do it in one. But I had to sneak it in after hours.

Mr. Merriam is right. It is beautifully written. I think it moves even more flowingly than "Lige Mounts." I think, too, you were less concerned with packing everything you knew into it. By this time you accept the unquestionable fact that we can't get all we know inside any two covers. There are always more covers; and for you always more knowledge to go inside them. Beyond Law is a beautiful book.

One reviewer can't get the title. I can see a number of things that title might have for its undertones. (Well, I'm smart!)

Here is a post card. Now what was there about that poem that was good. I have never seen anything in it except that a leaf fell. I do not want the card. But I did a real poem last night. The difficulty with it is that no one will have any idea what it means. Nevertheless I shall send it to you—and here it goes.

Mr. Bradley is here, and he is an old darling. I am glad I know him, just as one more fine human being. Few men are so sensitive as he, sensitive, I mean, to the other person's feelings. He knows when to move out of the room before I know that I want him to; and—he has been a sailor—at night he rather shyly begins setting the living room to rights before he goes to bed. His material isn't going to be of much service to me, directly, because it lies so far afield. If I were with him long enough to do creative stories, he would be an inexhaustible source. Some time I must do a story about the Indian who bet his lodge, with his young wife standing, fingers over mouth, astonished. I must stop.

Sincerely, Grace S Coates

Esahcawata Speaks

Bird-person, look at yourself,
And then listen to me: You are strong.
I have made you strong, Pin-tail,
Strong to dance by the trail
Where the Path-goer's eyes may see,
That his heart may dance with you.
You are strong with the buffalo's thew.
Your tail is the tree's seed-wing.
Your beak is the wolf's toenail.
The Path-goer's heart will sing
At your feathered feet in the snow.
I have made you to dance by the trail
That the Path-goer's feet be not slow,
That the Path-goer's way be not long,
And the Path-goer's heart may not fail.[16]

COATES TO MERRIAM, DECEMBER 30, 1933

Dear HGM,

I think we both have been gasping for air these past weeks. The season was full of satisfactions, as you so kindly wished for me that it might have been; and they came wrapped in rush. I won't dwell on that. In a few days or perhaps a few weeks I hope to have a minor nice thing to tell you about, that will please you.

Book reviewing for two months: I have this in mind. Let me know how it hits you. If there were more time, I'd make sure it was surely possible, and then ask you. If I could arrange for a very competent person, a personal friend of mine, to handle that work in Denver as a guest editor other review section, would that be satisfactory to you? The way of it is this: Pierre Kouchneroff, tb, by unfortunate circumstance cut off from personal ambitions as a concert pianist, finds his satisfactions in promoting other people. Consequently he has no enemies, and his friends are the most intelligent people of Denver. He could peddle those books out to such persons as Van Male and Mrs. Van Riper, and many others, and we would get a fresh note, and sound reviews, and attention among Denver people. IF? If, and if. I could make it very plain to Pierre as to what we wanted—sound reviews, but always kindly—no smarty stuff. His friends are writers, artists, musicians—If he will undertake it, do you see any objections? And I think we could depend on having it done on time.

The expense of sending books is of no moment—I can stand that for the time. Pierre was much pleased with the clipping I sent him on notes he had supplied for the lit col. For the setting of the man I'll just shoot along a letter (of course intimate and not at all formal)—but he knows people all over Europe and this country, and if he were doing the work I think he would find many correct ways of giving the Frontier publicity—and that is his hobby, promoting what he likes—publicizing the other fellow. It is his way of making life livable for himself. And his taste is impeccable. I thought that he, with access to telephones, friends, etc., might do the work, relieve us, and make it an all round pleasant job. Let me know. In the mean time I'll be finding out whether *if* we needed an editor, would he…

Never be afraid of saying "No," to me about anything.

I am sending some stories for The Frontier's consideration. I'd be grateful for their promptish return for a good many of the new mags are offering me space. Also poems, I am sure you are—I won't try to discuss it here, tho—right—I'll resume on the poem itself for clarity's sake.

I want to know whether you thought the last lit news col was good or bad. Please be quite frank.

After I saved time by sending you a torn scribble from Shipley, it occurred to me that he might have had a sly obscenity hidden in what he said. If he did, it missed fire, for I was oblivious at the moment of sending to you. It made no difference except that you should know I wasn't intending to pass along any moment's ribaldry. I'm so busy these days that subtle people need to take me by the ear and spell their stuff in italics—

That galley proof of NEWS NOTES was great stuff—it enabled me to clip, pasted on post cards, and send to the persons concerned and if you think they don't take notice, think again. Every one came back with more news, books, thanks promises of "I'll do this" etc. I shall hereafter always mail out the clips and try to promote subscriptions. Pull me 1 or 2 galley proofs—sometimes a certain clip should go to more than one person—and I know it will improve the flavor of the news notes I get.

I'm not half thru with accumulated things to say, but I won't try to say them all now. I take it for granted you are over busy, and I can handle the book reviews one way or another—but if the Denver way will work it will serve me as well as doing it myself would, and be easier. I am glad you said Feb 2—I was counting on Feb 20! All right.

Sincerely, Grace

I had a much appreciated card from Eileen and will be telling her about as soon as I can get to it—I like her, as you know.[17]

∞

Cleavage

Unfolding strange designs

On my mind's black velvet,

In the point of light

That presses forever on darkness,

I raise my eyes

And see rain slashing vigorous meadows.

Where is reality,

Within me, or without?

CHAPTER NINE

Grace continued to do an unbelievable amount of work through this period, despite periods of depression and exhaustion. She was going over copy for *The Frontier*, writing her column and doing book reviews, writing her historical series for the newspapers, editing others' books, writing news for the newspapers and of course, the many, many letters. She was working on the novel promised to Knopf and also managing the family accounts—she subscribed to *Barrons*, *Wall Street Journal* and the *New York Times*. There were trips to make appearances before women's groups and other organizations. There was also fishing and hunting with Henderson and entertaining her neighbors on occasion.

Her own work was well publicized in the Montana papers—she wrote her own copy, as evidenced by an item from the—*Great Falls Tribune* in 1934.

> Doubleday, Doran & Co., and the magazine, Story, jointly offer a prize of $1,000 for a novel by any writer who has contributed to Story. One Montana writer eligible to compete is Grace Stone Coates, of Martinsdale. Writing to Story's editors from the merchant steamer Mercury Sun, Cristobal, Canal Zone, Howard W. Quigley says:
>
> "No doubt Story has found its way into many remote corners of the world by now, but perhaps it would astonish you to learn that it is read even in the forecastles of rusty tramp steamers and oily tankers. About a month ago I actually heard a Norwegian able seaman and a Finn boatswain arguing about that story of Grace Stone Coates', 'A choice,' that story of all stories! What they said wasn't important, of course, but the fact that both of them had read that story is, if not important, encouraging. Looks like a tough winter for the 'pulps,' looks, also, like our sailor stiffs are going highbrow on us."
>
> Mrs. Coates says the story, "A Choice," is based on an incident from the childhood of Miss Frances Payne of Great Falls.

William Saroyan was busy writing and becoming successful, and letters became less frequent and finally stopped. As their letters slowed, the two writers had assured each other of continuing friendship.

SAROYAN TO COATES: NOVEMBER 28, 1932

Dear Mrs. Coates:

I forget where we stopped momentarily or if we stopped at all. At any rate, it seems to me that I ought to go on with our conversation. Of course in the meantime new topics worthy of discussion or silence have come up....

However, I like the name you have chosen. Portulacas in the Wheat is very fine. Naturally I had to look up that strange but delightful word, and its definition proved rather what I hoped. I hope the book is read and reviewed. Poetry will not sell. I suppose everyone's got to accept this fact. But I do hope the book is noticed, and I am glad you are getting out books. That is because I am glad when it rains (to steal your stuff) and when leaves appear on twigs and volcanoes issue lava. What ought to be ought to be, I mean.

But where have we been? I am afraid I cannot much account for myself, unless I have been in Armenia or in my father's trousers. The old man's photograph has been hanging before my eyes ever since I have had vision, and it is amazing how much I have grown to resemble the man. And as I grow older how much closer I get to the country he left. Nostalgia for Lake Van, Mount Ararat, the river Euphrates, the hills, plains, brooks, trees, the melons, and above all the talk. Well, I shall go there and be disillusioned or I shall stay where I am and write about it. But it's not really this bad. I mean I know a damned illusion when I've got one, and this is not one. I know there is no place like the place I see, but that doesn't make it any less real. My country, it is not of thee I sing. Besides, I am not singing, though I ought. I rather think I am being silent, if I am doing anything at all or if such a thing is an occurrence.

And I am not really writing about it, although being an Armenian is at least as much of a religious thing as being a Jew. Except that it has little to do with dogma of any sort. It is pretty ancient though, and it's in the language so that when you can speak it or think it or feel it, why, then you are an Armenian. And there is something about that old laughter, but I daresay my old man would have liked it if he had been mistaken for an Englishman. I can't understand how he could have had such a preposterous idea when his very appearance was utterly against him. I mean to say his moustache without which he might have been lost, and his eyes without which he certainly would have been lost. Well, perhaps he had in mind the focus of his vision. He might try to look at things the way Englishmen were in the habit of looking at them. I doubt if he could have done that much. But I love the English with him, and I know this feeling will grow as I grow. I mean as I grow in experience. I suspect that I've reached the top of my head and that my stalk now has its bark.

I am glad you sent me word. I have wanted to write for years, as it were, but what in hell can I say? So far, I am afraid, my life has been—well, an apology. I cannot open my mouth, literally or figuratively, without finding it necessary to apologize to someone or something or someone whose function appears to be to beg pardon. And I have been doing it for years. I have the idea that wherever I go and whatever I do or say, my going or doing or saying will in some definite way harm another. A misunderstood gesture, word, or presence. Therefore, even when it appears that I have done rather decently, I cannot draw off without asking to be forgiven, or forgiven, or whatever the hell it is. After all it seems to me to be a rather responsible thing to be alive and in the midst of things and among others who are alive. If I am the only person who thinks so then so much the worse for the others. I am not trying to make the world a better place. I would simply like to imagine I have made some effort to keep my world a reasonably, decent sort of place.

I am sure

Well, perhaps I am not. I was going to say I was sure I was boring you, and I thought perhaps you might not like me to say such a thing.

A Word to God is a good word, but (forgive me) you ought not to bother about justifying yourself to those who are different. I daresay it might do for them to justify themselves to you. When I say "them", however I am not referring (nor do I imply that you were in the poem) to specific entities, but rather to alien schemes of living, or alien ideas of the proper function of life. I imagine that I am a good deal more ordinary (in the streets) than many of my contemporaries who don't come onto an idea in three centuries. Nevertheless, privately I suspect that we live, or ought to live, in a different sort of universe. There is a relationship between the two, but it may not be as close as it seems. A man is obliged to be common among common things; elsewhere (and particularly in any sort of art) I think he is obliged to be uncommon, though not necessarily eccentric.

I am probably saying it is a good thing to take the world as it is, and a better thing to establish a more vigorous and absolute world for oneself. On the whole things are rather marvelous even when they are ridiculous and stupid or even ugly.

Which is about enough from me, I suspect. Young man go to the office. (I am remembering what my old teacher, Miss Grauthaus used to tell me when I interrupted her too often. But I think I used to interrupt the principal too, and that poor fellow hadn't anywhere to send me, but he did have a strap, damn him.)

I hope you had a splendid Thanksgiving and I hope you will have a joyous Christmas. I want to hear the Christmas music again. The silent nights and the holy nights, and the falling on knees (by God, those were splendid things when one could accept them and do them with the right sort of humbleness) and the inward piousness. I do think this depression is exactly what America needed, and the poor shall always be with us, thank God, and bless them.

How are you? And how is Montana? I sometimes wonder what your landscape it? Mine is the city but I can bluff myself when I am in Golden Gate

Park. We have several fake mountains there and a lot of real trees, but they are park trees. Still, it gives a man the right idea.

With good wishes, William Saroyan et Saroukhan[2]

Dear Will,
We didn't stop—we continued in silence.

Last May—no a year ago last May it must have been, I went to my old home in Kansas. There was my old uncle whom I had never seen, 93 then, and so like my father that he fitted right into my brain and heart. He and I loved each other, he hatefully and sarcastically in the way I knew so well; and his daughter watching us for a half-hour smile at each other almost without a word—having one of those intimate, wordless visits that my father and I always had, went to her room in tears. When I went up she sobbed, "I'd give anything in the world to know my father as well as you know him."

I sat on his chair arm and fiddled with his bald head, and contradicted him, and powdered my face in front of him—none of them dare. He is the loneliest soul, and probably I am the only living person who prefers to be with him rather than out of his reach. If he weren't so loaded with money I'd get him to come here—but you know the implications of a niece being so warmly affectionate to a nonogenarian she has never seen before—who has more than one million, allegedly. I may have mentioned all this—anyway it is on my mind, because I wish you could have the same experience with your own home in Armenia.

Oh, Will, why don't you come up to Montana—and herd sheep, I suppose! My dear 'Gene Saier has left me—he writes me beautiful letters in German that are a cry—he would come to my home and once more find peace. There is a little "melancholic" in his home because the depression begins to be felt, and the girls think too much of the times past in Germany—so he tells me. And I ache to be near him—ache some solace not localized in my flesh.

I'll write. Grace
The book keeps me busy, of course—there is an astonishing amount to do even when the printer is at work on a thing. And then more work, and more important work; and what does it all amount to?[3]

Saroyan had an interesting look at their relationship when he wrote,

It is very fine indeed to get one of the earlier kinds of letters from you again. I do not really understand what you say about me; (understand it perhaps, but cannot account for it) and must therefore believe that I am in your mind perhaps largely a myth, which is perhaps as it should be, even so. And with a mere correspondence contact how might we be to one another anything less than myths? That your friendship has meant more to me than that of almost anyone else I know goes without saying. The fact that our ages vary is somewhat insignificant to me; I say I am largely a myth to you because undoubtedly you have created the image of me you most desired; and I of you. In reality of course (when I am not writing you a letter) I must surely be a somewhat alien person, a rather slouchy character, an altogether commonplace (and perhaps disappointing) specimen. Even so it is worthwhile to me to drop this attitude now and then, to assume the appearance of something absolute, something similar to a work of art, to live perfectly for a half hour, say, as a good painting lives perfectly as long as its canvas does not rot. More than this I cannot say about myself. I know too well the truth; I know too well how disgusting are the imperfections of human life, how horrible decayed teeth, for instance, and how inconsistent with one's desires and intentions. As to yourself, I am certain, positive that I cannot possibly know the same individual you appear to be to those who know you as a human being, who have met you, spoken to you, and perhaps (like Knopf) see only that which is conventional, and wholly ignored that which is not. (This is all probably silliness, but to me it is the truth.[4]

In early 1934, she wrote to congratulate him on the publication of a story.

Congratulations on the story "The Daring Young Man on the Flying Trapeze". It is painfully beautiful. I hope that you may go far on your own flying trapeze.

I have always associated your courteous withdrawal from correspondence with me with your contact with Mrs. Jackson. It would make me more comfortable to know I am in error. I can take it on the chin—it is not understanding that is hard to adjust oneself to.[5]

Saroyan was quick to respond,

Many thanks for the note: silence happens: there is little to do about it. My withdrawal from correspondence with you occurred when I withdrew from everything else. I meant to stay out of the picture for five or six years: Story's acceptance of the trapeze tale (the first I sent anywhere in many months) started things again, and now it is thus: I am writing and so on: but not liking it a lot: ambition makes me miserable. Mrs. Jackson was delightful, one of the liveliest ladies I have ever met: I still think of her, and of her son, who was splendid, terrifically alert, wholly alive. He must be a great fellow by this time. If you see Mrs. Jackson, or if you write her, please give her my regards.

Story is printing another story of mine soon: Seventy Thousand Assyrians. They are holding others for consideration. The Magazine, from Beverly Hills, printed a story called 1 2 3 4 5 6 7 8…February issue: I told them to write you for a story. Covici Friede wants a novel: I don't feel well at all. The weather is rotten and I am being printed: it makes me feel blah…I am competing. The editors of Story, I think, are the finest couple of editors in this country: I like them a lot: they are trying to do all they can for me: I mean they are trying to do a lot of things for me: but what I like about them most is that they take a story and print it, and there isn't any fuss, any rewriting or working over, or anything else. That's how it ought to be.

I am also semi-famous: a news item from The San Francisco News, Friday, February 2, 1934: also a new version of my nose, etc. As I see it, if America is to ever emerge as itself, it will be through the pages of Story.

I am supposed to be writing: competing: keeping up: but I am not. I am trying, instead, to get back to the old quiet, which is a lot more important. For the sake of a little money it is all right to splurge once in a while, but I have money now: eight dollars and eleven cents: I don't need any more for a while. The Magazine paid me $30.59 for the story they bought and printed. A lot of money.

I'm still the same as ever.

Well, I've got to go over to my sister's and fix the clothesline.

> *Best wishes,*[6]

Grace responded immediately,

Thank you for your prompt answer to my letter. I want to tell you that I think your story in "The Magazine" is the finest thing I've read in long, long time. It is the kind of thing the Frontier would have hemmed and hawed over. Since I won't be bothering you any more, let me unload all my vexations—in confidence to you. Personally I thought the Frontier failed you completely. I was excited about your work. If I had been the editor I would have leaped at it, seized it, hurried to shout about it. After I sent your stories in, I all alight with enthusiasm, they would come back with the notation that I was to labor with you about them. Well, it is done. I say again, The Frontier failed you. It has helped lesser persons. That is its judgement on itself. I don't think it was I who was over-blind, even if it was I that tried to get you under the wire. I am always unable to embody Mr. Merriam's suggestion in my own work. Not that I am arrogant, but if I change what I have written it becomes something else, that I had no thought of writing.

Butch, I'm glad, no words for it—writing won't make you happy—but not writing will keep you miserable. The entire inside of me is tumultuous for you. I don't care whether you write me or remember me or not, so long as you go ahead. And I'll always know something of what you are doing. And I'll always be sardonic about the way The Frontier pecked and pecked at your work—blind!

I have read your letter, and given a big, loud HA HA at the beautifully subtle poignancy of my own! You know I'll bother you, and reach over and jiggle your elbow every time I get to thinking about you and wanting to. I thought The Frontier ran across genius and didn't know what to do with it, was up in the air and bewildered. Sounds as if I was tooting my horn and belittling Mr. Merriam, but I'm not. It is his magazine, and he distances me on everything me being a nut. But I shall reserve the privilege of saying hello to you when I want to, no matter how remote, how busy or how famous you become. Or how rich. Because you, everything you write, twangs my inside fiddle strings.[7]

As he was preparing his papers for the library, Merriam had a couple of letters of Saroyan's to Grace that she had forwarded to him. He circled the name Coates and wrote, "Asst. Editor of Frontier and F & M, 1927-1939. She handled most of the stories Saroyan sent to us. We published but one from him before Whit Pruwett discovered him and published his & also in Story."[8] Merriam also admitted later that he had "missed" some other authors who went on to establish a name.

"Thank you very much for the very friendly letter," responded Saroyan,

… it made me feel as happy as I used to feel years ago when a letter from you came to me: I am sure you could never have thought for long that I could or could wish to forget you: I could not and I could not wish to: and I have an idea that your friendship will be (fifty years from now and perhaps to the last minute and perhaps after the last minute) a remembrance that will come to me smiling

I am not much of a writer, though: and I shall never be famous and I shall never have much money. I hope to do some writing: which is living and the important thing. Fame is a form of fakeness and money is a form of impertinence: and to hell with each…I have had a bad day today: but writing to you is improving it a little. I shall not write often: I know you won't mind— we are after all pretty good friends and I think we really know one another and understand one another and we do not have to talk a lot about it. Isn't this so?[9]

Grace was pleased to tell Merriam, "Saroyan is in 'The Magazine' with a fine! Very fine piece of work.—So glad for him—2 pay stories placed!"

To Saroyan she wrote,

You are a permanent part of me, whether we write or not. All of you that is mine is inalienable, and silence makes a good cement. The May Frontier coming up has one of my stories, and not so good either—it has flaws. I have been ghosting mss for Caxtons. Back of this. Also, I wash and iron (for myself) Oh, dear. I take the stock reports.

I'm glad for you about the books. Random House is fine, and a book in print is an excitement that is as near as a man can come to bearing a baby. I am glad that I can write better than I do in letters, but anyway, a book is exciting, whether you pretend it isn't or not. The excitement and wonder subsides with each new book, and I doubt whether the 12th book is anything but a job.

I could tell you something worthy of a short story, but one can not write short stories on another's experiences, any more than he can digest another man's dinner. Until it becomes yours by process of either living or imagination, you can't do it.

Anyway, Henderson went sour on the stock market and turned our investments over to me to nurse. Then, with a load off his shoulders, he drew a long breath and demanded some social life, parties, bridge, cocktails and general gayety. Without the stock market, I could manage time for a little creative work, with it I couldn't until I had the thing systematized. But with bridge on top of that I was swamped.

It's a funny story if one can see it that way. I had a few brainstorms and then decided barnstorms wouldn't solve anything. Does he hate my writing, subconsciously, and are his unexpected demands on my time a subtle Freudian stroke?

One can tell a distant friend what he could not hint at to a neighbor. In addition, I needed money for personal matters not really up to him—broke relatives etc. So I ghost manuscripts. You wouldn't do that. You are geniusier than I.

Once you—once I asked you why you didn't thumb your way up here, and thought you were rebuking my vernacular when you asked 'Thumb? What does that mean?' I felt uncomfortable and chagrinned. Since you spoke of Mrs. — Jule's "pokey" I saw that you might have been in earnest, when you asked. I thought it the first sign of impatience with details of our friendship—and how well I know those signs.

I wish you would come up here this summer, and we could drive all over the country, get the neighbors to gossiping about us, laugh with Henderson about the comments, and write short stories and features. Come on. Uncomfortable house, but who cares. Come ahead

> *My love to you, Grace*

Do you know that you did not acknowledge two books I sent you? How come? Or am I at fault in asking this?[10]

When Grace wrote again, her typewriter was stuck on caps.

COATES TO SAROYAN: UNDATED

DEAR WILLIE
A MILLION YEARS OF SILENCE WOULD NOT DESTROY OUR

IDENTITY WITH EACH OTHER. I LIKE ALL OF MYSELF, OF WHICH YOU ARE PART.

SEE, WHERE YOUR LIFE BROKE OFF FROM MINE
HOW FRESH THE SPLINTERS KEEP, AND FINE.

I WORKED THIRTEEN HOURS YESTERDAY WITHOUT STOPPING, AND EXPECT TO WORK FOURTEEN TODAY. THIS IS A PLEASANT INTERLUDE TO WORK.

CURRANTS ARE RIPE. A FRIEND FROM FLORIDA VISITS ME TOMORROW. I AM ALWAYS HAPPIEST WHEN LIFE PILES UP AS IT HAS FOR THE PAST MONTH. I WRITE SILLY FEATURE STORIES* MONTANA HISTORY MOSTLY FOR SEVEN PAPERS WHILE THE REGULAR CORRESPONDENT IS HAVING A BABY. I'D RATHER HAVE THE BABY, BUT WE TAKE WHAT WE GET IN THIS HERE NOW WORLD.

NAW, NAW, DO NOT BOTHER ME WITH MY LETTERS NOW. KEEP THEM IN YOUR OWN WAY A WHILE LONGER, UNTIL I GET THE NEW OILCLOTH* NO LINOLEUM, ON THE KITCHEN. THOSE STARS ARE CAPITAL DASHES, AS YOU NO DOUBT SURMISE.

GSCoates[11]

COATES TO SAROYAN: MAY 24, 1934

Dear Will,

Somebody—Haniel Long in Space (a new publication) sent me back to Marcus Aurelius; who admonishes himself not to be often, or without necessity, to complain to friends of having no leisure. Not in letters, he says, do this. I have erred.

Ellen Glines asked me to write her a longhand letter, and I haven't done it yet. I wonder if you saw her new book, and her Mead and Mangel-wurzel poem? I mean period. Not ? And as for Port in Wheat, why should you feel guilty? I lost one friend over that book, one I thought steadfast. Said he would return it except that he didn't want to hurt my feelings. I told him to chuck it in the coalscuttle, and then laughter drowned me, because I kept from adding, "unless you are using the coal scuttle to take a bath." He is Jewish, and when he visited me he preferred the coalscuttle for his baths, because (I suppose) it was kosher. Anyway, I let laughter have it, and didn't say it; for I think I have not yet struck any person with a weapon he trustingly put in my hand. I couldn't imagine what ailed him, but got a clue later, when one gal wrote me he thought I had paid to have the book printed.

And Thumb, that too was guiltless—even if you had been showing impatience: to thumb one's way is to stand in the road and signal passing motorists for a ride—hold up one's thumb, in other words.

I was really sick, and it was so good to be sick and under no compulsion to get up and do anything. But the dreadful sickness of the mind that assails us more and more—all the slick paper magazines are telling why it is—because we have won freedom and now long for authority, because we are not big enough to run our lives without authority.

Will, Will, how are you subtle. Yes, you spoke of teeth gone wrong. I know, I know. My sister felt so helplessly degraded when she lost teeth she almost committed suicide. (She said I was the only one who helped her, and all I said was that her soul didn't reside in her teeth. But it does, if there is one, in the teeth as much as anywhere else.)

To whom belongs the humor that rises from a misunderstanding? "Leave in God's whiskers," you said; and I read, "Leave it in God's whiskers," and quoted it around as a wonderful resume of everything. Leave it with God. Leave it in His whiskers.

Your earlier letters to me helped keep me from jumping down the well. They meant so much to me, reverberated so widely, I could never write—not being able to write what I wanted, I wrote almost nothing. But you saved something in me otherwise gone down the drain. Whether you write or not, I'll be writing you again. There is something about everything you write that I care to read. I would read you if no one else did. I would read you if everyone else did. I care for what you convey to me. In the damned patter of the day, I have a distinct experience when I read what you write. I do not know whether I followed my intention of sending you a clipping from the Sat Review of Lit., which quoted Martha and the other editor as saying you sent a story every day for a month, and believe it or not, every one was a good story. I have seen things of yours I cared more for than the Mercury story—but I cared to read that, too.

> *Grace*[12]

SAROYAN TO COATES: JUNE 14, 1934

Dear Grace:

This morning I began writing the seventh novel I have tried to write this year: or I began to write a novel I shall write: or it is the seventh I shall abandon. A novel a day. This novel is called William Saroyan, and I think it is a good title. William Saroyan is a character in a novel by the same name, by the same man. I am very enthusiastic about this novel. I feel pretty good: no pain. Teeth in order. Everything in order: for the love of Mike, thank God. And how long will it be this time until I am again in agony?

I have read your letter four or five times: now it is before me, in the envelope, and I am answering it. All I ever do, though, is talk about myself. This novel I am writing may never appear in print, which won't matter much. And I will tell you something amusing about things being written solely for themselves, not for publication. I get a big kick out of this. Last year I put my typewriter in hock, so I could have a few dollars. For three or four months I was without a typewriter and I was miserable. I wrote on hotel stationery, on Y.M.C.A. stationery, and in little note books, and on all sorts of scraps of paper. But I was miserable because without a typewriter everything I wrote seemed unfinal: print is a form of finality. Well, finally I got my typewriter out of hock and I was so happy about it I had to write the sort of story I knew could never be printed. At least I thought so at the time. The story is called Myself Upon The Earth. I wrote it in about three hours. Three very happy and angry and bitter hours. After writing it I put the story in my trunk, among all the other things I have written.

Well, Story Magazine bought a story, and I began to write a story a day. When 1933 ended I looked over my work for the year, and came upon this story, Myself Upon the Earth. It seemed all right, and for some reason I sent it to Whit Burnett. He kept it. It will be in the book, although I said in the story that a century might pass before the story would be read, and I spoke of myself as an unprinted writer. Now this is the amusing part.

Mr. Angoff, of The Mercury, bought the aspirin story and asked for more. I sent him more and each he rejected with brief criticisms: obvious, verbose, etc. He rejected a very good one called Resurrection of a Life. I got sore and decided never to bother with him again. I mailed him nothing for over a month. Then he wrote and asked that I send him something. I felt ashamed for having been angry with his judgment and decided to try again. I had just written a little story called Ah-Ha, and while I felt certain he wouldn't like it, I mailed it to him just the same. He accepted it immediately, and when I read the proof I could see that it was a fine little story, a little over two pages long. In the meantime I had corrected the proof of my book of stories. Burnett took four of the stories to Angoff. Angoff selected Myself Upon The Earth. He said, Myself Upon the Earth is not merely a good piece; it is a great piece, and some parts of it reach the highest poetry. You are writing better every day.

Very amusing. I wrote the story over a year ago. Better and better every day.

My book disappointed me, but I suppose it won't be so bad.

I am reading the letter again: Leave in God's whiskers...? Who said that? I never remember anything I write. I don't even remember the mood most of the time, and the mood is probably all of it.

I write a story in two or three hours every now and then. Just to keep in practice. Half a novel I wrote in about thirteen or fourteen days: called Twentieth Century Blues. It has a lot of happy stuff in it, but I got bored with it and with myself and kicked it out. I hope Angoff prints Ah-Ha before he prints Myself Upon The Earth because I like Ah-Ha very much. It is so short and so complete and perfect that it is sure to satisfy everyone who reads it. Symphonic: it is surprising what can be done in two pages. Shortest story I ever wrote, and perhaps one of the best. I have a verbose style, too. Angoff's use of the word isn't wrong at all. It is because I do not want the reader to get even a slightly different impression than the impression I want him to get: so I have to put down prose that is like drawing, in a line.

Well, life continues somehow. Right now it is almost swell. I am not happy but neither am I miserable. I daresay I do not ever want to be happy any more than I want to be miserable. I want, I think, equilibrium.

I haven't asked you about your writing because I felt I ought not, since ultimately, finally, one cannot be of help to another, and ultimately when one wished to be, one makes a mess. I know nothing about poetry, but I do believe Black Cherries is one of the finest works of prose in English. I was corresponding with Malcolm Cowley a while back, and I mentioned your book in connection with the forgotten-books idea. He printed two lines of a long letter in "The New Republic, mentioning Black Cherries. Thus: The forgotten-books idea was good. How about Grace Stone Coates""Black Cherries". Finest prose you ever saw. Good wishes. (I do not know why he threw in the good wishes; of course it came at the end of my letter to him. I hope you won't mind his printing this note; or don't mind.)

I don't seem to be able to get into Scribner's or Harper's but I am trying; a bit of ambition humorously. I hope you will write to me soon,

William Saroyan[13]

Along with Saroyan, Grace was still busy writing to Merriam, Linderman— any number of correspondents.

After John Barrows had seen his stories serialized in the *Great Falls Tribune*, he sent the manuscript to Caxton printers. Merriam was concerned about the author's deal with the publisher, and passed his concerns to Grace. She told him of her part. As with Tucker's work, Grace wanted to protect her fellow authors from being exploited.

Since writing the rest of this letter yesterday I have your letter re John etc. Oh, the entire thing was clear to me. I knew as soon as Marg. asked me what publishing a book cost the whole story—in fact I surmised the trouble before that.

My whole mental query was whether it was any of my business. His plans were made long before I saw the mss. And if I interfere I am of course doing Caxtons a disservice and in doubt whether I would be doing John a service. It is none of my business I concluded. I told Mr. Gipson, in answer to his contention that he was trying to benefit—and we let it go at that. I also told Gipson that Mr. Barrows was an invalid deprived of his sight, and couldn't possible sell his own book—I wanted to see just what Mr. Gipson would do.

If he takes John's book and obligates John to sales or purchases then I know all I want to about Mr. Gipson. (And I do like him.)

He asked me what kind of a contract he would want Tucker, and I said, "Oh, one with plenty of words" and I also told him he needn't bother to send one asking Tuck to buy or sell books, because I should advise him not to sign it—and HE WOULDN'T—if I told him not to.

Mr. Gipson has made one unequivocal statement in Print: that they are absolutely dependent on Tucker for selling the book. Now, if they can't sell Tuck's book, what is the use stringing John along that they can sell his? They can't—they won't. BUT IT IS NONE OF MY BUSINESS. I didn't promote the deal.

But if Mr. Gipson is so heartless in promoting western literature that he takes money from John, I'm off everybody for life.

I have confined my letters to Mr. And Mrs. Barrows to the matter in hand. Haven't discussed any business or any person—he is a bit—Oh,—touchy. He told me not to try to change his style,—and he was like his cousin Margaret— and I said "Stop reminding me you belong to Margaret" and that is as near to personalities as I have come. But I had no secrets from you—it was as natural for me to try to sell someone else's mss as it is to pick a fourleaf clover—no gratitude due me. I knew I could sell it and did—no work especially. But the Caxton business isn't my baby, though I think it very unfortunate if John pays money when money is so scarce, or obligates himself in any way. And Caxtons CAN'T AND WON'T sell books—they just print them, and with God be the rest.

It might be I could stop John's doing anything silly—but that part is none of my business. "Say some more." I thought you might think the Tribune cheapened the material—but I take what I can get, these days. Now I have a serial of my own, and the Tribune is full up—so coals of fire, or is it bread cast on the waters, come home to roost!

> *Grace*[14]

MERRIAM TO COATES: JANUARY 20, 1934

Dear GSC,

You are a brick, and almost literally a gold brick in this instance, for interesting yourself in John's manuscript. I only hope that he does not take the $75 which the Tribune will pay him and turn it over to the Caxton Printers for publishing the book. I fear he may. You, by the way, can do more with and for John than I can, since he looks upon me as a youngster, something of an upstart, and worst or all, a college professor—worst of all because college professors are damned by the profession in his eyes. (This I am telling you in confidence.) I could not make out from the letter which Gipson wrote John what sort of a proposition he is making. It is a long, vague combination of words and sentences. Apparently he wished John to purchase a certain number of copies, the purchase price to be taken out of his royalty in case the book sells, and in case it does not sell, to be taken out of John's pocket. The sad fact of the matter is that John has no pocket. Or if he has a pocket, it is not filled even with air. Personally it seems to me that "Ubet"[15] would be a good book to follow up "Riding the High Country". It would not be so picturesque nor so striking a book, but it would be an authentic document of the West, interestingly written, and carrying behind its words a real personality. I think it was an excellent stroke to sell the manuscript to the Tribune, and it will work out well provided the Caxton Printers will issue the book immediately upon the publication of the last installment in the Tribune. Does that clear the matter at all?

Cordially yours, HGM[16]

With the press of work and some eyesight problems, Grace told Merriam she could no longer do some of the book reviews for *The Frontier,* and suggested again her friend Pierre Kuchneroff and others in Denver.

You know before I tell you, that what you do is always right with me, and that I have never known any one who would go farther to spare an associate any awkwardness.

What happened when you mentioned reviewing was my immediate thought of my eyes, already suffering badly—I was caught between the feeling that you should have any service I could give the magazine, and my own press of junky duties and eyestrain.

Then I thought of Eddie Custer (who is Pierre Kouchneroff) and his constant association with Denver writers, and wondered if you saw any objection to having all that reviewing done in Denver this time—you know how it is here, there are no persons in Martinsdale to hand the books out to.

I suppose it is ground into me to try to let the other fellow have the credit for things, if it gets them done. And my first suggestion was to let him figure as the editor of the column. He would not write any reviews, but he will pass over the books to thoroughly competent person, collect them, send them to me, and let me give them the once-over. But Pierre is like me, if you would prefer to have my name as the editor, Pierre would want it to be mine not his.

Of course as soon as I wrote you I wrote him, but told him it was merely tentative—might not be a vacancy was the way I put it—and he got busy at once, said Van Male (your advertiser and a book dealer and a darling) Linderman, caustic reviewer for the Rockymountain News and radio reviewer, now intent on making up to me for saying Port in Wheat was priced too high, and Mrs. Ladd head of Denver Library and Mrs. Von Riper who has been in

Paris finding out who Proust is (she is very finely intelligent) and this that and the other offered to each review a book for Pierre-me. (I know all these people, been in their homes, you see I got off almost too well in Denver two years ago when I was there.)

Now if this doesn't please you, there is no reason in the world to do it. If it does please you, I feel absolutely assured that we will get something fresh and high class, and that carries what it has seemed to me the magazine sometimes hasn't had—a sense of fun in the doing. (I'll take that right to myself, too, and get some of that into the henceforth news notes.) But if it does please you, and at the same time other arrangements have gone too far to change, let's do it for the May issue. This is what happened about the Wagner business (I can't locate the letter without too much eyeing of papers) I don't know her, but I have seen her writing on authors in ?The Personalist—I asked Mr. Kuhlman about her—he knows her and he is entirely safe—I asked him about her capacity for reviewing, and he thought it inadvisable to leave much responsibility with her and gave his reasons which seemed adequate to me. Not that she might not review a single book or two, O.K., but not to direct any work. So you were and are right here.[17]

With Merriam's agreement, Grace contacted Pierre who answered at once, saying, van Male was enthusiastic, and all the rest of them—and to come along any time. "He has written a card almost daily," wrote Grace to Merriam,

> ... adding ideas to his original ones and there does seem to be quite a bit of flattered attention account the suggestion. I think you'll get a good gob of reviews, and I have from the first said we didn't want any smartie panning, but sober, generous, honest review—honest opinions, but not with the idea of seeing how smart a reviewer can show himself to be at the expense of the author.

Grace had other news for Merriam.

> Following Times (N.Y.) book review and a radio broadcast Edwin C. Hill, Columbia Network, *Riding the High Country* jumped to Caxton's best seller (and that's nothing so hot) and Mr. Gipson immediately passed out more and wider publicity on it hoping for the best. *And* people from all over wrote me letters about the review and the radio talk, letters that almost had to be acknowledged at least. Hence the eye ache. Caxton said he had orders "from hell to breakfast" with a N.Y. jobber taking a small bunch—25.
>
> John Tucker, home from Europe, caught the review on the air in New Jersey and nearly died of loneliness listening to it.
>
> It's a good break. I am still hoping this year some time to do a little more for The Frontier in the way of money.

If you want those books passed around to the reviewers I have named whom I know, send them to Pierre Kouchneroff, 1050 Sherman street, Denver, and he will see that they are tended to. Mrs. Wagner's address is 409 Lewis Avenue, Billings. I can't possibly *read* any thing not imperative for a time.

When you have time, answer my question about whether the last news notes were any good. I did get some rather pleasant comments on them. Leafing thru an old Sat Review I found William Rose Benet's criticism, and admission that once in a while I struck off a fine line, like "The lighted rooms that the brave are," etc; and found several items about Port in the Wheat in N.Y. journals, hitherto unnoticed. The first book is so exciting, and all others increasingly less so.

I have a few good things—and by the way, turn down what you do not want of my stories at your convenience, for O'Brien is starting an English magazine and "invites" me to send him some stories. Good! Also, on strength of the Sibly and Hill reviews, the N.Y. Brooklyn Eagle also asked me for stories. I have a lot to tell you when once it gets ripe and is not still hanging fire.

Sincerely—all good and grateful thoughts, Grace[18]

Grace continued to hear from her other poet friends. Henrietta wrote from New York that she had "Concerto" published in *Kosmos,* a Philadelphia publication. Merriam had returned a story to her, saying most of the stuff had to be regional but saying it was "finely created and should like to see it published."

Henrietta caught Grace up on their mutual friends in the writing business.

What's new with you? Saw Frontier and liked your poem. Haven't gotten around to read your other stuff yet. Have to wait till I get some money. See where you reviewed—unfavorably—Nola Henderson's book. THIS MUCH IS MINE. She happens to admire you tremendously, and was a bit taken aback. Most of her reviews have been rather splendid. I haven't read the book yet; intend doing so this Saturday; but really don't expect too much. Depth isn't one of Nola's best points. She's nice tho. We've gone on bats together…Appel seems to be making good all around. Sold stuff in everything I lay my hands on. O'Briens's British mag. Has just taken something of his, too. DeJong's book BELLY FULLA STRAW should be out this week, if it isn't already. Heard its damn good. He just sold something to ESQUIRE. Let me hear from you, dear. I'm busy as hell—or else I'm afraid I'd be rather lonely. Heard Windsor Quarterly is folding up. A shame too. But God—how many to take its place in some form or other.

Love. Henrietta[19]

Merriam to Coates: February 14, 1934

Dear GSC,

Mr. Morrisette thought that one way in which we could improve, one, the writing being done in the Northwest, and two, the average of books published in the Northwest, would be to write very critical reviews of the poor books and publish them in our columns. I think there is something in that contention. However, he agreed with me that most of the poor books could be handled by simply listing them as "Books Received". I think that if we wrote to publishers for the most distinguished books, we might receive a surprising number of them. For the time being, I should like requests to go out from my office, largely because I can enclose certain publicity material, and because I should like to center the attention of publishers on Missoula and the State University; will you, therefore, send me the names of any distinguished books which you think should be reviewed in our columns a they appear, or if possible, before they appear. Kouchneroff and the Denver group in general, if interested, might be on the lookout for such books. In each case I will have the books sent to the person who requests them, or to the person to whom he wished them sent.

I do not know the final arrangements that Gipson made with John Barrows. I had a letter from Gipson a while ago stating that he knew I had written the book, or at least had had a large hand in the writing, and therefore he was going to propose to John that my name appear jointly with his—a la Coates-Tucker! This made me laugh, because, as you now know, John respects my literary judgment not at all, I think. Gipson got the idea in his head that I had written the book, and that if my name were coupled with it in some way, it would have a wider sale. He certainly gets queer ideas.

I meant to say that The Frontier does not ask for the "junky books", so far as I know. I am positive that I have not asked for them. Also, please feel free to keep any books which you review which you may wish to possess permanently...

...Windsor Quarterly is suspending publication, and has asked us to take over its unexpired subscriptions, and I am doing so.

Cordially yours, HGM[20]

Linderman to Coates: April 24, 1934

Dear Mrs. Coates

That bit you saw in the MNA[Montana News Association] was done 25 years ago, and I'd forgotten all about it. It appeared when the MNA was brand new. Percy Raban was with me when I took that photo, and he was then the MNA (with Wadsworth) Cheely was not in the game then.

My, Goodness, what a worker you must be! I couldn't do a tenth of the work you turn out even if I wished to.

Lovely here now. Flowers, birds, and high water already—and it's only Apl.

Say, I quit smoking two months ago and life's full of snags ever since. I haven't even smelled of a pipe or cigarette since I quit—and I think I'll stick, but I miss smoking.

I liked your article about BEYOND LAW. It couldn't have been better. And the darned book paid me $171.00

I think I'll do a kid's book on the grizzly bear now, and call the game out. And what a game it is! But it's a sickness, and there's so little one can do about it.

Yours sincerely, FBL[21]

COATES TO LINDERMAN: NOVEMBER 13, 1934

Dear Sign-talker,

I thought you might be interested in these clippings about Ashe. Do not return them.

In regard to one point, I did not make myself clear: bout the lesser personages. Just as Plenty-Coups' grandfather knew that the real point of the butterfly chasing was not catching the butterfly and rubbing the chest with its wings—that the real point was the strength and skill gained by the running and dodging—that the butterfly gave its speed and alertness only in a symbolic sense: just so, I asked, might not the wise men have taken the lesser Personages to be symbolic personifications of human traits. Old-man Coyote seemed to me so completely the counterpart of our subconscious monkey-traits that I asked the question. He is the thing within us that betrays us and laughs.

Perhaps you do not have the experience, but occasionally I hear a mounting tinkle of laughter from something that is not under my control, that laughs at me. It is my personal "Old-man Coyote"—and I do not think Indian and White Psychology is always so unlike as we assume. Text books comment on the Indian's way of squaring himself with the animals he is compelled—or impelled—to kill; but does any reasonably "white" person kill even an insect without a quick, tacit—perhaps infinitely condensed—moment of explanatory and apologetic justification of himself? I know I don't.

But you need not bother about going into discussion of this—I am mentioning it—incidentally—wile[sic] giving you a smile over Ashe.

Sincerely yours, Grace Stone Coates[22]

Grace wrote to many places and people to find information for the historical pieces she continued to write. She corresponded with the Barrows who had moved to California.

JOHN AND JOSLEY BARROWS TO COATES: APRIL 29, 1934

Your letter…has just been received so your questions are answered at once.
The Carroll Trail was on the south side of the North Fork of the Musselshell.
It crossed Flagstaff and Checkerboard Creeks and was between Fort Howie
and the North Fork. It crossed the North Fork at Gaugler's place when the
water was not too high…Copperopolis was nearly on the divide, about half
way between WSS and Martinsdale. It was the change station. I do not believe
that any stage made the practice of driving the 37 miles without change of
horses. It is possible that the Carroll Trail crossed and recrossed the North
Fork at Hall's ranch, but I think not. Consult Billy.[23] He knows the old road
like a book…[24]

JOHN BARROWS TO COATES: MAY 11, 1934

…I told you the other day that I was not sure that the old trail was south
of the North Fork in that section above Hal's Ranch. I could see reasons why
it might follow down the north side of the creek in that section…I think your
clap trap fenced line poetry is devilish clever, but your philosophy, if that
expresses it, needs over hauling…

I am dictating between groans and my wife is making notes between sniffles.
Heaven help us.[25]

JOHN BARROWS TO COATES, FROM SAN DIEGO: JUNE 10, 1934

…In accordance with my promise to send you only inferior stuff, I enclose
two shorts. The stage coach item is to help Johnny Reynolds, although you
may not be able to use it. I had planned to make it longer and include a
pageant of the road, showing the types encountered fifty years ago, but I have
been unable to decide on the form. I believe there is good material in it.

We hear you have had a rain. I hope you drown.

P.S. Perhaps I was too harsh. Please substitute "I hope you have to buy a
new umbrella."[26]

More responsibility for the Writers' Conference fell on Grace in 1934. Merriam
coordinated with Grace in June.

Dear Mrs. Coates, Mr. [Edmund] Freeman will submit a program for the
Writers' Conference to you within the next ten days. It will have to be final. I
am substituting for your talk on preparing manuscripts for editors the topic
"Contracts With Publishers". Bob Struckman who is down for the topic "What
I have learned from Magazine Editors" can very well incorporate the material
concerning the preparation of manuscripts. For your four o'clock talk on

markets I have substituted Bertram Guthrie of the Lexington *Leader* to talk on "Book Reviewing". The Bolleses[27] will be present. He will "stress the need for accuracy in depicting Montana backgrounds, to indicate some mistakes that are frequently made; and to list some convenient sources of references", and Mrs. Bolles wishes to "discuss literary competition from a general stand point…her experiences with literary contests, I maintain, dates back ten years, when she won the state essay contest for high school students. We have both kept track of all national contests for several years, and feel that these offer valuable opportunity the beginning writer." Harriette Cushman is going to give a report on an investigation in reading made by the 4-H Clubs. For the Tuesday evening meeting I have only a talk by Mr. Coleman on "Western Books and Writers". What else do you suggest. The rest of the program remains as originally sent to you.

Mr. Freeman will attend to such matters as room assignments, and you can consult him on any other matters you wish.[28]

Overwork was beginning to tell on Grace and friends and correspondents were beginning to notice. Max Lieber was a literary agent.

Max Lieber to Coates: June 22, 1934

Dear Grace:

My, my, what a sad and incoherent letter. However, I can understand, and I hope that things will be better for you soon. It's too bad that a fine writer like you has to fritter away so much of her time and energy on other stuff, and I certainly hope that after your writer's conference is over you can get the time and peace of mind necessary to write something that's worthy of you. So take it easy, my dear, and I'm sure that everything will be all right.[29]

Linderman to Coates: June 27, 1934

Dear Mrs. Coates,

I'll try to reach Missoula early Sunday, and I'll do my best to be of use there. And don't get skittish. Hell—there's nobody who's got you beaten in that game, so why get skittish. Be Injin. Heaven knows that an Injin never loses poise, that nobody buffalos him.

Just got back from the sun dance. I'm tired and reasonably happy. Had an interesting time, as usual. Verified some points, learned a little more, and tried to make the new deal clear to the painted-ones. Difficult, but worth trying.

Yes indeed, Mrs. Linderman would like the magazines. You can never do wrong by sending the Frau something to read—and she'll read it, remember.

Just before leaving for the sun dance I finished Frank Hill's "The Westward Star" a book-length poem. He has sent me chapter by chapter. Now, after I had offered the desired suggestions all the way through, he asked for another reading etc. I did it hurriedly, and sent the proofs back within 36 hours. I hope the work will make him some money—but I know it will *not*. It's a very splendid thing, with some wonderful spots. However I'm unfitted for such work. I'm not a poet in any sense. But I liked Frank Hill.

Frederic F. Van De Water's Life of Gen Custer comes out in October. Fritz tells me that careful research has proven the Gen. To be a (I don't use such words as Fritz used) I'll have an early copy of the book and will let you read it.

If you are the wagon-boss please let me know where I'll have to camp while in Missoula. I hope you tell me to take my old room.

Rain—rain—and I'm grateful

Your'n, F.B.L.[30]

After a successful writers' conference, Grace was again in good health and spirits.

COATES TO MERRIAM: JULY 28, 1934

Dear HGM,

It is bourne in on me how much I have to be grateful to you for. All my contacts at Missoula, however slight and brief they are, add much to my year's life. I don't know just where I'd be mentally if it were not for you and The Frontier and Missoula and the writers' conference. There isn't any way for a man who does things for other people to make a reckoning of how much he does do. Perhaps I get more letters from women with only one shirt (Who therefore can't come to the conferences) than you do; but even the fact that there is a conference and that they are remembered means a good deal to them. I had a rather poignant letter from one woman who told me, shamefacedly, how her poverty kept her from attending.

Because the publicity sheets carried my name I was flooded with letters of thanks for the announcements. The first were stereotyped, and I threw them away without thinking of sending them to you. But here is one that seems more personal, that I am sending on. You may know the woman, I don't

And Fred Ward [now publisher of the White Sulphur Springs newspaper, he had been principal of the Ismay school in 1931] was here yesterday! I am taking over the damned news work for Gerry Breen, again; she did it five years and is fed up. So I'll be telling Mr. Ward that Mrs. Piffle is having a party for Mrs. Griffle and no blizzard about it! I'm glad he is here. He ought to do me a lot of good. He is a real guy, and I hope I see him often.[31]

Linderman to Coates: August 6, 1934

Dear Mrs. Coates,

The fire situation is bad enough, and yet there are no fires that threaten Goose Bay just now. Nevertheless I'm sticking close. Thanks for your expressions of wonder.

The Frau has written you about her impressions of Anthony Adverse. I did not read the book. The Frau read me bits here and there—and if the author knew as little about all the subjects he touches as he knew about making clothes of a bear-hide (freshly skinned) he wouldn't interest me.

Thank you for writing your friend in N.Y.C. Maybe something will come of it. Hope so.

The Book is finished. It's a little one of about 16 to 30 thousand words. About like STUMPY. I began to type it—and then the darned pumping engine went on the blink. Had to spend three days tinkering the machinery. Now I'll get back to typing (maybe)

H.G.M. and his daughter were up for a day and night. He appears better. Hope he will go slower from now on. But I fear he will not...

...We are both distressed to learn that you are ill—or have been ill. Goodness, take care of yourself. "Chest" doesn't sound very good. It may mean too many things.

I've been so anxious to get away and go to the Crow country again. I so want to see old Pretty-shield. You know how much I think of her. Well, now, after months of waiting, I get a letter from a mixed-blood saying that she declares that "no woman danced the sun-dance" etc. She says (so I'm told) that she didn't tell me that a Crow woman *did* dance, etc. She says (according to this letter) that the interpreter made a mistake. GOSH—GOSH I'm plumb sick at heart over this. And of course she *did* tell just what I wrote, and she can't get around it. I just must see her, and make her admit one thing or the other. If she lied I'm out on a limb, because you see I have known many women to dance the sun-dance—but not Crow women. There's the rub in this damned situation. And nobody who is under 75 can have seen a Crow sun-dance (I believe) Nice sitiation [sic] isn't it? I just can't believe that her mind is gone, or that she lied to me. I *can't* I know you'll understand. If Nahpee would only send a lot or rain I'd get away somehow and go to the Crow country and have talk with P-S myself. I've *got* to. This may sound small to you but to me it's simply a mountain; yes, a range of mountains.

Best to you—Ho! F.B.L.[32]

As recognition of his work finally came to Saroyan, he was both embarrassed and thrilled.

SAROYAN TO COATES: AUGUST 12, 1934

Dear Grace:

I am becoming the most miserable literary success you ever saw, and it's spoiling my swell complexion, which burns me up plenty. Vanity Fair writes and asks me for some stuff: I sit down and write a story a day for three days and shoot them along. In no time at all Vanity Fair busy…buys…one of the stories for a hundred dollars and wires for a picture. I have pictures taken and shoot them along, too. And they've got me plumb dizzy this way. The story is called Little Caruso: it is solid American humor, a new kind of story for me.

I have an advance copy of my book and it is a swell looking affair. Advance copies will be arriving soon, and as soon as they do I am sending one to you, and I hope you are going to like what's in the book. Since the stories in the book were written, January of this year, I have written enough for a couple more books, and some other junk too. Did you care for An-Ha Ah-Ha in the current Mercury. A few writers here and there think it is something outstanding. I do too, but who am I vs. fifty millions?…[33]

COATES TO SAROYAN: AUGUST 21, 1934

Dear Will,

I am just back from Chicago. It's this way, Will, about what you write (for me): even what others might criticize in your writings is right—for me. You are right as the shape of an oak leaf is right; and your writing always seemed to me to bear the same relation to you that any aspect you care to name of the oak leaf does to the oak leaf.

That isn't exactly it, either, but it is part of it. Through your writing more than thru any other person's I knew, I understood your mind. Your writing was more nearly your mind in action than any one else's; and at no time was merely you manipulating words. That is why you are right even when you are wrong—and that is why it inwardly embarrassed me to play the pedant with you. An oak leaf (I'm not talking about your California liveoaks!) has a certain shape because it is an oak leaf, not because it saw that shape would sell, or saw a maple making that kind of leaves, or because it is a mathematical formula. Talent does what it can and genius does what it must, and I know you do what you must.

I'm in a hurry for your book—you know it, but you don't understand how much of a hurry.

I read much good writing that I am neither interested in nor enjoy, because it is my business to read it. But what you write I less read than immerse myself in. As for the Mercury story, all I can say is that it is perfect of its kind, whole-born, intelligible to a comparatively limited number, and entirely you. My surprise is that the Mercury had brains to use it.

Gosh, Will, I'm so glad for you. I can't even be sorry that the busting wide open as a success also has its flat side—If I could get a break and make $100 at a crack, my husband would respect me! (That's supposed to be partly humorous.)

Because I was in grief when you used to write me long letters, I could have sounded sentimental had I tried to write all I felt. But this moment I'm too sound—too full of autumnal wood smoke, August snapdragons and peach canning to fear being sentimental, so I'll try to express what I always feel about you this way, that something between us, some part of you plus some part of me, makes a unit, an entity. I could lose myself in your letters when not to lose myself in something was torture. I'm glad if, while you were helping restore my balance, I was of some service to you. How I'd like to be with you, but I'd want to meet you in unvitiated[sic] space—I can't know people, in any real sense meet them,—a person, I mean, not people—in crowds. When you recover from the rather dizzying experience of finding people want what you have to give, I hope you'll once more write what they can't possibly want, because it is too good. By that time maybe your name will sell them even what is beyond them. Anyway, I raise the pontifical fingers and bless you, bless you. And write if you want to, be silent if you want to be, it is all one. But send the book—sending or not sending that isn't all one!

  Grace[34]

Grace and her sister Helen Hyde attended the Century of Progress exposition in Chicago during the summer. The local paper also reported that Grace and Henderson had gone to Livingston to attend the eighty-ninth birthday party of Pat Tucker and then on to Salesville to visit the Hydes.

In late summer, Grace received a copy of William Saroyan's *The Daring Young Man on the Flying Trapeze and Other Stories*. It was inscribed:

Dear Grace: I do not know what to say, or how. This: not giving: perhaps returning. Anyway, in our time we have spoken together from a room in California to a room in Montana, and sometimes without words. I do not feel proud of this book of William Saroyan, a little, since he became nearly what he wished to become, though God alone knows why. Since he refused death, one way or another. As always, smiling. "good wishes" Will[35]

Grace was delighted and in her excitement rushed to send a telegram:

WILLIAM SAROYAN
348 CARL ST

I READ UNTIL EXCITEMENT MAKES ME PACE THE FLOOR AND
PACE UNTIL I AM QUIETED AND DRAWN BACK TO YOU THE TOUCH
OF WHAT LIVES QUICKENS AS THE TOUCH OF WHAT IS DEAD
BENUMBS AND I THINK IN WAYS NOT COME AT BY INTENTION YOU
WILL HAVE CHANGED MEN

GRACE STONE COATES[36]

Coates added a letter to Saroyan the next day:

Dear Will, reading a few words, and then closing the book thrusting it
from me; walking; to the end of the room, about, back again, and picking up
the book to read as long as I can until the inner pressure grows too great
again. Wanting to wire you, now, at once before I had even read more than
the preface—and tugging me back the feeling of sympathy for Henderson
and his perplexities…like digging a hole in the ground and burning a bill…I
wouldn't mind making him angry, but worrying him…worrying him because
I can not be made to realize the gravity of situations, so that I stop being
alive…and the enhappying conclusion that some persons must be dead and
worry because that is the way they are made inside, and that my sole necessity
is to remain inside the way I am…

The station agent took the message. His wife called me into their living
quarters to look at some sweet pease—or is it peas? Pease looks like that thickish
green soup that so reminds one of unhealthy chicken years. And while I admired
the sweet pease wishing they had not been jammed into a tight headed round
mass with every individual beauty lost, the agent came in to remark that the
message was too deep for him. He is a fatherly old soul with bright tired brown
eyes and fringe of white hair. "It is too deep for me" he said. I answered, "But
you aren't required to know what it means. Just send the words."

When I went through the office again he said, "I get it now. You are just
reading the book." Then both man and wife bend over the message, and when
I started to leave the woman detained me. They asked about you—and I was
once more betrayed—and spoke instead of remaining silent. When I had
finished the woman whose inherent foolishness has not been tempered even
by so much as a mastery of telegraphy said, "Is he married?" and when all I
could think of to say was, "Oh, my God, Oh my God," she pursued me with,
"Has he lots of money?"

As soon as I had wired you I became happy inside. I do not know why what
happens to us inside wipes off so many flea bites.

As I started cross lots for the station a man unloading boxes called to me
that the train was forty minutes late. As I crossed the street a woman called to
that I needn't hurry, the train was late; and as I took the crossing to the station

the agent's wife assured me I had plenty of time, the train was late. Each was aggrieved that I didn't in some overt way modify my conduct in accord with their information. Read that Wyoming story about the charge for gas in a recent STORY and you have my days and nights. When the rollers of my life are seated truly on their carriage I can extract the nutriment—it merely means sluicing a little more water thru my gills instead of a little less—but what about the days when my color fades and my gills fan weakly? If you do not mind fish riding on garage doors—

Grace[37]

Grace was finally able to accept the oddities of the life in the small town of Martinsdale. She wanted to assure Saroyan about the acceptance of his book.

SAROYAN TO COATES: OCTOBER 11, 1934 (POSTCARD)

Dear Grace:

I'm not going to be much interested in what the critics say. I know all about it. I saw Rascoe's blurb, and was pleased: hoping it might help sell the book. I want it to sell. I want money. Please thank Pierre Kouchneroff. And thank you for talking about the book to the University ladies. Oh there will be enemies of course, but I love them. I don't care what anyone likes to think. Mostly, everything I have written I have written for myself. Thank you for your friendship. Very good wishes.

Will[38]

Dear Will,

Of course I'll resent all your reviews, they will make me dance with impatience—not that they won't be good but because the reviewers will be so afraid of saying something that they'll have to temporize and minimize and if and hem and maybe.

I don't know how I missed this one, when I was watching so eagerly—until Pierre Kouchneroff of Denver sent it on to me. He has talked to all the bigwigs of Denver about you and the book dealers. He is a Russian pianist t.b. going to Los Angeles. Great friend. I love him. In the Jewish National Hospital, and is withered by that fact. Concert pianist who couldn't return to the stage to take his ovation at the conclusion of the first half of his debut—because he was off stage making an oblation of his lungs. Never could go on—I wish I had the setting—I'd write a story. He didn't tell me this—wrest anything of gloom from him if you can! Such a man—always sunny, always the one others take their glooms to. He would never whisper a word of personal stuff except by or with the most delicate reserve to a wholly trusted friend.

Anyway, he has the artistic world of Denver by the tail and I don't know exactly how.

But back to reviews and you—I am talking to the University Women in Bozeman, Mont., soon—and you are the subject—at least your book is what I'm talking about. I sic the bookstores on you and hope it will help. I say to such reviewers as those who find your work genius but irregular that artificial flowers have their petals, but they die—how do you spell die? Scrupulously uniform; but that I have never seen a living flower with petals identical. What enrages me is that where you are wrong you are right *for you* and fools can't see what I mean, and I, a fool, can't say it so they understand.

Well, back to the galley—My love to you—I didn't dare send you my love overtly when you were lonely for fear it might "take."

> *Grace*

I think I have not thanked you for the photo—taking it for granted you knew how much I cared for it. Yews, panther—I know. I've panthered a bit in my time—and I like all of them. You have a helpful mug, young man, helpful for a career I mean.[39]

In 1939 Saroyan wrote the play, *The Time of Your Life*, for which he received both New York Drama Critics' Circle Award and the Pulitzer Prize. He later refused the Pulitzer.

He was the one of the first American writers of his century to focus so much attention on immigrant communities, and treated his characters with what the *San Francisco Chronicle* called "the old Saroyan luminousness, which is to say with an insight fresh as that of an unusually perceptive child."[40] Such a similarity to Coates' work defines the like approach of both authors, or possibly the influence Coates had on Saroyan's work.

Grace's elusive novel continued to cause Merriam to chastise Grace, and in September he wrote,

> For some time I have been wishing to write you that my mind is set upon your submitting to Knopf before January 1 your second novel. I wish that you would set your determination to the same end. If you are going to continue as a writer—and you must do so—it is time that another book by you should appear. The book should be a novel and not another volume of poems. Knopf I know from recent correspondence with him wishes to see that second novel, the sooner the better. (By the way, Knopf has come thru for a page of advertising again for the year for F& M.) If you will get out the Lit News for the winter number of F. & M. I will excuse you (!) from further Frontier work. You should I think, even give over the newspaper tasks you now carry on, in order to concentrate on the novel. If necessary, you should isolate

yourself socially until the novel has been completed. You should clear your mind of all other matters and write the novel. You should, you should!

This is the first time, I believe, that I have intruded upon your private affairs. I do so now deliberately—and I hope emphatically—because you own to yourself and to the literature of our part of the country further writing. Forgive me if you can. However, I am used to not being forgiven.

The autumn issue of F. & M. is being delayed by publishers failing to send in copy for their ads, and we need their money so badly that we cannot go to press without the ads. The winter issue we shall bring off the press on Dec. 1. I should therefore like the Literary News material not later than Nov. 12.[41]

The story "Choice" was included in list of "Distinctive Short Stories in American Magazines" by Edward O'Brien in the fall.[42]

Grace was still struggling with her novel and wrote Saroyan.

…Touch me with your finger, Will. I need help. I am working on the novel that lies back of "Black Cherries" and I'm stuck, and need help. Only the living, I mean those who are alive, can help those who are alive—but stuck.

Will, did I ever tell you this? You know when you were writing to me in 1930, I was not able to write you as I would have had I not been psychically shellshocked. I was so nearly over the verge of real psychic shock that once when I tried to write a check in May I dated it November and couldn't sign it because I had forgotten my name. I had put too much out of my mind, and some things I wanted to keep had tagged along. But that is not the point: such small odd things were the first sign of wakening to life again. A stranger on the street, walking about the pace I was setting, helping himself to gum, fell in beside me and offered me gum. That wasn't funny, but my mind realized it would have been funny if I could have felt it at all; and a few days after that, when I stepped to the front porch the air smelled good (Montana air has a peculiar spicyness every one comments on at first experience) and because it did feel—smell—good it hurt me so I began to cry—and in a week or so, as I lay in bed, I noticed an insulator on the radio wire sparkle back of my hand (as my hand lay palm up on the lower sheet) felt the sheet rub my hand as it ever so faintly muscularly *thought* toward the bright bit of glass—exactly like a baby's response. I knew then I was coming out of it—but such a slow, slow process.

It was your book that wakened me enough to set me to my own novel again. And what the hell good did it do me now I'm stuck!

Well—here goes—I send you seven kisses—for the seven sins…of the Virgin or whatever…

Grace

With all our letters, I have never written you freely—my freedom is a certain wild humor that a person has to take long steps to understand and keep up with. You see, when I am truly I, I do not say the next thing but the one after the next; and unless one can keep up he—men especially—get frightened and think I'm trying to do God knows what. I did not write freely to you, because when you were young and hadn't written a book, I was afraid of injuring you in some queer, unexpected way. And I was right, for the psychically sick spread their disorder, and most especially where they...don't want to.

G.[43]

She expressed some of the same thoughts to Linderman who rebuffed them.

LINDERMAN TO COATES: OCTOBER 11, 1934

Dear Mrs. Coates,

Nope, you aren't sick; you're just ornery. Say, that was a good letter. And you're right. My pride's hurt in the Pretty-shield matter. That, and losing faith in that old woman, hurts. As for my being honest in "spots" I'll admit that the spots are tiny, that it's only a rash, an occasional rash. However Pretty-shield's error becomes my own, because if I really knew my stuff I'd have prevented her from saying Crow women dance sun dances, you see. I think your suggestion is good. I'll see what my publishers will do about a "sticker" in remaining books—and all that come out in future. The Frau got an awful kick out of your comments on clubs etc. And you are dead right about Alice Frost. She's a sure-enough person. I wish you'd write to her once or twice. She would appreciate it I'm certain; and she can't get much attention where she lives. I wish I could start something good her way (and I reckon your letters might be good)

Have you seen Frank Hill's "The Westward Star"? It's a fine thing. I wish it might make him some money, because I know he needs money; but I don't see how it can. He believes his story will be picturized. Let's hope so. Goodness, he has put in a lot of hard work on The Westward Star.

And Van de Water's book on Gen Custer ought to be a good one. I know that he has done lots of research work for the thing. He calls it The Glory-hunter—and when it gets here I'll give you a look at it—if you're interested.

You never saw such weather. Everything's so beautiful. Of course that cold snap killed the leaves on the maples so that they lack their usual fall color. The tamaracks are just turning now, and the hillsides are wonderfully bright in the sunlight. Better come over and visit. I reckon I'm going to give our dog to somebody who has sheep or cattle. He's a darn pest at night. He will yap at the deer, and they are cake-walking all over this place, right up to the windows. It's their season for visiting, it seems, though it's a bit early. And goodness,

FRANK BIRD LINDERMAN

Montana Historical Society, Helena

how they ramble around. Anyhow I'd rather see wild creatures from the windows than the dog—and he just will not permit even a chipmunk to live within sight of the house (though they manage it somehow).[44]

LINDERMAN TO COATES: NOVEMBER 9, 1934

Dear Mrs. Coates

By golly I was *goin'* to. Then this morning along came your letter. Thank you for both the newspaper article and the letter—and also for your determination to say something to the Women's Clubs about Montana authors.

The Frau is baking cake. I can smell it—mebby you can, too. It's loud enough.

And did you notice the election? Gee! (funny, but I'm glad of it, me) Sic 'em, say I.

When are you coming over here? Better do it pretty soon, or there will be no Goose Bay to come to.

Got the darn Bear-book all typed, and now I'm telling about an old dog I used to own. Think I've got the wrong idea of telling the dog story, though. I'll see later.

Why can't you come over here? I'll meet you and fetch you, and I'll feed you flapjacks—and everything.

Fritz Van de Water's book, GLORY-HUNTER is a whiz. It shows up Gen. Custer and proves statements. I wrote a short review of it for the publishers, but I do not know the first thing about reviewing a book, me. A child could beat me at the game. Wish I did know how to do the job. People are beginning to ask me for reviews, and I have to tell them I'm incapable. But I just had to try in this case. Beautiful here today—

> *Ho! F.B.L.*[45]

LINDERMAN TO COATES: NOVEMBER 14, 1934

Dear Mrs. Coates

Gosh—gosh, but we laughed over your club story. One couldn't believe such things if he hadn't seen and heard such clubs in action. But here's a new one; and you'll appreciate it because you told me that the woman who plays the lead assured you that she "always got to the heart of things", that she'd get the "*truth*" about the Pretty-shield affair. Well, she *did*. She went right after it just as a dog goes after fleas. Yesterday I got a letter from her, beginning with the statement that she had "*a good report to make*". She says, further, that whoever told me that the Crows *didn't dance the sun-dance* either lied or didn't know what they were talking about. She says that several old Crow women told her that Pretty-shield *told the truth about that sun-dance* and the shooting of Sitting-heifer, that the only *mistakes* she made was in saying that Sitting-heifer *danced,* and *pledged* the sun-dance. Now, I needn't tell you that there never was any controversy as to whether the Crows danced sun-dances. Everybody knows they did. Quite unconsciously the investigator *proved* that Pretty-shield made *misstatements,* or *lied,* when she said that the Crow woman *danced* and *gave* the sun-dance. *These,* alone, were the points in question, not the darned sun-dance itself. In other words the investigator, in getting "at the heart of the matter, ran onto a gizzard and thought it was a heart." It shows that the lady had never read the story she was investigating, and that she knew not one darned thing about it. She just clucked and clucked, God bless her. "Tucker and Cortez" Yep, I savvy, Me. We are in perfect accord. The then, the common, barn-yard variety of any of Nahpees's species are but space-fillers, potential mud for crack-filling.

However, I had long ago admitted that I'd permitted Pretty-shield to make misstatements about that sun-dance, confessed my error to a man who knows less about the Indian than the club-woman-subject of this letter.

I hope your novel will have a woman's club in it—and that you'll get it all so fast that you'll be surprised. I'm so disgusted with the darned game that I don't expect to play it any more. And yet I earnestly wish you to go on—and WIN, and you can win, I'm sure. But don't forget those Nahpee poems.

The Frau had a good laugh over your story.

Sincerely, F.B.L.[46]

Linderman was shocked when Grace told him of her trip in a small plane.

Dear Mrs. Coates…

I'm glad that you're glad, and I'm tickled at your "crowing", but see here, Lady Grace, you stay off them things. "Over the snowies in Burt Walker's plane" indeed! Want me to have to follow along behind, or on the trial of the darn tin, and he'p scrape you off the scenery with my jack-knife—Goodness knows that you're up in the air' *enough* without employing gasoline to lift you *higher.* Be satisfied to let your spirits go up, but keep your feet on the ground, dog-on it.

I let you know about the Texas thing as soon as I got the news myself. Couldn't do more, could I? And because I'm telling you all I know about this literary game I'll let you in on what the figures actually mean (as far as helping me to stay here at Goose Bay is concerned) Elmer Green, formerly with the World Book Co, and my close friend, has written that last year a book, "The History of the American People" which he got out with the help of one Dr. Robbins, went to its tenth printing. He says that last year they sold to the schools 26,000 copies of the book and that his royalty on the 26,000 copies amounted to $260. (which was half the royalty paid by the Book Co) The other half $260 went to Dr. Robbins. So as far as money goes there's nothing to excite one in the news from Texas. And yet I'm tickled pink over it, because it's a distinct boost, a wonderful recognition, and I'm grateful for it I can tell you. And I surely did glow over your words concerning it. It's good to learn things about this game we play, to know that always an author gets the small end of the play, and it's good to know the truth when we see it, even though few will tell the truth in the field. So far I've had two selections by the Junior Literary Guild, and an interest (a small one) in a Book of The Month selection, and there was little in any of them. I even refused to let the Guild have BEYOND LAW, which was mistake, because the book paid but $171.00 so far. My share of the Book of the Month Club's selection was $32.50, and I never got a cent of it. And this year AMERICAN, by the World Book Col, paid $8.42. I'd like to stay here, and go on, but nearly 18 years of trying to make a living with books has shown me, at last, that I must move while I'm able. Don't you see? Or do you think me a piker? I've tried my best, and no magazine will take a second look at what I turn out—and goodness knows that books do not pay. If I hadn't managed to earn money other/wise we'd have been in bad shape. But, thank goodness, I've always been able to make a little money when I set out to do it. But, of course, I wanted mightily to play this game, and I've stayed with it dangerously long. I believe you'll savvy, and not believe that I'm wanting to *run*. You'd better come over and eat some flapjacks. Ho!

F.B.L.

You've got me to wanting to see your new book. Can't you fetch the m.s.? Maybe we could all sit around the fire-place and listen—and have a big time.[47]

Dec. 1934

If this were my last Christmas bell
    As sure as I'm a born'er
I'd scrub my knees and elbows well
    To get 'em ready for the coroner.

I'd frisk my husband's wardrobe clear
    Of pants with mended fannies—
I know how grief makes relatives peer
    In all the nooks and crannies!

I'd knock unfinished work for a goal,
    Be sure that my hair was curled;

And with you and a bottle and dish of ravioli

I'd sit on top of the world.

COATES TO SAROYAN: CIRCA 1934

Dear Will, I could say a lot but haven't time and it is all horse feathers anyway. I made 500 girls Saroyan conscious, and did you the favor of NOT telling them to write you any letters. I picked you for the subject, or victim, not as a favor to you but for easy material for myself. So needn't say thankyou. I get most of the N.Y. reviews, that is I get the NYTimes Herald-Tribune, Sat Review, and numerous literary "littles" and I get fun out of the stir about young man Saroyan. I note you reviewed—can't recall the name of that mountain tragedy. You should have begun in the middle—but, hell, you don't want criticism from the sticks.

I thought the last half of your review good enough to atone for the first part. And it's better to rise than to start high and peter out.

I have very individual—I mean also clear-cut and definite feelings about death. But if I should try to express them, at once I am set down as a coward whistling to keep up my courage; or a pessimist too sluggish to want to live. But before I was 5 or 6, and I got the entire matter adjusted all at once, someway. It seems obvious to me that death is all that gives life any value. I don't say I'm right for you, but right for me; and surely if we grow old we ripen for death and welcome it. I believe we grow hungry for death—quite above the region of "sick of life" ishness or pessimism. Well I didn't mean to get started on profundities.

Congratulations Paul Engel etc etc and ETC

Either I don't know my San

Francisco or I was thinking of

Two other men.

GSC[48]

Grace's delight at another new Saroyan effort caused her to wire him:

MARTINSDALE MONT DEC 23 1936

WILLIAM SAROYAN
5959 FRANKLIN HOLLYWOOD CALIF
LONG TO REMEMBER BUT NEVER LONG ENOUGH TO FORGET PERIOD I READ YOU IN CORNET WITH DELIGHT AS ALWAYS PERIOD YOU HAVE MADE ME THREE TIMES HAPPY: IN THE MOMENT

COMMA IN ANTICIPATION COMMA AND IN LONG HOURS OF READING TO COME

GRACE[49]

Merriam continued to urge Grace to write. The promised novel following *Black Cherries* was still not finished. Illness again forced Grace to ease up on the work she was doing at the end of the year.

MERRIAM TO COATES: JANUARY 17, 1935

> Dear G.S.C.,
> I have deliberately not asked you to give us help with the *Frontier* for some months in the hope that you would be pushing along the writing of the novel. I shall be happy when again you feel that you can give us some time. I hope that your recent illness was not due to too persistent application to the novel. Mr. Branch has taken over all matters of make-up; he also reads all manuscripts that come into the magazine. He is a prodigious worker. So far this year he is the virtual editor. Fitzgerald,[50] who is now in Hollywood, has done nothing for us since June. Financially we go into debt with each issue.[51]

Grace did send Merriam a story for the Summer issue of *The Frontier*—"Far Back, Far Forward," another in the series of her childhood. There are few stories based on Montana experiences.

MERRIAM TO COATES: MARCH 6, 1935

> I suppose you have heard of Courtland Matthews' project, the publishing of Northwest Literary Review. If he makes a go of that it seems to me that we would not need to run our Literary News column. What do you think? Matthews wishes a 1500 to 1800 word write-up of Frank Linderman. I am asking Bob Struckman if he cares to do it; if he does not, would you undertake the task? Of course Matthews cannot pay for material. He would want this essay by mid April.
> *Good wishes. HGM*[52]

Although letters in 1933 had indicated that the novel was drafted, Grace continued to refine and research. She turned to her family in Kansas for information.

ANGELA STONE TO COATES: MARCH 13, 1935

> Dear Grace: this information comes from the man who makes my farm loans and who has been in the business for 25 years, so it is correct. A crop

under usual failure conditions is given up for good some time before April 15th. We both enjoyed your delightful letter. Will reply some of these days. The "book" is news to us. Will await more news.

> *Love. Angela*

> Spring wheat sowed None planted in this part of Kansas
>
> Winter wheat sowed From Sep 15th of Oct 20th
>
> Cutting begins From the 13th to 20th of June
>
> Threshing begins combining begins about June 20th
>
> Spring plowing begins From 1st to middle of Feb
>
> Corn is sowed when From April 1 to May 1st.

Olive added to Angela's letter,

> I called up the County Agricultural agent for this information so it must be O.K. Some country rules are: Plant corn when the hedge begins to bud. Cut corn when the drought has burned it. Considerable corn is husked on the stalk and the stubble grazed and later burned. A letter sometime

> *Lovingly, Olive*[53]

There is little trail to follow this second novel although Grace sent it to an editor for editing and critique. A carbon copy surfaced in the 1980s along with parts of *Black Cherries* in a box Grace had stored in the attic of the Coates Brothers store.

COATES TO "I.M.P": APRIL 14, 1935

> I'm going to answer your letter; but not until I can say: SHE'S IN THE MAIL. Partly self-discipline, and partly consideration for your time.
>
> Knopf was the publisher. They have been waiting for this book with consideration and patience. I appreciate your generosity more than I can tell you. Nothing you would say could be impertinent—a person capable of impertinence wouldn't be aware of the possibility. If I desperately need something I'll ask you, but I won't pester you needlessly. I know you'll get results, whether you hit the nail on the head or on the thumb. Thank God— and I know you'll be glad to know this, too, gentility and nice people, family with a capital F, are no worries of mine. As you suggest, such concern, for a writer, would be like handcuffs for a swimmer....But I'll say the rest some other time. In the mean time, my thanks for just the help you have given me. And my cordial wishes for your own work, too.[54]

Grace continued to promote Linderman's work. He sent her information to write the article about him that was in the *Literary Review.*

LINDERMAN TO COATES: APRIL 29, 1935

Dear Mrs. Coates, Herewith letter from G.N. Ry. Co, so "you may fire when you're ready, Gridley."

I called my story OUT OF THE NORTH, because the Blackfeet came out of the North, from Lesser Slave Lake, to their present location. They were driven, slowly, by the Chippewas—and in turn, the Blackfeet drove the Snakes, and—*perhaps* the Flatheads, Kootenais, and Nez Perce, from the Northwestern plains, where they settled down to become plainsmen more than 200 years ago. The story gives much of their social customs etc. Of course you know that the Blackfeet, (the three tribes, Pecunnies, Blackfeet, and Bloods, forming the Blackfeet Nation) were the scourge of the Northern plains (after they obtained horses and guns)

Winold Reiss, the artist, is famous. He will teach a class in painting somewhere in Glacier Park again this year, as he has done for *several* years. I reckon this is about all I can give you, except that the book will be published by *Brown & Biglow,* the calendar-makers, in May. Do as you please about naming the publisher. Anyhow they do produce wonderful prints in color.

I ran across Vern's letter (the one I said was mislaid) Here's what she said about your article "I thought Mrs. Coates' article on Daddy was *beautiful.* (the emphasis is Verne's) It was interesting to me from many angles, the personal, the reportial, the ethnological, etc."[55]

LINDERMAN TO COATES: MAY 31, 1935

Dear Medicine-woman

Got yours. Don't understand where John Frohlicher [Frolicher, a Butte newspaperman] got into the game, since I have not mentioned him to you—or to Mr. McGillis. You did call the fact to my mind that John was working for the Brown & Biglow concern—that's all. However that makes no difference that I can see.

Think the enclosed clipping, showing that Englishmen insisted upon knowing just what they were getting back in good old 1700, will tickle you.

And about that mining article—the papers took it from Kalispell correspondent. Don't understand why they didn't take it from you. Thought I was handing you something.

As requested I'm returning the Struckman sketch. Didn't you get the magazine?...

If you should wish to use any of the scene of my meeting with Red-Horn I'll send it along. Please return it.

Darn if I know what else to send or write. Wish you could ask me what you wish to know—and that I might answer with spoken words.

First Blackfeet I ever met (and I didn't meet *them* for years afterward) stole a muzzle-loading rifle from my cabin, a rifle that had belonged to my father. Never saw it again. I brought it to Montana Territory with me, and used it for several seasons (until I could afford a more modern rifle) The above are just pannings. Maybe you'll find a color or two in the pan.

Cuss me if you feel like it. I'm doing my best. I just am a blank at this thing and know it. (and in other matters)

    F.B.L.[56]

LINDERMAN TO COATES: JUNE 2, 1935

Dear Medicine-woman

I'm returning Mr. McGillis' letter to you. It's fine. IM glad you have made a hit with him, and hope that something good will come of the acquaintance.

Can't understand the Frohlicher connection—but there's no good in thinking about it.

Sent you some dope, most likely it will madden you, and yet it's the best I could think up. You might wish to hint that the mention of my name among the Cree-Chippewa Indians gets attention.

Say—Elmer Green, my old Yonkers friend, says that the talk in New York is that Pearl Buck is going to shed her husband and marry Dick Walsh. He sent me clipping from Baltimore paper containing the story, and Mrs. Buck is quoted as saying that she could neither affirm nor deny the story since it was a personal matter. GOSH! I spent several days in the Walsh home; fine folks, nice family, two children, son and daughter; lovely lady, Mrs. Walsh—GOSH!

Yep, I'm swelled up over the hit which the story Out Of The North seems to have made.

What about your new book? Has it gone to the publishers? Don't wait to let me know what they say. Nahpee knows I wish you luck with it. Hoi!

    F.B.L.

Of course I'll send you some dope on Injin use of pigments because you want it, and I'll do the best I can, letting you write the article yourself—[57,]

Grace lost her dear friend Pierre Kuchneroff in the summer. He was a dear friend to many. His daughter was among those who wrote.

MARY RUFFNER TO COATES: JUNE 21, 1935

My dear Mrs. Coates,

Pierre presented me with a copy of your latest lovely poems and I want to tell you that I think they are very wise and charming, and delicate as well. I am glad you like snow-flakes and flower petals and can express your love for them. It takes me back to a young girlhood when a snowstorm was the most exciting and satisfactory thing in my existence. I wish you could have seen Pierre's delight in your poem dedicated to him. It was very touching, both his emotion and the poem as well. Also, when my mother read the poem, tears came to her eyes, for it seemed to her to fit perfectly my father.

So you see, you have brought beauty and tears to us in one little book—

With kindest wishes to you, Mary Ruffner[58]

RUFFNER TO COATES: UNDATED

One of Pierre's last thoughts: that you should autograph your first edition of Black Cherries, (returned to you yesterday) with a message to his unknown Russian friend in New York who sends him daily the postcards which he must have mentioned to you. And send this to her as a mutual friend.of P.A.K. She is Mrs. K.N. Rosen, first name, Ekaterina, (he was careful that I should understand this name) 410 Riverside Drive, New York City.

This request was made to me Monday when he had such difficulty in speaking. He wanted to say other things but had not the strength, so was going to say them "later" Not even then did he think or mention death.

One of the last things he said to his nurse was "Twissie, tell me something funny!" not woefully, not painfully, but as if he would have enjoyed it…And he would. When she was trying to give him a drink of water and asked him to take it, he said in semi-delirium, but of course roguishly, "What, honey?" I love to think of him, but gaily. Never with gloom. It would be…not sacrilegious, but great tactlessness, insensibility, to think of Pierre with gloom.

I sent your rose with mine. I think I must tell you that they were Talisman roses with white buttons of chrysanthemums, and the only cut flowers. They stood beautifully at the side of the room or chapel and were not taken to the cemetery. I went back later to get the container, and happened in on another funeral, this time, a pathetic one with a scattering of people and few blooms stood there on the table helping out a lot. (as regular, Pierre touch) There was a black bearded rabbi mumbling something in a corner in an almost bare room, except for the pews.

We had no rabbi for Pierre, as he knew none and I have never known Pierre to be surrounded by strangers, but always friends. We had organ music for twenty minutes, flowers and meditation. Some would want otherwise, but then always some want otherwise.

Funerals are such a problem. I am sure Pierre would have stayed away from his own funeral it he could, just as he stayed away from his own death. I wonder where he is now. I am sure he is not where we put him.

By the way, the two other books, the Spender and Auden, were given to him a few weeks ago, and he wanted me to send them to you. I believe he read the Spender but did not have much of a chance at the Auden.

Thank you for your letters. I did not get a chance to read the last two or three to him, but told him of them.

With love to you. Mary[59]

RUFFNER TO COATES: JULY 5, 1935

My dear Grace—

I have done something that should never be done. I have waited and waited until "just in the mood" to sit down and write you a letter of superior elegance and quality (which is the ambition hour own letters five to one) and, instead of achieving anything in the way of quality or elegance, the only thing I achieve is a blank and too easily misunderstood silence—How you are ever to know the real glow of friendship which greets any message from you. I am at a loss to suggest. You will just have to take me on faith, my dear—

I suppose I am trying to live too many lives . First there is the social worker, which takes up the major portion of my time and energy. Then there is the striving to have a finger in the community pipe. I am one of those things called a "woman voter" and this year have undertaken to be the president of the Denver League of Woman Voters. Of course, we attempt and fully expect to change the political map of Colorado. Then there is the mad social whirl. I love to dance and stay up very late. Consequently when a leisure moment rarely presents itself. I find it necessary to catch up with myself and gather together the few remaining shreds of sanity and consistency. Reading? It has vanished into the mists of a far distant past. Writing? I push it off into the far-distant future by means of vague promises and regular cohorts of good intentions. So my friendly correspondence slips between half a dozen stools. I also have a passion for beautiful songs and try at odd moments to learn them and to sing them. You may, unfortunately, think of me as a creature who does an incredible variety of things incredibly badly. My [epitaph] is already written. "Pray for this poor child of the age! She lived and died riding off in all directions!! Now her ashes are as scattered as her efforts. R.I.P."

At the present moment, I am actually at rest—in a 70-year-old log cabin in the mountains, seven miles from Central City. We have just finished reading aloud some of Thomas Hornsby Terril's poems about these mountains and this "ghost town," in which the summer Festivals will begin tomorrow with the gala opening of "Central City Nights," in the 50-year old[sic] Opera House. This will be the fourth annual""event" staged by Robert Edmond Jones. They have all been lovely in their way, though with more color than substance. My Communist friends would call his stagecraft "decadence"—He gave us a very much emasculated "Othello" last summer—Nevertheless, one is grateful for any gift of beauty even though offered from a drooping and somewhat sapless stem.

You have seen Central City, haven't you? It has had an amazing rebirth, what with the quality people of Denver buying up the faded old houses for $100 and transforming them with neat paint and a thousand or two more dollars into something so tastefully decorated and set out with pink geraniums and terraces that their original hard working owners would never recognize them. From a grim and rocky old mining town hewn from the mountainside, Central City has become a city of costumes and play boards—as fascinating as a fairy tale.

There is some property near here I have my eye on. Soon I shall be lured into the bosom of this make-believe (though not in town—eight miles off and isolated) and I think it would be fun if you would come and have a house party with me someday.

Now I must go and take a bath, without a bathtub or hot water—eat a meal, without any fire in the range, and hustle to town to watch for the five o'clock motor car (bringing more week-enders) Oh, what fun!

I am very eager to hear about your book though I do not deserve to have any word from you for a week of Sundays. I shall still hope for it nevertheless, in the course of the years

I often think of Pierre—and of you. My love to you,

> *Yours ever, Mary*[60]

Another of Grace's stalwart correspondents was Helen Maring, a Seattle author and editor of the *Northwest Review* and a long time friend.

MARING TO COATES: EARLY OCTOBER, 1935

Dear wonderful Grace,

Just an extra copy of a poem I was typing to send H.G.M. Have just spent the afternoon with Ethel Romig Fuller, preciously, on the precipice edge of the Sound, and before a huge fireplace—Romig's wife gave a tea—Ethel read her "Origins of Beauty" from Spring '35 American Scholar. I'm taken with it—going to send for a copy to possess the poem—her mood of "Mountains Talk"—but so far above and beyond it. Did you see it? My soul needed some kind of a major jarring to start a new poem—she did it. How I wish you too were here.

And the most exquisite collection of seashells! Ethel picked them up on the seashore near Carmel. She has them graded in size and mounted in shallow boxes on cotton, varieties sorted. Some of them are infinitesimal—and the loveliest shades and sheens, pink and blue and mother-of-pearl, orange, and salmon—real poet's loot. Only Ethel could have found them.

This is just a hello between spasms of typing poems. Must get back at the grind. Since Aug. have sold two small articles to Sunday school markets. And have placed poems two at a time in Love Story, with the Baptists, etc. Lorrin is going to sell Real Estate instead of "bone-conduction instruments for the hard of hearing". Started yesterday—The Model T is graduating to a 1933 Terraplane, and I learning to drive beginning Monday. (Didn't learn—got sick)

There goes a slice of our "old Age fund"—or the emergency bank account for appendectomy or something. I'm so please to think that we won't go on having our backbones crystallizing from the constant jarring of an old Ford! The plunge. It's worth it and then some. Hurray! As soon as I get so that I'm not climbing telephone poles, come on over and I'll give you a ride. We're still living in Mrs. Murphy's parlor.

Dear, dear Grace. I've neglected you for weeks, but I haven't written anyone as much as a whisper. On the next plane, thoughts will suffice for letters, and you'll get one every day.[61]

MARING TO COATES: NOVEMBER 12, 1935

My dear and wonderful—
That beautiful book on the "Blackfeet"—I'm crazy about it. Have read and looked and loved it thru and thru—Thank you so very much. The whole family loved it.

The old shadow back over me—didn't snap out of the flu—getting florescoped first of week. One hemorrhage, and everyone thrown into spasms. I've prayed to live at the beach—it this is the way it comes, okay. I've been running fever, and the emotional gamut. Moralizing in verse to keep up my morale on minute, and enjoying it all the next. Two years at the cabin—it would be wonderful! Glorious! I'm ready for it. I'd have the squirrels eating out of my hands, and wild birds lighting on my shoulder. And everyone oh-ed and ah-ed and marveled. A spasm was thrown about not getting it back into its cage, and I did it in two try's and about ten minutes. Most fun I've had for a long time. Guess I'll buy myself a canary. Never had one....

Is this any good?

Armor

Pride will make you poor,
Pride will make you thin—
But never let laxity
Enter in.

Pride will shun a favor
Pride will never whine—
Pride will keep you walking
On a straight chalk line.

Hold your head higher
Looking for a star.
They glow brightest where
Black spaces are.

Blackness on blackness
Such is defeat.
So, walk with a strut
On the man-made street.

Pride is sword and armor
Holding at bay
The brute, self-pity, …

Quoting you, "life is so mysterious, and also cock-eyed."

I'd like to either stand on the top of a mt. And look off into space, or get drunk.

Beautiful music over the radio—Old Doc. Wouldn't let me out to hear Paul Robeson tonight, I guess I've been gnashing my teeth over it subconsciously. Sometimes music is the necessary hashheesh real music, not jazz.

I love you dearly, Helen
Did Martinsdale get any earthquake?[62]

MARGARET MARSHALL TO COATES: NOVEMBER 16, 1935

So long you have been in my mind and in my heart too—and days are so full, nights so short! Grace, can you believe he [Pierre] is gone, can you realize that not again shall we take with great joy a letter from the mail box, gay, charming, chatty, whimsical so wholly individual? Some times when I am alone I am filled with such bitterness, such horror and hatred for this thing called life and what it can do to us that I am afraid I put on hat and coat and stride out over the hillside in sun and wind and find solace and compensation in tall golden tress, in rusty red shrubs, the flight of birds and the sudden dart of a squirrel across my path. But I am filled with loneliness that goes unappeased.

Twice in the last four months I have watched death triumph. How defenseless we all are! Imagine my utter despair Grace when all out of a clear sky one Monday Oct 15th I decided to go to Denver. I left Wednesday Oct 17th to be greeted on arrival, with the news of Pierre's serious illness. I know Mary Ruffner has written you details. I asked at once if anyone had written you and she said she had after the transfusion. It was a long and weary fight. Jack came on Thursday and his coming was a great delight to Pierre. They are such a devoted family and Pierre was the idol of them all. Jack was so overwhelmed from the very first it was extremely hard to be with him and toward the end the strain and uncertainty told on him enormously. So many, many times he bowed his head and sobbed out his grief and wrung our hearts, already over full.

Mrs. Van Riper, Jamie Holm, everyone who knew him came to the hospital many times to offer anything. Everything even their life's blood but to no avail. Dr. Tingerman had felt from the very first it was a losing fight. His faithfulness and devotion to Pierre, his unfailing efforts in his behalf I shall remember always.

There was a good deal of drama about it all Grace. I wish you could have been there…wish I could see you to talk it all over with you. I shall hope always to know you. You seem so very near and dear to me. Some time I am sure we shall meet and I shall be more glad than I can express. Won't you find time to write me and if there are any questions I can answer please ask them?

Do you know about the funeral, only soft, organ music no words spoken at all? Some how it seemed just right and he rests there in Denver at Lovely Mt. Ebo. This quotation has occurred to me again and again as I think of Pierre.

"He loved the stars too well to fear the night."

Grace this letter is more meandering than I meant it to be My heart is very full these days I seem utterly joyless. I must quit it I know.

Heard Christopher Morley last nite first one our town Hall Lecture Course. I would much rather read him! I hope you are well and that you will write me.

I love you much.[63]

The novel, *Clear Title*, never appeared in print.

There is no record if Grace told Merriam that her novel had been rejected, or anyone else near her. She did confide in her friend in Ohio. Knopf rejected it, "…questioning its salability. They did say it had some beautiful writing. But that washes me up with Knopf & I'm sorry."[64] Grace sent the manuscript to Caxton and J. O'Brien took it to England to show it there, but to no avail.

Grace told Merriam the plot of the story.

Man, by reason of childlessness in first marriage, and his wife's business competence, is relieved of all responsibility for wife's support. Financially competent himself, but visionary. Wife protects her (later arrived) children by her will, leaving her property to them. Died suddenly, when the man is at a crisis in his finances…A woman, well balanced, religious, sane, healthy, normal pops up and marries him within a month of the time she meets him. How a woman who is all that does that particlar thing is something tht takes some writing to make go down. She does it—and I haven't made this point in the story, but it is fundamental and should be there, because instead of acting intuitively, she lets her intellect vitiate things, and wants to pass his intellectual qualities on to her children—wants to give her children a wonderful father. (Personally I think that is a fatal reason for marrying a man. A woman is thinking too far ahead—nature defeats such civilized behavior)…Can you make head and tail to what I'm saying?…

The man has never had any training in treating a wife any way at all and since this second wife immediately is hampered economically by pregnancy— successive and constant pregnancies, bad health, financial reverses et alt., he contrasts her unfavorably with the smooth slipping first wife.

The plot, in so far as there is a plot: The second wife lets the man coerce her into signing a paper with her own name, but under such circumstances that give it the weight and authority of the first wife's. She conveys to her husband the first wife's property left in trust for the children. When things go to pot the father tries to inspire the children to lay claim to their alienated property. In the title chapter—"Clear Title" the step daughter answers her father.

A damned critic in the Nation called Black Cherries 'gloomy.' Well, the novel is somber; but I did have the grace to steal one of Bud Shipley's titles and head the last chapter: HAPPINESS IS A LONG LANE TO FLOWER. In it Teressa, Veve and Augusta discuss the past events of their lives, as they go back to the place of their childhood.

That chapter from "Clear Title" includes the following passage:

They were within sight of the now almost treeless house. There was genuine concern in her tones:

"I meant to tell you—you mustn't count too much on getting inside the house. There are tenants living there, and I don't suppose they'll let you in."

"Not let me in?" Veve's tone showed her astonishment. She had lived long in the West. "Why, of course they'd let us in! When I tell them that I haven't been back for a long time—that I was born there—why shouldn't the let us in?"

"I'm just telling you. Maybe they will. But the chances are they won't." She smiled her difficult smile: "You're not in Montana."

An outmoded touring car stood opposite the house, on the road in front of them, as they swung into the denuded "cottonwood" lane. In conversation with the two men on its front seat stood an unkempt giant of a man. His foot was on the running board of the car, and he rested his forearm across his knee.

The incoming car stopped a few yards from him, and he looked at Veve and Tahta without greeting them as they opened the car door and stepped out. A woman, big like the man, stood some distance behind him. Her dress was nondescript, worn; not noticeable, except that her shoes were misshapen, and she stood bareheaded under the hot sun. Veve went toward her, smiling. "Goodmorning," she said. The woman looked toward the man, presumably her husband, and looked back at Veve, without speaking.

"I used to live here," said Veve…"Years and years ago, when I was a little girl. I was born in this house," her hand indicated the porch and open kitchen door. Since the woman remained silent, Veve added, "May we look around the yard?"

The man turned his head slightly in the woman's direction, and back toward the men in the car. He gave no further recognition of his wife's words, or the strangers' presence. They were but women. He continued his conversation with his peers.

But Veve was off to the front of the houses—the same porch, two steps— the same pillars. She caught the left corner pillar with her left hand and swung round it, once—off the porch and over the void and back to solid porch again—to see whether she could do it; her skirt was chalky with the dry, white paint she brushed against; and then her hand was on the front doorknob.

It was there! Covered with a slipshod smear of white paint from the woodwork, but unmistakably there, the bronze doorknob whose balance and contour had been gratifying to her father's hand. It felt small to her, slender, almost. She understood why her father had called it delicate. The sensation she remembered was of her hand stretched to grasp it, almost unable to bring purchase enough to make it turn. That only, of all she saw, fulfilled the accustomed prophecy that childhood's world, revisited, appeared dwarfed. The dimensions of all the rest, house, granaries, yard, she had apparently readjusted year by year…*a mile long –as far as from here to the railroad crossing….A four-room house—an attic; as large as the fourth house from the corner* ….So she had adjusted her recollections to reality.

"….My father brought this from New York City and put it here in place of a clumsy white one. He always mentioned liking to feel it under his hand…"

…They stayed in the house but a few minutes longer. The kitchen made Veve restless. She could see her mother standing ironing, in the middle of the night, after the rest of the household was in bed…She could not walk to the north window to look out, where she had seen her mother stand and gaze over the empty reaches.[65]

Perhaps Knopf thought the story had already been told. From 1930, she had submitted less work and ended in 1935 with work in *The Frontier* and

Opportunity: Journal of Negro Life. Prophetically, perhaps, the poem in Opportunity is titled "Moment-Flare." The final stanza:

> If my life must throb let it vibrate only
>
> To the piston-thrust of a driving will—
>
> But my heart contracts to something chill,
>
> Desperately small and lonely.

As she put aside the novel and concentrated on historical pieces, another window opened for Grace. From the *Great Falls Tribune,*

> The latter part of November, 1935, Mrs. Coates was appointed district supervisor of the federal writers' project with head quarters at Billings, and supervisor of a second project at Butte, under direction of State Director H.G. Merriam of Missoula, where the state office is located. Mrs. Coates returned from Billings to spend the Christmas holidays at her Martinsdale home.

Marguerite Bair had offered to write the local news while Grace was in Billings at the WPA office, and one of her first news items was about Grace leaving.

BILLINGS GAZETTE: JANUARY 3, 1936

> Mrs. Grace Stone Coates of Martinsdale, one of Montana's best-known authors will appear for the first time in 1936 "Who's Who" and "Principal Women of America." Inclusion in these reference works is based on fitness and a paid biography has never appeared in their pages. Mrs. Coates is assistant editor of the Frontier and among her books are "Black Cherries," "Mead and Mangel Wurzel" and "Portulacas in the Wheat." She was co-author with Pat Tucker in writing "Riding the High Country," which is now in the second publication.

∞

Insult Out of Amity

Weigh it in your hand like a counter, a gold penny,
    A shrouded, uncut ruby, a ball of colored glass;
Touch it with curious finger, questioning; *Has it any*
    Value? Lay it by, and let time and question pass.

Weigh in your mind's palm this insult out of amity,
    Finger it with thought, then drop it into your breast.
Is it the uncut gem, jewel against calamity,
    Or a subtle Borgia token scarring its way to rest?

CHAPTER TEN

Grace Stone Coates was excited about the Federal Writers Project and the opportunities it provided to help writers during this depression—an excitement that soon paled. One of her first letters was to Martinsdale to the Bair family:

That was a good send-off you gave me, Marguerite, and raised my stock in the WPA some 100% Everybody clipped it for me and brought it to me. Thank you for it.

I have most of the office to myself and a good stenog and life is rosy as a red pigeon's wing. I enjoy this work more than any I ever attempted. Lots of nice persons to meet; and my work gives me an excuse to go butting in to anybody I want to meet. Mr. McDonald of the N.P. [Northern Pacific Railroad]—chief geologist—came bringing me Willard's Geol of Montana and I have been reading it nights. He is a peach of a man—not many busy persons would take the trouble to come in with the book. Reminds me I better write him and tell him so.

Work moves along. Of course I was swamped because work piled up while I was waiting for office accommodations. They moved all the finance department over to Helena and now I guess they are in such confusion that Mr. Whitten wants to come back. Hope they won't come because the crowding is out of all reason for all of us.

Henderson wrote me he dined with you—and had a fine time. That was nice of you. I wish I could put my arms around Mrs. Bair's neck and get a good kiss; and smoke some 7 cigarettes with Alberta.

I couldn't be happier than I am. If only I am sure Henderson is all right I haven't a care in the world. If I think up any news that Marguerite can run I'll send it along. Maybe this job will yield some one of these days. We do dig up a lot of interesting things.

I'm going to talk to the City Federation of Woman's Clubs Tuesday, in order to advertise the work of the American Guide. Wonder if I can dig up a clean dress. You'd be astonished at the number of long nails I have—two dozen at least!

I send you all a great deal of love. You have been wonderful friends to Henderson and me ever since you came to Martinsdale. Just as soon as I have a few more days of long work I'll be caught up and more human, and perhaps will find more time to drop little letters your way to remind you that I remember and appreciate your kindness. Maybe I can sneak home some day. If any of you are in town give me a ring, at Mrs. Eames or the office—WPA number is 4101-Ex. 3—my room is 215—and the stenog, Mrs. Baltrusch will always be here and will always know where I am—maybe.

Fondly, Grace[1]

Grace was still enthusiastic about her job several months later when she wrote a friend, "I am adapted to this weird work of WPA. It is just enough of this and that to suit my talents. I like it; also I overwork at it. Anyway, I like it."[2] She planned to stay in Billings until the finish of the work, although she was supervisor for a similar program in Butte and traveled there periodically. She got home to Martinsdale as often as possible.

News came shortly that the book, *Riding the High Country*, written by Patrick Tucker and Grace Stone Coates, had come out in a British edition. It was a distinct merit for the book, although too late for Patrick Tucker who had recently died.

Grace was still hoping to see her second novel published and sent it to Caxton. She wrote to Powers, who helped sell her books, that Caxtons "...will keep Black Cherries in print; and they will probably want CLEAR TITLE. Have had no word from O'Brien; and of course he has not had the book mss long enough to be pestered by my questing questions yet."[3]

The manuscript was finally relegated to a box in the general store.

While Grace was working for the WPA, she found a new correspondent with Charles Kuhlman, continuing the exchange of letters long after she left the federal job.

Kuhlman had had an interesting life. He was born in Iowa on a small farm and went to school at Grand Island, graduating from high school in 1892. To earn money for college, he taught in a rural school for a year and raised sugar beets for a local sugar factory. He attended the University of Nebraska on a fellowship and received his BA in 1897 and his MA in 1900. A professor urged him to continue his studies in Europe and he researched the Breton Club, a precursor of the Jacobin Club of French Revolutionary fame. His thesis was accepted for a Ph.D. by the university at Zurich, Switzerland.

Back in the United States, Kuhlman became an instructor at the University of Nebraska, but was forced to give up teaching when his hearing deteriorated badly—a result of an attack of measles and mumps in earlier days.

He left the university in 1903, married Minnie Wilkinson, and moved to Loveland, Colorado, to become a sugar beet farmer. When that venture failed, he moved to Joliet, Montana, and again failed at the sugar beets. He then tried his luck at truck farming in Billings with better success.

When the bottom dropped out of the farm market in the late 1920s, the farm was foreclosed. In 1930, his wife Minnie died, and Kuhlman went into a deep depression. Drugs he took to make him sleep affected his motor nerves and he lost fifty pounds.

In 1935, Kuhlman's grown children took him to a visit to what was then called the Custer Battlefield, today Little Bighorn National Monument, where he became interested in the history of the battle and the location of markers on the battlefield. For the next 16 years he did a close analytical study of the battle and came up with a new interpretation of the Custer defeat. He wrote to Grace about having his work published in some form, and through the years of the late 1930s, the two became friends. He finally put his findings in a book in 1940—*Gen. George A. Custer: A Lost Trail and the Gall Saga.*

Coates found herself again in her old role of helping fledgling writers get published, and wrote to Kuhlman about submitting work to the papers.

"Forgive me for being slow," Grace wrote,

> I am overworked. The MNA [Montana News Association] necessities, as to length, are well defined; 1200 to 1500 words, preferably the shorter; and "shorts" up to 500 words for fillers.
>
> The Tribune might be an outlet for the longer story, tho they say they have features for a year ahead. Still, a year goes fast—and sometimes they pay before publication.
>
> Certainly I'll read the story. I might be able to suggest a market, or I might not be lucky enough to be of any service.
>
> No, you did not annoy me by anything you have said recently. I liked the birthday letter very much, even though I did not make any response. As for "love," one can not confine his affection, his love, his what you wish to name, to one person without robbing that person cruelly. I think my father was too far ahead of his time. When one is too far ahead, one is recalled by crucifixion.
>
> Write anything you want to write. I am sorry that I am not ample enough to meet the demands on me.
>
> Many a letter on my desk is answered solely because the writer puts his address on *the letter*. My practice is to break my mail and discard the envelopes, leaving the letters in the basket to attend to later. I seem not to cure myself, and writers seem not to cure themselves, so some letters get no answers.[4]

A tragedy occurred when Kathryn Corwin, a student in college in Billings, was killed by a car. Her family lived in Martinsdale. Grace wrote to Henderson about the funeral and then brought him up to date on domestic chores.

> You should go over to the Corwins, you do not need to speak about Kathryn at all. I never saw a better example of composure and good taste than they

showed…Their grief is too deep for them to want people to rush up and begin talking about Kathryn, but you could go in there and tell them you are glad they are back …

I have seen few people more loved and more eulogized than Kathryn was around Billings and in the Eastern Montana Normal School.

The Martinsdale people attending the funeral were: Mr. and Mrs. Petrie, Mr. and Mrs. John Duncan, and Louise Cameron. Give this to Marguerite for a news item if you want to—and of course, me. Maybe I'll write Marguerite a letter. I spent a good deal of time with the Corwins and felt desperately sorry for all of them. The entire church was a bank of flowers and the service was very short and simple.

I thought I told you about the newspapers, etc. I can get time to read Barron's and the Financial World, but not the Wall Street Journal. I am sorry I was slow about telling you. You should have had a letter Tuesday because I mailed you one Sunday. It is the 29th of April and I haven't got word yet from a Miss Ann Furier, whom I was trying to get for your housekeeper. Work is slacking up and I am not half as driven as I was earlier in the Project.

In Hardin the dandelions are all in blossom. I wish I could see you.

Yours with a lot of love, Grace Stone Coates[5]

Along with the WPA Writers' work, Grace tried to keep up some work with *The Frontier*. She continued to write the writer's column although she no longer contributed material.

In June, she heard from her longtime friend, Helen Maring.

Dear Precious Grace:

Why do I back up and turn into stagnant water? A million amoebas and algae and scum and slime and mosquito-wigglers in the pond of my mind….I need rain of emotions, and torrents of thinking—winds of discordant intellect to shake me from lethargy. Arguments—passion—violence. Or is it youth that is the torrent?

Come on, Pegasus, where are your wings? Don't tell me you have become a draft horse, or even a mule! Oh, so it is a water-buffalo you are, come to plow the pond? Go to it, old awkward with mud caked on your flanks—plow!

Rainy Sunday—poetry papers piled high—and I'm lazy as a bum. Spring fever has hit me a couple of months late. Just wanted to talk to you for a minute and see if I could snap myself out of it. Bless you! I think it's worked!

Love, Helen[6]

In September, H.G. Merriam returned to the campus in Missoula to find his work piled up and "much confusion in FRONTIER matters." Douglas Branch was in Missoula on vacation, and offered to get the autumn issue out. Grace had not been doing the literary news column, but had sent instructions to Missoula on how to handle it. Merriam was concerned that it would not please Grace.

"By the way," Merriam wrote,

> I have used a fifty pound paper in this autumn issue instead of a sixty pound as before, therefore cutting the number of pages from 100 to 92. These changes will save me about $30.00 an issue. Since we are now about $700.00 in debt, it seems to be wise to cut our running expenses without injury to he magazine. Have you any practical suggestions for a reduction of that debt?
>
> Will Murphy, who is a lawyer for the A.C.M. Company, suggests that now is a good time to send an appeal for donations to wipe out that debt. Can you think of any names that belong to generous persons who could be interested in such a matter?[7]

Grace replied,

> Dr. Branch must have unbounded energy. Linderman, Eileen and I had one session at your hospitable house, with Branch as the subject of our hilarity; all of us wishing we had his verve.
>
> As for the debt, I'll think about it. Conditions are so damned peculiar here that—well, I can function normally in supporting or enlisting public support of my interests. All the once wealthy persons are broke; tho they still go on living well and piling up bills. You should have offered me a job on condition all but my actual expenses go to The Frontier. I'd have taken it just the same....I suppose you turned right around to Will Murphy and asked what you could put *him* down for![8]

She also included some personal notes:

> Several persons who had seen you after you returned from Oregon mentioned to me that you looked refreshed; that your summer had done you good. I am glad if this is so. Life is good when one is well and not over-burdened; and hard to take when one is.
>
> Don't worry about my column appearing satisfactory to me. It never has, yet. If I once make a col. that suits me exactly I'll issue warning that I'll excommunicate anybody who changes a comma on it. Your kindly wish has added zest, because the col. states that I have just finished a novel, and had my goofy humor accepted by Red Book. I wanted to wire, "Who's goofy now?" in emulation of the late brother of the late Bob Chanler. Already Mrs. Linderman has written me that she is watching the issues of Red Book eagerly. I surmise that somebody had me in mind as he wrote the item—perhaps the real lady's name is Grace, and the rest came automatically.[9]

Both Merriam and Coates became disillusioned about the work of the WPA Writers' Program. When he was able to see the end of the project, he expressed his relief to Grace. She wrote to reassure him.

> I can understand your relief about the WPA. The work is disintegrating; but I shall never cease feeling grateful to you for letting me out of my prison momentarily. I came so near losing my prison altogether that the realization busted me out of the spiritual imprisonment, and I am feeling inordinately blithe as a result—not worrying about writing a bit, knowing that a person can only do so much, working hard, and letting the solutions take care of themselves. I am gratified at several things about the project: that four of my workers now have supervisory jobs of one kind or another; that two of them have made new markets—they are kind enough to thank me for pointing out to them; and that Archie has a book that I'm enthusiastic about practically done—that started with his interest in Butte drama. Elmer Baird (the Christer) is married; Frank Kniepp is off to school—I think; Mrs. Baird, the last I heard of her, was under arrest and bond to keep the peace! Accused of creating a disturbance in the sewing room. (She's another Christer)
>
> I note that John Mason Brown is to lecture at Washington University. The surest way of making the news notes better is to cure me of procrastination…[10]

Grace and Merriam were not alone in their disappointment in the writers' project. A friend working for the project in Iowa wrote,

> You talked as if you had your Guide book almost written. Well, we haven't. We need a lot more time and I don't believe we'll have it anywhere near finished by July 1st. I suppose we have more towns to write up and likely haven't gotten the background of historical research and study you folks have out there. We have a fine HISTORICAL SOCIETY that has gotten together much information but it hasn't always been available. I've worked like the Devil and am in need of a vacation. We have a nice office but it's noisy and these writers are all temperamental. I used to work as an accountant and have been a school teacher and preacher and I know what files, order, discipline, and such things mean but—damn the writers who talk about socializing the country and then are anti-social. Most of us are individualists at that and should let all this politics go. But we get hurled into it.[11]

Grace later wrote to Merriam,

> The writers project: if I started to talk about that I'd not end. I am out of sympathy with making big-bellied loafers of persons too inclined that way in the first place. The Montana writers project was a joke from the beginning. I think I have seldom seen such waste of misdirected energy. Crane is as good

as the project he heads. You well near wrecked my theretofore peaceful end of things by demanding statistics on the relative numbers of the A.F.L. and the C.I.O. in Butte—a hot spot if ever there was one, to ask an outsider to deliver closely guarded statistics on. We delivered 'em. Chad is a delightful person. I like him. He is not always magnanimous, but few persons are. Crane was here the other day. I was pleased with myself that I could overlook the drunken louse's having called me at 3 a.m.—and Helen Elliot—commentary on Chad's firm disciplinary hand on the reins. Anyway, I was courteous to the low-grade dement, and took the nicest specimen of moss agate he had when he told me to take my choice!…I might as well get this off my chest, too: you resent Hart's saying he could assemble material from the railroad guide books, but the first thing your office asked me to do when I got to Missoula was to take a Great Northern holiday *tour.* So Hart's comment didn't strike me as far astray.[12]

The culmination of the Writers' Project was a book, *Montana: A State Guidebook,* published in 1939. Credit is given to Merriam for his contributions, but Grace's recognition is in the text as an author who ranks with Myron Brinig and Frank Linderman as the state's best.

James B. Rankin of New York City began making a catalog in the mid-1930s of the present location and ownership of all the original sketches, paintings and modelings of Charles M. Russell. He wrote widely to people in Montana, hoping to find pieces that had not yet been publicized. Grace was one to whom he wrote. There soon developed a lively exchange of letters, sometimes steering Rankin to Russell information and sometimes enjoying the friendship that developed. Grace put an item in the newspapers announcing that James B. Rankin of New York City was making a catalog of "present location and ownership of all original sketches, paintings and modelings of the late Charles M. Russell. He has written widely to Montana associates of the artist, hoping to uncover hitherto unpublicized originals. His interest is not in purchasing material but in cataloging all that exists."

"I get a kick out of your letters," Grace wrote to Rankin,

but, honestly, I have things to do besides write (to you). If you want to do something nice why don't you jot down some of the interesting things you have encountered in locating Russellana—things you are not planning to cash in on yourself, and send them to me for continued news stories. *Names make news* and Cobb's, Will Hart's and Will James's and a lot of others make news in Montana. Linderman by the way has been away from home, and is under the difficulties of a houseful of relatives at the moment; if that helps any, in case he hasn't written. I have a vague feeling that Sid Willis did die—will ask. OF COURSE Russell was glorious—who doesn't think so?

JAMES B. RANKIN

Montana Historical Society, Helena, Montana

Mr. Frank Bird Linderman has many illustrated letters from Charles M. Russell; none of them for sale. He has much other material. I suggest that you write him, (Goose Bay, Somers, Montana) but under no circumstances mention "Riding the High Country" to him. He and I are friends; such good friends that he felt free to say that the book represented all that he hated in spurious westerns. Then he added in a fury of resentment: "Blue eyes! Bah! Russell's eyes were yellow as a wolf's."

But, again, the book has a certain naive charm.

My husband knew Russell, and played poker with him lots of times. I knew him, but not intimately. I have met Mrs. Russell, but she would probably not remember it. In approaching any old timers, like Mr. Linderman, do not mention her. She is persona non grata to Russell's old friends.

Mr. Linderman could tell you a lot. I've tried to give you tips about what *not* to do, at least, in case you write him. The—their name escapes me—in Butte, have some murals etc. if you will write to Mrs. E.J. Settle, Martinsdale, Mont., asking her if she knows anyone in Butte who has etc etc, she can tell you. C.M. Bair, Martinsdale, has some Russell originals. I can not tell you what. I suppose you know about Sid Willis' collection. If not, address him, Great Falls, Montana. He is your best bet. If you want more information, write me, and I'll do what I can.

> *Sincerely yours, Grace Stone Coates*
> If there was a stamped envelope in your letter—didn't see it.[13]

COATES TO RANKIN: NOVEMBER 13, 1936

Dear Mr. Rankin,

Thank you for the stamps; my little dig was really directed toward your getting by with persons more Scotch than I. But I'm Scotch enough to appreciate them.

Well, one ear on the radio and the other on this letter—if you get me— waiting for Lon Hughes to "bring you now the latest news from the business world together with last minute reports direct from Wall street" I say: that I can give you a lot about Russell, most of it incorrect, probably, as personalities usually are. The Butte woman's name which I suggested you get from Nell Settle is Mrs. Charles Schatzlein (I may go to Butte Monday and if I do I'll see whether I can get anything for you.)

The last time I saw him was in Glacier Park—where one of his $15,000 pictures hangs in the Lewis hotel…Malta hotel: no. Write the postmaster at Malta.

Joe De Yong [western artist, protégé of Charles M. Russell]: ask Linderman—he can tell lots but probably won't. B. and sister: I don't know.[14]

Coates to Rankin: November 21, 1936

Owen Smithers—a good place for material—has a Photostat of the first pay check Russell got as a cowboy….Unless you have written news you scarcely realize what unconsidered trifles make news—as that in response to the news item you got a letter from Anaconda—and the Chinook item—and Cobb's loan loss—,…So you must have much material that is of no loss to you if released and good publicity for you around here. So if you care to, (accommodate me) send it along. Owen Smithers may neglect letters; but he'll talk till tomorrow if he gets a chance. I know a lad, who, for a small fee, might collect bits of info for you. He is on relief—used to work under my supervision. All good luck to you…Billings Gazette also carried your item, substantially as the rest.

> *GSC*

Try Miss Ida Sternfels, Butte Public Library
Lewis Hotel (manager of) Glacier National Park
(Lots of big bracket mushrooms there with Russell's sketches cut in them— he'd be walking thru the timber, stop to rest at a bracketed tree and cut a cowboy or a horse on a hard mushroom (fungus to you) Russell was lazy— his friends characterize him as the laziest man they knew. 'Nother source of friction between him and Mrs. R.

> *GSC*

What are you really doing? Getting out a book?
I don't think Russell was any poker fan—he preferred to draw. But he played poker, make no doubt of that.

Here is a postscript, to be read first; I opened the envelope to insert it.
Mr. Coates says he never played poker with Russell, and never saw him sit in a game; and was under the impression that he never played. After discussion pro and con, while I waled but you SAID you had played poker with him, and he disavowed ever having said any such thing, I reminded him at last of a conversation he could recall, when he and Pat Tucker were talking here at the house. "Oh, yes," he said, "but that was a Russell at the old town, a cowpuncher that liked to play cards." It developed that they had been talking about *the* Charley Russell when I left the room; and had switched to the unknown Charlie-hoss when I returned.
I then went to Jack Coates, who knew Russell better than Henderson did, and he said Russell never, to his knowledge, played cards at all.
So much for getting misinformation even from honest persons.

> *Sincerely yours, GSC*[15]

In a later letter, Grace continued about Russell.

Russell had a farobank layout over his studio door—I think it was Jew Jake's but it might have been anybody else's. Anyway, I associate it with what Russell hated, a reception for schoolteachers at his studio. The gal ahead of me had vivacioused [sic] at Russell—he hated gush—"Oh, Mr. Russell, is that Square Butte? Can you see it from here?" "Can if you look," Russell grunted. I had intended to pass and keep my mouth shut, but I caught sight of the far' bank layout—the case keeper—over the door and had to tell him about Henderson's attempt to buy one—hunted all over Butte, finally tried the second-hand stores: a Jew, rubbing his hands and following Henderson to the street, loath—is it loth?—to miss a sale: "Ve have no case-keepers but ve haf suitcases!"

Malta hotel: no. Write the postmaster at Malta.

Joe De Yong: ask Linderman—he can tell lots but probably won't. B. and sister: I don't know.

Relations of Mrs. Russell—her relation to him and his success and to his old friends will have to take another letter. Ask Mrs. Lincoln, sculptress, Great Falls—Mrs. Edmund R. Lincoln 1817 3d avenue North Great Falls—you do put me to a lot of trouble looking up addresses—she was the won [sic] who won in the contest for a Russell bust for the hall of fame; and due to Mrs. Russell hasn't got it accepted yet. I could give you tips but do not know how discreet you are—one story is that Mrs. Russell had a slick young artist on the string and wanted him to do the bust. It may be a canard. I dunno. You see some of the gossip is too hot to pass out to a stranger. Anyway, I watched Senator Wheeler do a good political politic stunt, dodge a hot issue, by being too busy to go look at the bust and say whether it was good or not. Mrs. Senator and I took tea there for a preview, but of course Mrs. Senator isn't Mr. Senator. Burton K. Wheeler can still say he hasn't seen the bust.

Tip: write W.W. Cheely, recently returned to M.N.A. Great Falls (his address) from NYC. He hates Mrs. Russell with a godly hatred; and he may not answer you; but write him.

And write Mrs. Lincoln—and with what I've told you, be tactful;—, And if you want to, send me more stuff that I can use for a feature story that will give your address, and perhaps pull a lot of information from the submerged tenth which Russell loved—and Mrs. Russell didn't!

What are you really doing? Getting out a book?

And remember that, to strangers, a stamped, self-addressed envelope has a pulling power that sometimes makes them answer a letter; the envelope lies looking up at them reproachfully every time they turn around, and finally in sheer self-accusation they say something and send it back. Not everyone indulges to such an extent as I in what J.T. Shipley of the *New Leader* characterizes as "the whoring of the artistic spirit"—i.e. letter-writing.[16]

COATES TO RANKIN: DECEMBER 2, 1936

Dear friend, James B,

Are you of the Missoula Rankins? Housecleaning and refurbishing sounds as if there might be a Missus James B. If as and when, my obeisance.

Stamps: you have sent me all of 4. If I hold to post cards, I'll make a profit. As soon as Alberta Bair showed up I asked, not whether she had had a letter from you, but whether she had answered your letter. She thinks now I'm clairvoyant. (I asked her at once whether you had enclosed a stamp.)

I saw your BOOKS item. Good. Glad to hear of the results.

Yes; seismographic; and your best friend won't tell you. But go ahead. The material is the man's who gets it. Don't let the wet blankets damp your spirits. Of course I think Linderman should have written a life of Russell long and long ago. Only his fine sense of not wanting to capitalize a real friendship restrained him. And does he hate Nancy! But that I have no business to say, since I am only surmising.

Wondering whether you tried Mrs. Lincoln, and if you didn't, why????

Have you thought to ask Alex Leggat, Leggat Hotel, Butte, about Russell? Legget has the best collection of Montanana in the state. Or one of the best. He is a fine person. (Mr. Linderman always says "a nice dog-person" where lesser men say a nice dog—or pooch.

Indeed I'd be delighted with the book catalogues—I wish I were in New York. I haven't been there since the Empire building was half way up—Radio City just in the raw.

Just did my news. Tomorrow I make a news item out of your nice and most amiable letter.

In one of Russell's stories—I could look it up if I were not lazy—he tells one on *Billy* Coates. Trails Plowed Under? I think so.

I must run—mail almost ready to close. When are you coming West to pursue the elusive inner manliness of the artist Russell?

> GSC

Do you know Berton Braley in NYC? Gwendolyn Haste? (There's a tip for you) She didn't know Russell in his youth of course, but may have some dope.[17]

COATES TO RANKIN: DECEMBER 6, 1936

If it is a case for G-men, as you suggest, what have I in the morning's mail but a personal letter from J. Edgar Hoover, commending a story of mine on the lately retired J.H. Dickason of Butte. My heart was in my mouth as I read, "My attention has been called…" I wondered what boner I'd pulled *now*.

Sid Willis: typical inarticulate (by pen) westerner. Josephine Trigg: prim and snooty. Tom Mix: letters a drug on the market. Will James drunk—in boots too tight. Gary Cooper—try his mother. She was recently in Helena. He's a spoiled pet, too, probably.

Interlude: temperature rose 32 degrees in 30 minutes this morning. At 8:a.m. 10 degrees below zero, east wind biting the face. But the eyes in the face could see a west wind fogging the wnos [sic] along the northern foothills, at the base of the Belts [Belt Mountains]. At 8: 30 a.m. the thermometer registered 20 degrees above zero. But west of here they reported a rise of 32 degrees, against the 30 degrees here.

Henderson says Sid Willis is alive, and that the Mint is still the Mint. I've been in it often—in fact talked to Sid Willis the last time I was there. I believe he—no it was his cook—wrote me a letter not so long ago. Wanted to give me a story. There are some nice robust ribald pictures of Russell's in the Mint. How can you get by with the typical ribald-obscene-story of Russell's? In your book?

Get your psychoanalyst to tell you why I transpose letters. That *snow* above there is the worst I've yet done. It is either genius, insanity, fatigue or inertia.

I shall do a good story, reserving it until a day when there was no lutefisk dinner in town to shout about, and send you the clippings. I am glad HGMerriam writes letters to somebody—he certainly has treated me with scant courtesy in regard to queries I've shot at him re the Frontier and Midland.

By the way, I have a story in the December JUNIOR RED CROSS JOURNAL illustrated by the Washington artist, Charles Dunn. He says he had a grand time doing the drawings.…

GSC[18]

LINDERMAN TO COATES: DECEMBER 7, 1936

Dear Medicine-woman

The Frau delivered your message "Tell him to write to me" Just like that—when you already owe me a pair of letters. I'd be crowding to write more before hearing from you; wouldn't I?

Been to Missoula, been to Helena, been to Havre, since hearing from you. They had to blind-fold me and back me onto the cars, too. Been workin' for fun, as usual. But I'm going to make WOLF AND THE WINDS a better story by letting him live the years after leaving the village. This will require a lot of time—but I think it will pay in satisfaction. That man, Whicker, of the English department at Missoula is a most surprising individual. I couldn't see anything in him at first; but Mercy, the man knows heaps—and he's the most heart-breaking worker I ever saw. But I'll bet he will quit teaching one of these days. Better look him up, and don't shoot too quickly. Wait—wait, and lead him out first.

Sally pulled a fast one. I heard the following in the hall—Jim: "Sally, if you'll swear you will not follow Rick and me for a whole hour I'll give you back this old doll-head." Sally: "All right, God *dam* you."

They keep us stepping, and they are so lively and bright. But GOSH Gosh when the confounded radio is going (theirs) and they are jabbering it's no place for a plodder like yours truly.

Better come over. We'll feed and take care of you. And I'm glad you like the tepee. Tell Henderson that even though I don't kill deer I brought in venison this fall. Our buck-law is damnable. Men kill does and don't pack them out, leaving them where they fall. One morning while going up for the mail I saw a bloody trail near our gate. I followed it, and jumped a young doe with both legs shot off on one side. The poor thing couldn't run. Going back to the shack I got my rifle and shot her through the head. She was young and fat— but I could have twisted the man's neck who had shot her and left her to die. I phoned the judge, and kept the meat. The kids, all of them, helped me dress the deer, which was an experience for them; and they might never have learned otherwise. We have painters come often, and some of them give time to the kids. And the two boys are going to pose as models for the high school mural, which pleases them immensely.

Somebody, a souvenir-hunter I suppose, stole the sign from our mail box so that I have now to make another. Isn't the white man just about what I think him? Golly it's snowing, coming straight down. Looks like a real one to me. The kids are prayerfully waiting to see the snow fall deeply so they can play in the wet.

I've sent off a short story to Colliers. It will be back by return mail I suppose—and I'd like to show you some work that lady, Mrs. Lochrie [Elizabeth Lochrie] did in painting bears for the book, BIG JINNY.

Yours sincerely, F.B.L.[19]

COATES TO RANKIN: DECEMBER 16, 1936

I have no time to write this letter to you. Alberta Bair was in, last night…

Sometimes I don't tell you things, because I didn't know Russell. What I say is gossip, and is confidential. I've told confidential things now and then, to give the setting, the atmosphere, and been embarrassed to see them blazoned in print, and not as I conveyed them. Authors have no conscience as a rule. Judge Calaway—two ll's—told me he talked freely to—who was that guy who snuk [sic] in here and wrote Vigilantes for the Satevepost? Birney? Not supposing Birney failed to understand what was given in confidence and what for use: and that he wouldn't have permitted some of the things Birney told in print for

$500 or any price. I think that is dirty. I don't know just how you are handling your material, whether you are generously advertising the persons who say this and that, or not—digression from a deviation, but did you notice how Isabel Paterson said that so-and-so, "not understanding the uses of publicity, failed to mention the title of his forthcoming book"?——————but I, for instance, wouldn't resent anyone's quoting me as quoting Linderman in his strictures on my book; but it would put an altogether different aspect on what he said if he were quoted as saying it to anyone but me. He and I are friends, and it would put him in a false light to suggest that he criticized my work except directly to me. I'm using this as an illustration of what I mean. So now here is some gossip re Russell, not to be pinned to its source and blazoned to the world. I asked Alberta just why all R's old friends hated Nancy. She said because they felt she commercialized everything so, and forced Russell to meet persons she considered valuable to his note as an artist, whom he hated to bother with.

When Russell died Nancy solicited all his old friends for funds for the Russell memorial (his studio in Gt Falls) and they contributed; and after that she came again and again (so the story is), and they were indignant and more or less disgusted.

This, for instance: Bair knows the man who owns the original Russell, "The Last of Five Thousand" done on the end of a cracker box. Nancy has tried and tried to get the man to give it to her. He will not. Every time Bair appears in her vicinity she rushes and gushes, but invariably tips the secret reason of her cordiality by urging him to use his influence to get this picture away from the owner.

(You know Cole, of course, and his NY collection."Nuther [sic] interlude)

Once the Bairs were at the Ambassador hotel, Los Angeles. Alberta at table; tap on shoulder. Charley Russell there. Long talk. Until Nancy intervenes, calls Alberta to the table behind her, introduces dinner guests—Groomed, stiff, important, wealthy, European. (Russell was in tux and sash) Alberta sits at Nancy's table; Russell in great discomfort and boredom, answering only in monosyllables when spoken to. When he gets a chance he asks Alberta, "Has Charley" i.e. Charley Bair "heard from Pink-eye Smith lately?" "Oh, yes" and Alberta was off—Pink-eye had just killed a man, and had written her father to say that the killing was entirely justified, and that if Bair will send him money for a lawyer for his trial, he will work for Bair for nothing for the rest of his life (Pink-eye was at the time 85)—and Russell and Alberta spend the evening having a good time with Pink-eye, while the European prospective moneyed purchasers stiffen up and Nancy bides her time to say what she thinks.

Russell didn't want to wear tails, and didn't want to run after moneyed people to buy his pictures; and Nancy wanted to cash in on her husband's talent; and both were right. So there you are.

I waste an AWFUL lot of time on you.[20]

Coates to Rankin: December 14, 1936

Dear JBR,
Did I go cryptic on you, just when I thought we understood each other?...

She thirteen times repeats his single seasons

And may be many women in a night.

　Between them lies

A strange, uncalendered day

No leap year can set right.

Your letters are extremely interesting to me.
Gal was supposed to type for me this morning, and she ai'n't [sic] here.
I've done a huge washing this morning—rugs and ev'ry [sic] thing.
These are facts, startling in their clarity. Like 'em?
I'll tell you somebody to approach on the Russell business: John Barrows, author of UBET (which you should examine) who lives in San Diego. 3775 Utah Street. I mean San Diego, Calif, in case there are any others in these United States. I was thinking of somebody else, too, the other day; but now his name escapes me.

Don't think, when I say Russell was reputedly lazy, that I mean it as a criticism. It is a fact, like the color of his eyes, which Linderman calls "yellow as a wolf's." I know too well the disaster of trying to push one's physical energy and activity, when also doing creative work. Part of Russell's genius was accepting the necessity, unconsciously probably, of being lazy. That was the one difficulty—one of the difficulties—between him and Nancy. Russell said he couldn't paint pictures the way one took a job of sawing cordwood. But Nancy wanted money, and that was the way Nancy worked—systematically, like doing a good neat job of sawing wood. She wanted Russell to work according to the clock; she say no sense in writing a letter, convulsively [sic] illustrated, to sent to a sheepherder—even tho [sic] the sheepherder had once been a cowboy and a pal.

She saw a great talent, and could see no purpose for such a god-given gift except to make money—for her, for them, for social position and prestige. She didn't want old cow hands showing up, coming round to the house and embarrassing her before her swanky guests, and being greeted by Russell while the toffs were ignored; and worse, tolling Russell off to take a drink, when he might be painting a picture to sell for $500. She wanted Russell to be eccentric, yes, if he must; but consciously so—his eccentricities all under control, turned on and off as the advantage lay. In other words, Nancy was a schoolteacher. Like me.

And when old roughnecks did show up, to Russell's hospitable delight, she showed her disapproval, and didn't hesitate to be rude to Russell along with the guest; and, so those who knew her say, she was a trouble maker even between Russell and his friends of high standing. She was always alert to see if someone wasn't going to reap some advantage from Russell; and since doing his friends a good turn was Russell's life, of course they weren't always so happy over this.

I'm telling you the essence of what I believe regarding them. I am sure she was, in her way, a fine woman; and Russell owed her much. But he owed her both success and all that spoiled the success. A man, every man, and most especially every artist, has to choose. But Nancy made Russell's choice for him; and the very core of an artist is the necessity of making his own choices. So, it has seemed to me, knowing nothing about it—as who knows anything about the human soul, even his own?—that Nancy made Russell, and in making him destroyed him. She blocked his natural outgoing carefree service of all his friends, the devotion of his art to the fun of friendship and coerced him into commercial success.

But what artist has a right to be married, anyway?

Sulzer[Seltzer]—is that the way he spells his name?—in Great Falls, Russell's pupil—his wife sitting with folded hands, hardly daring to breathe, because Sulzer was painting. Sulzer, letting his art, his temperament, his nerves have full right of way; getting somewhere, gut hell to be around. Consuming his wife's life in order to be an artist. That isn't right either, it is?

IL think if I go to bed on Proust every night, by the end of 1937 I'll be able to write a sentence that doesn't end until the next letter.

Many delicate deaths we die

Besides wide-eyed innocence and

And sleep's peace across the eye.

Pretense dies stubborn;

But we see

All are tender blossoming,

Spicy buds of the Dark Tree.

     Yes

     GSC[21]

∞

The Lady Speaker

She ended, competent and serene;
   And in the silence that followed after,
The hinterland of her mind, unseen,
   Crackled with imps' derisive laughter.

As the ladies patted her grave applause
   She was alert in her soul's defense,
Parrying thrust of *deed* with *cause*,
   Wresting honesty from pretense.

Gracefully one by one withdrew
   With a courteous word for her larger vision;
Hung on an inner cross she knew
   The biting laughter of self-derision.

CHAPTER ELEVEN

G race Stone Coates began the year 1937 with thanks to James Rankin for books that he sent her.

> I was wholly delighted, and 2/3 provoked, with your pleasant thought of this bookless region and my necessities. What I want to do is lay a mortgage on your Russell, if as and when. Long silent Will Saroyan, my dear friend, sent me his three books—Daring Young Man, 3x3, Provoked, I happen to be one of those persons when—how shall I say it?—haven't learned how to enjoy being given gifts...A little self-advertising—like sending you P. in W. [Portulacas in the Wheat] —now coming up—that is different.
>
> When I'm sane again I'll write.[1]

Merriam continued to struggle with the economics of the *Frontier and Midland* and expressed to Grace his concerns.

"I hope that you have received the six copies of the Winter issue of F&M—You may have as many free copies as you wish of each issue; just tell me the number you want and that number will be sent to you—especially if you can get J. Edgar Hoover[2] to set some of his G-men on the trail of defaulting subscribers.

"I am definitely stating," he wrote,

> that unless I can find some way to reduce the present indebtedness of FRONTIER AND MIDLAND I shall close out the magazine with the Summer issue—although I don't really expect to be able to get around to that task that early. Can you give us any suggestions or other help in this problem of reducing indebtedness? Could you give us the names of any persons with some money who might be interested in helping us; or would you write some letters for us? I do certainly hope we can manage to keep going. I have always sworn that I would not enlist the support of a number of patrons at say $5 a year. Would you suggest that we descend to that devise? I shall certainly appreciate any suggestions you would make. I hope you feel, as I do, that the magazine is partly yours (this does not mean that anyone but myself be responsible for any of the indebtedness!)[3]

Grace immediately answered,

Last night's train brought me your letter, which meant a great deal to me…Your letter meant much to me, partly because I have wished to find a mood in which I could explain something of my own circumstances to you, without raking so much cactus and brambles over my (Oh, sweet and sound,) artichoke heart.

About the magazine: it would be impossible, of course, for me to envisage what my days would have been without all it has represented. To take from me what my writing has meant, would have left things drab indeed. There was a time when I had the world by the tail here in Martinsdale; and could have done a good deal in a financial way for it. But it happed [sic] that just at the time when the Frontier was launched I had lost prestige; and with the depression coming on and the pressure for public funds greater and greater, there never seemed a time when I could attempt any of the money raising things we once did. This is all by the way, but it is a fact that for some inner or outer reason I always felt estopped when it came to trying to raise money for it.

You have carried a load, with that magazine; and have had large draughts of inappreciation [sic]; and been able to swallow them and go on. And you have had inestimable pleasures from it, I feel sure. (It does seem as though a great university…) I will do some thinking and write you soon—the Hidekopers have money and might do something; the Bairs have money (and keep it.) OF COURSE I'll write letters, any number, any time. Most of the big ranches around here are broke—my friends who once had money keep on acting as though they had, but the banks hold their mortgages and the stores are stuck with their bills. (My best bet would be to smile at some of the drunken sheepherders when they come in with their year's paychecks!)

Henderson this moment came in with, among other things, a letter from Archie…Archie is capable of unusual courtesy and deference, and he exercised both whenever he spoke of what you had done for Montana. He asks me if I care to read any of his mss before he sends it off, so I surmise his "Gallant Troupers" is almost completed. If he has luck there, it may be the making of that boy; but, Oh, dear, depending on any Irishman who drinks is "leaning your elbow on the wind." So I expect nothing, not even a letter; and then whatever comes is so much to the good.

This letter has grown too long to accommodate anything about the status of my own writing, which I wanted to tell you about. But I can't now; and will some day when telling you seems important.[4]

Conditions on the University of Montana's campus brought a hiatus in Merriam's correspondence to Grace. She was still doing the literary column, but her story and poem contributions stopped and she was doing less editing.

The give and take of the correspondence between Rankin and Coates had brought a new interest in Grace's life. She recalled her love of New York through his letters, remembering the delicacies and delights of the city and some of her experiences from the times she spent there.

COATES TO RANKIN: FEBRUARY 2, 1937

> Dear Mr. Rankin,
> I'm not doing so well by you; but give me time.
> Mr. Coates has been sick—nothing serious; but it threw some of his work on me.
> Your letters are always delightful. Once I used lots of time writing many expansive letters. For some reason the desire left me, and I'm not so eager as I was.
> I am always busy, and usually over busy. If you know how I hated to sit down and make a cleaning on this desk tonight you'd know I have a strong conscience. Now I have to go mix Henderson an eggnog, and mebbe [sic] drink one myself. I dunno.
> Anyway, I appreciate your fine letters.
> > *Grace Coates*
> A friend separated from me by miles of 10-foot snow has my Repplier.[5] One of these days when the big thaw comes, I'll get it back.[6]

LINDERMAN TO COATES: FEBRUARY 17, 1937

> Dear Medicine-woman
> Thanks for the clipping—enjoyed it. But Golly what a winter this has been— and yet *is*. Deer, heaps of them, are in sight every day—and at night they even enter our woodshed to nibble hay which I bought for them, and which I scatter near the porch so the kids may watch the feeding. Ice on the bay is two feet thick—never saw such before—and the snow is yet deep—but so far no deer have been killed by coyotes, thanks to the softened condition of the snow.
> I'm afraid that affairs at the university are not so fine. I'm sorry. I'm afraid that some of the English department will quit. I'm going to try to pay Missoula a visit soon—and then I'll learn what's going on.
> I'm trying desperately to make that novel you read (CHICK) into a long short story, but maybe I shall fail. Sent WOLF AND THE WINDS, BIG JINNY, MIKE, and two short stories to an agent in New York on the suggestion of two of my good friends in that city. Don't expect anything to come of the venture—and when the ms returns I'll send the bear story to Houghton-Mifflin, who have said they'd "read it with a view of publishing the story"; and I think they'd like it. Can't even make a guess on the other things. I told

you that I re-wrote the last part of WOLF, letting him live the 30 years for the reader. Maybe I improved it. Anyhow the job's done.

Wish I lived where I might chat with a writing-person once in a while. But, Say, this house isn't so still these days. The kids have a great time (but you, yes, even an enemy of mine, could have the radio) Better pay us a visit. Ho!

F.B.L.[7]

Linderman's allusion to the English department at the University concerned their friend, H.G. Merriam. Following Dr. C.H. Clapp's death, an interim president was appointed to run the institution. Merriam was on a committee to seek a new president. The low pay and lack of benefits made the search for an outside person fruitless, although a poll of the faculty had indicated that they would prefer an outsider.

A downtown business and professional group proposed Dr. George Simmons, an Assistant Professor of Zoology with two years of service on the faculty. Although letters to previous employers indicated that Dr. Simmons would be a poor choice, the downtown group was able to push through Dr. Simmons' nomination. The faculty committee considered this a sharp rebuff and thought the action of the downtown Missoula group undue interference in University affairs.

One of the first problems that arose regarded censorship. After a history professor had appeared before the Board of Education in August of 1936 to complain about the bad moral conditions on the campus and read, out of context, objectionable passages from Vardis Fisher's novel *Passions Spin the Plot,* the board passed a ruling that the novel and all books of a similar character should be removed from the shelves of the libraries of all of the units of the University System. The novel had been placed on the leisure time reading shelf by the librarian, Professor Phillip Keeney. It had also been offered on a bulletin board of the Department of English at a reduced price if combined with a subscription to *Frontier and Midland.* Professor Keeney was particularly loud and persistent in public denunciation of the ruling.

When the new school year opened, Dr. Simmons received two petitions, one protesting censorship and the other asking the Board of Education to rescind its action. He in turn proposed to the faculty that a campus community committee be set up to see that "proper standards" characterized choice of library books, student publications, dramas and exhibits.

Although the censorship itself was not mandated, Dr. Simmons influenced the choice of drama and articles on the campus. He wrote to Keeney and Merriam that

...if the two of you set a proper tone for your departments there would not exist at the present time the campus turmoil shown by The Kaimin...such turmoil and lack of teaching efficiency cannot be tolerated.[8]

Friction on the campus was accelerated when Professors Keeney and J.P. Rowe re-established a chapter of the American Federation of Teachers, an organization which was affiliated with the American Federation of Labor. The members were concerned about faculty rights. The president did not outwardly object to the formation of the Union, but many people of the community construed the union as socialistic, if not communistic.

The problems came to a head when the Board of Education, upon complaints from Dr. Simmons, placed Rowe upon month-to-month tenure. At the same meeting, Keeney was dismissed without a hearing. After an appeal that went into court, Keeney was reinstated. However in 1939, the board investigative committee from the legislature recommended that Professors E.A. Atkinson, P.O. Keeney, N.J. Lennes, H. G. Merriam and C.E.F. Moller be dismissed. After Keeney had been reinstated by order of the Supreme Court of Montana, Merriam was told by friends that he might be under fire and requested appearance before the committee but was not granted an interview. He learned of the board's action in the morning's newspaper. Merriam immediately resigned and took a position with the University of Oregon. His resignation was later changed to a leave of absence and he returned to Montana after a year in Oregon.

COATES TO RANKIN: MARCH 9, 1937

Dear Mr. Rankin,

Your gentle and most courteous letter of March 3 would prompt me to write one as pleasing, if I knew how.

I hadn't supposed anything said about either M&M [Mead and Mandel-Wurzel] or PinW [Portulacus in the Wheat] could please or displease me; but your comment pleased me—and two other recent comments from women pleased me: one that M&M was a ferocious book; and the other that it made her hurt, as she hurt when her babies were being born. God bless 'em all—but yours pleased me for two reasons, one that I think your good opinion worth having, and the other that I think well enough of your sincerity to believe you could have found a noncommittal platitude within the frame of courtesy if that had been what you wanted to do.

Because you don't know my agony of lostness for NYC you can not understand what such things as your Clavilux program do to me. And all the rest that you send me. I haven't even told you about enjoying the book catalogues and putting them away, and last week *finding* them again. I must have a traumatism—indeed, I know I have—about unfamiliar things where only the known is supposed to be; and I looked at the catalogues in fascinated horror until I had them placed again; and then read in them once more. It is only recently that I can go to our silly village masquerades, for the shuddering horror in my spine at the faces. Most of the causes of my occasional quirks reveal themselves to me in my sleep, like slivers gradually working to the surface; as this one did. I am not neurotic, nor am I hysterical, tho of the hysterical diatheses I suppose. But for attacks of pseudo-hysterics, no, not for me. Mr. Coates came into the kitchen, behind me, as I was lifting a steak from the broiler to the platter. He spoke, but as I turned I saw him in an unfamiliar black oilcloth apron a prune peddler had just given him. I threw the platter of meat and screamed, and went into a second attack of hysterics I had ever experienced. Weeks afterward, awakening one morning, I found myself living again an experience of infancy: My father standing in one corner of the kitchen in a yellow "slicker" coaxing me to recognize him; I in my crib—or cradle? In the opposite corner, laughing as long as he stood still and talked, uncontrollably screaming when he started toward me, no matter how slowly. He had thoughtlessly come in, I was told long afterward, wearing his slicker and had picked me up abruptly and sent me into convulsions. These things are of no interest except to the chance person who happens to like diving below the surface. *Black Cherries* is a series of childhood remembrances of things past. I believe I have a more marked memory for things of childhood than some persons. One of the stories, The Way of the Transgressor, started with a peculiar feeling of tension in my wrists after a poet, Dr. Neumann, had written me that we—he and I—were like two steel blades hanking at each other. His name is Newman, by the way: Israel Newman. And after weeks the memory and the story came. I do not know why I am writing you all this, except that your letter was gentle and made me cry.

...And, yes, another thing I have saved up to say to you: Tovarish, with due allowance for Greenwich Village and Martinsdale, the very atmosphere of my home. Can you see me all slicked up waiting for Captain somebody on a certain midnight train; a literature who was to give me a story—the Captain not arriving—I still reading at 2:30 [a.m.]—my dress, doubtless, awry; a knock; I answer, forgetting the unusual hour—remembering might have made me afraid. A queer creature with a bed roll, who introduced himself as Captain Bride. He had just arrived by freight. He came, and he stayed—but I can not spread my entire life on paper, can I?

Oh, yes: Borscht and pumpernickel. Yes, indeed...As my father grew old it became impossible for him to accept any gift. He always returned gifts, with beautiful courtesy and finality—and I am very like my father, except in courtesy...You remember Fra Lippo Lippi—"...my whole soul revolves, the cup runs over, the world and life's too big to pass for a dream And I do these wild things in sheer despite, and play the fooleries you catch me at, in pure rage!"

The drifts are going fast. One of these days I shall descend on my friend and get Repplier and read it; and tell you (she doesn't come here because she still owes me for some books she had me order!) and in the mean time I'll cuddle my cat—it is distinctly not a cuddley [sic] cat. (That was not nice of me to say that about the gal and the debt)…Did I tell you to ask George P. Mallon[9] of 272 Murphey Ave. Sunnyvale, Calif., about Russell. He knew him well. I suggest you do not use my name. Linderman got a kick because I sent him the excised portion of letter you sent me about killing the widow.

And all good fortune to you.

GSCoates[10]

It was a late spring in Montana. Grace wrote to Rankin that the hills were still covered with snow and ranchers in the foothills were buying hay for $25 a ton, but the prospects for the range were the best in years. She would not plan to garden earlier than May 15.

The fishing was ruined, she reported, between dry riverbeds last summer and game hogs. One can find fishing in spots, but the automobiles were able to take the men to the "happy hunting grounds" and the hunting is thereby doomed, and the grounds cease to be happy.

Out of Martinsdale, Mr. Bair was blasting to change the Musselshell River to make a new channel to go in front of the house while Alberta and Marguerite were visiting in Portland.

Oh, yes: yesterday, by dint of letter-pressure, I got back Repplier IN PURSUIT OF LAUGHTER. As I say, I am doing a 14 hour stretch, minimum, but one of these days I'll be expressing renewed gratitude for Agnes [Repplier]. My Persian cat, well, my cat….

Sincerely yours, GSCoates[11]

COATES TO RANKIN: UNDATED

Dear Six-floors-up,
One of these days I'll fool you by sending a blue envelope from somebody else.

Bear with me: the word was *gentle* not *tender*. The terms are not interchangeable. An old hoss is often gentle, but even a young critter isn't always tender. I felt that your letter had the gentle courtesy with which a competent alienist approaches a lunatic just before he claps a straightjacket around him.

Forgive me for not mentioning the Cary business; yes. Send me, say, four, and I'll see what I can do; and will return them. You bus' my heart with schedules and programs.

GSC[12]

Several of us got fun out of the Coronation issue of the New York Sun. Much of my joy came in again seeing the Sun's masthead. When we were very poor, father, a New Yorker lost in the wilds of Kansas, kept up his subscription to the NYSun; and once when he asked me, a five-year old, what I had been reading in the Sun, I answered "The murders and suicides"—i.e. the—*cream of the telegraph* column—short items, brief and to the point, and short enough to attract a child's eye.

I have not met Mr. Marchand. Since to attend a movie means a night drive of 60 miles, I see few movies and have not seen The Plainsman.

…Answer to when my next book will be off the press: God knows.

I am leaving for Billings Monday; for Rochester, Minn., soon after, *perhaps.* But I'll get the Cary story in when the moment strikes me. I am looking forward to a drive to Crow Indian reservation while I am in eastern Montana— a girl droll of humor lives there. I wish I had saved her comments on that Indian airhostess, Miss Pease, to send you.

Your coronation edition of the Sun finally reached the hands of a good Scotsman here, who surely must have enjoyed at least portions of it.[13]

In May Grace wrote to Rankin that she was leaving for the Mayo Clinic in Rochester and when she came back, she expected to find a pair of Martin Larsen shoes awaiting her feet. Beginning then, she wrote, she would be ready to grow backward and resume her youth. "Nothing the matter—I'm tired all the time and want to find out why. Until I am rested I can't write—unless I fall in love, and then I'll be tired of that. Persons who have to be in love to write love lyrics are not poets. Vide Eddie Guest."

Still helping him find information about the Russells, she told him,

Dan Conway disappeared in more or less disgrace, persona non grata to the Montana Newspaper Association. I think he conspired with Mrs. Russell to chew the hand that had fed the public publicity for them.

A woman, 31, came to visit me for a few days; she has been here five or six weeks, and says she prays every night (only one knowing her godless soul would understand the figure of speech) that Henderson and Grace won't send her away—will let her stay another day, was what she said I believe. She is going to stay here while I go to Rochester—and let the natives howl; and in the Fall has a chance to work the state likker [sic] store while the owner goes to Rochester. She is smart and amiable, and I've always wanted to have an amiable person around, having been cursed with situations most of my conscious life. I hope we can like each other even after several months of contact—usually quick joys had sudden ends; but we don't like each other, so much, as we play amicably together, and neither takes offense at sharp thrusts to parry.

Sincerely yours, GSC

I have just promised the Montana Standard to do the Cary story for them when I get home [14]

COATES TO RANKIN: JULY 2, 1937

Dear Mr. Rankin,

What fun to look forward to seeing whether you are 250 pounds and bald, or 140 with a black mustache.

Billings is on the Northern Pacific and we are on the Milwaukee, and it is a disagreeable trip, so find a way of coming by auto if you get a chance. C.M. Bair is often in Billings at the Northern Hotel, and you might happen to hit him at the right time and place. But do come over, spite of discomfort, for we would like to see you. I am sorry that, as usual, I have two guests, and can't find a trundle bed for you. (One of my guests might be complacent!) But we always eat. The Bairs are at hand, only around the corner a quarter of a mile away—our corners are large in the wide open spaces.

I'm either sick or limp or something and have entirely stopped what was once my soul's delight—spreading myself on letters. But letters or none, we look forward to seeing you; and talking with Charlie Bair will be well worth your time. And by all means see Linderman in Western Montana. He and I are rather especially good friends, and I think I might make a good approach for you in that quarter. Mr. Linderman likes the dislikes with good Western fervor.

If things were not so tough with us we'd come after you. But Henderson is already swamped with obligations, half-dead dipsomaniac partner—flighty wife—age creeping upon him—lame hip. I think if I asked him to drive empty miles to bring home a stray male I'd attached by letter, he'd give me a dirty look. If it were a bathing beauty, now...

If you will let me know when you are coming I'll dig out your letters and the Cary material and try to make it look as if I were writing a story. (My difficulty is a violent flare-up of arthritis in my hands, heigh-ho, which makes using the typewriter set them singing and me talking to myself.) If you want to have a hint as to my relative baldness, weight, temperament, etc., I'll type on the other side something that cost me a friendship with another unknown who wrote me sentimental letters—how he passed thru Martinsdale, broke, on a stock train, and saw a beauteous vision of someone he thought was me playing tennis. God be with you till we meet, and afterward.

Sincerely, Grace Coates[15]

COATES TO RANKIN: JULY 13, 1937

Dear Mr. Rankin,

Taking your recent letter from the office, I mailed one to you at Billings. Disregard it, of course—what else!

Mr. Linderman will be happy to see you. I had written him about you, assuring him that by all the signs and portents you were not a pest. (It is a dangerous thing to rely on a stranger's sense of humor, otherwise I'd tell you that Henderson seems to think you are wandering around the country, betraying friendly dogs—devouring them, like eccentric slices of watermelon.)

Do try to make this small town—for the Bair's sake; if not for mine; and in Helena see W.W. Cheely, who runs a unique news service—Montana stuff only, county paper syndicate. It would be fine to see the Huidekopers while you are here. Their American ranch is worth seeing. We could manage that, I am sure, from here.

Did you see the—paint people—Linderman can tell you who I mean—in Butte. Or…but Mr. Linderman will know everything you should do. In Missoula make contact with H.G. Merriam, State University, editor of the Frontier & Midland, and my onetime boss. Schatzlein—that is the name I couldn't think of.

All good fortune to you.

Sincerely, GSC[16]

LINDERMAN TO COATES: JULY 17, 1937

Dear Mrs. Coates

Will you hand this note to Mr. Rankin when he stops at your fire?

Mr. Rankin—I forgot to ask you if you had talked, or are going to talk to Percy Raban of Los Angeles. He could tell you much about Charley's life in Great Falls etc. I do not remember his address, but having worked on the newspapers in Los Angeles you should have no trouble finding him—you may say that I suggested talking with him. And then there is Josephine Trigg, of the Gt. Falls Public Library—she ought to prove valuable to you. I'd see her. Good luck to you.

Frank B. Linderman, FBL[17]

In July, Jim Rankin made a trip to Martinsdale and stayed with the Coates. He was able to visit with C.M. Bair about Russell.

Although correspondence between Merriam and Grace was scant these years, *The Frontier* was still part of Grace's work, and she wrote to Merriam in August that the literary news would be on time for the fall issue. She said she had had company continuously since April 1.

COATES TO MERRIAM: AUGUST 13, 1937

"Noivous [sic] women! Two goiters at one time is three too many."

Augusta and I talked the past until she, with high cheek bones and Indian blood and what she supposed was acquired stoicism beside, had hysterics. I think that is a real accomplishment, to make a stoic go wild.

Enough about myself.

I'm glad about your book. I've wanted to—not explain but state to you my own writing status. There is no use telling the would-be kind friends like Gipson who urge me not to be discouraged that they are barking up an exotic tree that doesn't grow in my garden. It sums up to this, that I became aware that I was trying to do this and that from outside pressure, when what I wanted to do was get outdoors and make garden. I have only one life, and if gardening is what I want, writing becomes silly. The only reason to write is because one has something he wants to say. And my writing is in fine shape, I'm doing what I want to do, and when I get the damned company off my hands if when as I do write, I'll be again writing what I want to write.

You being my guardian angel of the writing province had that much of an explanation coming to you.[18] There is more to it, but that's enough. My writing and I are at peace with each other and have been ever since I decided to run my own machinery.

Forgive me for spilling on to the second page. I've got to the place where, I loathe the sight of letters, either to read or write.

I had a sudden, violently fast-spreading arthritis that alarmed me. I haven't got it subdued yet, but think I'm on the right track. Incidentally, I had a great clarin-up spree, and mentioned to the usually understanding Dick Lake that I was burning up loads of stuff, getting ready to die. I meant they had passed permanently out of my life, and any conclusion is in a sense a birth but a death as well. But Dick, it seems, told all and sundry I was on my last legs. So…

How about Archie? Every time The Tribune comes out with the right head on the wrong story, and more typo errors than usual I worry about that lad.

Don't write. I'll shoot along the lit news. Yes, I get the poetry bulletins. I have a brand new racket adventure, but probably rackets are an old story, and boobs are ordained to be sold anyway.

Sincerely, GSC

Letters to the NYTimes about the F.W.P.[19] have been increasingly caustic.[20]

The unrest at the University continued. Grace expressed her concern about *The Frontier*, the Administration, Merriam and incidentally the Keeneys:

COATES TO MERRIAM: AUGUST 13, 1937

> I'm desperately sorry that the English department isn't getting the support it deserves and has earned. I'd be sorry to see a Communist put out of a job he was filling well because he was a Communist. I'm even sorrier to see a man kept in a job because he is a Communist and his comrades make a noise about him. I would regret individual injustice to the Keeneys or any one else; and regret more seeing properly constituted authority lie down to the plumbers union, et al. Mrs. Holbrook, with her flair for inaccuracy, assured me you had taken The Frontier to the coast. I saw her in Minneapolis.[21]

As the summer waned, Merriam wrote and apologized for not writing more. Grace immediately set his mind at ease.

> Dear H.G.M., Your correspondence, committed or omitted, has not seemed unsatisfactory to me. I think of you only as a friend who lets me write whatever pops into my head when I sit down without taking any of it seriously. Few of my letters bear any relation to what I intended to say.
>
> The seething present is so full of things to ponder I wish I could stretch myself enormously to cover more of it. The Standard carries note of Viking Press "American Stuff" (WPA) and current Scribner's has an article about Conrad Kohrs old ranch. If possible include the few notes I send with this. — or maybe they might wait for better mention in the Winter issue.
>
> I can't read for Frontier for at least a month. Something is simmering that has come up in the last few days. I can tell you about it later. Gwendolen Haste sent me a lovely poem for comment, not for publication; saying she wants to submit material to you later; asking about the magazine. She is married, you know, but keeps her name and her good job with General Foods. Has a recent promotion and private office; gives lectures on literature to employees. Perhaps a note to her—same address—might please her (from you.)
>
> If I could send you a letter from Marg Chagnon, which I probably can't, and you could understand it, which you couldn't, men would understand women, which they don't. By the way, I forgot to make note that according to supersensory data assembled thru 26,780 experiments in Columbia University, women show 50% greater capacity for supersensory "savvy" than men. However, any good grammarian could point out the absence of antecedents for my whiches.[22]

It was sometimes necessary to chide Grace to get her literary notes for *The Frontier*. He also chided her for her outspoken views about the Writers' Project.

MERRIAM TO COATES: OCTOBER 30, 1937

> Dear G.S.C.,
> Anytime now that you are ready to send in the Literature News section for our Winter issue of December 19, I should be glad to get it. I am in somewhat of a hurry because The Missoulian will work on FRONTIER copy only at moments when it does not have other work on hand; this means that if I get material late it is likely to not get set up on time and the issue is likely to be delayed. In regard to this number delay would be fatal because I am trying to get advertising on the basis that the issue will appear in time to advertise books for Christmas purchasing.
>
> McPhee's letter did give me a chuckle. Of course, you are under no necessity of accepting my advice, but I think you would do well to "lay off" the Federal Writers Project. You had plenty of grief handling it, no doubt, but you also had good fun and you got paid. It seems to me that you and Chadbourne and I ought not to do anything harmful to the Project.
>
> I am still looking for a story or some poems from you for FRONTIER. It has been a long time since we have printed your name over material.
>
> *Sincerely yours, HGM*[23]

COATES TO MERRIAM: NOVEMBER 13, 1937

> Dear HGM,
> We are always at cross purposes. I stomped a lot of Guide book material into the stove because I thought that was what you were advising against. I haven't been because I am abashed that I have been silent: I am going to entertain the Lutheran Ladies Aid and have been trying to bring my house to that standard of glowing perfection perennially maintained by these Norwegian women. Right now I'm taking a rest from waxing (and waning) the kitchen floor.
>
> Dr. Phillips: The Tribune runs a column, "Getting acquainted with the University." In it I noticed the item that he had resigned, and that no one else could take his place in this and that. That was my sole information about him. I supposed he had resigned because he was ready to and wanted to.[24] You left me with my jaw down. If I had known he was in trouble I wouldn't have picked that time to be flippant about his odd behavior of a year or so ago. He had been quite courteous and cordial to me as of other years, and had given me historical material; so that I looked on him if not as a friend, at least as a good guy. When I was last in Missoula I met him in front of your

WPA office, and naturally spoke—blithely I suppose. He looked at me without speaking, so I added still blithely, "I'm Mrs. Coates." He answered, "I know you are Mrs. Coates," and that was the sum total of our conversation for the rest of the summer. Now what had got into the historical-minded gentleman? I had had no communication with him, no dealings with him our paths hadn't crossed, I was the same Mrs. Coates he had been (as I say) quite courteous to. Is it just that everybody gets queer who works for the Great White Father? Or say, who is immersed in the atmosphere of the Missoula campus? Have you any idea what ailed him?

The Keeneys: Marg Chagnon wrote me that Angus had spent a grand week there, sleeping on the floor on a hard mattress and eating the abominable food she cooked, and having a wonderful time; and that Mary Jane was in the Blackfoot country. I had supposed their troubles were settled, and in their favor; but of course Marg's words made me assume that in this I was mistaken. So I asked about them.

AND me: Perhaps I have said or written something oversmart, that I would blush for if I had to read it out loud in cold blood. But in general, I believe if whatever I have said or written were repeated in toto, and with reference to the comment to which it was a response, there wouldn't been much I need feel painfully ashamed of. There was a scamper of lively limericks, but since I got rapped over the head quite as wittily as anyone else, I thought it was all good natured. I did land on Taylor well and often; but in the end he said he agreed with much I had said, and expressed his good will; and still writes from time to time, casual stuff about his work and his plans. And I have maintained, and still maintain, that the thing I consider wrong about all this relief work is that the administrative costs are too high. The money goes where it is not vitally needed. This criticism hit me as hard as any one, so I felt the more free to express it. And I still say this, in season and out; and must perforce address those ears which I can reach. If I knew where to say it to better effect, I would. Of $2,000 spent for relief in Meagher county, $1,500 went to its administration. That is wrong.

I feel sorry the Keeneys are in suspense; but an impartial person might feel that their incessant and acrid tongues do not make for peace on the campus.

I'm sorry you can't bust loose with a white and cleansing rage at things as they shouldn't be. I like to watch angry persons, acting in anger. In anger a man shows himself unmistakably—white, pink or yellow, or only purple.

Thank you for your letter. I haven't a new thing to offer you. One of these days I'll be writing again, and it will be when I have something I want to say, and am saying it.

Thank you, again.[25]

Alice Roosevelt Longworth and Theodore Roosevelt, Jr., published *The Desk Drawer Anthology* in 1937. They sought to give preference to good verse by little known Americans on American subjects. Next they planned to use favorites from American poets of the last hundred years, and the final category composed of English poets of the same period. Grace's contribution revealed her feelings of her childhood home

Prairie Birth

I was born on the prairie;
   I know how a partridge rises
Like a bullet out of the grain fields.
   I have watched the coveys of quail
Running along the road
   In front of a loaded wagon
And the wagons hurrying to the barn
   Ahead of the rattling hail.
Here the valleys lift
   Toward pine-swept peaks above them;
I hold my peace when their dwellers
   Disparage the level sod,
Canyon and cliff are vast;
   My heart is glad that men love them.
But no less for me on the prairie
   Has rested the hand of God.

Roosevelt sent Grace a copy with this inscription, "To Miss Grace Stone Coates, I hope you'll like this anthology—By this time you must be pretty well snowed in—Best Wishes Theodore Roosevelt."

Roosevelt had corresponded with Court Durand in 1927 congratulating him for putting elk on his dude ranch, but there is no record if he ever visited in the area to know Grace personally.

Coates to Rankin; November 16, 1937

Dear Jim,
You are warm in our hearts; but I am getting ready to entertain the Lutheran Ladies Aid; and as I did once when I served my first goose, I've asked everybody

I ran across to come. The consequence is I'm beginning to wonder where I'll get the sandwiches, and who'll make 'em.

So this is short and earnest, this note. I appreciated the Longmans Green *blotto*—and laid down a waitress' tray to scamper in here and write this to you.

Hunting season. Henderson out every day and every day; this sitting up till midnight—on my temperament—and getting up at 4 a.m.—on his is devastating.

Thank you over and over for your various greetings; send me some more Book Fair news. I take the NY Times, but recently only the Sunday issue. I miss the daily Times, but it was taking too much of my time to even skim it. I hope your big book is going good. I had a letter from Archie Clark recently, mentioning you (impersonally, as a Frontier news note. Did you know you were a news note?)

I am sorry we did not see you again. Will you visit us again, sometime? I— but never mind. I'll say it next time. I feel sorry, sorry, about the dog.

> *Grace*[26]

Coates to Kuhlman; December 11, 1937

Dear Mr. Kuhlman,

When I acknowledged receipt of your Billings article I had not yet read it—for amusing reasons. (I had received it when in the throes of entertaining the Lutheran Ladies Aid, and in oooshing everything extraneous out of the way, had put the story away so carefully I couldn't find it.)

This morning I hunted it down and read it, with great interest. I like your fine way of expressing what you have to say, forceful without being forced, and animated without being glib. I shall send it to Mr. Linderman on the chance that he will enjoy it as well as I did. Thank you, again, for sending it to me.

It seems to me this ought to be a magazine sale. It is in print, to be sure, but could be modified enough to pass for a wider market.

> *Sincerely yours, Grace Stone Coates*[27]

Coates to Kuhlman: December 30, 1937

Dear Mr. Kuhlman,

"Easy" writing makes hard reading—a bromide of the trade. But your story struck me as the kind of "Easy" reading that comes from clear thought and honest weighing of your words. Before a thing is logical and smooth on paper it has had a lot of turning over in somebody's mind.

The Tribune and the MNA[28]—also the Montana Standard, are good outlets for any Montana writing on historical themes. Good, too, for discussions of present conditions—take the land around you—it was—it is…

Did I suggest the American Region Monthly: try it.

Have you followed the Duke University experiments in supersensory knowledge? One night some weeks ago I thought of you, for some reason. The next morning—and this is really a most curious thing, as only a person who knows Henderson could understand, Henderson asked me what had become of you. And the next day came your first letter. I think that for some reason of supersensory—"wavelength" you and I communicate after a fashion.

I understand what you mean about havoc among friends; and tho I do not applaud making havoc among friends, I believe I understand how it happens, something of the state of mind that leads to the having, more fully than many persons. I don't do it much, myself; but I've seen it done, and understood.

I'll read your introduction if you wish this. It isn't necessary, but I'll do it.

Sincerely yours, GSCoates[29]

Coates to Rankin: December 29

Dear Jim,

You are too good to me. Like each new book I get, yours will be passed around and give pleasure to plenty of my friends. Let me see…I had confirmation of your questioning statement that Mrs. Russell has been confined to her bed for three years or so; following an automobile accident, I believe…You mentioned the Buckskin Kid, Marble. He wrote me asking if he could send me his mss for possible publication. Of course he considers it grand, a bad sign. Unlettered persons present difficulties in book business. They had exaggerated ideas of their worth, and so when they make no money, think some one is stealing from them.

I wrote him I'd read his mss and tell him what I thought of it for $10 (my first attempt at being a capitalist at the expense of honest merit!) I though this would head him off; and it did, for a time. He waited for months, and then apologized for not answering my letter, and sent the mss, asking me to tell him what I thought of it. I sent it back, saying I thought my earlier letter covered the field. I suppose he is now my enemy. (Only in jest.)

Those lads if lucky get a book published, and then because they make no sale they think some one is gypping them. I want no more of their books. More than that, if I do the work and the publisher turns them down, they are again aggrieved.

I hope, with confidence, that your Christmas was good. Mine was. Always something charming comes my way unexpectedly—as did your gift. My only criticism of the writing was that killing off the protagonists suggests lack of resourcefulness on the part of the author. I thought the descriptions were vivid as paintings could have been. A Kansas artist who spent 1936 in Japan did a small self-illustrated brochure from her notes on flower arrangement

"Elegant Amusement" that is like herself delightful. She was good to remember me when she signed and mailed them.

If I have not answered your various queries or comments write me again.

I've been catching up on social obligations—two more dinners to go and I'll be thru. I hate big dinners, when I have to either get them or eat them. Yesterday I prepared a 19 lb turkey and now will I be able to get it in the oven? I wish you were here to join us for you are such a very soothing and amiable guest.

...I've just turned around and switched off the light—the *morning* light—and raised the curtains; and find it is nine o'clock, and I have a stack of letters beside me—and three news letters off on the 7 o'clock train (that I overlooked by reason of the turkey, yesterday)—so you know I started early.

With all high hopes for your work and you.

   Grace[30]

After several years of silence, William Saroyan wrote and asked for the letters he had written to Grace. In a candid letter to Will, Grace had some rather blunt observations about H. G. Merriam.

COATES TO SAROYAN: JANUARY 11, 1938

Dear Will,

Did you ever want to do something so much that it kept you from doing it?—Your letter—the last one, not this current note: I have answered it mentally every day, I suppose, since I got it. I wanted to indulge myself in an adequate answer (one of those letters written for the good of the writer, not the recipient) I wanted to get a lot of things off my chest about Merriam, which I would say (probably) to no one but you. I've taken a civil service exam, sprained my wrist, entertained the Lutheran Ladies Aid, got caught up on all but one of my dinner obligations (why, why do people want to stew over big dinners, when a smaller dinner and a little more intelligence would go down easier.) Joke on me. Today I was invited as I supposed to a dinner—I am no breakfast eater—so I went empty, to a 1 o clock gathering. Discovered it was not a dinner but a female set around and talk afternoon. At 3:00 pm. Coffee and 14 kinds of Christmas cookies, and if I eat sweet things I begin to hate the world.

That was what kept me from getting your letters off today. They shall go tomorrow express. I can't see anything to move my emotions about your asking for them. I'd like very much to have them back, but after they get into your hands they are yours, and if you don't want to return them, o.k., I won't be resentful. But I'll be deprived and sorry.

In toto the letters, one day some time ago, said something to me they had not said, one by one.[31]

COATES TO SAROYAN: JANUARY 15, 1938

Dear Will,

I don't know whether my body is going to be sick, and is discussing this with my soul; or my soul is sick, and is telling this to my body. Anway, my j'ints ache. For one thing, I fell backward and sprained my wrist—which I was aware of, and dislocated various ribs—which I am becoming aware of. Forgive my lack of order or sequence in my filing (and recovering) of these letters. If I were at my best I'd surely sort them to persuade you I was orderly.

I do hurt so in all my dark corners. Do you think it means I've been overeating, or that I'm going to have a poem?

You will be delighted with these letters, and wonder how you ever happened to be so felicitous here and there (as I always do when I run across a "cold" letter that I've forgotten.)

Your writing still seems to me entirely alive, and would make me feel the weight of anything that has grown inert in me.

Grace[32]

COATES TO SAROYAN: JANUARY 20, 1938

Dear Will,

Here are more of your letters; and there may be more. I did not go thru all I sent you to see that no alien breath intruded, for I was too impatient. I do not know why reading your letters makes me cry, except that I am not writing. Not writing is for me a way of being dead. Being dead is all right, but not while one is alive. I hope you do not find anything funny in your letters that should have been seen by no eyes but mine, but if you do it makes no difference—I mean some other letter, not yours, that accidentally was slipped into them.

There is something in these that is not yours that I left on purpose.

How can one have a gyroscope in him so that he stays steady in all the hellish currents (hellish was an interpolation of the instant.)

About HGM: I am inclined to carry the childhood habit of thinking the other fellow is a compendium of all virtues. After years, when at last persons told me HGM was jealous, I remembered that time after time my own unworded state (of mind) was that if such a thing were a possibility—which it wasn'tn'tn'tn't[sic]—, it would seem as tho HG didn't want this or that to be so well done that it attracted attention; and at last I realized that the idol had sticky feet. Granted that he is opinionated, stiff ("A slender man of jointed glass, Thru which discomforts and culture pass?" I once said of him) impossible to work with, taking credit, giving none, socially snobbish with no reason—since he has sufficient entree—; toadying, worshipful of success—

not profound, trying to do far more than he could do well; unfair—grant all this, there is still something more and better, I don't fully know what, that commands respect and loyalty.

One thing he can do: he can "take it" and remain silent. I have done things to him that would make me want to harry the doer to my last breath, and he has accepted it silently. But from the first he had a queer antagonism toward you. Whether it was because I gave such a joyous yip to heaven when I first read your mss, and he resented my cocksure admiration; or my discovery; or my assumption of critical acumen in acclaiming you instead of inquiring whether he was seeing what I saw; or what. I always felt as if he got a lot of his resentment of me off his chest by not applauding you. That is merely my feeling. May be nothing in it. And he was always jealous of Story, which did what he attempted. With the breaks we might have had their success—he feels I think we would have had to be less stodgy to get anywhere….A young chap whom Merriam has befriended, helped, admired, worked with, who worked under him said of him: "You make him uncomfortable. HG is always uncomfortable when anybody puts their cards on the table and expects him to do the same." And I think that is so.

I am going to Butte; teeth; then Havre—talks—don't want to but think it good to compel myself to meet that degree of social amenity. If I followed my bent I might grow too careless in my dress and behavior.

Grace[33]

COATES TO SAROYAN: APRIL 20, 1938

Honestly, Will, only God's silence is awful!

I was going to write just that on a post card, and then felt that it was being oversmart.

Noone ever *owes* me letters. I succeeded in alienating my best female friend by trying to make her understand that, but it remains true.

Those letters are yours. I care for them, and they have comforted me at unexpected moments—leafing [sic] thru my files, catching a paragraph, snatching at a word. That mistyped word makes a nice new one, doesn't it. It reminds me of the time I listened eagerly while a ranch woman told me how to make a wonderful spicy condiment whose base was cashba. I waited eagerly for her to conclude the recipe, so I could find out where to get the exotic cashba. She was tonguetied, and trying to say "cabbage."

Funnier still, my sister-in-law, who is stupid (aren't all sisters-in-law stupid?) never did discover that the *corn radish* she acclaimed so vigorously, as though it had sprung from her own soul, (never giving the poor ranch gardener any credit) was *corn relish*. And the recipe for Corn *radish* appears in a church cookbook, to confound a future antiquarian.

Will, will you please send me with a bill, a copy of either of your later books, Little Children or Love, Here's My Hat, autographed:

For Ida Christine, whom she loves, from Grace Stone Coates

With (here insert any sentiment you want to, from "with my loud Ha Ha's" to anything less banal, just so it gives you a chance to sign your name.) Your quick sensibilities will tell you that the book without the bill would be an embarrassment. I do not love many women, but Ida Christine is one I have known in person but briefly, but continue to love. I met her at a summer session of the U of Southern Calif some—can it be 25?—years ago.

I hope you'll have time to do this for me. I've been waiting quite a while to ask you….This is my sister's birthday, and writing to you has called my attention to the date….Please don't have consciences around me.

Grace

I meant to tell you, we sold the store—for cash—and Thank God are free. Town booming under the impetus of a million dollar Federal dam project. Shacks going up everywhere. Headaches to come later[34]

COATES TO SAROYAN: APRIL 26, 1938

Thank you, and again, for the book. You left me feeling not in the least uncomfortable, and I'm entirely willing, such is your grace, to let the pleasure be yours. I'm also enclosing a check, to share in the pleasure.[35] I do not know whether I mentioned this, but I can open one of your books most anyplace and begin to read, and in a moment be bawling out loud, not because you are saying anything pathetic, but because (to me) everything you write is a living thing, and the movement of life is painful, necessarily, under certain situations. The only way I could be happy under the circumstances of my present life, it to be dead; and to be dead I refuse. So, I live in your living and consequently hurt.

"The awful eagerness of people to be special." That is worth having said. I have said something the same when I berate a certain Catholic friend for desiring miracles—i.e. special miracles. "You can't see a miracle in the grass, when it comes up green—that isn't miracle enough for you; you'd have to have it spotted blue and pink before it would be a miracle." A dandelion isn't a miracle—they want a rose from a dandelion plant—either disease or hocus pocus, before it's awesome and holy…But why belabor the point. You've said it. And to complete the picture—all being grist to a writer's mill—your appreciation reminded me that what got "cashba" across to me was her really fine hands unmistakably shaping a nice cabbage head—one got the rich green of the curling outside leaves, and the compact inner head, all from her shapely, work useful hands…There's a Norwegian rancher here who can make you see a deer bound over his fences better with his hands than you can with lazy and accustomed eyes…You recall Browning's painter's question: "Have you seen my scullion's hanging jaw? No? Give me a bit a crayon, and you'll notice it next time!…

How did I get *here* with this letter—when I began by saying that I thanked you for sending the book, and intended to stop at that… "Incompetent with anything of bulk." We have always had the store to wrap books in—and now the store is sold—did I tell you?…the town teeming over a million dollar Federal dam project (better take your vacation here, when the book is done for, and committed to the publisher)…I meant to say by way of news merely that Henderson and I had come a long ways—we can clash head-on, expend our unreason, walk apart; and meet with chuckles and a devised compromise on each side. Our latest encounter concerned my ultimatum that an outside toilet was neither the place for objet d'arte nor rakes, hoes, tin container "that might come in handy some time, if I happened to have a little paint left over," or anything except devoirs.[36]

Saroyan used his letters to write a summary of his life and also his appreciation of Grace's friendship. He acknowledged the extreme impact she had made in his writing

I cannot begin to tell you how fine your criticisms are, and I only wish they were not in vain, for I feel greatly obliged to you for your sincerity. I am more than convinced now that is just these apparently insignificant details that make a story good or bad, and with your suggestions before me I must admit that the work of correcting the story. I can see the difference, the new sharpness of each sentence, the clarity and completion of each thought.[37]

Coates to Rankin: February 18, 1938

Dear Mr. Rankin,

Your latest letter sounds as if you were sugaring off on me. Probably nothing would make me so insistent on writing to a man as the idea that he wanted to stop.

I am sure it must have been two other fellows that said all that about Mrs. Russell. All I wished to convey was that she was intent on the financial returns from her husband's work and failed to appreciate, his friends thought, the peculiar aspects of genius.

I am sure if you look your information over you will find I didn't say anything about her making things hot for you. She won't want anything that interferes with her getting all possible returns from Russell's fame. That is all.

Nancy asked for that letter (Riding the High Country) and Tucker said she couldn't have it. I doubt whether he, I, or the publisher knew there was any law about publishing letters. Russell had promised to do illustrations for Tucker; and tho Tucker couldn't have proved Russell said he could use the letter, Nancy couldn't prove he didn't—and I do not think the book worried her, anyway. I am no lawyer. Ask B.K. Wheeler, Chief Justice Hughes, or Cummings. Ask Roosevelt—and have him make a law covering it, in your favor, and announce it in effect.

The Bairs have gone to Portland. Marguerite had a letter written to you but never got it copied on the typewriter. Honest.[38]

COATES TO RANKIN: FEBRUARY 26, 1938

Dear Jim, for promptitude: Your letter is scarcely 3 seconds out of the shell—and here I go.

Don't buy Ubet from the publisher: buy from the author, (who is expected to sell his own books) at 3775 Utah Street, San Diego, Calif.; address either Mrs. Or Mr. John Barrows—it will give them a thrill to get another order, and from NYC. The Caxton Printers, Ltd., Caldwell, Idaho, are the publishers.

John Barrows is bedridden and blind. I have one of the two books personally autographed by him—except those for his immediate family. I think Linderman has the other. Was I proud: His wife is fine—exchanges a cake for a violin lesson for her baby—a girl say 15 or so; does anything, anything to turn a dollar. If they sell the book they make one on it. The family are all musical—one son had records simultaneously broadcast from Boston and Portland, Ore., which was an oddity for a premiere of an unknown lad. Anyway, they are an up and coming family. Leslie (Mrs. John Barrows) offers us northerners—I've forgotten the name of it—jelly from her own trees, when her crop is too heavy—at so much per, and always in a way that leaves one entirely free—no salesman pressure.

I mention all this because her energetic ways and freedom from self-pity and whining; and from all false pride interest me a lot.

It is a shame someone can't do publicity on Ubet, for it is a good book of its kind and should be in the library of many persons and institutions as a factual story of the real West, well written by an honest and lettered man.

Having said all this about Leslie, I want to add that the spark struck into

This is bitterness;

Make no lie that it is sweet,

Be my last success

To accept defeat.

Spare me the last gall

Your pretense that all is well...

Came from John's reaction to Leslie's eternal optimism. Tell a man blind from glaucoma that everything is sunshine in the best of all possible worlds!— My innate sympathy went to John in his bitterness, even while I realized that Leslie's spirit was admirable beyond words.

Grace[39]

Coates to Linderman: August 18, 1937

Dear Sign-talker,

When the brick looks bigger than its gilding….(Next day)….it is time to select one's crematorium.

Aug. 20.— This is getting funny. I think I have lifted my fingers to this attempted letter at least eight times. That is as far as I would get.

The Rankin sent me a nice picture of you on your vine arched porch; you and Mrs. Linderman, your lovely daughter and adorable children. Mr. Rankin is most punctilious about his minor obligations, at least. He is still in Great Falls, attempting what he calls his Gargantuan task.

When I started this letter I was going to sound off a wail about the entire world; but since then I dug in the garden, hauled leaf mold, and ran the pum to soak it down, and got so much sunshine in my blood I have forgotten what it was I was grieving about—lack of a reference library I guess.

Reverting to the sale of the lodge: I hadn't supposed Rankin had any money, but thought he might be in touch with opulent persons. All signs point to a revival of interest in western land. The financial journals predict it, and easterners are inquiring. When *Der Tag* comes, it will be the safest place to be. There is a crooked dude ranch near here that attracts many square persons. I'll see if any of them nibble. Dr. Cole was in Billings, by the way….When I am tired of our ugly immediate surroundings I often content myself thinking of your lake and the blue, blue shining water.

Summer almost done, again; and I have been ridden with guests all summer long, to a degree unusual for me. Now I am alone and for the moment happy….One of the dude guests was a Mrs. Hager whose "Big Loop and Little" is off the MacMillan press. She is a feature correspondent on aviation for the Washington Star, and a most interesting person. More interesting than anything is the funny relation of "dudes" to natives here. The "dudes" will hang on some dead beat we have known as a nonentity for years, and tell us what a marvelous person he is—but perhaps they have the seeing eye.

If I were several persons all but the one of me that has to stay here would come and see you.

May all good things be with you. Grace Coates[40]

It was a crushing blow when Linderman died in Santa Barbara, California, after several years of ill health. Grace received a letter from Mrs. Linderman telling her Frank's last days. She replied immediately.

COATES TO MRS. LINDERMAN: MAY 25, 1938

Dear Mrs. Linderman,

You were so understanding and good to write to me—gracious is too cold and formal a word—but I didn't want you to feel any burden of needing to write. I do not know why I sob and sob. I am very sure Frank is near to you, entirely, forever near; closer than when he sat beside you. His devotion to you and your generosity toward his work and his friends was all part of the friendship that I felt. I think women are more generous to men's work than men are to women's work outside their household duties—in the main, I mean. This is the first good picture I have ever seen of Frank.

If I write you from time to time do not feel that you must reply, unless you are rested and really want to. I felt comforted by your word of a happy winter. Not knowing, I had imaged a continued losing fight, and perhaps part of my sense of loss comes from having intended many times to write, and putting it off.

Oh, yes—the day I learned of Frank's going, I fell—on a level floor—and broke my nose. It was really a bad fall, and for several days I was confused and used queer words instead of the ones I meant. There was no one around me to entrust with anything of real meaning to me.

A Boston Insurance company has asked for a 15 min. radio script of Frank's work. I do not know whether you even want to think of such things at the present. If the script is prepared, I'd rather do it than have some one else; and I believe (Frank liked the little sketch I wrote for "Blackfeet Indians") that I can keep it in good taste; I mean I believe you can trust me with the work. If you want me to do this, perhaps one of the girls will send me the autobiography, which I had for several months, to give the work freshness and keep it authentic; and I'll return it very promptly. If you do not want this intrusion at this time, do not even bother to explain, for I will understand. Some time I want the privilege of reading the biography again for my own delight.

With love and affection, Grace[41]

MRS. LINDERMAN TO COATES: MAY 27, 1938

My dear Mrs. Coates:

Replying to the fourth paragraph of your letter of May 25th asking for material to be used in a fifteen minute Radio script by some Insurance

Company of Boston, Massachusetts, I hardly know what to say because you did not state for what purpose the fifteen minute Radio script would be used.

If you will be good enough to advise name of the Insurance Company and for what purpose the script is wanted I will try to furnish such material as my seem best. I assure you that I have the greatest of confidence in your ability and if such a thing is to be done at all I would appreciate it very much if you would be good enough to write the script.

I trust that you will write me at your earliest convenience and give me the benefit of your judgement in the matter.

With love, Mrs. Linderman[42]

Martinsdale boomed in 1938 as construction crews came in to build the DuRand (now Bair Dam) and the Martinsdale Reservoir. Grace and Henderson had eight trailers on a traveler camp to look after as well as taking in boarders occasionally. It made for a busy summer.

The town itself woke from a long sleep as workers poured in. There were nine places along main street where one could buy liquor. South of town was the Slab Shack, a place where workers could go to dance with girls. Patrons had to buy a drink and one for the dancing partner, but word was that one was buying only tea for the girls.

Grace carefully recorded the history of the building of the dams for the newspapers, recording such facts that the peak employment in September and October was 326 men, with a peak payroll of $9,500 a week. Skilled labor was paid $1.50 an hour and unskilled labor, 65 cents.

Fred Ward took over the *Meagher County News* and found out about the "politics of local news" and about a small town. Some were sending in news without giving them to Grace, who received a small stipend for writing the news. Ward was strict about not publishing any news that was not signed and not using the "assigned" correspondent. He wrote to Grace,

Copies of two letters are inclosed.[sic] They will explain themselves. Juilian Bell wired items from Lennep to Ed Betzel at the depot and Mrs. Cameron wrote in. I can't see why she failed to give this to you but believe this letter will straighten things out down there.

Maybe you will understand me when I say that I have a definite ambition to make this paper open to all the people and to have it devoted almost exclusively to the people of this county. I get enough government propaganda to fill 10 papers and enough chances to plug some commercial enterprise like a world's fair etc to fill 10 more papers. But local and rural news is harder to get. It stirs up more repercussions when it isn't right but I think it makes a rural paper. The folks have been encouraged to bring in items. Some of them are rather self conscious about it the first time and I try to make them feel that they are doing me a personal favor and the result is that I get notes, cards and word of mouth from all over the county. The city reporters call these their pipe lines.

Of course you knew I was kidding when I quoted the bible about the gnat. I want to keep my pipe lines open but I am glad you wrote me because it put me wise to a thing or two. There is no good reason why the policies followed here should create any embarrassment to you. Covering the entire east end of the county is not an easy job.

What a day. They drained my car last night. Had a row this morning when I told a guy his attempt to build a $1500 club house and a few minutes ago a car ran over my dog. I am not a sentimentalist but that hound came bawling to me and I thought they had broken his leg. But I guess they didn't. What the hell.[43]

COATES TO RANKIN: MAY 19, 1938

Dear Jim just wrote you a post card—but now, using these 2 Russell items for the Frontier, and quoting your letter a bit (I hope not to your embarrassment) in the column, I find I can send these on to you. Jim, Jim, Jim, I fairly fizz with the romance I know (and few outsiders do) about Francis Parker. You can use some of it discretely, but one of the principals is still living and in Helena.

I'll give you the low down on my request for a Russell sketch: I am incapacitated by my egregious broken nose: and right at this juncture have a call for radio sketches of my own chosing, [sic] 1600 words, no adjectives— at least not many—of central Montana—especially Lewistown. They want minor emphasis on the background of the character before he came to Montana; major emphasis on the person, as opposed to the Montana history. The program is for an Eastern Insurance company broadcast from Great Falls. If I can send them something snappy, quick, I'll get all the work I want to do. And can a blue nose and black eyes go get material????? Except from friends? On paper?

But I know what it is to be busy and my request may be utterly beyond your kindness. If you can do this, the draft may be rough; and you will be able to use material that you do not mind having broadcast, not some precious secret. The general title of the series is "Montana in Review." All your letter is duck soup for that kind of thing. Are these clips of value to you, or do you get them thru a clipping service?

With all good wishes, Grace Coates[44]

COATES TO RANKIN: JUNE 10, 1938

Dear Jim, Mrs. Pat Tucker spent a day with me. I do like her a lot. She will sell the Tucker mss. She will sell—maybe—the original Russell—watercolor. Have you any idea at all as to what the watercolor might be worth? Or the mss? Caxtons asked me to try to get them, and Mrs. Tucker asked me to set a price—I am at sea. Also: she thinks Joe De Yong is dead—he always wrote from time to time, and now he does not even answer her letters. You knew, perhaps, that he was a deafmute, and that he is—or was—going blind...Glad you got the citation. I wrote HGM—not that I am thinking this moved the mountain. Do not bother with this until you can snatch a moment...I too have a hospital patient in NYC, my cousin, an artist, broke, dying of cancer of the liver in a hospital. I am writing to find out.

Thank you, and don't let me bother you unreasonably.

Grace[45]

RANKIN TO COATES: JUNE 8, 1938

Dear Grace,

American belles lettres have been sadly lacking in a great romantic quality and I know that I have brought to light the person who can conjure up this missing treasure. That last letter of yours about Frances Parker is a real gem of the finest water. Don't pooh pooh me, you have the stuff that is required to go to town.

I got a perfectly swell kick out of that message and you wrote from the heart. That is why it was so fine. Gal, if you'd only let yourself go, you'd write a greater ANNA KARENINA, but you're too afraid of trampling on somebody's corn patch. Montana is just aching for someone to tell her story with a terrific wallop. I just can't help the—pun but like the Atlanta Constitution's "Like the Dew it covers the South", your own battlecry would be "Like the Snow Coates covers Montana."

The good old U. of Montana finally sent me the citation read to CMR in '25 when he got the LL.D. It must have taken a might effort to locate it but at least they did send it, so hooray! I'd have given anything to see Charlie's face when he got the degree. A certain New Yorker, formerly of Montana, was on the team that gave Charlie the "works" when he entered the ?Elks. He has related with full details the effects of this treatment on CMR so I know how he reacted to the university cap and gown and the citation. The question is, did anyone every call him "Dr. Russell" or even "Doc"?

Several months since, Mrs. Astor has closed her stables and N.Y. is the poorer. No longer do we know what her w.k. horse said each Monday morning to the gentleman with the cart and long broom. He probably takes his ease like the immortal little bull, Ferdinand, under a cork tree and passes the peaceful days smelling the fragrant air of the country flowerbeds. Ah me!!

To play hookey is always real sport. Last Thursday I sneaked away from the big stem and lit off for Washington Irving's Sleepy Hollow. Tarrytown, about 20 miles to the north of here, reeks with folklore, charm and good cooking. The ladies of the Historical Society entertained me all afternoon with giant volumes of epitaph Ana and genealogy. Then I turned in at the Copper Beeches, so reminiscent of Sherlock Holmes that I couldn't pass it by, and ate supper on a sweeping verandah that commanded a magnificent view of the Hudson. Thence down the old Boston Post Road past the statue of Major Andre on the very spot where that gallant gentleman was rounded up by three scapegrace continentals and subsequently hanged as a spy, across the bridge that supplants the one cover which Ichabod Crane and the Headless Horseman galloped one midnight long ago, and into the old Dutch burying ground. You didn't know it but my weakness has been for just such places as this. The wooded hillsides are covered with tottering stones with memorabilia in Dutch, Latin and English, The See family haunted me everywhere. What a fruitful lot they were and how many of them lie interred in that magnificent Westchester County graveyard! But I went to shed a tear on the forebears of Charlie Russell, one branch of the family, and to gaze at the last resting place of the gentle Irving of Sunnyside, not far distant from this last home. There also were the Fargos of Western fame and Robert Hoe, the scion of the printing press Hoes and the great American book lover and collector. Wandering through the cemetery, I came across a group of new-Americans bent on strewing flowers on their family plot. To my query where Washington Irving was buried, they all looked amazed and bewildered. One ventured to say that he had heard of him but did not know the location of his grave. When they understood that he had been laid to rest in 1858 they agreed that he was in the old section, near the Dutch Church, and there he was, securely guarded in the center of a large square of Irvings, flanked by iron railings and privet hedges.

Do you know Mrs. Vesta O. Robbins of Bozeman who is in charge of the art committee of the Montana Women's Clubs? She told me a long while ago that she hoped to come to N.Y. next year as a delegate to the World's Fair from Montana. I suggested at that time that Montana send a collection of Russell paintings to the Fair instead of giant pumpkins and hunks of copper ore. She has never answered so I wonder if I've hurt someone's feelings. In the 1933-34 Chicago Fair the most fascinating state building was the one from Indiana. It had stunning, thought provoking murals by Thomas Benton, which were a sensation at that date. The girl in charge of the information desk told me that many farmers came to see what their home state had contributed and were outraged at the "senseless waste" of the Indiana taxpayers' money. Let's hope that the world has developed sufficiently since then!

In the current Caxton Press bulletin I see that you have edited a book about the world war experiences of a mule skinner. More power to you but how about that romance! You've simply got to do it and the sooner the better we will like it. Let me know about that. If you knew Frances Parker, how about Alice Harriman, Carie Adell Strahorn, Bertha Mussey Sinclair-Cowan (B.M. Bower), and the rest of that throng who wrote for Charlie's Illustrations?

Best o' luck and write again soon, ere I set out for Washington, D.C. to finish the bibliographic end of the Russell book. More hot news later, or do you like it tepid, cool, or what? Let me know and I'll dish it up to the queen's taste (not Queen Bess).

> *Jim*[46]

Grace was beginning to show the pressure of the summer with the work created by the reservoir construction. In late summer she wrote to Merriam,

> It crowds me beyond endurance to get news out. Happy solution, yield my place to Romig Fuller as guest newser, and run her infinitely dull New York account. I enclose it. If I could get out notes without making myself sick I'd do it, but I can't.
>
> (Henderson asked the characteristic question, once, when he saw me midnight-oiling on the Frontier, what I got out of it. I said I got the privilege of having my name misspelled for the past several years as assistant editor.)
>
> If this pressure still presses at the next issue of the mag I can't do the news work. I await its early ending. House may be empty by September.
>
> *Sincerely yours, GSC*[47]

COATES TO RANKIN: SEPT. 6 AND I CAN HARDLY BELIEVE IT IS:

> Dear Jim, I never know whether—do right or wrong when I put you in print this way.[newpaper articles] If you wish I wouldn't just say so.
>
> Eight roomers. I have enjoyed the experience and had a happy summer. Henderson has a new boat (my present to him. He paid for it) and he came in with a fat salmon—silver salmon trout; he was hungry and I cooked it for him. The lakes around here will bring more tourist business. Henderson looks years younger since we got out of the store.
>
> I have done more housework this summer than in all my housekeeping years combined. Knew it was in the cards for me to do it, sooner or later; and I'm glad I didn't do it sooner. We had 8 trailers on a trailer camp, whom I herded and disciplined—the camp is clean, and we managed to remain friends. I even reduced my please to doggerel, to make them take it.

Here you are—and you will be similarly appearing in Frontier and Midland. I hope you are as happy as I am.

Grace[48]

MERRIAM TO COATES: SEPTEMBER 28, 1938

Dear GSC,

Why not try a batch of new names in solicitation of news. Here are some: Dean Vernon McKenzie, The School of Journalism, The University of Washington; Franklin Pierce, Seattle; Stuart Holbrook, 2842 Northeast 56th Avenue, Portland; Professor W.F.G. Thatcher, The University of Oregon, Eugene; Vardis Fisher, Boise (response may be none too cordial); Mrs. Schemm, Great Falls; Professor George Savage, Jr., The University of Washington, Seattle; and Newton Reilly, *The Chronicle*, Spokane.

I am glad you are willing to go on with the News Notes; but I want you to let me know the minute you do not find the task of interest or value.

I note what you say about Linderman. I do not expect to be able to evaluate his work; I only expect to call it to some public attention. If you do not see an article that you can do, well and good. Have you suggestions as to what the issue should contain or might contain that would be of general interest?

Cordially yours, HGM[49]

Merriam was still concerned about Grace's criticism of the Federal Writers' Project, but Grace was always honest in her opinions.

Dear H.G.M., With the letter I sent you I had enclosed three sheets of burlesque news notes; but, remembering that much of my difficulties with poets like Dr. Newman, and all my difficulties with Henderson come from a divergence in our respective senses of humor, I reluctantly ditched 'em....I thought I was giving the project a leg up. The controversy between Easley and Alsberg was widely publicized; and, when there was so much of significance to say about the project, I thought Alsberg was dumb to emphasize quantity of output in comparison with something else "that took 15 years to write." I am not sour on the project. As I said to McPhee, if I have occasion to speak of the project I'll say what I think, or such portion of what I think as seems appropriate to the occasion. I used that stuff last issue of the Frontier because I was short of anything else to say. The only two grievances I had when I worked on the project under you was a sense of injustice that I had to stir up all the communist nastiness I had avoided by getting CIO information—which seemed to me foreign to anything proper to a Guide book; and that I was ordered to save Chadbourn's face by issuing dishonest checks to NYA workers. I didn't see why I should be the one to pay country school teachers who were simultaneously teaching school and drawing down NYA checks, when I wasn't the boob who had put them on the project. Those were my only gripes. And I didn't see why you should be so unfair as to order me to. (I challenge you to read that CIO sentence except by the light of your prior knowledge of what I'm trying to say.) Perhaps, like Roosevelt, you hold there are matters of such import that personal unfairness but there goes the question of humor, again, flirting its disappearing tail over the hill.

And, anyway, something else wells up in me: just because a person was paid when he worked hard, does that mean that his lips are sealed against his knowledge of waste and laziness and slovenliness and the established policy of grab while the grabbing's good? The pretense of disinterested service covering a dubious political machine? Have we completely sold our integrity because we once worked on the WPA? Healthy things don't require a shush-shush atmosphere for their growth. Montana didn't have any destitute writers; it had some hungering potential supervisors—who probably once had had ideals and integrity (of sorts.)

I wouldn't be surprised, if I keep on, if I wouldn't be writing a poem![50]

Gwendolen Haste's husband was killed in New York in an automobile accident. Grace's sympathy went out to her long time friend.

COATES TO HASTE: DECEMBER 12, 1938

Dear Gwendolen:

For days you had been in my mind, and I was feeling that I must write to you, when a letter from Mrs. Kerber told me of your sorrow. I am so sorry that grief had to come into your life, and such grief, just when you might have hoped for serenity and happiness. What can I say—except that life is damned hard to stand sometimes.

I hasn't been hard for me this last summer. I've had a houseful or roomers, and enjoyed them. I do not mean I've enjoyed their society, but enjoyed not having to stand any of it. This curious house is so arranged that I can rent almost any part of it and not need to give the entrance to kitchen or living room. So I have had as many as 10 roomers, without seeing any of them except when they poked rent thru a crack in the door…And I've written poems about them.

They are building dams on the Upper Musselshell, and the shortage of rooms for the temporary population was my opportunity.

The Bairs have built a grand new house that spreads spaciously over the Grant ranch location—where the old Grant ranch house stood. They moved several old buildings and unified them—had a good artichet (not an artichoke) architect and the result is more than pleasing to the eye. Why don't you visit me and see what we are doing here?

We sold the store—perhaps I have not told you—sold last April. Jack is practically helpless, went on one too many drunks and has never come out of it. Josephine carries on in her usual competent if slightly histrionic fashion. Marion approaches 40, with a 27-year old beau whom I hope she permanently engages. I am fat in the hips. Oh, yes, William Coates died recently. Margaret looks bad. Henderson is still persuaded that one can not combine seemliness and convenience. So we take the inconvenience along with the ugliness…Dear, dear Gwendolen, I hurt inside for you.

My love to you, Grace[51]

❦

Tarnish

I wish I could walk to the farthest hill,
The farthest hill under dappled sky,
Questioning life till it tell me why
I have grown tawdry, I have grown drunken,
My golden hour of promise shrunken
To a foolish word and a flaccid will.
Skies that leaned, and peaks that thrust—
A wisp of vapor, a pinch of dust.

Chapter Twelve

Henderson's brother Jack died in January of 1939. Grace was still contributing her column to *The Frontier,* but apologized to Merriam for not doing a better job for him. Although discouraged and tired, her sardonic wit was not diminished.

If the Coates's will stop dying, for a while, I'll get letters off to the persons you named in your letter of September 28. I can't realize that that letter has lain on my chest all this time—and here it is January.

As you know, Jack[1] died Sunday; was buried Tuesday. He was unconscious two weeks before he died, and the Sunday before his death ardently embraced the Catholic faith. (I'll submit a poem for the Frontier on the back of this sheet.) He and William, who died last October, were not young, and their deaths were natural and so, not agonizing; but the only son, 38, of the oldest brother Talt Coates, died in an emergency operation out of apparently perfect health, and to leave his old father is a tragedy.

I am so busy writing obits and marriage notices I can't even find time to put a chuckle on paper about Mrs. Rudkin. When you told me about her sitting in on an Oxford Scholarship committee meeting, I didn't associate the name with the person I knew. Several years' association with minor reporters on New York papers have made her merely a more glib ass than before. "But, *Da-a-a-a-'* ling!"

I noted Mrs. Walker's photo in the SatRevLit—Mildred Walker, new book. Gwenna Haste's husband was killed in a traffic accident....I wish I could write the Frontier col as I want to—it would be too undignified for the magazine. I have never determined what the column is or should be aiming at. A col. Which it is a distinction to "make"? No, that isn't the function of the magazine. (why not?)

Warm as summer here, and has been right along.

Grace's little poem reflected the nature of her brother-in-law's death.

As he stood before the Throne
In his heavenly vesture
And crooked his elbow
In the old earthy gesture

He looked surprised
And said,
"Holy Moses!
I thought this rosary
A shot of Four Roses."[2]

Merriam was quick to reassure Grace about the column.

> Why don't you try writing up the literary news column as you wish to? I don't think the dignity of the magazine is so great that it would suffer. Work out your own style and let's see what the result is.
> Hastily but cordially[3]

"You are dependably long-suffering," Grace responded.

> Of course you have always given me a free hand with the col. My letters, as you have observed of my verse, are throw-offs; and I was so low when writing the last column that I was constantly discarding wisecracks. I can't depend on being low every time, however.
> (We have had so many sweeping changes in the routine of life during the last year that I would like to lie down under a cool, heavy boulder and rest for a year or two.)

Grace regretted that her column would always be "cold meat" because she didn't have contact with writers and libraries to browse in to find information not generally available to the public. She thanked Merriam for the contacts he had given her.

> It is a compliment to you, since I asked in your name, that every one of the persons you mentioned as possible sources of news responded. Vardis wrote briefly that he was in Boise, sick from overwork—to remind him again in March.
> I enclose Stewart Holbrook's notes without retyping. You won't overlook them, I know. And there will be a few more, as soon as I go thru the mass of material I have chucked away day by day for the past 3 months.
> I appreciate your friendship, though I seem always going after its foundations with a pickaxe to see whether it is really substantial. Let me know the deadline, if I do not get all the notes in before it approaches. I hope you, Mrs. Merriam and the children all had a pleasant holiday season—by the way, Mrs. Jack Coates is leaving for Calif. tomorrow, so she will doubtless see the Barrows before long.[4]

In the June 1939 edition of *Frontier and Midland,* Merriam announced that the September issue would be the last. He cited lack of support from the university administration, lack of his own time to administer, edit and find the finances to produce the magazine. It had been a long good run. H.G. Merriam went to teach at the University of Oregon for a year.

In 1964, when Merriam made a speech about the history of *The Frontier,* he mentioned that Grace Stone Coates had been an original contributor and the editor of the "literary news column." Merriam reported that he had borne the "many years of the magazine's publication, the responsibility of supervising, of circulating, and of financing each issue as well as the burden of reading manuscripts and editing the magazine, of course with much loyal help." The many years of work at editing and publicity Grace contributed were indeed, loyal help.

The friendship that developed between Charles Kuhlman and Grace while she was working on the WPA project continued sporadically. He wrote to her in September of 1939.

> Dear Mrs. Coates,
> This is, I believe, the first letter this year from me to you. Your last one to me is dated Jan. 24. Of course, the *only* reason I am writing now is that I am afraid you will not read the Jubilee number of the Bismarck Tribune which you probably received today. I want you to turn to Section Four and read the splash about me and also the article on Mark Kellogg. Unless I tell people that I have become famous they will never know about it. The Keogh article is merely a corrected reprint of it as appearing originally in the Billings Gazette. I did not [send] it to them to publish, but for their information. If the Gazette gets on their neck it will not be my fault!
> Your last letter was a study in warfare. It was full of hidden trenches, false batteries, real batteries camouflaged to deceive the enemy into thinking them fakes—wooden, flank and rear attacks, faints and false passes, bombing by air, and I don't know what else.
> Poor girl! I don't blame you. I am very trying. No doubt of it at all, and if you were not really very good-hearted you would do something to get rid of me effectually and permanently. What saved me so far, if I must always believe a lady, was a single pound of popcorn, the last of which is certainly gone by now; so I am putting on leather pants before this gets to you. I am sorry about the popcorn. I could easily grow some more and keep you supplied gratis, and be glad to do so. But it is the one thing to grow it here in the edge of town and quite another to harvest any of it. I have about five acres of field corn, and am not at all certain I shall get much of it. Many of the stalks were broken down by mischievous kids and bushels of ears have been stolen up to

date, even before it is ripe. What would they do to popcorn? You have one guess, but don't strain your brain making the guess.

If, like the late Frank Linderman, I were one of the initiates in psychic matters, I should not have to be, or rather make "pretentious comments"; but unfortunately I have to depend on my crutches, the same as other ordinary folk, the power of analysis, slow, plodding when compared with the inspiration. Remembering that, I hope you will say that I did a smart job in reconstructing Mark Kellogg's fate, so you can see him clearly with the mind's eye during his last hour. What a story we have missed because he did not manage to escape to the river and timber and finally to Gibbon! Perhaps part of that story in his handwriting lies buried in the archives of the War Department, for, according to Mr. Megregor, editor of the Tribune, his papers were recovered and turned over to the Department by Colonel Lounsbury, then owner of the Tribune. His diary of the march from Fort Lincoln to the mouth of the Powder or Tongue, you will find reprinted in the edition of the Tribune you have.[5]

A few years later, Kuhlman wrote again after Grace was listed in acknowledgments in Kuhlman's work on Custer.

> Fair warning: my typewriter has got religion and is afraid to print the letter "d"—does not want to take the name of the Lord in vain.
>
> I knew "kissing goes by favors" (who would want any other kissing?) and the principle holds in the matter under discussion. But you are all wet if you think there was no substantial ground for putting your name along with the rest in the "Acknowledgments."…
>
> …No, quite aside from "favor" your name belongs there. Others sent me much material on parts of the story not concerned directly with the action on Custer field, the thing that especially interest most people. They sent me *nothing* that helps on this part of the story. I can explain the "Custer mystery." I cant [sic] explain the sub-conscious hocus-pocus that is involved in this study, and has been involved from the first. That is always true where intense interest exists, I think, but it passes all past experience in this case, as far as I am concerned. Hard boiled materialists will scoff at this. Let them scoff.
>
> When you wrote years ago "I think we always know everything there is to know, only we don't know that we know it," you said a mouthful. The sense of "interest" connects you more or less with that world, so I am guessing.
>
> I am very sorry you are so in the doldrums. I can understand about the Luce review. The book is hard to review and give the writer a square deal on all points. I knew about the literary difficulty, or thought I knew. I will explain to him you are "all in" for the present. *You* do not owe him anything,

so need not worry, though I appreciate your good intention in trying to help me out in this.

I shall certainly appreciate it a lot if you will give me a good report to Northwest Books…

…If you have read *David Harum* you may remember the wonderful soft-boiled egg he ate while the guest of a big bug in New York. There seemed no end to it and spread out over everything in the most surprising way. Well, that is the way it was with that McClernand article!

> *Sincerely Yours, Charles*[6]

When Coates responded to Kuhlman she continued to complain of the "doldrums" she was in. This was a long period of depression for Grace. She became abrupt in her writing with Kuhlman and Rankin, and complained that the joy that was hers once to write letters, had now become a burden.

> No, your letter did not annoy me. I am not annoyed with you any more. What probably caused me annoyance in you was what annoys persons in me: in-season and out-of-season irony.
>
> And you must not be annoyed with me when I say I could not review Luce's book. I am like a watch with the main spring broken. Nothing ails me, but I don't go, any more. Free lancing is hard in any line, and there is practically no such thing as free lance reviewing. I tried to force myself to review the book, but I can't. I wanted to do it as a courtesy to you; but unless I review sincerely I can't review at all, and I wasn't impressed with the book. It was unorganized. On its valuable side I was incompetent to comment, and on its literary side I was ag'in' it. But entirely apart from that, I don't tick any more. I directed Mr. Falconer to return the book to you—in fact, I was so distracted that I sent him the book without a covering letter and put him to the trouble of asking whether he should send it to you or me. The reason for this lapse of courtesy was that I have the kitchen all torn up, and had company in the house for two weeks just about that time. I am still torn up, and am living in the living room, whither I have just moved all the kitchen washing paraphernalia, to be warm while I use it.
>
> The comment on Luce's book in the Gazette prevents further stories in any other state paper; and I have no outlet for reviews….the only outlet I have is the MNA, and I can write a …story for that if you—and Luce want me to. But it would be more a resume than a review. But later. I have no energy in me now.
>
> I am delighted about your booklet. *There* is something I could throw my heart into. I feel pleased that I shall have a copy. I like to know all the things you tell me. I *hate* the man who cheated you of the gold medal—they should have given two medals….As for Luce's book, I would feel aggrieved if I had

paid—is it 3? For it, unless I was free to rehash it for the MNA for 5. He was good to send you the de luxe copy—and he says he has sold all his books. Good!

I have just read a single, good book: Birchlands, by Jorun Kirkland. The story of a Norwegian girl who visits her relatives in Norway—she is a Big Timber [Montana town]girl, and writes a sincere, honest story.[7]

Life became more commonplace for Grace and she wrote the local news and found time to work with the Community Aid and serve as a judge at elections.

Henderson took pen in hand to write to Cornelia Otis Skinner about her book, *Our Hearts Were Young and Gay.* Skinner came from Moberly, Kansas, where the Henderson Coates family lived and where he grew up. She replied immediately.

Skinner to Henderson Coates: December, 1942

How nice of you to be so enthusiastic about Emily Kimbrough's and my book and to write me such a charming letter. It was nice to hear from a friend of mother's—and one who had lived in Moberly. I am writing a book about my family, Mother, Father and me and I wish I could talk with you about those early days and your memories of Maud Durbie. How lovely she must have been! She was always lovely for that matter.

Thank you again for writing me. I so hope sometime my travels will take me out your way.

> *Sincerely yours, Cornelia Otis Skinner*[8]
> P.S. Please remember me to Alberta Bair.[9]

There was an occasional letter from Merriam, although with the demise of *The Frontier,* there was little reason to correspond regularly. He wrote in April of 1944 to request some copies of *The Frontier,* if Grace had duplicate copies. "There is still talk of reviving FRONTIER," he wrote.

The Administration keeps telling me that it wishes the magazine published, although it does nothing to make publication possible. We are having this summer a "workshop in creative writing" for six weeks. We are also having six weeks School of the Drama. I shall be kept sufficiently busy this summer. It would be pleasant if you could drop in on our summer session at sometime during the first six weeks. Are you, by the way, still writing; and if so, mayn't I see what you are doing now. It has been so long since I have had personal news of you that I do not know what your days are like.

Our daughter finally got released from her job with the Navy at Panama last August and joined her husband, who is now an officer in the Army stationed at Fort Benning, Georgia. Our son has been in the Army Air Corp for a year, has been in seven camps, has finished training in both chemical warfare and in the generation of oxygen for high altitude flying The last address we had was an A.P.O. and that was more than two weeks ago; we therefore assume that he is overseas, but we don't know where.[10]

Grace responded immediately to assure him she had sent the magazines off.

I wish I could spend the summer in Missoula—that is if the atmosphere was less maddening. But I can't, and won't. My days would not amuse you, and of course I still write; and have nothing to submit to you just now. Among other things that my days embraced was working at a grading table from which the army took 27 cars of potatoes. It was fun for me, though nobody seems to understand why I thought so, and I wrote some poems, none of which got set down on paper—"wrote" being a generic term here.

It jolted me to realize that the war had caught up your son and daughter, whom I can think of only as children. Mabel Nelson—you will remember she worked in your office—is now married. She is a Yoeman ? in the personnel department (she was married Saturday in Washington, D.C., and rated half a column in the Washington Post, God bless her!)

Gwenna Haste is still writing. She says she has a good many requests for her work for anthologies and regional collections. The only verse I continue to sell is "Prairie Birth." I see I should have gone in for the gently pious attitude (instead of the one this remark connotes)…

I was glad to send the mags, and glad you could house them.[11]

Merriam conceived the idea for a Montana Institute for the Arts in the early forties, but it was not until 1948 that the first organizational meeting was held. He tried to get Grace interested in the concept. During the war years, Grace had been living a less active life, although she helped with the war effort by helping with the potato harvest at Harlowton. In answer to a query from Merriam about her activities, she wrote,

You wouldn't believe how my time has been absorbed by spuds—I mean the vegetable not the cigaret—and after our local Gestapo took the fine Mexican crew away things were tougher than ever. Potato shipments have begun at Harlowton now, and I'm preoccupied with doing a good job there. There ought to be a story in it. Some time when I see you I'll explain a bit about my writing, since the quirks of writing and writers has an impersonal (as well as personal) interest for you.

I didn't mean to let your letter wait so long. There has been no failure of courtesy on your part, I'm sure, ever…I miss the contacts, the friendly relations that magazine [*The Frontier*] brought me; and of all of them Helen Maring and Queenie B. Lister were the two I loved.

...Tell me more about your thoughts regarding a Quarterly; what do you aim at, what hope to accomplish? There is everything to be said here (in Montana) as in any other place for that matter. What would the nature of the quarterly be?...It should be something more specific than vaguely literary. Yes?...You see I *can* be interested. I hadn't known I could...[12]

One of her new friends was Hal Stearns, who took over the Harlowton paper in 1946. He remembered meeting her in Missoula and visited her to chat about their mutual esteem of H.G. Merriam.

I went to Navy in 42 and it was not til 46 I met her again. She had an enchanting, musical sort of rhythm to her speech—not at all put on or uppity—she was really a lady who didn't take her talent seriously. She also critiqued some of my own writings—I took a stab at poetry writing and of course she was most helpful on western research. Grace gave me a copy of *Black Cherries* and *Riding the High Country*...I know so little but I loved her very much. She took a real interest in me and wrote so in notes regrettably not kept.[13]

One of the chores Grace did over the years was to serve as a weather observer. Countless observers in small towns and on farms and ranches helped the weather bureau maintain records, and Grace reported for Martinsdale. As usual with her, she made friends in the "service." A letter from the supervisor in Portland, Oregon, in 1947, thanked her for her vivid account of the happenings of one of the observers out of Martinsdale, and added,

Something in your last letter, the "glowing tribute to the cooperative observer", tells me that I shall have to justify that statement. Else I shall be damned as the author of glib, trite, honeyed pep talks to observers concocted with heels atop my desk. As I believe I once told you, my contacts and my work have been largely with the field service. What did I learn through the years? Well, I shall take your favorite contraction, QC, to mean in this case "Quiet Conviction", a quiet conviction that I was dealing with a human cross-section of USA. And this sample of USA was not the one which I could glean from the headlines of our newspapers,—that of wars, murders, intrigues, wealth gained and lost, eternal bickerings over *who* should control *what*, in short, human Selfishness! The quiet, day by day saga from the observer has been to me a sample, or a cross-cut of the real USA...thanks a million for having kindled the flame of memory by the spark of your thought. This being certainly not official business, but rather the irresponsible effervescence of the Irish, it shall go forward to you under postage.[14]

Merriam continued to talk about his concept for the Montana Institute for the Arts, and in 1948, Mary Brennan Clapp, Naomi Babson, Paul A. Grieder and H.G. Merriam sent a letter to about eighty Montanans who they felt might be interested in becoming founding members. After meeting in April at the Placer Hotel in Helena, more artists and writers became interested and by the end of the year, membership was at 300. Merriam served as the first president and later edited the quarterly for seven years.

It was at a subsequent meeting in Great Falls that Margaret Bell Dobin approached Merriam at a meeting of the MIA about a manuscript she had written. It was her memoir from her childhood.

Born in Great Falls in 1889, she was only eight when her mother died, leaving her to an abusive stepfather. There were three younger half sisters in the family as well. The stepfather took his family to Canada to live on a ranch where one of the daughters died. When he decided to try his luck in the Klondike, he took the girls to a convent school in Washington. From there, Margaret finally made her way back to her grandmother and uncle in Montana. Her memoir covered these early years, ending with the return to Montana and reconciliation with relatives.

It is an absorbing tale of the hardships of a youngster on the frontier in a bad family relationship, and Margaret wanted it told.

She made several attempts to have the story published, with Grace in 1947 and again in the late 50s.

Grace described her work and frustrations with the manuscript in her letters to Merriam and to Margaret herself.

COATES TO MERRIAM: NOVEMBER 7, 1947

Dear H.G.M.

My various silences when I'm actually feeling grateful to you are more a matter of circumstance than intention. First, regarding Mrs. Bell, whom you sent to me: she spent the past month with me, and we got something done on her projected book. We are both tough, so we survived the close association in an inconvenient, non-modern house.

I'm interested in her manuscript, but it is almost impossible to do anything with it at long distance from her. All one can do is to state more felicitously what she has put down; and she hasn't put down on paper the necessary things. Her book has a dreamlike quality, in that characters appear and disappear without motivation, as in a dream; they are unnamed; she lives 8 years without one word of household conversation—even her little sisters remain just that—little sisters, sometimes one, sometimes two, sometimes three; and after she has reduced them to one, sometimes two of them appear hand in hand at the crest of a dreamlike hill. What she hasn't put down is a wealth of humor and entertainment that relieved the "almost unbearable agony" of her story. (I quote from Sloan Associates.) It is a disservice to her for well-wishers to lead her to believe she has an acceptable mss. at the present time.

But Mrs. Bell is not the subject I'm writing about: the Institute of Letters, Arts and Crafts. For the invitation I thank you, and am considering accepting. The little joker on the last page, "It is hoped…more than a year's dues…"—just how big a little joker is that? One hundred dollars? Four hundred? Five? Ten? I wouldn't wish to join and appear stingy, but we who are on fixed incomes suffer somewhat under the disadvantage of inflated prices; and as you know, Henderson has retired—AND SO HAVE I!

And I want to thank you, too, for the various prize announcements. Keep me posted, if you will. I want Mrs. Bell to submit two stories to the Atlantic "I Personally" award contest, but she can't write them—she talks about "cute aprons" and" "dainty fragrance" and some of her sentences are longer than Mrs. Bloom's soliloquy—but she's a remarkable woman, tough (in a fine sense) as mountain alder—and free of cynicism, and determined as a Missouri mule.

Our greetings to you and Mrs. Merriam, and all your growing family.[15]

MERRIAM TO COATES: NOVEMBER 10, 1947

Thanks for your good letter of November 7. I am pleased to hear that something is being done with Mrs. Bell's manuscript, for both Joe Howard[16] and I both thought there was something there that should not be dropped.

We who are organizing the Institute had been thinking of yearly dues of a dollar and a dollar and a half, and of the contribution of founding members as being anything from a couple of dollars up. However, the matter of fees is to be determined by the organizational meeting, which we hope will be in Butte or Great Falls early in December. In any event, I think that the founder's contribution will be entirely voluntary, and I am sure that no one need be embarrassed by any sum that he might offer to get us started.

My daughter, who has now two daughters herself, has returned to Panama and the family is living there. My son, Alan, was married in August to Barbara Williams (Williams and Pauley Ranch at Deer Lodge family). He is a graduate student in music at Northwestern University, and his wife is a junior in music there. Doris and I plug along with routine duties, trying to pep up life once in a while with some project like the Institute. President McCain seems to me about ready to reestablish *Frontier*. I'll send you word later[17]

Coates to Merriam: September 16, 1949

Dear H.G.M.,

In spite of a Collier's cartoon with the caption: *I just hate Marie; she answers letters the day she gets them!*, I'm sitting down at once to tell you how happy I was to get your note. I had been afraid one or other of my free-wheeling letters might have sounded unintentionally ungracious, and had annoyed you.

How very happy you and Mrs. Merriam must be with Allison and her children, and with your son. As for your kindly wishes about my summer, life is getting so short I can't waste my time not being happy, or being not happy.

Mrs. Bell is a fine woman. Any service I have given her, if such it was, has been free. I did re-type and correct her entire mss., and told her she now had a beginning to work on—that she had a skeleton to work from. But she is determined and headstrong, and in spite of my expressed opinion that she should wait about submitting her mss until she had it as perfect as she knew how to make it, she let Howard[18] send it to his publishers, and others. I advised her to stop chattering about her "book" until she had one, and not to associate my name with it until I gave her permission; and on top of that prohibition appeared an item she had given The Tribune, that GSC etc was cooperating with Mrs. Bell etc. I told her again that in my opinion she would save herself embarrassment if she would refrain from publicizing her book until she had one.

She wrote me that she had been in Missoula, and received invaluable information, instruction and renewed enthusiasm; and I refrained from writing her that that was good, if she considered lack of enthusiasm her main deficiency. So, you see, I'm mildly sour, mildly cynical—but *mild*, which is new for me. Mrs. Bell is a warm-hearted, completely generous person; and she is not in debt to me or to life; she has paid her way...

Eunice Wallace has revived "The Harp," or is reviving it. I'll have something in it—just be accident, because she asked for one. (a poem) It concerns one of your former students who once told me (after her marriage) that when her husband's sister's brothers-in-law came to the ranch to buy cattle she had put on her lace table cloth and served the luncheon buffet style, and (with triumphant satisfaction) "they didn't know what to do."

The verse is based on that incident, and I got as much malicious satisfaction from the poem as she did from disconcerting her in-laws.

Virginia City might be a fine idea. There are three sets of conditions under any of which I might get a great deal from the MIA.[19] At present none of them prevail, so for the time I am more a friendly on-looker than a participent [sic]—but surely I wish you well with everything you seek in the organization.[20]

COATES TO BELL DOBIN: MAY 30, 1949

Dearest Margaret:

I feel like a heel for not getting my letter to you written before I did. CONGRATULATIONS again and again on the wonderful, wonderful results with Harpers. And the success of your New York—all coming to you for your determination and courage.

Margaret, I think you know (or I wouldn't say it) that I have never had any eye on pay or profit out of your book. I shuddered when I began reading about the Jew. KEEP AWAY FROM THEM. Don't let anybody have any 50%, in the light of the fact that Harpers has advanced you, or promised you an advance. Margaret KEEP YOUR BUSINESS TO YOUR SELF. Don't let those leaches find out you have anything coming to you. More than that, $500 would be an adequate payment for ghosting your book. Don't let them fool you.

Don't give those birds a percentage. You can do the roughing in yourself, and I'll gladly help with the smoothing. I— Ohm/ what's the use trying to write! The Gilstraps are coming over here (Nelsons are "bumped"[21] and the kids are coming over to get their things sorted here.) They'd be glad to bring you over for a talk. I just have to see you and talk with you (I'm full of good advice, and you know the ole saying "Advice that costs nothing is worth what it costs.")…I'm going right over to Nelsons to find out what I can about the kids coming, and whether they would bring you, get their address from Mrs. N. and write them about you.

Would you consider coming over here again for a month, say? I know I was upset and nervous when you were here before, and probably disagreeable; but that was because I had one idea in mind (not to let you be a household drudge) and you had another (not to let *me* be.) But I wouldn't be embarrassed about my house this time—it's my house and my business if I want to let it look like hell—I can do your book *with* you. I know what you are up against— just what Howard and you and I didn't want—a romantic, fictionized story interest—but we can do it if we have to—even if we have to take sex hormones to get in the mood!

Damn the MIA anyway—I had my teeth out—have to go to Butte but can't go until June 17 (weather work June 8-17 holds me here)

The looting of the bank by that pious skunk upset all of us and has cost the town its chance to amount to anything—he forged checks on depositors accounts—ranch hands; relatives, millionaires, every body—…even let the community give them a big party and present them with dishes and silver and several hundred dollars on their 25th wedding anniversary—are about $250,000 short in the past 15 years—again I say, the pious skunk.

Mrs. Nelson just came to the door for lilacs for her little twin grandchildren's graves—Needless to say I stripped the bush—And I asked her about Jack and Mabel—they are coming today: But: the Nelsons want Mabel to take her car and go look up a place for the Nelsons to live, while Jack goes back to Great Falls in the old car; then he will come and get Mabel—and that is your chance. Mrs. Nelson will arrange things, I'll see them today—or whenever they come—and maybe we can make it possible for us to have a talk without too much expense. But don't, don't don't don't let anybody talk you into signing that book away. And don't let Jack devour your time. You can do much more for him if you get going on your book.

Forgive me for butting in—I'll keep you posted about the Gilstraps (Capt. Jack Gilstrap in the fone book I imagine.) I was down, and depleted—Helen is so sick—the bank business knocked us all silly…

Real persons like you, of whom there are few in the world, meet kindness everywhere, big city or little;—you and New York would get along fine, I knew that—so glad you had the courage and gumption to go. I was so MAD at Henderson, bless his good heart, for wanting to discourage you in the n.y. trip; and I wrote a letter that sounded so snooty about "stick-in-the-muds" that I tore it up.

God bless you—do come over if you can; and if you care to have me help, come ahead and I won't be so upset about my ratty house as I have been in the past—you know what to expect now.

Grace[22]

The Montana Institute for the Arts met in Virginia City in May. Grace did not attend, but she received a letter from a Montana writer who did attend.

Mildred Walker was a novelist who lived in Great Falls, married to Dr. Ferd Schemm, a noted cardiologist. Like Coates, Walker led two lives. Her daughter, Ripley Hugo, remembered growing up with a mother,

…keenly aware of a mother who insisted in her role…of a doctor's wife in a Montana town…who insisted on decorum, performance of correctness in front of those outside the family; a mother who dressed and held herself exactly as other children's mothers we knew, giving afternoon teas, selling tickets for the Junior League, conducting dinner parties at which we could overhear her entertaining guests with vivid, humorous descriptions of our latest escapades. A mother who was not easy to live up to.[23]

Her other life was that of a writer of thirteen books, imaginative and insightful. Like Grace, she wrote in her journal, "Once committed to writing—writing is one's life—but it makes for desperation…when nothing goes ahead."[24] It is understandable that they would appreciate the voice of each other.

WALKER SCHEMM TO COATES: MAY 30, 1950

This is just a note to tell you that the most intense impression that I brought back from the MIA at Virginia City was from the volume of your poems that I bought there,

Mead and Mangel-Wurzel. The weekend would have been interesting …amusing…but on the flat side but for that. And my husband and I read most of them aloud the night I got back. What a genuine and original and thrilling poet you are!

I wish you had been there, selfishly because I would so like to have talked with you again. It was fun to have the festival in Virginia City. Norman Fox wrote some rhymes for the occasion and the punch line was particularly apt: "For cultch had come to Alder Gulch". Naomi Lane Babson talked on the short story for the Writers' Group and was interesting though she dealt almost entirely with the "outward signs" rather than the inner. Maybe there's no use in trying the latter, though. And the usual group of women "writers" asked the same questions they always do about agents and magazine tabus and markets etc. She is a charming person, herself. A Mrs. Place talked about non-fiction but it didn't interest me greatly. There was a good deal of activity and enthusiasm in the art and weaving and pottery groups and I heard the drama group put on some artistic productions. It would have been rewarding to have gone to hear about other crafts than that of writing.

Well, that's all, only I wanted to tell you about your poems. Don't stop writing, please.

With sincere admiration, Mildred Walker Schemm[24]

At Christmas, 1949, Grace sent a card to her neighbor, Deene Rognlie,

I no longer send cards, but to a few friends who I think will tolerate them I send rhymes in response to their cards: so here is yours

Attainment

Moisture less than a tear,

That has no need to fail,

Presses my inner eye.

A nerve twists in my thigh

Like a snake. So I draw near

The quiet I have awaited.

Small pride can not lie

Silent where it is hated

As a great pride can lie.[25]

In October of 1950, Grace lost her sister Helen, and then in less than two years, her husband Henderson.

Henderson Coates was 85 when he died in the Butte Community Hospital where he was hospitalized following a heart attack. The *Great Falls Tribune* of March 19, 1952, reported that he had, with his brother Jack, operated the Coates Bros. General store. Along with Grace, survivors included two sisters, Mrs. Elizabeth Tolle of Kansas City and Mrs. Lucille Blunk[26] of Oklahoma City.

Henderson Coates was cremated, and Grace scattered his ashes at his favorite fishing hole. At the same time, she made provision for her own death. She, too, wanted to be cremated and her ashes scattered on Gordon Butte, the hill near Martinsdale where she loved to walk. This same butte is featured on her book, *Portulacas in the Wheat.* At that time (1932) the suggestion came from the poem "The Cliff."

Grace was seventy-one. She had lived in Martinsdale for forty-two years because she was married to Henderson. She stayed, now, because the memories of Henderson were there. The passionate voice of the writer, trapped, was muted. There were no more petulant outbursts to her friends of the letters about her "prison." She was content.

There was no family left except two nieces of Henderson's—Marion Coates of Martinsdale and Lucille Blunk of Oklahoma City. There was no rapport with Marion, the postmistress of the village, but Lucille continued her summer visits. She remarked to a friend, "Grace first introduced me as Henderson's niece, then it became *our* niece, and now it is *my* niece." Grace gave her the statue mentioned in the short story *Plaster of Paris.*

Grace worked in the Community Aid, helping put on the annual Smorgesbord and other seasonal affairs. She attended church and even went to the showers and tea parties given by the ladies of the community. Stopping to pick up a neighbor for the walk to the center for a shower, she was always on time. "We have to get there early enough to get a chair and play those stupid games. But they do serve good food." And she wrote the news. She walked for exercise. A neighbor dropped in one morning. Grace called to come in, she was "stretching." And so she was, one leg stretched to the top of the refrigerator.

Great Falls Tribune: October 26, 1954

Martinsdale—Grace Stone Coates has received word from J.H. Gipson of the Caxton Printers, Caldwell, Idaho, that he has sold to Universal-International movie rights to the late Tommy Tucker's book "Riding the High Country."

Mrs. Coates was co-author with Tucker of this story, which first appeared as a serial in The Great Falls Tribune under the title "Old Cow Trails." It was illustrated by the Great Falls artist, O.C. Seltzer.

At the time of publication Mr. and Mrs. Tucker were residents of Livingston. Mrs. Tucker now lives in California, where her daughter, Margaret, a nurse, and her sons, John and Roy, have established themselves.

Charles Kuhlman continued to write to Grace. Their correspondence had lapsed into a casual exchange over the daily routine of life. He gave her advice on her gardening and told of his work with the Historical Society and brought her up to date on his latest work on General Custer.

I hope that by this time the theolept has completely lepted [sic] himself out of your life. If so, good riddance. For while he may have been of some use to you for a while it seems to me that as a permanent ficture [sic] he would be what the French call de Trop!

Yeah, I should know what a psychosis is. Like sin it can be multitudenous [sic]. One is company, two is a crowd.

But how are you now? And how are your iris? Mine are out, the tallest blades about 4 inches long. This afternoon I cleaned them up, fixing the ditches along the sides of the rows to hold the irrigation water. Also; I spread some Milorganite over the rows and in the ditches and thoroughly watered them down. The milorganite will not harm plants if it comes into direct contact with them. It acts like barnyard manure. We are having a light rain here, successive showers that probably will not mean much. Nor do I need the rain. My ground is in perfect shape for working. All I have planted so far is cabbage in a cold frame with 10 sections of "plexiglass" for cover. The plants are just coming up and should be ready for planting about the end of the third week in May, if the sun and temperature are normal.

Last night Fay and I went to a dinner of the Yellowstone Historical Society. She has the job of taking notes on the speeches and proceedings and I foot the bill—a good trade for me, though the stuff for some reason or another is not very interesting to me. That may be due to the fact that I cannot hear the speeches and the notes are necessarily very brief, since Fay does not know how to use shorthand; and if she did I would not be able to read it.

I have been hung up all winter on that blasted Hughes article accusing Custer of disobedience. A week's work would have done it had I been in the shape I was only a few years ago. Trouble is chiefly loss of memory. But I am getting results, I think. I am supposed to have it ready by the middle of June, though that is not an absolute "must." There will be some real fireworks in it—definite proof of deliberate lying on the part of Hughes—the writer of the article.

This article of mine, if it is published, is sure to raise a storm on the part of the Custerphobes. I hope it does, for that will spur the sale of Legend not History. The late Colonel Graham wrote me not so long after the book was out, that it, the book—was sure to be attacked severely sooner or later, but added "not by *me*." Which was nice of him, since we are so far apart in our ideas. You know, of course, that Graham died last fall—October—I think. A few days before his death, when he was in the hospital, he told a close friend that he had been trying to get a probe into my story to see if he could not find a hole in my reasoning, but admitted that he had not been able to so, saying "Kuhlman—Kuhlman and his damned deadly logic." This was not said in criticism, but rather in admiration. And since Graham was the best student on the subject, this "tickled" me, you can imagine. But this is strictly on the "qt." Graham was deadly serious in his studies on the Custer subject and usually very fair—as nearly free of bias as is humanly possible, I believe.

Well, again, "How are you?"

All good wishes. Sincerely yours, Charles[27]

KUHLMAN TO COATES: JUNE 5, 1954

Dear Grace:

A million thanks for your letter. It did do me some good, I find, after a day or two. Somehow the subject dropped out of my mind, and when it returned it was very much less painful. Perhaps during sleep our subconscious minds touched, as happened years ago, and a sort of "damper" was put on the sore spot. This is, I suppose, about what the psychotherapists do. But whatever the mechanism, something unusual has been at work; for ordinarily I cannot shake off anything like this except through long torture.

I wish you would tell me more about that "theolept". I looked in my *Webster's Collegiate* and couldn't tree the annimile [sic]—except in two pieces—*theo* and *lept*. That was some hours ago, and I will not look it up again; but if you put the two together it seems to say "Little God." There are so many "Little Gods" in Greek and Roman Mythology, that I cannot even make a guess who your theolept is. But evidently he is good for you. Luck to you and more of it.

Now a word more about iris. I don't see why I did not think of it before. Next fall plant some under the eaves of your house....

Charles[28]

Charles Kuhlman was seventy-nine when his book *Legend into History* was published, followed six years later as *Did Custer Disobey Orders at the Battle of the Little Big Horn?* They were reprinted together in 1994, and Grace Stone Coates is still listed in acknowledgments.

MEAGHER COUNTY NEWS: AUGUST 1956

Mrs. Grace Stone Coates and her niece Lucile Blunk were in Bozeman Monday, and found Mrs. Coates' brother-in-law L.S. Hyde had been hospitalized there.

After many years of little contact, Merriam sent a Christmas card in 1957 inquiring about her.

COATES TO MERRIAM: DECEMBER 14, 1957

Dear H.G.M.—
What a delightful card! I shall remove the letter and send the face of the card to my sailor boy, who (now home) is sending me a teakettle from Pusan. He is a musician. It will make him cry.

It will be a pleasure to tell you something of my life—as presently lived. If I wait for *time* to do this it will never be done; so here I sit in a house that has had no housework done for this, the sixth day.

You know Fred Ward of course, editor of the local county paper. Some years ago he suffered a stroke, and the office called on me to come and help while Fred was in the hospital. I have helped off and on. He is leaving for Needles soon, so I continue to work. Mondays and Tuesday and sometimes other days I get up before 5 a.m., take the school bus at 7:30 and return on the bus at 5:30 or on the Canyon bus at 8:00 p.m. The work isn't hard when Fred is away, but sometimes almost unendurable when he is there—not because it is hard, but because he has streaks of wanting—and needing—to talk; and I am the available person to talk at. The other day he had told me something for the third time, and I said: "Mr. Ward, you have told me that three times, and if you tell me six times more I won't know it any better, than I do now." He was ruffled, and said, "You are just trying to make it appear that I am tiresome." But he left me alone for two weeks. His ability to put punch into editorials is unimpaired. Tho I put a little lunar caustic in the honey sometimes, I do feel profound sympathy for him in his hunger to still be needed and wanted.

As for my inner life, for some reason I have found a degree of tranquility, an inner happiness that persists even when I'm tired or irritated or momentarily crying outside. Sometimes I feel luminous inside…I'm still convinced that the creative principle of the universe is laughter. They are considering—in fact have decided—to move the Episcopal services from Martinsdale to Harlowton. As a correspondent for the Harlowton paper I wrote a careful and studied story for the paper and at the end, putting around the personal remark the time-honored circle of prohibition against print I wrote: "Mrs. Coates says Martinsdale first lost its red-light district, then its bank, then its Milwaukee trains, and now is losing its church." The editor put my story in the middle of the front page, and my unfortunate remark in the middle of the story. I haven't heard such bursts of belly laughter in years.

Life is good. I do not mean my life, but life itself; and I wouldn't forgo any of it, not the pain, not even the wrong—except only the pain that those I loved endured. Their pain is now the only pain I know.

Circumstances of my workdays make it hard to attempt any sustained writing; and my things are still the throwoffs you condemned me for. I did start a story for you some time ago and it was going to be a good one and I would have enjoyed writing it. I am working on a poem, but I was thinking of sending it to "The Living Church" of which Martindale's late rector is now the editor. (He was a wonderful man but he ran out of church—I mean that in the sense that a seamstress runs out of thread. He reduced two churches— yes, three,—to non-attendance. He was too far over the people's heads.) His successor, a man whose granite-like qualities I have learned to like, is a former policeman. He got down to a more popular level, drank a bottle of beer in one of the joints and was ostracized by the holy. But he fought back in righteous indignation, and the Bishop backed him up. He was a juvenile protective officer in Baltimore. He looked at me with his honest policeman's eyes and said, "Why, we always drank beer."

From what I write about you can catch the tenor of my life—trivialia, [sic] but a carved cherry pit means as much to me as those faces that insult the Black Hills—or whatever the mountains are.

I have written this because you asked about it, and my narrow life contrasts with your wider life and the interesting life of your children and their families. Often I've walked the brushy lake front between South Evanston and the University grounds when I was growing up—a changed scene now no doubt. Some one met you on your travels to or from Buenos Aires, and brought me word from you. I am happy to hear from you, and send my greetings to Doris. The Time-Life bureau is not interesting to me. My sub. to Time began with the first issue. I'll be reminded of you every week.

Thank you for the greetings, and all good wishes to you and your family.

Grace

This is some paper the print shop printed up for its galley slaves. G.[29]

Coates to Bell Dobin: May 13, 1957

This paper has been in the machine two days waiting for a letter to start—a letter to you.

I have my house painted inside, my books cleaned—and rain has interrupted the outside painting for a month. Well, sometime—

How are you, and how is your sister? And how is the fund for the book progressing? I still work at W.S.S. but am going to stop. The movies are crazy for new types of material—yours has such possibilities...A friend sent me Alan Swallow's column from the Denver Post, in it he said unexpected things about me.

Rainy days are no good—I like the sun. But when we read of the horrors in Texas I am ashamed of complaining about our inch of rain. There is a new telephone in town right at our corner, so I make my weather reports easily...Life's not much good without Henderson. I wish you could come over and see me. What uneven typing I am doing. Tomorrow I go to W.S.S. and am getting so I dislike the trip more and more. I go on the school bus and it, recently, leaves the oiled road for a lateral to pick up two new pupils, and it makes a round trip of 90 miles and I DON'T LIKE IT.

I think of you and know how good you are. Give my greeting to Roy. My memories of his home are pleasant indeed.[30]

There was still some publication of Grace's work. Bob Fletcher was doing a column in the MIA (Montana Institute of the Arts) quarterly in 1958 and H.G. Merriam wrote to ask Grace's permission to use "Suspect" in the next issue. Her old friend Taylor Gordon was retired and living in White Sulphur Springs with his sister Rose. He held on, too, to some of the days when his work was applauded and turned to Grace for advice about possibly reprinting *Born to Be*.

Coates to Taylor Gordon: November 21, 1959

You and Rose are welcome, any time. At present Thursdays are my freest (free-est) days. I write new Fridays. I have no fone, but if you do call, call station one—it is at the hardware store across the street, and they can reach me more easily than the other station can.

I think you better wait for the weather to moderate—the blizzard, or rather having to service the weather station[31] during the blizzard, knocked my heart out of kilter somewhat, and I'm doing more resting right now than anything else. But, say, after Thanksgiving I should be myself again.

It pleases me that George [Ward] used your story in last week's paper.

I wish I could be at the church dinner tomorrow.

P.S. I am afraid there is no chance of Caxton Printers reissuing your book unless you had bought the plates from the publisher. Then they might. I think I know a better scheme than that, but of course go ahead and ask Caxton's, but I am sure they are, as they told us, loaded for at least two years.[33]

The main street of Martinsdale ran north/south—from the depot on the north end and one of the grocery stores on the other. The Coates houses were on an east-west street that brought traffic into town. Grace would walk to the corner where the Coates Brothers general store was now a grocery store owned by Kay Berg, make a right and go up the street past the barber shop and bar (which had been the livery at one time) to the post office. Another grocery store and another bar were further south. Across the main street were the two garages and a hotel.

In the later 1950s, Grace could be seen walking up and down the main street with her pencil and pad in hand to get the local news—hat on, the loose housedress. Neighbors don't remember her without the writing pad. She would shop in the Berg grocery, and visited often with Kay Berg. He looked forward to her visits and the good conversations, and some animated discussions over politics.

"She still had her wry wit, which Kay enjoyed," recalled his wife Ardella.

Sometime after 1960, however, neighbors noticed a less attentive Grace. She would sometimes go to shop for items she had gotten the day before, then another day would be her old self.

She received a Christmas card from Merriam in 1959, and wrote back in February, but didn't get it mailed until June.

COATES TO MERRIAM: FEBRUARY 20, 1960 (RECEIVED JUNE)

My friends Mr. And Mrs. Merriam:

Living alone, life reaches a point where it is hard for one to maintain the decencies of life, and the amenities go by the board. I appreciate your always pleasing Christmas greetings, but I am losing friends who object to August acknowledgment of December good wishes.

You occasionally ask for a poem for the M.I.A. Quarterly, Mr. Merriam. Here is one you can have if you wish. *You* can caption it (and possibly get it wrong) or I'll try to condense its essence into a word (I'm taking a lot for granted.) Or just drop it in the waste basket. I wrote it years ago out of immediate experience, but it is only recently that I know what it means.

Sincerely yours, with appreciation of what you each have meant to Montana.

Grace

Grace Stone Coates OVER [on the back of the sheet:]

Dear Mr. Merriam—I've worked through a mountain of accumulation, and happened on this—of last February. I decided I didn't want the verses in print. Readers were not so intimately associated with the thing so I had the advantage of them in knowing what I was talking about. Probably you know that I am not so hilariously well as I used to be. AnyWAY (I'm battling a newly acquired typewriter) the note serves to convey my warmth of friendship as of last February…Jere Coffey of the Acantha is dead, and I am grieved. His parents treated me as no other parents ever have.

Grace[34]

In 1960, she submitted work to a publication in Denver, and was rejected. The editor, an old friend, wrote,

"hank[35] and I both LOVE your fable of the busted trinity but feel its just not quite right somehow for the gentle POOBLic of the pottery form…but DO send us anOTHER!…thiiiiink what that two dollars WOULDn't do for you in martinsdale, dear heart…and how ENVious it would make the BAIR girls…how ARE that priceless pair, by the way? I have Always been madly and secretly in love with both of them with a slight bent toward Alberta…and rest assured: now that we have achieved THIS much I shall expect NOTHing further from you till it arrives…IF it ever does…for I know all too well how 'TIS, from time to time with both of us…if you don't MIND I may, whilest on the crest of the wave again, inflict myself upon you with more frequency than you do me…on the other hand, THIS may be my SWANsong…one simply doesn't KNOW when one no longer has an THELma THYroid glissINDa guh-LANDS to guide him through these bewildering times…and what do YOU lack, dear falcon of the crazies?…s'hell while our slumps LAST but isn't it wunnerful in between times[36]

Grace was still trying to help Margaret Bell Dobin get her memoir in print. She tried Kathryn Wright at the *Billings Gazette* to suggest running it as a feature item in the paper.

WRIGHT TO COATES: JULY 17, 1961

Have been vacationing a week—working at home—we live in the country—and found your note and the diary at work today.

Read the diary tonight and found it interesting—but scanty. Which—of course—is the way early day westerners wrote diaries—when they wrote 'em.

I believe it would make a fine feature for The Gazette. Hedges' background is given in detail in many Montana histories. It would be no trouble to give the reader a foundation. I think there should be an introduction by you or at least an introduction telling how you happened to have the diary, etc., and something of your writing career. As you know, I've been an admirer of yours for a long time.

You mention coming to Billings. Do hope it's for the correspondents' day The Gazette is planning July 24. It would be wonderful to see you again and have a good talk.

If you think my brief plan for the diary is all right, I would like to see the original. You know, describe the writing, penmanship, etc. for the readers. Do let me know.

Thank you for sending the manuscript and all my best wishes.

Kathryn[36]

Nothing further came from the attempt to have the diary printed in the paper. Grace continued to have periods of anxiety and suspicion. Her friend Helen Maring replied to a letter in the spring, reflecting the letters received from Grace.

MARING TO COATES: MAY 19, 1962

Happy Birthday!

I have long put off writing because I have been extremely busy, over-tired from hard labor, strangely lost in the darkness of bright lights, and extremely confused by comments in two of your last three letters regarding the content of my epistles and the publicness [sic] of sealed letters in the U.S. Mails.

Let me explain. No, first, let me ask…..Did you receive a long letter written from Ukiah shortly after my return from South America. It was long, personal, and contained a letter from a third party (my current landlord in Seattle) which should have explained, along with my letter, my motivations for taking the Seattle job and the alleged conditions of my residence at the address I have there. This letter was written shortly after receiving yours which mentioned your surgical operation, etc., and in which there was a paragraph, seemingly out of context, which lamented purloined letters, etc. I did not know, nor do I now, whether the statement referred to times past and letters written by you or to you or if it referred to letters between you and I—in the past or present? Somehow, although the statement confused me I did not FEEL it an admonition to censor my correspondence. I had intended to inquire about this but episode Seattle interfered (sp?) and when I again wrote it was a usual sort of letter. Your answer which mentioned that you had shortly after the operation, broken your knee and been hospitalized again also mentioned

that you had found a sealed but unmailed letter *to* me which you had destroyed
and also stated that if I didn't heed your admonition about content of my
letters you would have to discontinue our correspondence! ??????? Perhaps in
the unmailed letter was an admonition?....[37]

In 1962, Grace packaged the letters from Linderman and donated them
to the Montana Historical Society in Helena, putting finis to that long-ago
strong friendship.

Then, on a blustery, wintry night February of 1962, Ardella Berg looked out
her window to see Grace standing in the middle of the street in her night gown,
her hair in a long braid down her back. She had no coat, no shoes or socks. The
Bergs rushed out into the night and brought her to their kitchen where Ardella
wrapped her in a blanket and gave her hot coffee. She didn't appear to know
where she was.

When Kay went to Grace's house, he found all the doors locked and had to
jimmy a window to get in. The Bergs put Grace to bed, and in the morning
called Marion Coates, Henderson's niece, the postmistress. She was the only
family in Martinsdale.

Coates had made arrangements to go into Hillcrest, a retirement home in
Bozeman, and now it was time to go. Her books and papers went, for the most
part, into Marion's garage. Some of the books were sold.

Grace started living at Hillcrest in 1962 and with help and good food began
to have better days. She became content with her new home and relayed that
to her friends.

COATES TO ROSTAD: JANUARY 11, 1964

Hillcrest is preeminently a place where one can get nothing done. There is
too much to do.

Yesterday Dr. Sabo said to me, "You're not taking advantage of the things
this place offers. I'll warrant you didn't go to that lecture last week (a lecture
by Ashley Montagu on the Biosocial Nature of Man.) I retorted, "I not only
went to the lecture, but I read his book before I went." Incidentally, I told him
somebody in the college music department was making a collection of
Montana verse, had set a fragment of mine to music and had been up here to
sing it for me—and a few more things. So he concluded I was doing all right.

I follow some of your activities in the Meagher County News. Both local
papers keep me on their mailing list, and I appreciate this. I've just come
from a lecture on Oriental thought—very well presented and interesting; but
this letter is about the 1964 Centennial and the very interesting note paper
you sent me. It is just the thing to send my eastern friends, and I appreciate it

more than you would guess. I had no anticipation of a Christmas season so abundant and beautiful. Everyone seems to have forgiven me for my sins of omission and commission, and I love them every one.

I'm waiting for summer to bring more of my friends over here, but I love these winter storms, the swirling fog and snow, the black Bridgers and the snow covered Spanish Peaks.

I thank you very much for your kindness to me. I have something to tell you about the delicious venison, but that will keep until I see you.

Greet Phillip and the boys for me, and tell any friends who chance to mention me that I am happy—and come to see me.[38]

COATES TO HASTE: AUGUST 7, 1964

Dear Gwendolen—

I'm having a good time. A college town is a drastic change from Martinsdale. As for Alberta, I believe I mentioned to you that some real famous—at least widely known—man of the college wrote, asking a bit of information, and she ignored his letter—You see, she has so much money she doesn't consider courtesy necessary. Well, she was always o.k. to me, and I had no delusions about the quality of her native fiber, so nothing she does surprises me. When one is useful to her she is a friend—when the usefulness ceases, so does the courtesy.

Love to you, Grace[39]

COATES TO HASTE: DECEMBER 15, 1964

Dear Gwendolen:

The last account I read about Central Park implied it was a pretty tough place. In spots, at least. My father, as I may have mentioned, was a New Yorker, and told us much of his days there as a young man. He is gone and the family is gone, and I am the only one left. At least, that leaves me no one to worry about.

Beauty is in the eye of the beholder, and in moments of exasperation I have called this a Jerrybuilt monstrosity; and others, more competent observers doubtless, eulogize it. Personally, I'd settle for less show and fewer leaks. We are well wrapped in falling snow right now, which bothers me not in the least.

Somebody, writing me, hoped I'd find some persons I could like. There are plenty—some I like extremely, on the campus. Few here at the Home that I do not like, But in general a highish class crowd. The long-distance talkers are somewhat wearing, but I can dodge them. On the whole I'm happy but wish there were more men of the kinds I like, or more important, of the kind who like me…Jeanette, I hear is in New York. The Bair girls maintain silence. They were afraid I might prove a liability I guess, God bless them! I would return Alberta's gift to me, a costume jewelry crane from Holland, but its eye dropped out the first time I wore it, and I wouldn't want to embarrass her! If I were intent on such high minded conduct, I could return a really lovely corngarum (I can't spell it) Dave gave Mrs. Bair, which she passed on to me.

Love and mischief, Grace[40]

H.G. Merriam had not forgotten his long-time assistant editor and friend and in 1964, the *Bozeman Chronicle* reported that the third booklet of poetry published by the Montana Institute of the Art Poetry Group, entitled "The Death of John Bozeman and Other Montana Poems," was published in celebration of the Montana Centennial—1864-1964.

The booklet was dedicated to Grace Stone Coates, author of the novel *Black Cherries,* and two books of poetry.

H. G. Merriam, professor emeritus of English, Montana State University, was the editor of the booklet.

Her good friends, Taylor and Rose Gordon continued to keep in touch.

COATES TO THE GORDONS: DECEMBER 20, 1965

Dear Rose & Taylor—

You will forgive me for making one letter serve for two. I would do better, but I had an accident to my arm—a funny one—but the doctor assures me it is not funny. Looking at me morosely he says, "There is nothing funny about that hand!"—a lot of broken blood vessels that may raise hell with me.

I thank you for your lovely card, and kind letters, and all the news. It happened we were speaking of you and those other two spiritual singers at the breakfast table today—a woman who had taken a course in N.Y.C.

It is climbing toward noon, and I should comb my hair and prepare to go down the cafeteria line for dinner.

My arm still feels best in an ice-bag, and it is hard to write, but it is fine to hear from you. God bless you both. I got to talking with a woman who was full of grievances, and it made my hand hurt! Funny what nerves will do!

My best wishes to you both, and thank you for writing.

Grace Coates[41]

Her last few years were isolated by illness, and alone and quietly she died in the winter of 1976.

BOZEMAN CHRONICLE: JANUARY 26, 1976

Grace Stone Coates, 94, of Hillcrest Retirement Apartments, died Sunday at Bozeman Deaconess Hospital.

She was born in Ruby, Ka. May 20, 1881, the daughter of Mr. and Mrs. Henry C. Stone. She was a widow.

Her body will be taken to Croxford's Mortuary in Great Falls for funeral services and burial.

Survivors include a niece, Mrs. Lucille Blunk of Oklahoma City, Okla.

There were no services, and the body was cremated and scattered on Gordon Butte out of Martinsdale as she had requested.

I shall make my way alone

Past the green alfalfa tillage

At the far end of the village,

Skirt the coulee, dropping down

Till the rounded knolls behind me

Hide the chimneys of the town

With their small insistency,

And no curious eye can find me;

Only then shall I be free

For the prairie and the foothills

    And the cliff that summons me.[42]

Grace seemed forgotten, but a few people were discovering again the talent that had languished in the little town of Martinsdale. Coates was included in the Montana anthology, *The Last Best Place* in with her short story, "Black Cherries" and several poems including "Ransom," "Topers," The Answer," "Village Satiety," "Nights of Evil" and "Country Doctor."

John Updike chose her short story "Wild Plums" to represent 1929 in his *Best American Short Stories of the Twentieth Century* in 1999.

Then, in the 1990s, a copy of Margaret Bell's memoir appeared in one of the boxes of Grace's jumbled papers and letters. Margaret Bell's book, *When Montana and I Were Young*, was finally published by the University of Nebraska Press, edited by Mary Clearman Blew. *Black Cherries* was reprinted by the University of Nebraska Press in 2003, and reviews found it as moving as when first published. A reader from Oregon declared *Black Cherries* "a work of genius, written in vital fluids, illuminated by lightning, quivering with truth."[43]

Strangely, the poet from almost a hundred years ago seems very current. People are still reaching out from their "alien lands" for friendship and love.

GRACE STONE COATES

END NOTES

Introduction

1. Coates to Rankin, undated, James Brownlee Rankin Papers, Montana Historical Society, Helena.
2. Coates to Saroyan, October 27, 1930, William Saroyan Papers, M0978, Stanford University Libraries, Stanford, California.
3. With Grace's mastery of the written word, this is probably a purposeful misspelling of manic.
4. Kay Redfield Jamison, *Touched with Fire* (New York: Free Press Paperbacks, 1993).
5. Robert Burns, *Common Place Book,* quoted in Jamison, *Touched with Fire,* p. 72.
6. Jamison, *Touched with Fire,* p. 109.
7. Coates to Powers, Undated, Grace Stone Coates Papers, MSS 422, K. Ross Toole Archives, The University of Montana, Missoula.
8. Coates to Saroyan, January 20, 1938, Saroyan Papers.
9. Coates to Merriam, December 14, 1957, H.G. Merriam Papers, UM 5, Box 19, Folder 1, K Ross Toole Archives, The University of Montana, Missoula.

Chapter One

1. Letter from Coates to father, August 8, 1914, private collection.
2. A.A. Knopf Collection, Undated, 1314.2, Harry Ransom Humanities Research Center, Austin, Texas.
3. Henry Stone to sister Jennifer, December 21, 1919, private collection.
4. *Black Cherries,* p. 199.
5. *Black Cherries,* p. 177.
6. *Black Cherries,* p. 176.
7. Coates, unpublished, in the author's possession.
8. Ibid.
9. Coates to James Rankin, Nov. 13, 1936, James Brownlee Rankin Papers, Montana Historical Society, Helena, MT.
10. Charles' name was Henry Charles Stone, after his father. He named his only son Mel Stone.

Chapter Two

1. Actual conversation between Grace and Henderson as told by their niece, Lucille Blunk.
2. Coates, unpublished, in the author's possession.
3. Coates to Merriam, undated, H.G. Merriam Papers, UM5, Box 18, K. Ross Toole Archives, The University of Montana. Missoula.
4. Letter from Grace to Helen, undated, private collection.
5. Anna Haugan, a next door neighbor.
6. Alberta Bair, another neighbor.
7. Grace to Helen, June 1, 1950, in the author's possession.
8. Unpublished notes, in the author's possession.
9. Helen to Henry Stone, August, 1921, private collection.
10. Spelling preferred by Miss Haste.
11. Coates to Saroyan, April 25, 1930, William Saroyan Papers, M0978, Stanford University Libraries, Stanford, CA.
12. Residents of Martinsdale and the surrounding areas sought medical care at Butte or the Mayo Clinic—both more accessible by train than other medical facilities.
13. Coates to Haste, February, 1922, private collection.
14. Lake McDonald Hotel.

15. Coates to Rankin, November 13, 1936, James Brownlee Rankin Papers, Montana Historical Society, Helena, MT.

16. Although it was motorized, old timers continued to call the bus the stage.

17. Coates to Haste, April 39, 1923, in the author's possession.

18. Coates to Haste, June 21, 1923, in the author's possession.

19. John T. Frederick to Coates, undated, in the author's possession.

20. Haste account of visit, in the author's possession.

21. *The Midland*, June 15, 1925, published at Iowa City, Iowa.

22. Coates to Saroyan, Undated, Saroyan Papers.

23. From the Greek, "running before."

24. Coates to O'Brien, May 10, 1930, Saroyan Papers.

Chapter Three

1. Esther Warford, *Montana Arts*, July 1968, Vol V, No. 6.

2. Ginny Merriam, *Montanan*, Autumn, 1985, Vol. 3, No. 1.

3. Coates to Merriam, October 12, 1927, H.G. Merriam Papers, UM 5, Box 19, Folder 1, K Ross Toole Archives, The University of Montana, Missoula.

4. Merriam to Coates, October 8, 1927, Merriam Papers.

5. Merriam to Coates, November 10, 1930, Merriam Papers.

6. Coates to Merriam, undated (October 9, 1927), Merriam Papers.

7. Taylor Gordon, *Born to Be* (New York: Covici Freide Publishers, 1929).

8. Ringlings had land investments in the area.

9. Coates to Saroyan, February 17, 1930, William Saroyan Papers, M0978, Stanford University Libraries, Stanford, CA.

10. Coates to Saroyan, May 18, 1930, Saroyan Papers.

11. Gordon to Coates, April 16, 1927, Emanuel Taylor Gordon Papers, Montana Historical Society.

12. Gordon to Coates, July 2, 1927, Gordon Papers.

13. Gordon to Coates, August 24, 1927, Gordon Papers.

14. Coates to Merriam, Undated, Merriam Papers.

15. Merriam to Coates, June 29, 1928, Merriam Papers.

16. Coates to Purnell, September 30, 1927, 1314.2, Idella Purnell Papers, Harry Ransom Humanities Research Center, Austin, Texas.

17. Coates to Purnell, October 27, 1927, Purnell Papers.

18. Coates to Merriam, May 24, 1927, Merriam Papers.

19. Coates to Merriam, May 26, 1927, Merriam Papers.

20. Merriam to Coates, June 13, 1927, Merriam Papers.

21. Coates to Saroyan, Undated, Saroyan Papers.

22. Coates to Saroyan, Undated, Saroyan Papers.

23. Merriam to Coates, November 3, 1927, Merriam Papers.

24. Pierre Kuchneroff.

25. Merriam to Coates, Undated, Merriam papers. The poem was "Modulation" and the six lines were;   As I love the caves of thought
      Where no other mind has moved.
      Have you seen a cereus bloom
      Drowned in silence, on the floor
      Of the pale enchanted sea
      That the moon knows how to pour?

26. Coates to Merriam, November 3, 1927, Merriam Papers.

27. Coates to Merriam, November 21, 1927 Merriam Papers.

28. Merriam to Coates, November 18, 1927, Merriam Papers.

29. Coates to Merriam, November 21, 1927, Merriam Papers.
30. Merriam to Coates, November 29, 1927, Merriam Papers.

Chapter Four
1. *Meagher County News,* August 26, 1936.
2. Grace Stone Coates to H. G. Merriam, January 5, 1928, H.G. Merriam Papers, UM 5, Box 19, Folder 1, K.Ross Toole Archives, The University of Montana, Missoula.
3. Merriam to Coates, January 10, 1928, Merriam Papers.
4. Merriam to Coates, January 11, 1928, Merriam Papers.
5. Merriam to Coates, January 15, 1928, Merriam Papers.
6. Coates to Merriam, January 22, 1928, Merriam Papers.
7. Coates to Merriam, January 27, 1928, Merriam Papers.
8. Coates to Merriam, Undated, Merriam Papers.
9. Merriam to Coates, April 27, 1928, Merriam Papers.
10. Will James did the frontispiece for November 1929 issue.
11. Merriam to Coates, May 16, 1928, Merriam Papers.
12. Coates to Merriam, May 20, 1928, Merriam Papers.
13. Coates to Merriam, Undated, Merriam Papers.
14. Merriam to Coates, June 23, 1928, Merriam Papers.
15. Gwendolen Haste.
16. Mary Roberts Rinehart (1876-1958) wrote dozens of very popular novels, hundreds of articles, and plays, once having three of the last open on Broadway simultaneously.
17. H.G. Merriam to Grace Stone Coates, June 28, 1928, Merriam Papers.
18. Coates to Merriam, July 18, 1928, Merriam Papers.
19. Taylor Gordon.
20. Coates to Merriam, July 1, 1928, Merriam Papers.
21. Merriam to Coates, July 21, 1928, Merriam Papers.
22. Coates to Merriam, September 23, 1928, Merriam Papers.
23. Merriam to Coates, October 2, 1928, Merriam Papers.
24. Coates to Merriam, October 22, 1928, Merriam Papers.
25. Merriam to Coates, October 31, 1928, Merriam Papers.
26. Coates to Merriam, November 5, 1928, Merriam Papers.
27. Coates to Merriam, Undated, Merriam Papers.
28. Coates gave the sculpture to niece Lucille Blunk, after she admired it, without revealing the value.
29. Coates to Merriam, November 26, 1928, Merriam Papers.
30. Merriam to Coates, November 28, 1928, Merriam Papers.
31. Merriam to Coates, December 26, 1928, Merriam Papers.

Chapter Five
1. Coates to Merriam, March 9, 1928, H.G. Merriam Papers, UM 5, Box 19, Folder 1, K. Ross Toole Archives, The University of Montana, Missoula.
2. Coates to Rankin, December 6, 1936, James Brownlee Rankin Papers, Montana Historical Society, Helena, MT.
3. Coates to Rankin, February 19, 1937, Rankin Papers.
4. Merriam to Coates, February 6, 1929, Merriam Papers.
5. Coates to Merriam, March 3, 1928, Rankin Papers.
6. Merriam to Coates, March 3, 1928, Merriam Papers.
7. Coates to Merriam, April 28, 1929, Merriam Papers.
8. Merriam to Coates, April 24, 1929, Merriam Papers.
9. Coates to Merriam, April 26, 1929, Merriam Papers.

10. Grace had arranged for Shipley to mail out *The Frontier* in the New York area.

11. The DuRand dude ranch.

12. Coates to Merriam, May 8, 1929, Merriam Papers.

13. Merriam to Coates, May 18, 1929, Merriam Papers.

14. Merriam to Coates, June 27, 1929, Merriam Papers.

15. Coates to Merriam, July 1929, Merriam Papers.

16. *Born to Be.*

17. Coates to Merriam, July 1929, Merriam Papers.

18. Gordon to Coates, July 28, 1929, Emanuel Taylor Gordon Papers, Montana Historical Society, Helena.

19. Merriam to Coates, July 27, 1929, Merriam Papers

20. Coates to Merriam, Undated, Merriam Papers.

21. Merriam to Coates, July 19, 1929, Merriam Papers.

22. Merriam to Coates, July 22, 1929, Merriam Papers.

23. Coates to Merriam, August 5, 1929, Merriam Papers.

24. Coates to Merriam, August 17, 1929, Merriam Papers.

25. Coates to Merriam, August 17, 1929, Merriam Papers.

26. Merriam to Coates, August 12, 1929, Merriam Papers.

27. Coates to Merriam, October 25, 1929, Merriam Papers.

28. Coates to Merriam, October 30, 1929, Merriam Papers.

29. Coates to Merriam, January 18, 1930, Merriam Papers

30. Coates to Saroyan, April 17, 1930, William Saroyan Papers, M0978, Stanford University Libraries, Stanford, CA.

Chapter Six

1. Coates to Saroyan, January 25, 1930, William Saroyan Papers, M0978, Stanford University Libraries, Stanford, CA.

2. Saroyan to Coates, February 1, 1930, Grace Stone Coates Papers, K. Ross Toole Archives, University of Montana, Missoula.

3. Coates to Saroyan, February 6, 1930, Saroyan Papers.

4. Saroyan to Coates, February, 12, 1930, H.G. Merriam Papers, UM5, Box 18, Folder 17, K. Ross Toole Archives, University of Montana, Missoula.

5. Coates to Saroyan, February 17, 1930, Saroyan Papers.

6. Coates to Saroyan, February 22, 1930, Saroyan Papers.

7. Saroyan to Coates, March 3, 1930, Saroyan Papers.

8. Coates to Saroyan, March 6, 1930, Saroyan Papers.

9. Saroyan to Coates, March 10, 1930, Saroyan Papers.

10. Saroyan to Coates, March 11, 1930, Saroyan Papers.

11. Saroyan to Coates, March 12, 1930, Saroyan Papers.

12. Coates to Saroyan, Undated, Saroyan Papers.

13. Saroyan to Coates, April 17, 1930, Saroyan Papers.

14. Coates to Saroyan, Undated, Saroyan Papers.

15. Coates to Saroyan, Undated, Saroyan Papers.

16. Coates to Saroyan, Undate, Saroyan Papers.

17. Saroyan to Coates, Undated, Saroyan Papers.

18. Coates to Merriam, undated, Merriam Papers.

19. Coates to Merriam, undated, Merriam Papers.

20. Coates to Saroyan, Undated, Saroyan Papers.

21. Merriam to Coates, Undated, Merriam Papers

22. Coates to Saroyan, Undated, Saroyan Papers.

23. Coates to Saroyan, Undated, Saroyan Papers.

24. Saroyan to Coates, February 20, 1930, Saroyan Papers.

25. Possibly those with Israel Newman.

26. Coates to Saroyan, April 24, 1930, Saroyan Papers.

27. Saroyan to Coates, April 24, 1930, Saroyan Papers.

28. Coates to Saroyan, February 21, 1930, Saroyan Papers.

29. Saroyan to Coates, February 25, 1930, Saroyan Papers.

30. Saroyan to Coates, Undated, Saroyan Papers.

31. Saroyan to Coates, March 14, 1930, Saroyan Papers.

32. Coates to Saroyan, March 17, 1930, Saroyan Papers.

33. Saroyan to Coates, March 20, 1930, Saroyan Papers.

34. Coates to Saroyan, Undated, Saroyan Papers.

35. Coates to Saroyan, Undated, Saroyan Papers.

36. Saroyan to Coates, March 24, 1930, Saroyan Papers.

37. Coates to Saroyan, Undated, Saroyan Papers.

38. Saroyan to Coates, March 24, 1930, Saroyan Papers.

39. Saroyan to Coates, March 25, 1930, Saroyan Papers.

40. Coates to Saroyan, March 28, 1930, Saroyan Papers.

41. Coates to Saroyan, Undated, Saroyan Papers.

42. Saroyan to Coates, March 25, 1930, Saroyan Papers.

43. Saroyan to Coates, April 1, 1930, Saroyan Papers.

44. Saroyan to Coates, April 3, 1930, Saroyan Papers.

45. Coates to Saroyan, Undated, Saroyan Papers.

46. Coates to Saroyan, Undated, Saroyan Papers.

47. Coates to Merriam, Undated, Merriam Papers.

48. Coates to Saroyan, April 8, 1930, Saroyan Papers.

49. Saroyan to Coates, Undated, Saroyan Papers.

50. Saroyan to Coates, Undated, Saroyan Papers.

51. Saroyan to Coates, April 14, 1930, Saroyan Papers.

52. Saroyan to Coates, April 16, 1930, Saroyan Papers.

53. Saroyan to Coates, Undated, Saroyan Papers.

54. Coates to Saroyan, Undated, Saroyan Papers.

55. Coates to Saroyan, Undated, Saroyan Papers.

56. Saroyan to Coates, April 23, 1930, Saroyan Papers.

57. Coates to Saroyan, Undated, Saroyan Papers.

58. Knopf to Merriam, November 19, 1930, Merriam Papers

59. Merriam to Knopf, November 26, 1930, Merriam Papers

Chapter Seven

1. Coates to Unknown, January 30, 1931, in author's possession.

2. Coates to Saroyan, Undated, William Saroyan Papers, M0978, Stanford University Libraries, Stanford, CA.

3. Coates to Saroyan, January 26, 1931, William Saroyan Papers, M0978, Stanford University Libraries, Stanford, CA.

4. Coates to Saroyan, February 7, 1931, Saroyan Papers.

5. Coates to Saroyan, Undated, Saroyan Papers.

6. Coates to Saroyan, February 20, 1931, Saroyan Papers.

7. Saroyan to Coates, March 2, 1931, Saroyan Papers.

8. Saroyan to Coates, March 12, 1931, Saroyan Papers.

9. Coates to Saroyan, March 17, 1931, Saroyan Papers.

10. Saroyan to Coates, March 20, 1931, Saroyan Papers.

11. Coates to Saroyan, March 23, 1931, Saroyan Papers.

12. Coates to Saroyan, March 24, 1931, Saroyan Papers.
13. Saroyan to Coates, March 26, 1931, Saroyan Papers.
14. Coates to Saroyan, Undated, Saroyan Papers.
15. Coates to Saroyan, Undated, Saroyan Papers.
16. Coates to Saroyan, March 30, 1931, Saroyan Papers.
17. Brassil Frederick, assistant editor of *The Frontier.*
18. Coates to Merriam, March 31, 1931, H.G. Merriam Papers, UM5, Box 18, Folder 18, K. Ross Toole Archives, University of Montana, Missoula.
19. *Wichita Eagle,* May 17, 1931.
20. Linderman to Coates, May 31, 1935, F.B. Linderman Papers, Mansfield Library, University of Montana.
21. Coates to Saroyan, Undated, Saroyan Papers.
22. *Northwest Verse: An Anthology,* H.G. Merriam, ed. (Caldwell, ID: The Caxton Printers, Ltd., 1931).
23. Richard Roeder, "Grace Stone Coates: Forgotten Poet and Writer," unpublished, @ 1985. Montana Historical Society, Helena.
24. Coates to Merriam, undated, Merriam Papers.
25. *Oregon Sunday Journal,* undated clipping, Coates Pape.
26. *Frontier* 12 (March, 1932), 282-283.
27. Mary Brennan Clapp, February 4, 1932, *The Montana Woman,* Butte, Montana.
28. Roeder, op. cit.
29. *Contempo,* Mid-July, 1931 (Vol. 1, No. 6), Chapel Hill, N.C.
30. Tony Buttitta, *After the Good Gay Times* (New York: Viking Press, 1974).
31. Coates to Abernathy, June 18, 1931, Contempo Records, #4408, Folder 19, Southern Historical Collection, the Library of the University of North Carolina at Chapel Hill.
32. Coates to Powers, Mss 422, Grace Stone Coates Collection, K. Ross Toole Archives, Mansfield Library, The University of Montana, Missoula.
33. Coates to Powers, November 30, 1931, Grace Stone Coates Collection.
34. Coates to Saroyan, July 24, 1931, Saroyan Papers.
35. Saroyan to Coates, June 29, 1931, Saroyan Papers.
36. Coates to Saroyan, September 3, 1931, Saroyan Papers.
37. Coates to Powers, August 17, 1931, Grace Stone Coates Collection.
38. Coates to Saroyan, October 10, 1931, Saroyan Papers.
39. Misspelling probably intentional, since Grace had amazing command of words.
40. Coates to Saroyan, October 15, 1931, Saroyan Papers.
41. Henry Louis Mencken, writer and critic, editor of the *The American Mercury.*
42. Saroyan to Coates, October 27, 1931, Saroyan Papers.
43. Coates to Saroyan, October 28, 1931, Saroyan Papers.
44. Saroyan to Coates, November 18, 1931, Saroyan Papers.
45. Coates to Saroyan, December 16, 1931, Saroyan Papers.
46. Billie Burke, actress best known as Glinda, the Good Witch, in the 1939 film *The Wizard of Oz.*
47. Coates to Merriam, undated, Merriam Papers.
48. Coates to Merriam, undated, Merriam Papers.
49. Merriam to Coates, October 5, 1931, Merriam Papers.
50. Coates to Merriam, undated, Merriam Papers.
51. Merriam to Coates, October 17, 1931, Coates Collection.
52. Coates to Merriam, November 1, 1931, Merriam Papers.
53. Coates to Saroyan, November 17, 1931, William Saroyan Papers, M0978, Stanford University Libraries, Stanford, California.
54. *Northwest Verse.*
55. Coates to Merriam, undated, Merriam Papers.

56. Grace Stone Coates, *Mead and Mangel-Wurzel*, (Caldwell, ID: Caxton Printers, Ltd., 1931).
57. Coates to Merriam, December 8, 1931, Merriam Papers.
58. Coates to Abernethy and Buttita, December 15-16, 1931, Contempo Records, Folder 2.19.
59. Merriam to Coates, December 18, 1931, Merriam Papers.
60. Coates to Merriam, December 22, Merriam Papers.
61. Coates to Abernethy, Contempo Records, Folder 2.19.
62. Buttitta to Coates, July 24, 1937, Grace Stone Coates Collection, Montana State University, Bozeman.

Chapter Eight

1. Wife of William Coates, relative to John Barrows.
2. Coates to Merriam, July 11, 1933, H.G. Merriam Papers, UM 5, Box 19, Folder 1, K.Ross Toole Archives, University of Montana, Missoula.
3. Coates to Merriam, undated, Merriam Papers.
4. Vardis Fisher.
5. Coates to Merriam, October 1, Merriam Papers.
6. Caxton to Coates, March 6, 1933, in author's possession.
7. Frank Bird Linderman, *Stumpy* (Chicago: E.M. Hale & Co., 1933).
8. Coates to Linderman, Undated, Frank Bird Linderman Letters, Montana Historical Society, Helena.
9. Coates to Rankin, December 16, 1936, James Brownlee Rankin Papers, Montana Historical Society, Helena.
10. Coates to Bairs, May 1, 1933, in author's possession.
11. Poetry contributor to *The Frontier*.
12. Merriam to Coates, August 31, 1933, Merriam Papers.
13. Coates to Merriam, September 2, 1933, Merriam Papers.
14. Linderman to Coates, September 12, 1933, Linderman Letters.
15. Coates to Linderman, November 22, 1933, Linderman Letters.
16. Coates to Linderman, November 24, 1933, Linderman Letters.
17. Coates to Merriam, December 30, 1933, Merriam Papers.

Chapter Nine

1. "Cleavage,"" *Mead and Mangel-Wurzel* (Caldwell, ID: Caxton Printers, 1931).
2. Saroyan to Coates, November 28, 1932, William Saroyan Papers, M0978, Stanford Univ. Libraries, Stanford, CA.
3. Coates to Saroyan, December 1, 1932, Saroyan Papers.
4. Saroyan to Coates, Undated, Saroyan Literary Archives, M870, Folder 12.
5. Coates to Saroyan, January 31, 1934, Saroyan Papers.
6. Saroyan to Coates, February 5, 1934, Saroyan Papers.
7. Coates to Saroyan, February 8, 1934, Saroyan Papers.
8. Saroyan to Coates, February 12, 1930, H.G. Merriam Papers, UM5, Box 22, Folder 21, K. Ross Toole Archives, The University of Montana, Missoula.
9. Saroyan to Coates, February 13, 1934, Saroyan Papers.
10. Coates to Saroyan, April, 1934, Saroyan Papers.
11. Coates to Saroyan, Undated, Saroyan Papers.
12. Coates to Saroyan, May 24, 1934, Saroyan Papers.
13. Saroyan to Coates, June 14, 1934, Saroyan Papers.
14. Coates to Merriam, January 21, 1936, Merriam Papers.
15. John Barrows' book. Ubet is the name of the stage stop where he lived.
16. Merriam to Coates, January 20, 1934, UM 5, Merriam Papers, Box 19, Folder 1.
17. Coates to Merriam, January 10, 1934, Merriam Papers.

18. Coates to Merriam, January 12, 1934, Merriam Papers.

19. Henrietta to Coates, March 8, 1934, Grace Stone Coates Collection, Montana State University, Bozeman.

20. Merriam to Coates, February 14, 1934, Merriam Papers.

21. Linderman to Coates, April 24, 1934, Frank Bird Linderman Letters, Montana Historical Society, Helena.

22. Coates to Linderman, November 13, 1934, Linderman Letters.

23. William Coates.

24. Barrows to Coates, April 29, 1934, Coates Papers, Burlingame Special Collections.

25. Barrows to Coates, May 11, 1934, Coates Papers, Burlingame Special Collections.

26. Barrows to Coates, June 10, 1934, Coates Papers, Burlingame Special Collections.

27. Mr. and Mrs. Jason Bolles, Jason a frequent contributor to *The Frontier.*

28. Merriam to Coates, June 18, 1934, Merriam Papers.

29. Maxim Lieber, "authors' representative," 545 Fifth Avenue, New York, New York.

30. Linderman to Coates, June 27, 1934, Linderman Letters.

31. Coates to Merriam, July 28, 1934, Merriam Papers.

32. Linderman to Coates, August 7, 1934, Linderman Letters.

33. Saroyan to Coates, August 12, 1934, Saroyan Papers.

34. Coates to Saroyan, August 21, 1934, Saroyan Papers.

35. Inscription in book, in the author's possession.

36. Coates to Saroyan, Undated, Saroyan Papers.

37. Coates to Saroyan, September 3, 1934, Saroyan Papers.

38. Saroyan to Coates, October 11, 1934, Saroyan Papers.

39. Coates to Saroyan, Undated, Saroyan Papers.

40. www.barnesandnoble.com

41. Merriam to Coates, September, 1934, Merriam Papers.

42. *Great Falls Tribune,* September 14, 1934

43. Coates to Saroyan, Undated, Saroyan Papers.

44. Linderman to Coates, October 11, 1934, Linderman Letters.

45. Linderman to Coates, November 9, 1934, Linderman Letters.

46. Linderman to Coates, November 14, 1934, Linderman Letters.

47. Linderman to Coates, November 20, 1934, Linderman Letters.

48. Coates to Saroyan, undated, Saroyan Papers.

49. Coates to Saroyan, December 23, 1936, Saroyan Papers.

50. Brassil Fitzgerald, assistant editor of *The Frontier.*

51. Merriam to Coates, January 17, 1935, Merriam Papers.

52. Merriam to Coates, March 6, 1935, Merriam Papers.

53. Angela Stone to Coates, March 13, 1935, in the author's possession.

54. Coates to I.M.P, April 14, 1935, in the author's possession.

55. Linderman to Coates, April 29, 1935, Linderman Letters.

56. Linderman to Coates, May 31, 1934, Linderman Letters.

57. Linderman to Coates, June 2, 1934, Linderman Letters.

58. Ruffner to Coates, June 21, 1935, Coates Papers, Burlingame Special Collections.

59. Ruffner to Coates, Undated, Coates Papers, Burlingame Special Collections.

60. Ruffner to Coates, July 5, 1935, Coates Papers, Burlingame Special Collections.

61. Maring to Coates, October 1935, Coates Papers, Burlingame Special Collections.

62. Maring to Coates, November 12, 1935, Coates Papers, Burlingame Special Collections.

63. Margaret Marshall to Coates, November 16, 1935, Coates Papers, Burlingame Special Collections.

64. Coates to J.A. Powers, Undated, Grace Stone Coates Papers, MSS422 Box 1, Folder 1, K. Ross Toole Archives, The University of Montana, Missoula.

65. Coates manuscript, unpublished, in the author's possession.

Chapter Ten

1. Coates to Bairs, January 4, 1936, in the author's possession.
2. Coates to Powers, April 14, 1936, Grace Stone Coates Collection, MSS 422, Box 1 Folder 1, K. Ross Toole Archives, Mansfield Library, The University of Montana, Missoula.
3. Ibid.
4. Coates to Kuhlman, April 26, 1936, Charles Kuhlman Research Collection, Montana Historical Society, Helena.
5. Grace to Henderson, April 29, 1936, in the author's possession.
6. Maring to Coates, June 7, 1936, Grace Stone Coates Collection, Montana State University, Bozeman.
7. Merriam to Coates, September 16, 1936, H G. Merriam Papers, UM5, Box 19, Folder 1, K. Ross Toole Archives, The University of Montana, Missoula.
8. Coates to Merriam, September 24, 1936, Merriam Papers.
9. Ibid.
10. Coates to Merriam, Undated, Merriam Papers.
11. Raymond Resensky to Coates, June 6, 1936, Grace Stone Coates Collection, Montana State University, Bozeman.
12. Coates to Merriam, August 13, 1937, Coates Collection, Montana State University.
13. Coates to Rankin, November 21, 1936, Coates Collection, Montana State University.
14.Coates to Rankin, November 13, 1936, Coates Collection, Montana State University.
15. Coates to Rankin, November 21, 1936, Coates Collection, Montana State University.
16. Coates to Rankin, November 13, 1936, Coates Collection, Montana State University.
17. Coates to Rankin, December 2, 1936, Coates Collection, Montana State University.
18. Coates to Rankin, December 6, 1936, Coates Collection, Montana State University.
19. Linderman to Coates, December 7, 1936, Frank Bird Linderman Letters, Montana Historical Society, Helena.
20. Coates to Rankin, December 16, 1936, James Brownlee Rankin Papers, Montana Historical Society, Helena.
21. Coates to Rankin, December 14, 1936, Rankin Papers.

Chapter Eleven

1. Coates to Rankin, January 3, 1937, James Brownlee Rankin Research Collection, Montana Historical Society, Helena.
2. Hoover had written to Grace about an article she wrote on the FBI.
3. Merriam to Coates, January 30, 1937, H.G. Merriam Papers, UM5, Box 19, Folder 1, K. Ross Toole Archives, The University of Montana, Missoula.
4. Coates to Merriam, January 31, 1937, Merriam Papers.
5. Agnes Repplier, *In Pursuit of Laughter* (New York: Houghton Mifflin Co., 1936).
6. Coates to Rankin, February, 2, 1937, Rankin Research Collection.
7. Linderman to Coates, February 17, 1937, Frank Bird Linderman Letters, Montana Historical Society, Helena.
8. H.G. Merriam, *The University of Montana: A History* (Missoula: University of Montana Press, 1970), p. 86.
9. George P. Mallon and Marie McCoy Mallon were witnesses for the wedding of the Coates.
10. Coates to Rankin, March 9, 1937, Rankin Research Collection.
11. Coates to Rankin, April 3, 1937, Rankin Research Collection.
12. Coates to Rankin, Undated, Rankin Research Collection.
13. Coates to Rankin, April 23, 1937, Rankin Research Collection.
14. Coates to Rankin, May 9, 1937, Rankin Research Collection.
15. Coates to Rankin, July 2, 1937, Rankin Research Collection.

16. Coates to Rankin, July 13, 1937, Rankin Research Collection.

17. Linderman to Coates, July 17, 1937, Rankin Research Collection. Merriam Papers

18. Merriam was concerned about Coates' not writing for several years. She continued to do the column for *The Frontier* and historical pieces along with editing about eight books for Caxton.

19. Federal Works Project.

20. Coates to Merriam, August 13, 1937, Merriam Papers.

21. Coates to Merriam, August 13, 1937, Merriam Papers.

22. Coates to Merriam, August 28, 1937, Merriam Papers.

23. Merriam to Coates, October 30, 1937, Merriam Papers.

24. Dr. Phillips was accused of improper behavior. The accuser later recanted the story.

25. Coates to Merriam, November 13, 1937, Merriam Papers.

26. Coates to Rankin, November 16, 1937, Merriam Papers.

27. Coates to Kuhlman, December 11, 1937, Charles Kuhlman Research Collection, Montana Historical Society, Helena.

28. Montana News Association.

29. Coates to Kuhlman, December 30, 1937, Kuhlman Research Collection.

30. Coates to Rankin, December 29, 1937, Rankin Research Collection.

31. Coates to Saroyan, January 11, 1938, The William Saroyan Papers, M0978, Stanford Univ. Libraries, Stanford, CA

32. Coates to Saroyan, January 15, 1938, Saroyan Papers.

33. Coates to Saroyan, January 20, 1938, Saroyan Papers.

34. Coates to Saroyan, April 20, 1938, Saroyan Papers.

35. Saroyan did not cash Grace's check. It still resides in his papers at Stanford.

36. Coates to Saroyan, April 26, 1938, Saroyan Papers.

37. Saroyan Papers, M870, Stanford Library, University of California, Stanford.

38. Coates to Rankin, February 18, 1938, Rankin Research Collection.

39. Coates to Rankin, February 26, 1938, Rankin Research Collection.

40. Coates to Linderman, August 18, 1937, Linderman Papers.

41. Coates to Mrs. Linderman, May 25, 1938, Linderman Papers.

42. Mrs. Linderman to Coates, May 27, 1938, Linderman Papers.

43. Ward to Coates, April 28, 1938, in the author's possession.

44. Coates to Rankin, May 19, 1938, Rankin Research Collection.

45. Coates to Rankin, June 10, 1938, Rankin Research Collection.

46. Rankin to Coates, June 8, 1938, Rankin Research Collection.

47. Coates to Merriam, August 28, 1938, Merriam Papers.

48. Coates to Rankin, September 6, 1938, Rankin Research Collection.

49. Merriam to Coates, September 28, 1938, Merriam Papers

50. Coates to Merriam, November 12, 1938, Merriam Papers.

51. Coates to Haste, December 12, 1936, private collection.

Chapter Twelve

1. Jack Coates, Henderson's brother.

2. Coates to Merriam, January 13, 1939, H.G. Merriam Papers, UM 5, Box 19, Folder 1, K. Ross Toole Archives, University of Montana, Missoula.

3. Merriam to Coates, January 29, 1939, Merriam Papers.

4. Coates to Merriam, February 2, 1939, Merriam Papers.

5. Kuhlman to Coates, September, 1939, Charles Kuhlman Research Collection, Montana Historical Society, Helena.

6. Kuhlman to Coates, February 24, 1942, Kuhlman Collection.

7. Coates to Kuhlman, February 20, 1942, Kuhlman Collection.

8. Skinner to Henderson Coates, December, 1942, in the author's possession.

9. Cornelia Otis Skinner and Alberta Bair were classmates at Bryn Mawr.

10. Merriam to Coates, April 22, 1944, Merriam Papers.

11. Coates to Merriam, April 28, 1944, Merriam Papers.

12. Coates to Merriam, October 31, 1944, Merriam Papers.

13. Harold Stearns to author, undated.

14. George Murphy to Coates, March 13, 1947, Grace Stone Coates Papers, Montana Historical Society, Helena.

15. Coates to Merriam, November 7, 1947, H.G. Merriam Papers.

16. Joseph Kinsey Howard, Great Falls newspaperman and author of *Montana, High Wide and Handsome* (New Haven: Yale University Press, 1959).

17. Merriam to Coates, November 10, 1947, Merriam Papers.

18. Joseph Kinsey Howard.

19. Montana Institute of the Arts.

20. Coates to Merriam, September 16, 1949, Merriam Papers.

21. Railroad personnel were sometimes moved by someone with more seniority.

22. Coates to Bell Dobin, May 30, 1949, Margaret Bell Dobin Papers, Cascade County Historical Society. Great Falls.

23. Ripley Hugo, *Writing for Her Life* (Lincoln and London: University of Nebraska Press, 2003), p. xiii.

24. Schemm to Coates, May 30, 1950

25. Coates to Rognlie, December 20, 1949, private papers.

26. Lucille was a niece.

27. Kuhlman to Coates, April 24, 1955, Kuhlman Collection.

28. Kuhlman to Coates, June 5, 1954, Kuhlman Collection.

29. Coates to Merriam, December 14, 1957, Merriam Papers.

30. Coates to Dobin, May 13, 1957, Dobin Papers.

31. Volunteers monitored the temperature, rainfall and snow depth for the state in various places. The program is still in effect.

32. Coates to Gordon, November 21, 1959, Emmuel Taylor Gordon Papers, Montana Historical Society, Helena.

33. Coates to Merriam, February 20, 1960, Merriam Papers.

34. Henry W. Hough, editor of "Poetry Forum" in *Sunday Empire*—a Sunday supplement of *The Denver Post,* Denver, Colorado.

35. Unknown (signed "Will") to Coates, March 23, 1961, in the author's possession.

36. Wright to Coates, July 17, 1961, in the author's possession.

37. Maring to Coates, May 19, 1962, Grace Stone Coates Collection, Montana State University, Bozeman.

38. Coates to Rostad, January 11, 1964, in the author's possession.

39. Coates to Haste, August 7, 1964, Sue Hart Papers.

40. Coates to Haste, December 15, 1964, private collection.

41. Coates to Gordons, December 20, 1965, Gordon Papers.

42. "The Cliff."

43. *Statesman Journal,* May 11, 2003, Salem, Oregon

About the Author

Lee Rostad was born in Roundup, Montana, graduated from the University of Montana, and spent a year doing graduate work in London before marrying Phil Rostad, a rancher in the Musselshell Valley. Like Grace Stone Coates, she took her turn at writing the local news for the weekly newspapers and took time from her ranch and cooking chores to write magazine articles. She is the author of *Honey Wine and Hunger Root, Fourteen Cents and Seven Green Apples,* and *Mountains of Gold, Hills of Grass.* She is co-author of *Meagher County Sketchbook.*

In 1995, Lee received an Honorary Doctor of Letters from Rocky Mountain College and in 2001 received the Governor's Award in Humanities. She currently serves on the Montana Historical Society Board of Trustees.